Void's Enigmatic Mansion

2

D0048337

HeeEun Kim
JiEun Ha

Yen
Press

Void's
Enigmatic
Mansion

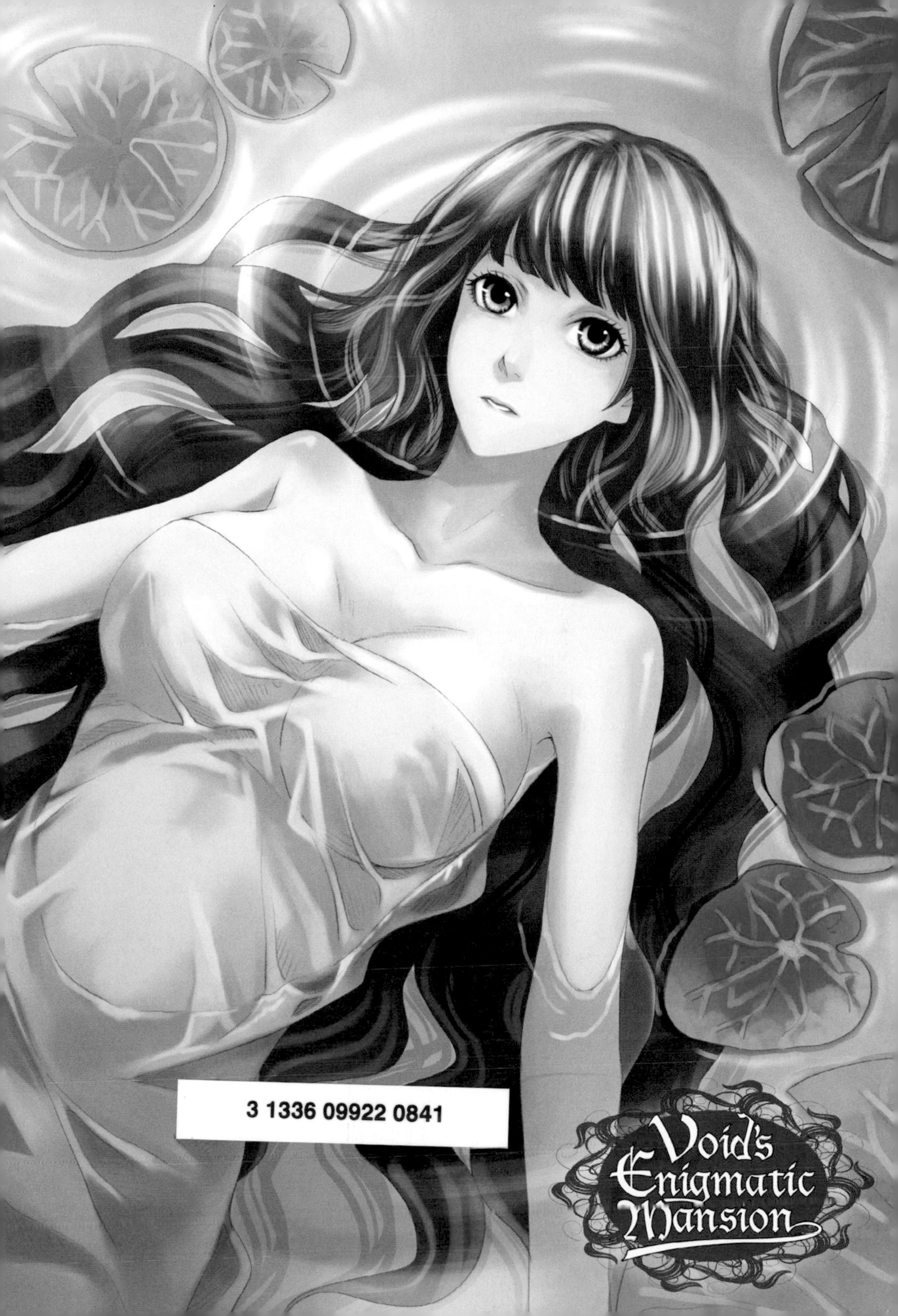
Void's
Enigmatic
Mansion

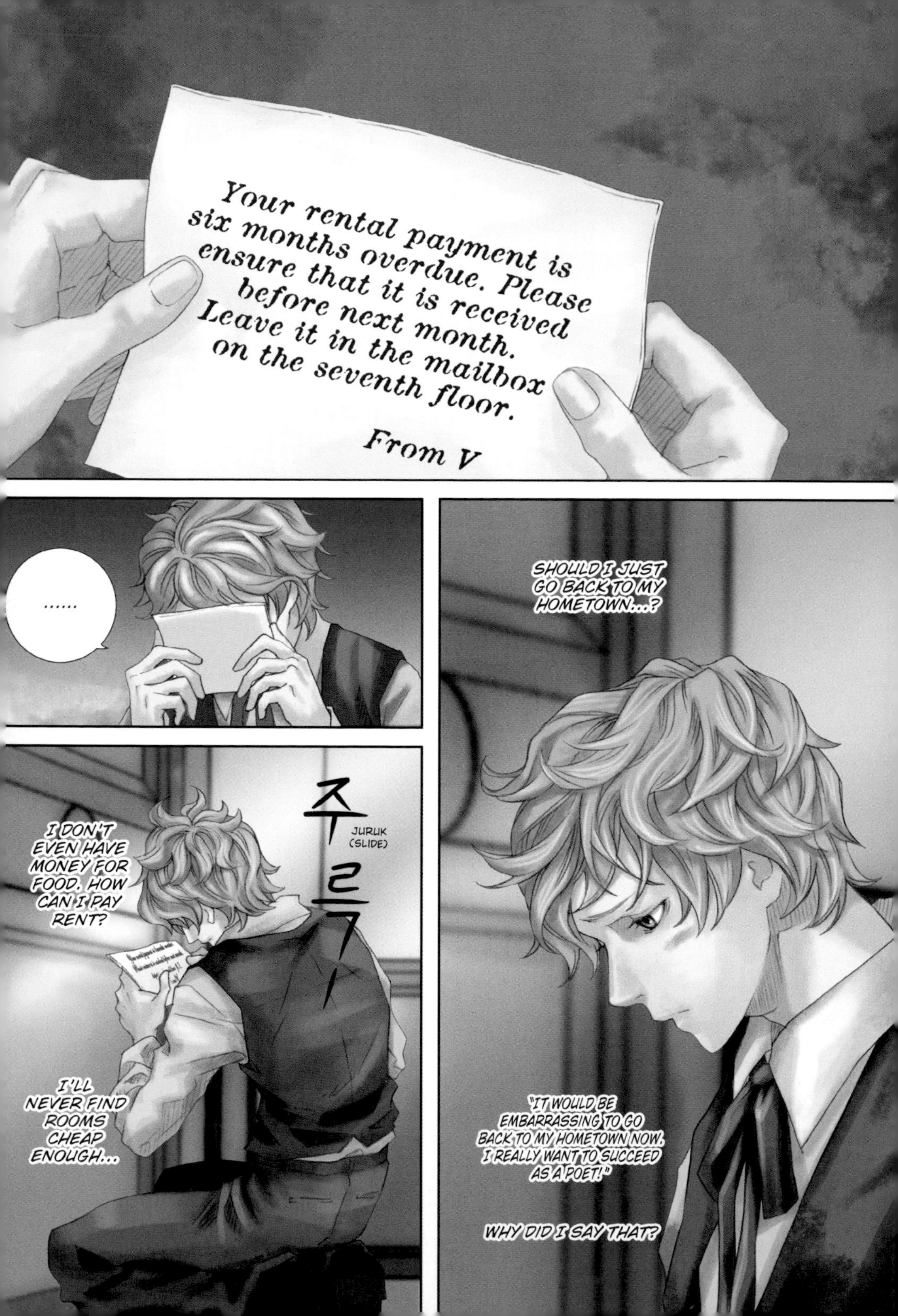

Your rental payment is six months overdue. Please ensure that it is received before next month. Leave it in the mailbox on the seventh floor.
From V
......
I DON'T EVEN HAVE MONEY FOR FOOD. HOW CAN I PAY RENT?
JURUK (SLIDE)
I'LL NEVER FIND ROOMS CHEAP ENOUGH...
SHOULD I JUST GO BACK TO MY HOMETOWN...?
"IT WOULD BE EMBARRASSING TO GO BACK TO MY HOMETOWN NOW. I REALLY WANT TO SUCCEED AS A POET!"
WHY DID I SAY THAT?

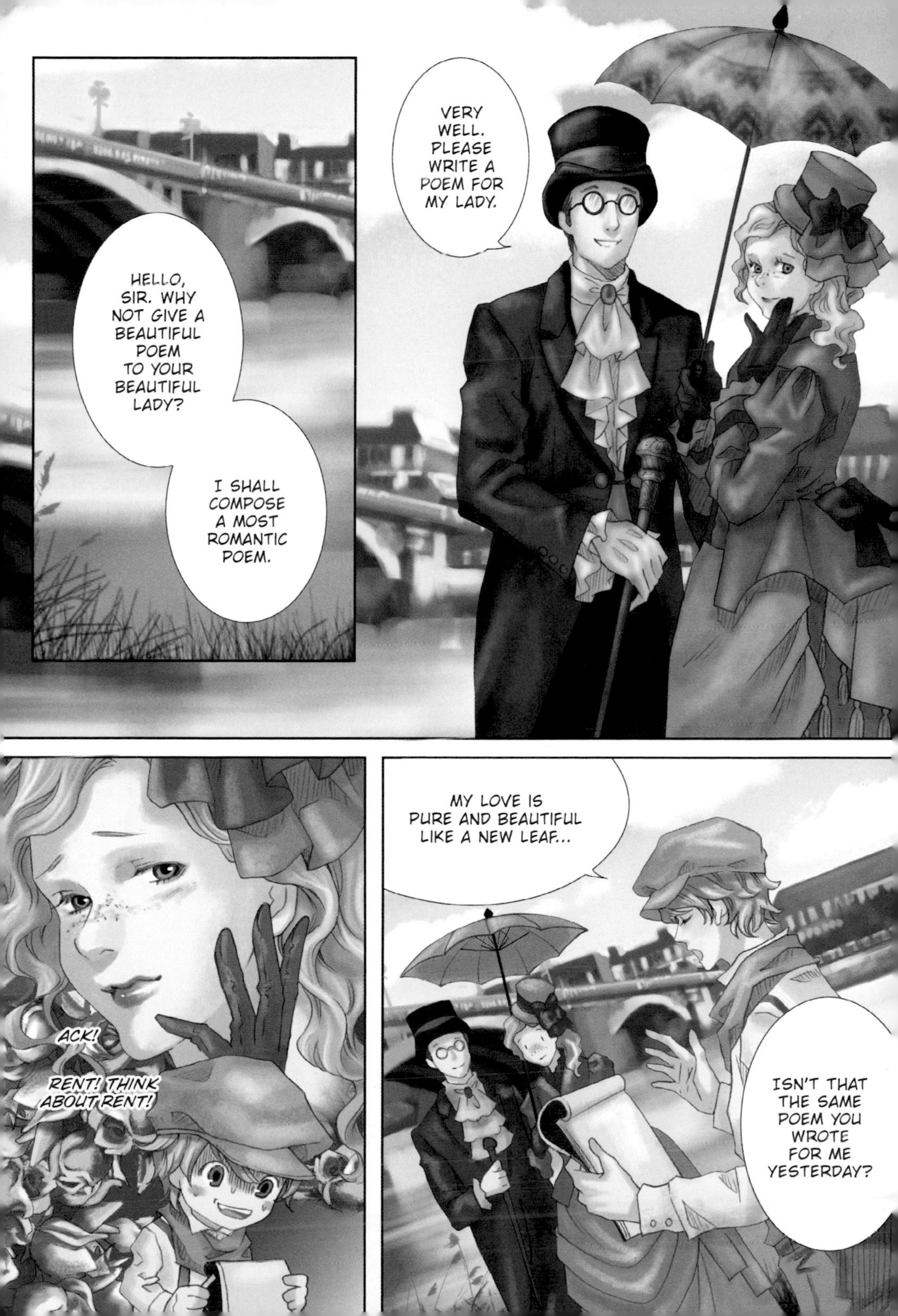
HELLO, SIR. WHY NOT GIVE A BEAUTIFUL POEM TO YOUR BEAUTIFUL LADY?
I SHALL COMPOSE A MOST ROMANTIC POEM.
VERY WELL. PLEASE WRITE A POEM FOR MY LADY.
ACK!
RENT! THINK ABOUT RENT!
MY LOVE IS PURE AND BEAUTIFUL LIKE A NEW LEAF...
ISN'T THAT THE SAME POEM YOU WROTE FOR ME YESTERDAY?

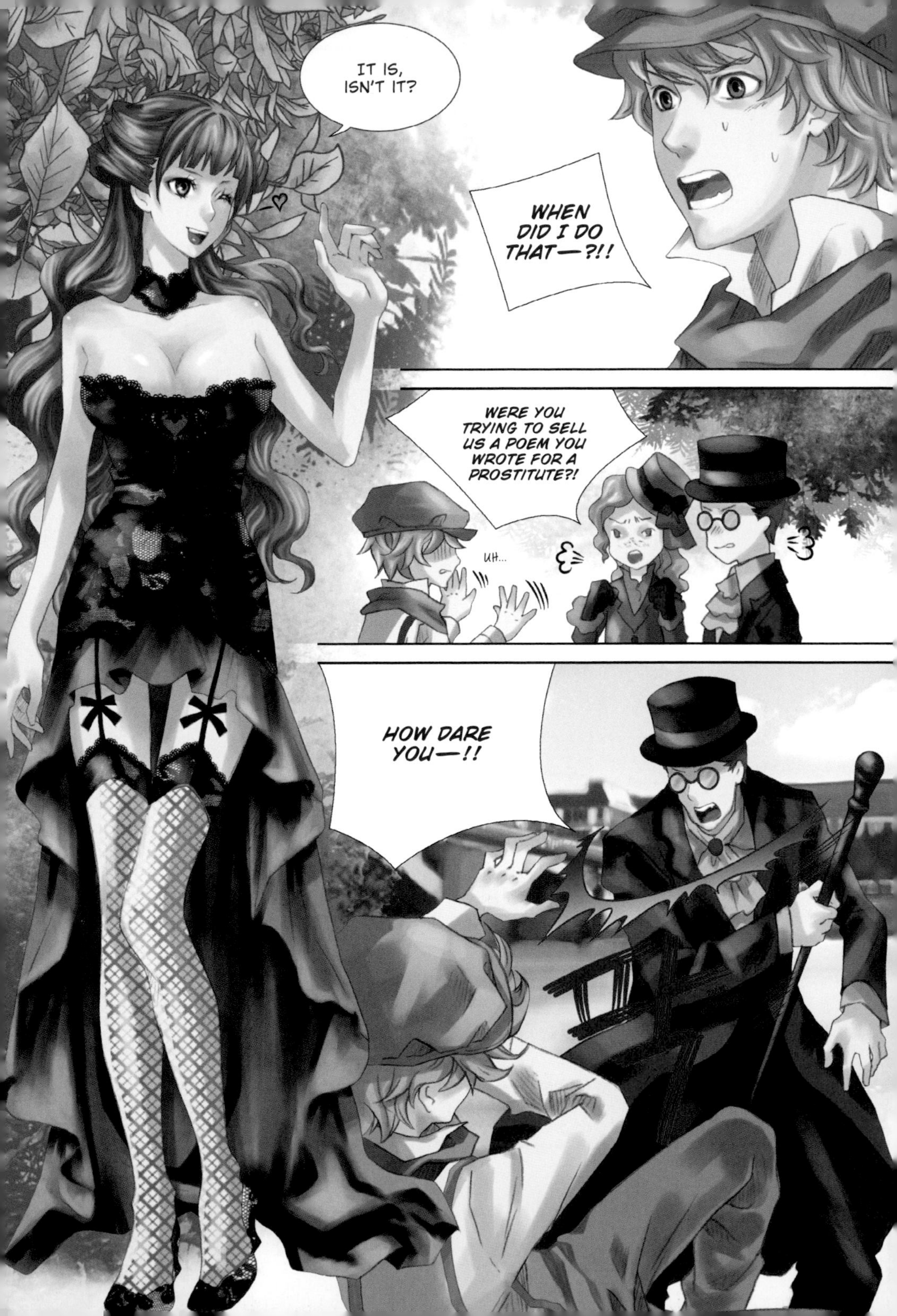
IT IS, ISN'T IT?
WHEN DID I DO THAT—?!!
WERE YOU TRYING TO SELL US A POEM YOU WROTE FOR A PROSTITUTE?!
UH...
HOW DARE YOU—!!

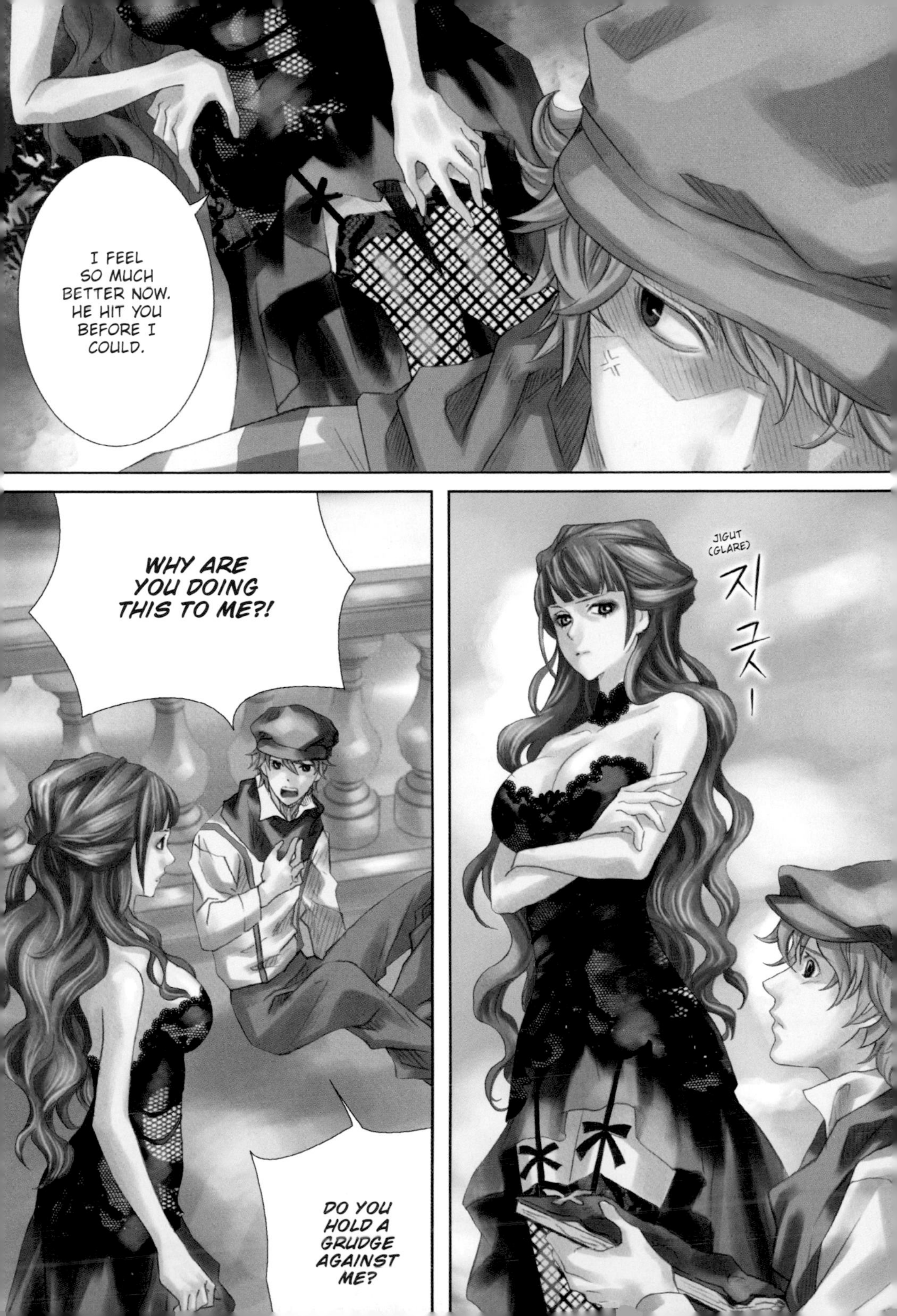
I FEEL SO MUCH BETTER NOW. HE HIT YOU BEFORE I COULD.
WHY ARE YOU DOING THIS TO ME?!
DO YOU HOLD A GRUDGE AGAINST ME?
JIGUT (GLARE)
지긋-

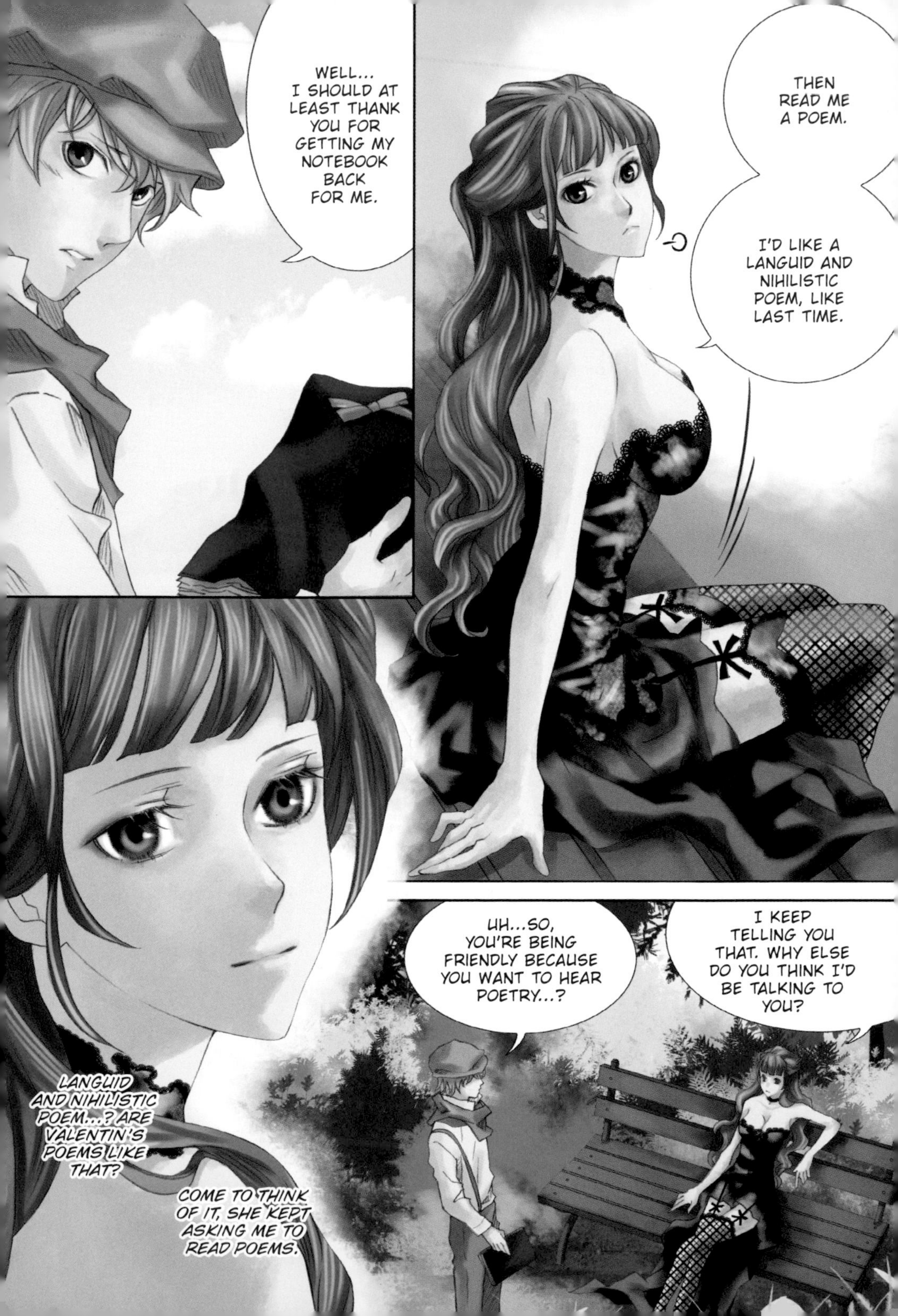
WELL... I SHOULD AT LEAST THANK YOU FOR GETTING MY NOTEBOOK BACK FOR ME.
THEN READ ME A POEM.
I'D LIKE A LANGUID AND NIHILISTIC POEM, LIKE LAST TIME.
LANGUID AND NIHILISTIC POEM...? ARE VALENTIN'S POEMS LIKE THAT?
COME TO THINK OF IT, SHE KEPT ASKING ME TO READ POEMS.
UH...SO, YOU'RE BEING FRIENDLY BECAUSE YOU WANT TO HEAR POETRY...?
I KEEP TELLING YOU THAT. WHY ELSE DO YOU THINK I'D BE TALKING TO YOU?

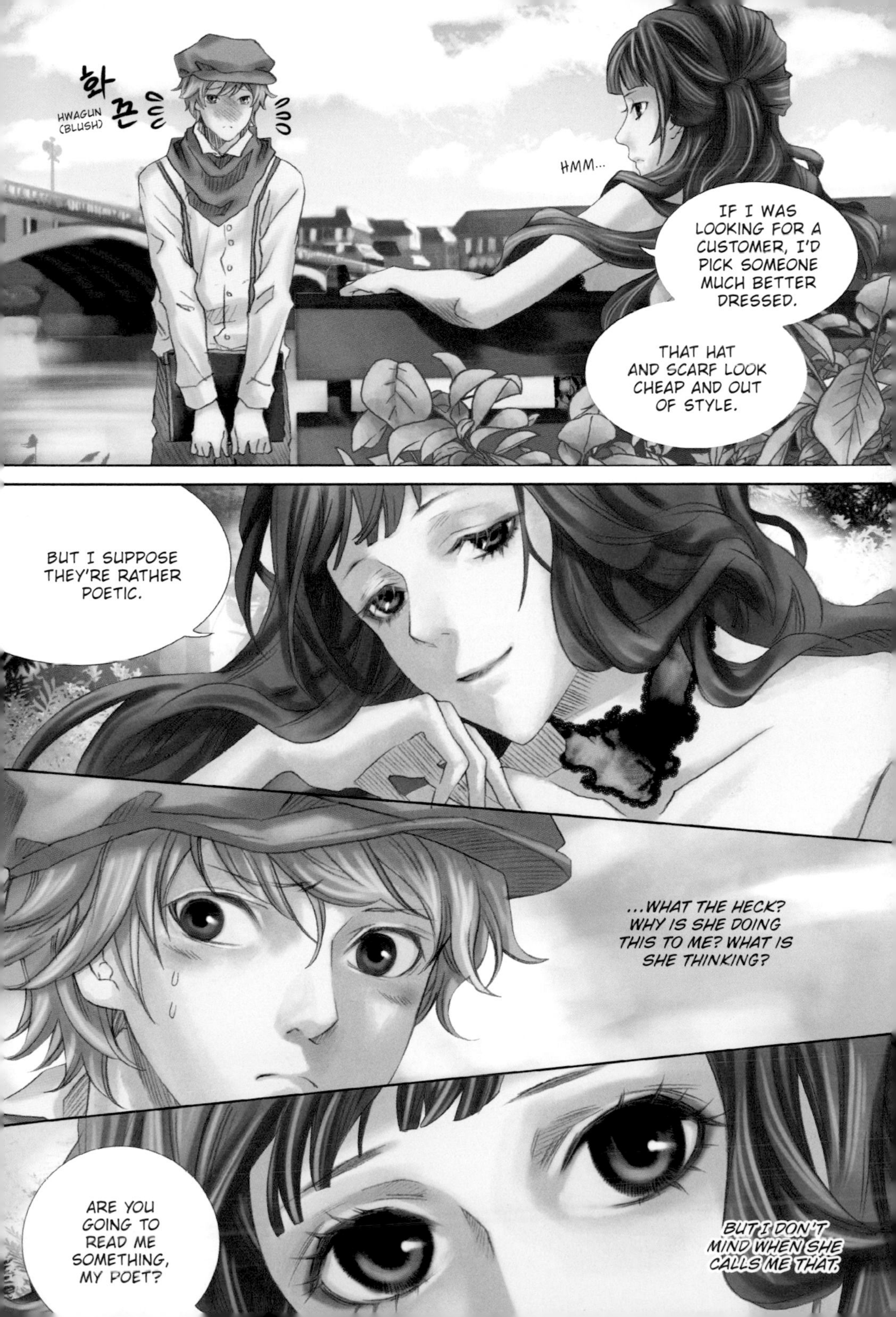
화끈
HWAGUN (BLUSH)
HMM...
IF I WAS LOOKING FOR A CUSTOMER, I'D PICK SOMEONE MUCH BETTER DRESSED.
THAT HAT AND SCARF LOOK CHEAP AND OUT OF STYLE.
BUT I SUPPOSE THEY'RE RATHER POETIC.
...WHAT THE HECK? WHY IS SHE DOING THIS TO ME? WHAT IS SHE THINKING?
ARE YOU GOING TO READ ME SOMETHING, MY POET?
BUT I DON'T MIND WHEN SHE CALLS ME THAT.

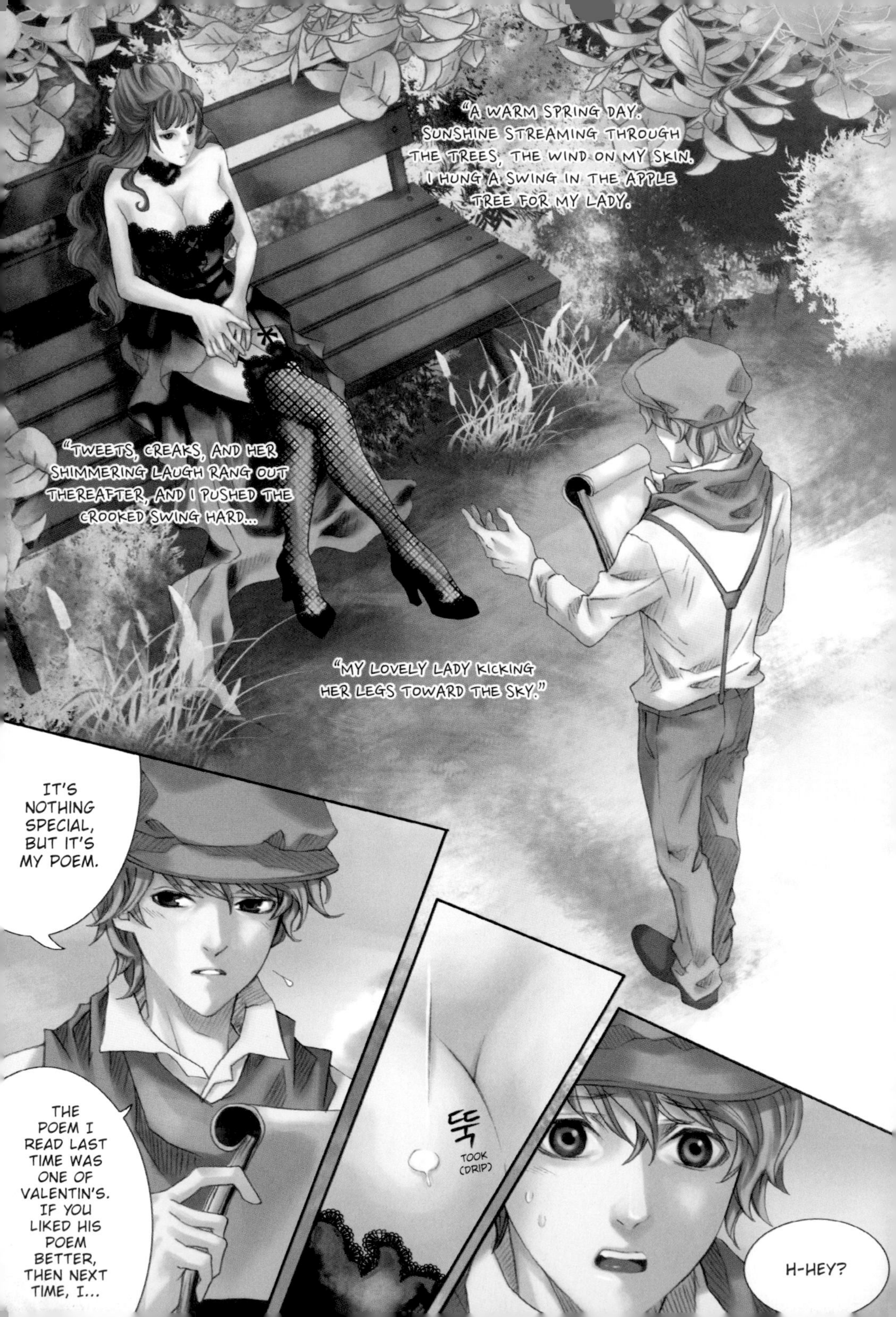
"A WARM SPRING DAY. SUNSHINE STREAMING THROUGH THE TREES, THE WIND ON MY SKIN. I HUNG A SWING IN THE APPLE TREE FOR MY LADY.
"TWEETS, CREAKS, AND HER SHIMMERING LAUGH RANG OUT THEREAFTER, AND I PUSHED THE CROOKED SWING HARD...
"MY LOVELY LADY KICKING HER LEGS TOWARD THE SKY."
IT'S NOTHING SPECIAL, BUT IT'S MY POEM.
THE POEM I READ LAST TIME WAS ONE OF VALENTIN'S. IF YOU LIKED HIS POEM BETTER, THEN NEXT TIME, I...
뚝
TOOK (DRIP)
H-HEY?

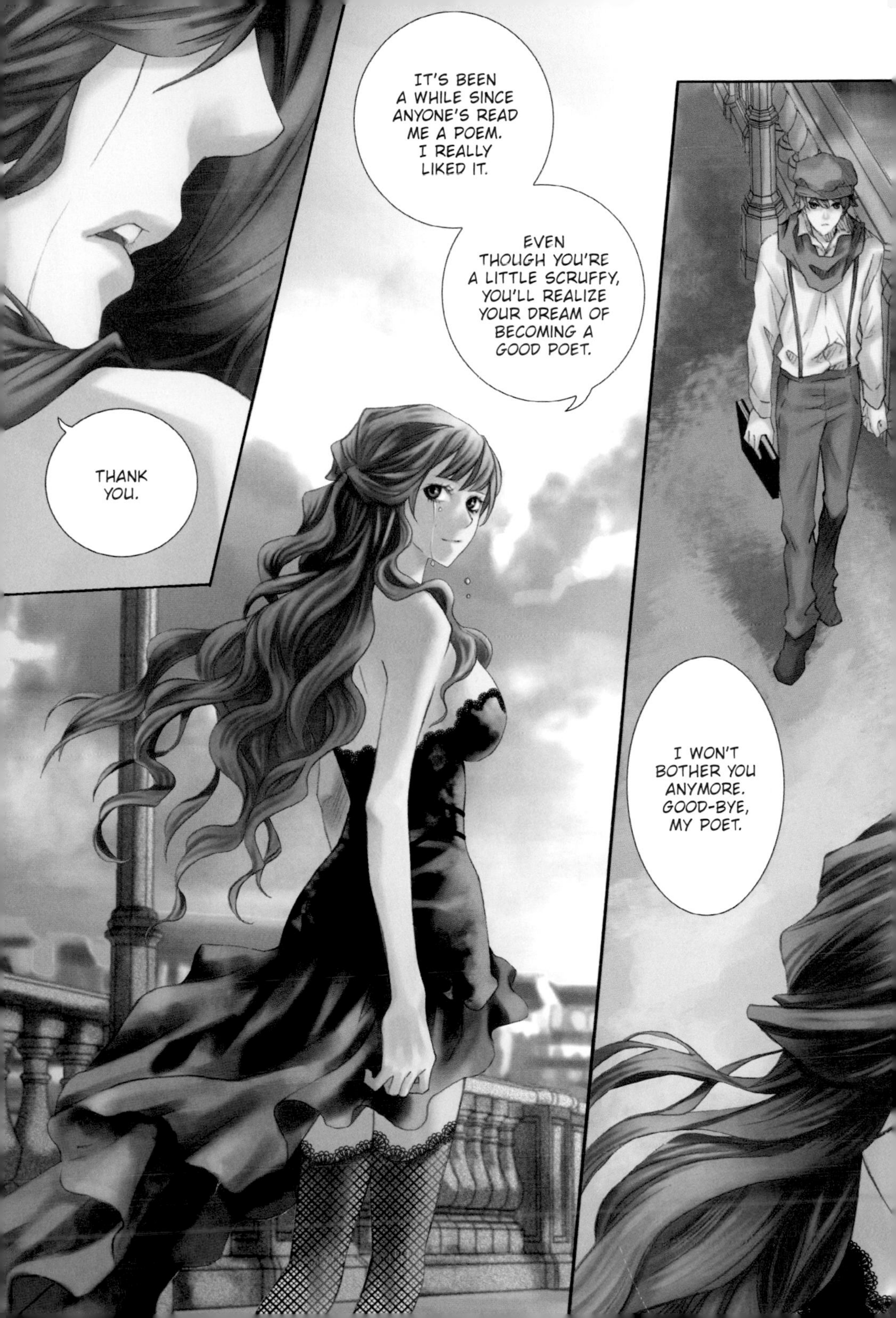
THANK YOU.
IT'S BEEN A WHILE SINCE ANYONE'S READ ME A POEM. I REALLY LIKED IT.
EVEN THOUGH YOU'RE A LITTLE SCRUFFY, YOU'LL REALIZE YOUR DREAM OF BECOMING A GOOD POET.
I WON'T BOTHER YOU ANYMORE. GOOD-BYE, MY POET.

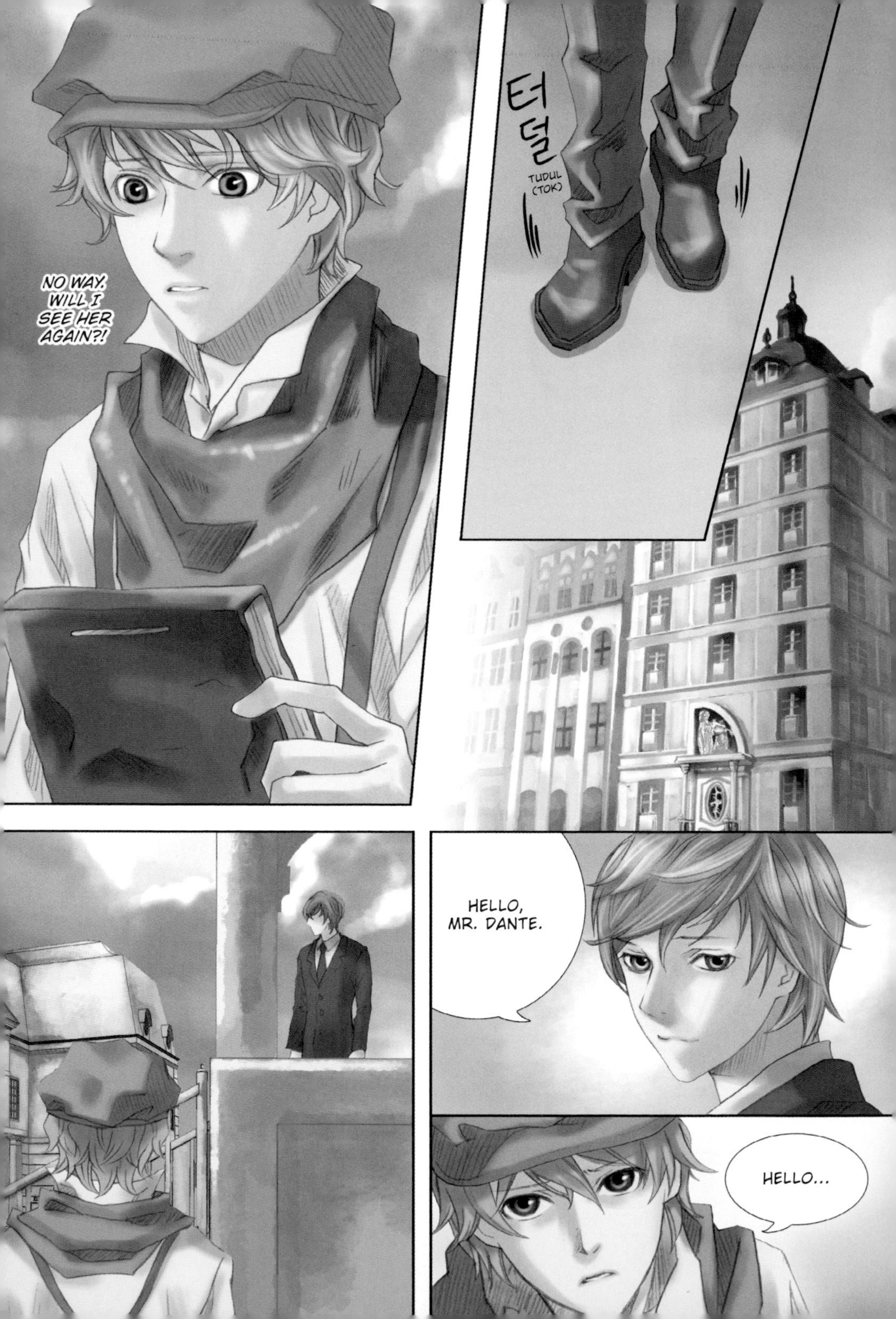
NO WAY. WILL I SEE HER AGAIN?!
터덜
TUDUL (TOK)
HELLO, MR. DANTE.
HELLO...

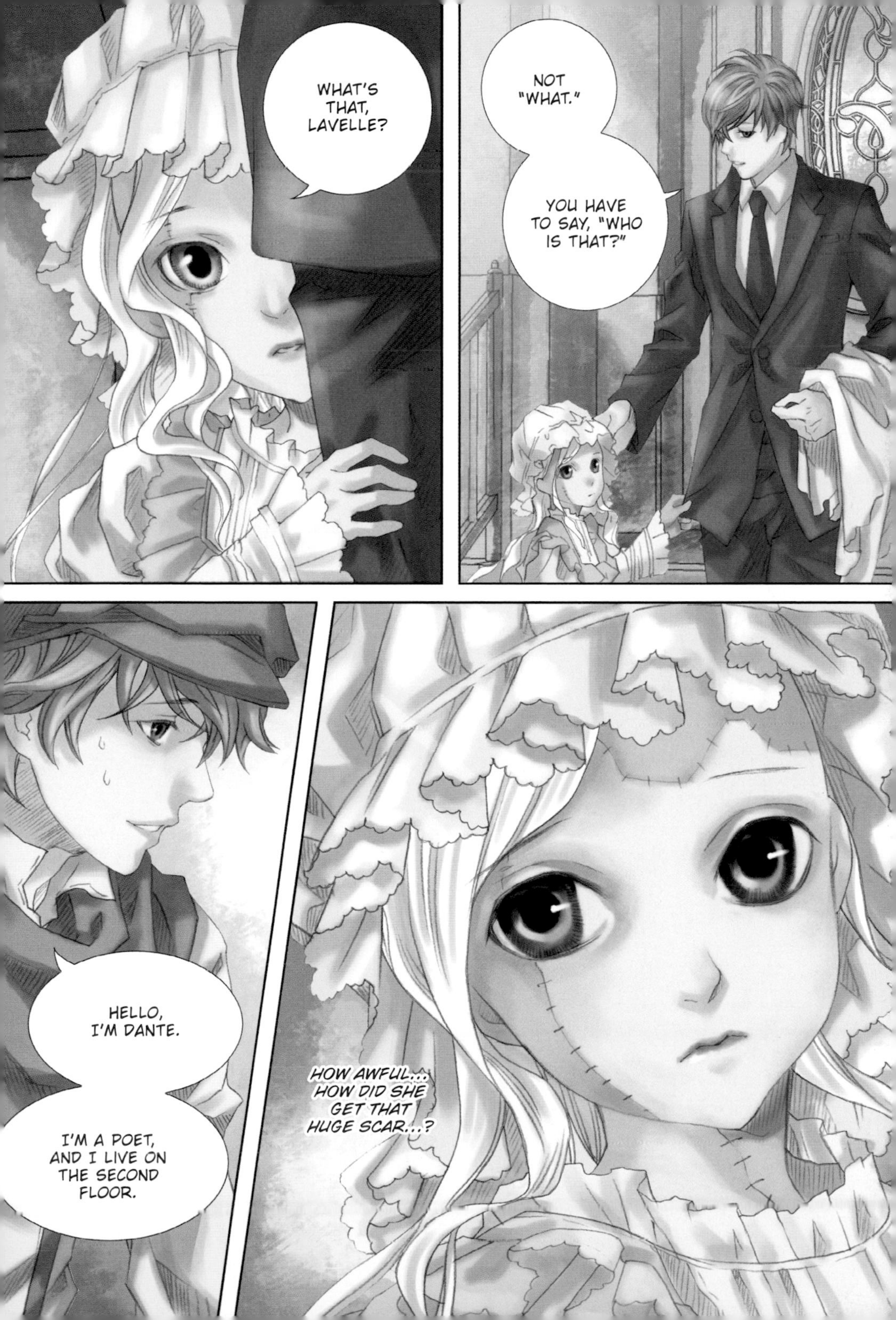
WHAT'S THAT, LAVELLE?
NOT "WHAT."
YOU HAVE TO SAY, "WHO IS THAT?"
HELLO, I'M DANTE.
I'M A POET, AND I LIVE ON THE SECOND FLOOR.
HOW AWFUL... HOW DID SHE GET THAT HUGE SCAR...?

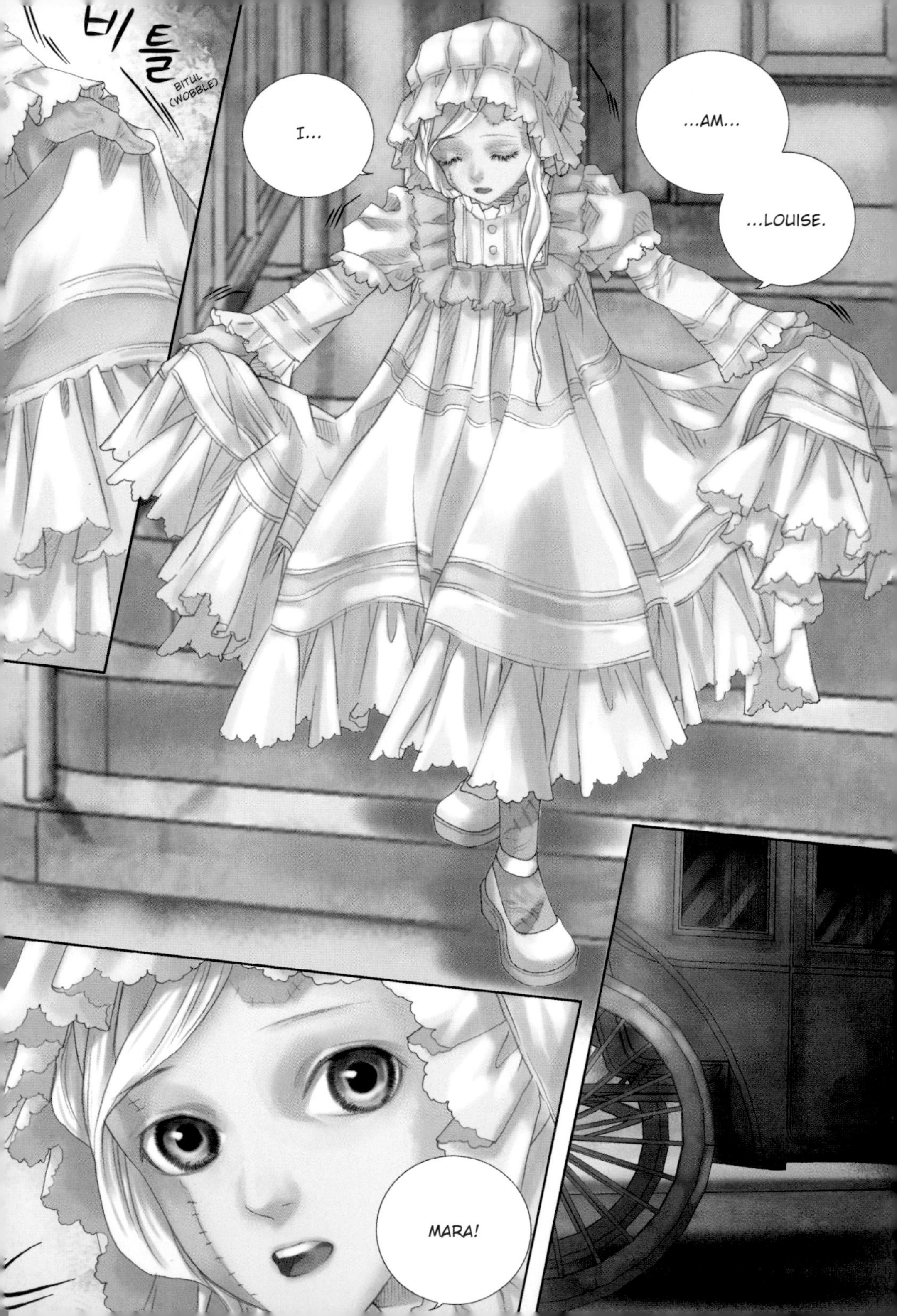
비틀
BITUL (WOBBLE)
I...
...AM...
...LOUISE.
MARA!

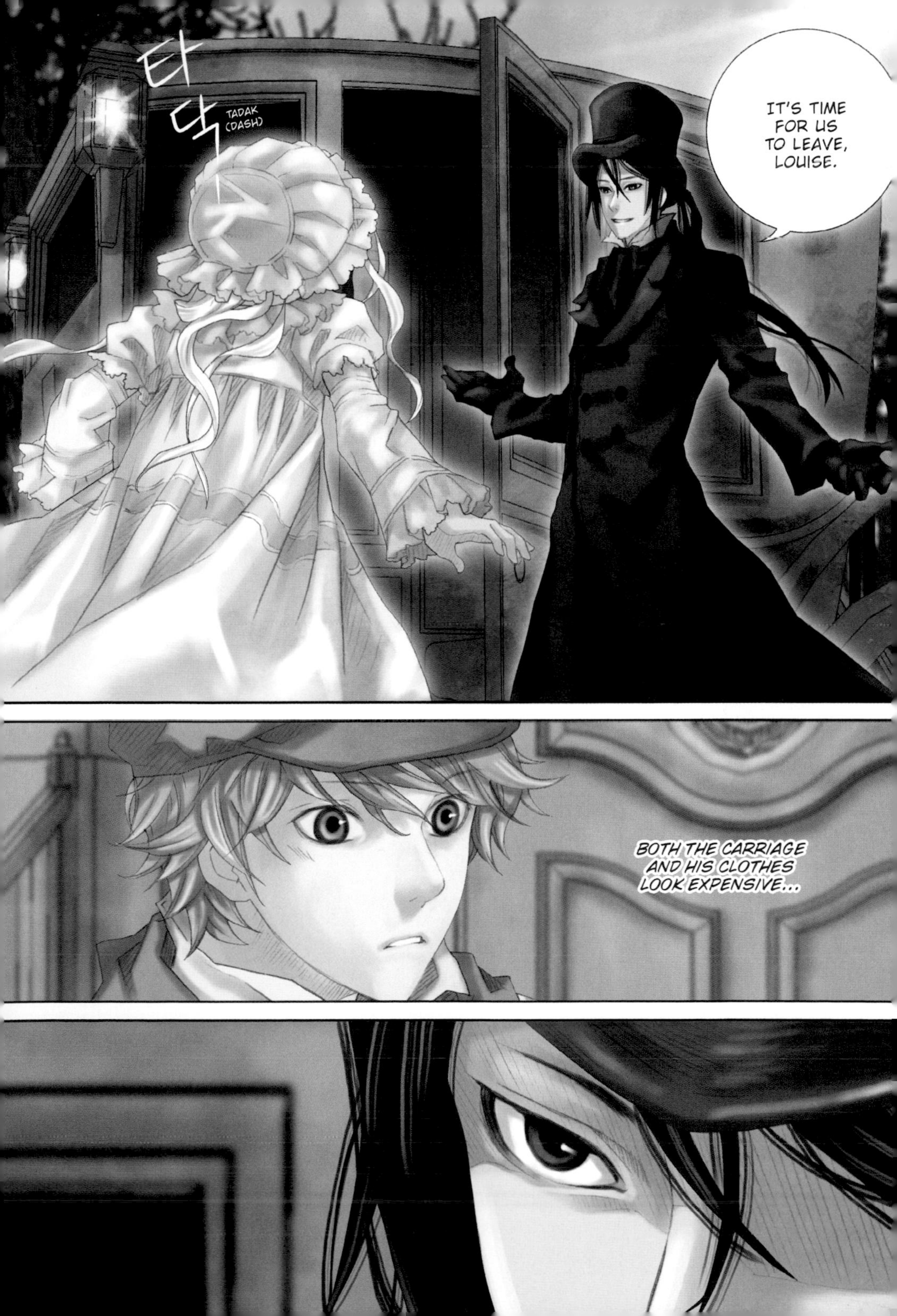

타닥
TADAK (DASH)
IT'S TIME FOR US TO LEAVE, LOUISE.
BOTH THE CARRIAGE AND HIS CLOTHES LOOK EXPENSIVE...

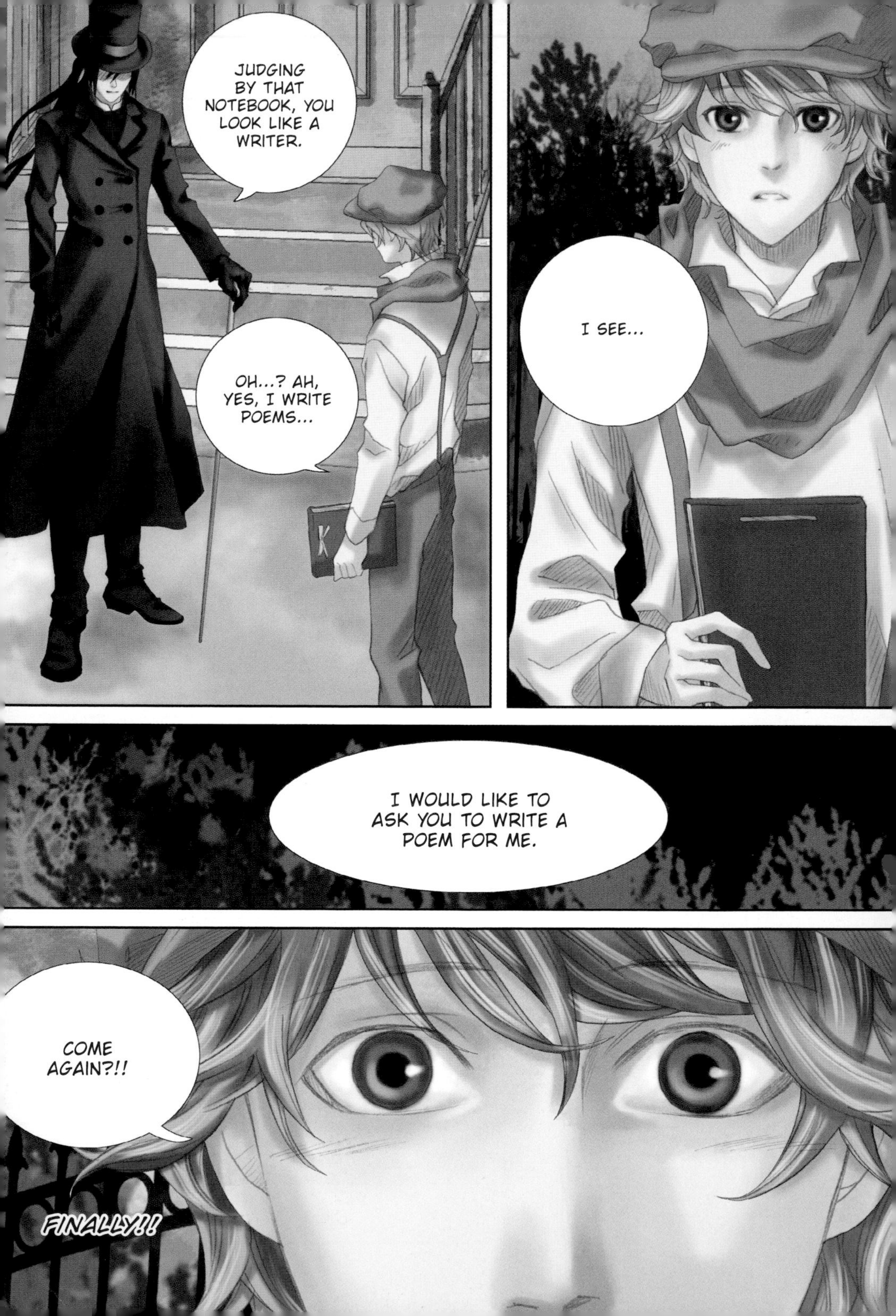
JUDGING BY THAT NOTEBOOK, YOU LOOK LIKE A WRITER.
OH...? AH, YES, I WRITE POEMS...
I SEE...
I WOULD LIKE TO ASK YOU TO WRITE A POEM FOR ME.
COME AGAIN?!!
FINALLY!!

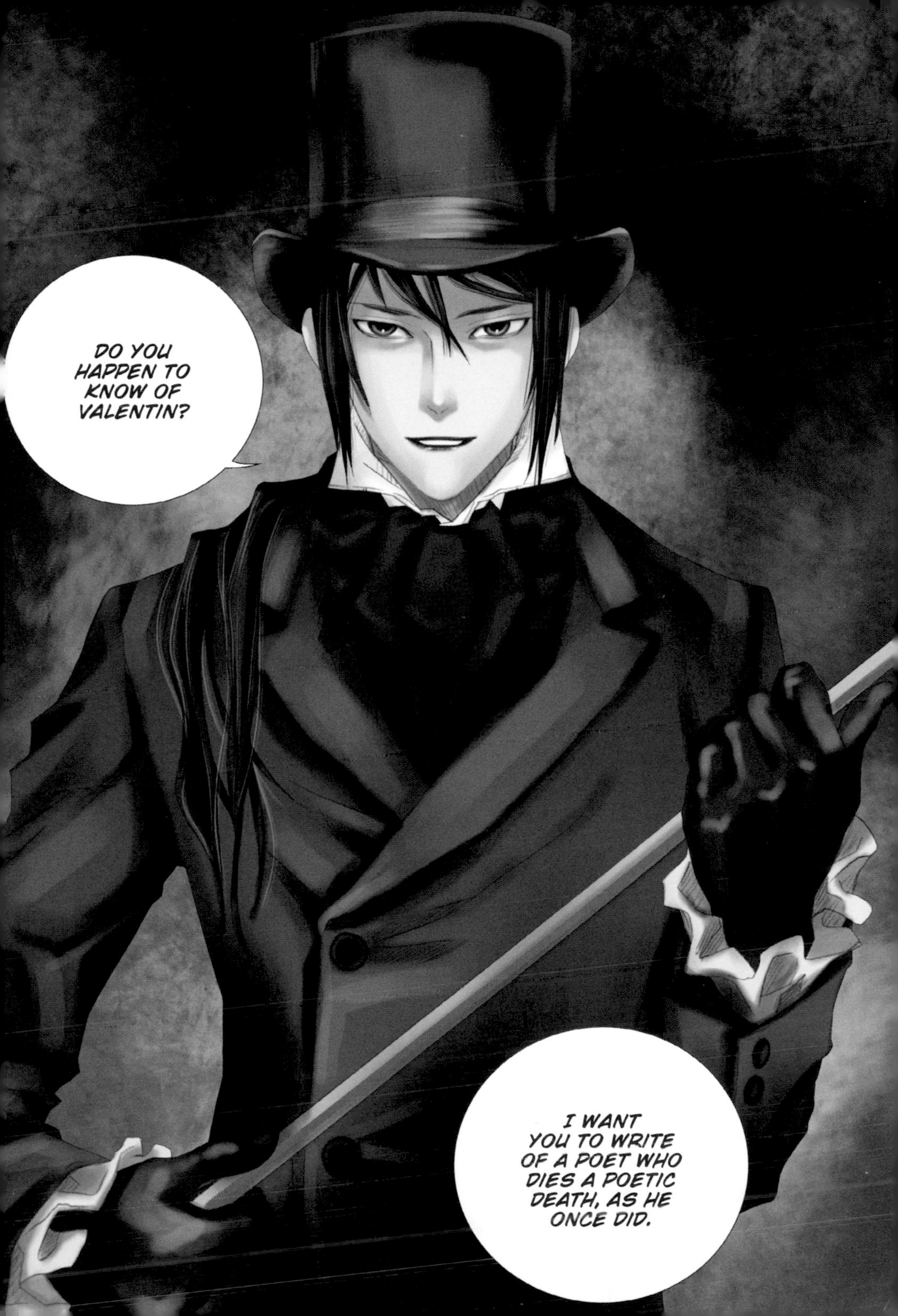
DO YOU HAPPEN TO KNOW OF VALENTIN?
I WANT YOU TO WRITE OF A POET WHO DIES A POETIC DEATH, AS HE ONCE DID.

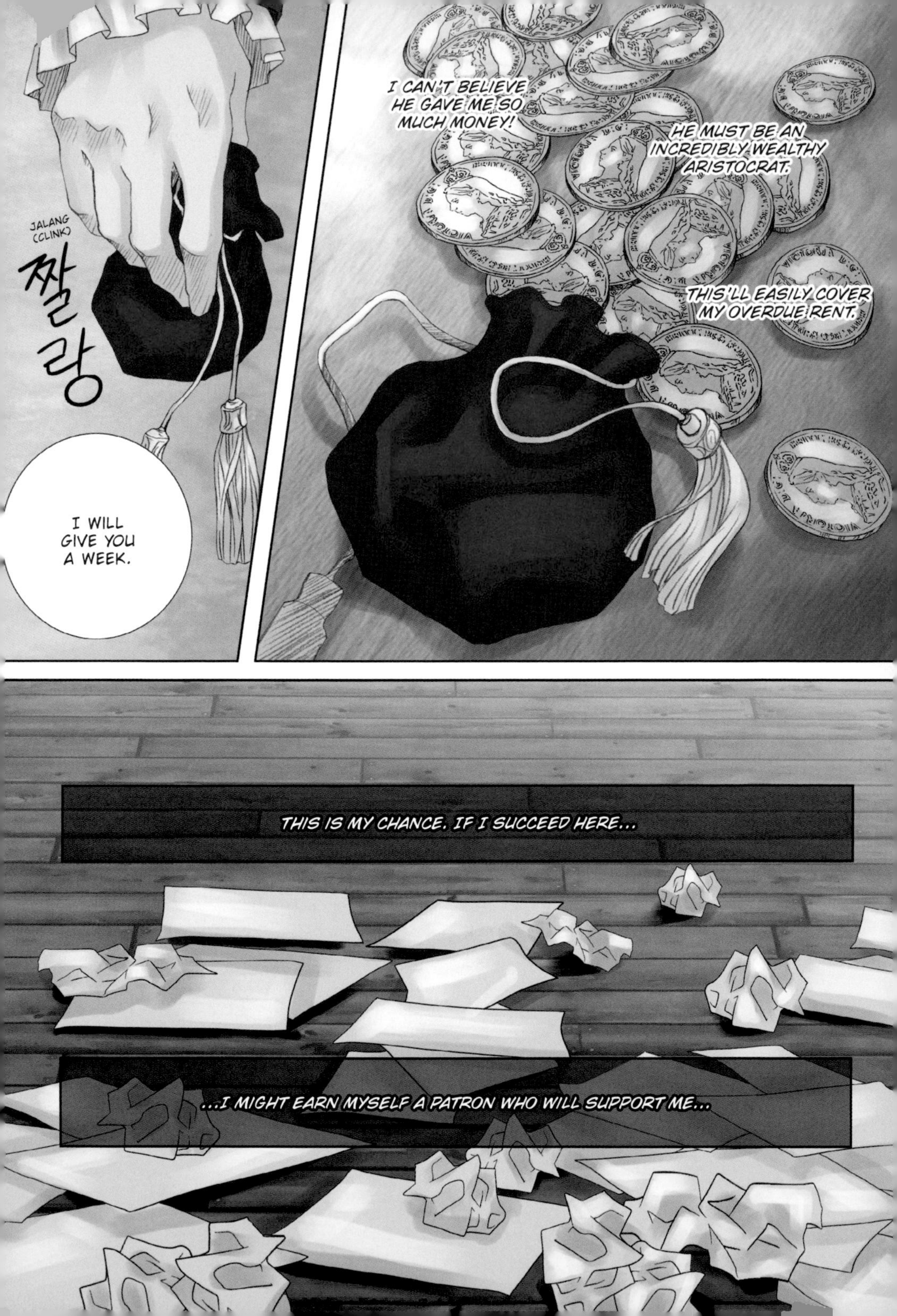
JALANG (CLINK)
짤랑
I WILL GIVE YOU A WEEK.
I CAN'T BELIEVE HE GAVE ME SO MUCH MONEY!
HE MUST BE AN INCREDIBLY WEALTHY ARISTOCRAT.
THIS'LL EASILY COVER MY OVERDUE RENT.
THIS IS MY CHANCE. IF I SUCCEED HERE...
...I MIGHT EARN MYSELF A PATRON WHO WILL SUPPORT ME...

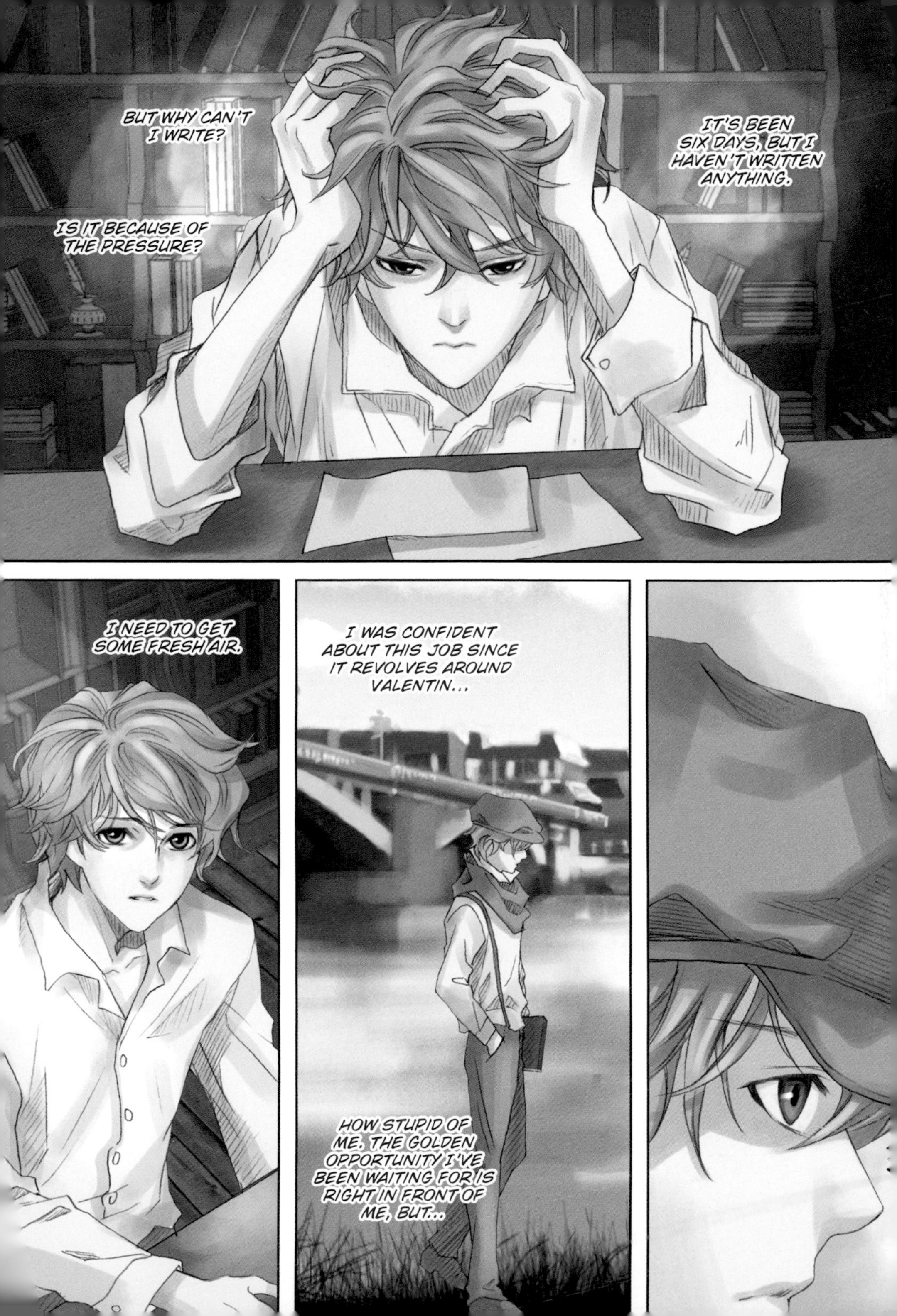
BUT WHY CAN'T I WRITE?
IS IT BECAUSE OF THE PRESSURE?
IT'S BEEN SIX DAYS, BUT I HAVEN'T WRITTEN ANYTHING.
I NEED TO GET SOME FRESH AIR.
I WAS CONFIDENT ABOUT THIS JOB SINCE IT REVOLVES AROUND VALENTIN...
HOW STUPID OF ME. THE GOLDEN OPPORTUNITY I'VE BEEN WAITING FOR IS RIGHT IN FRONT OF ME, BUT...

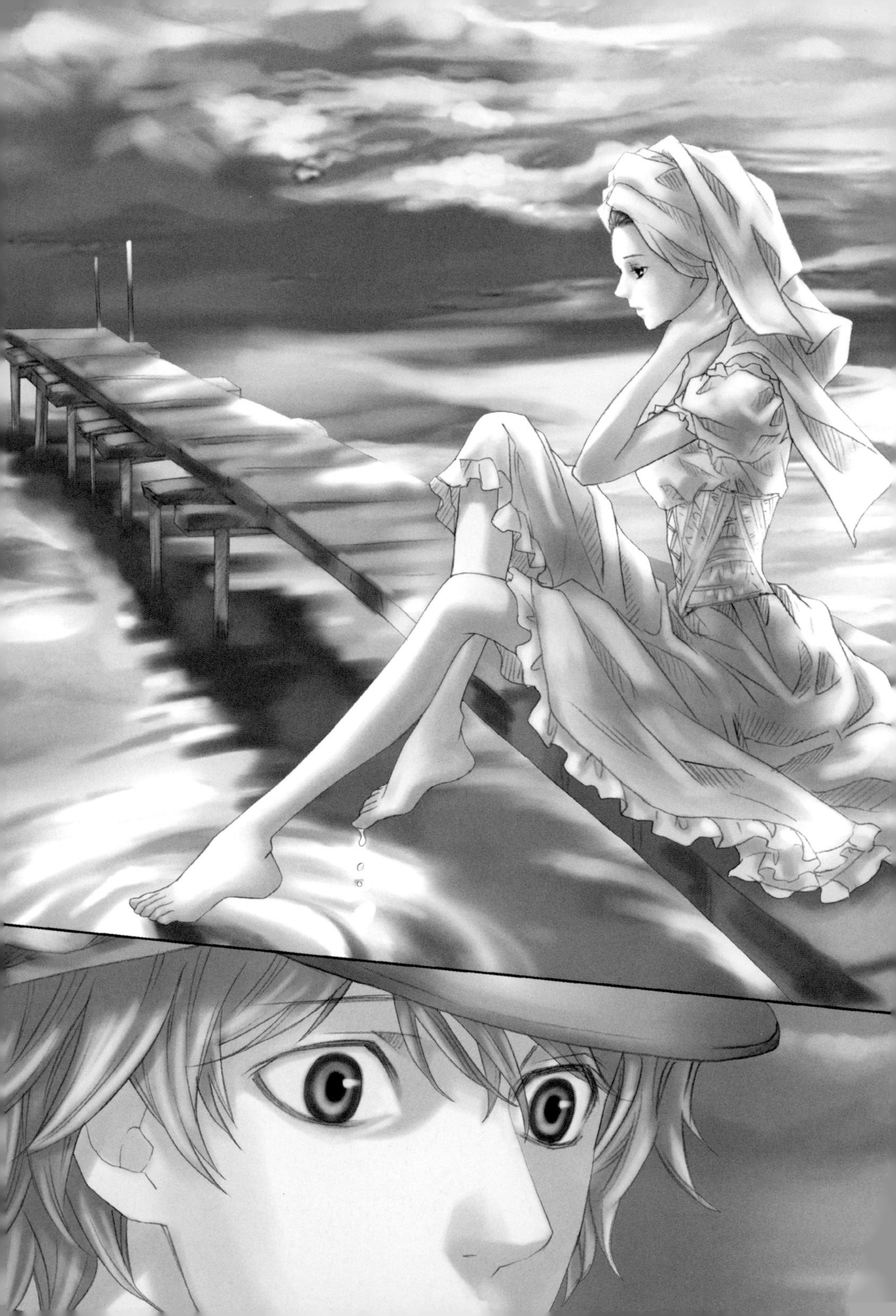

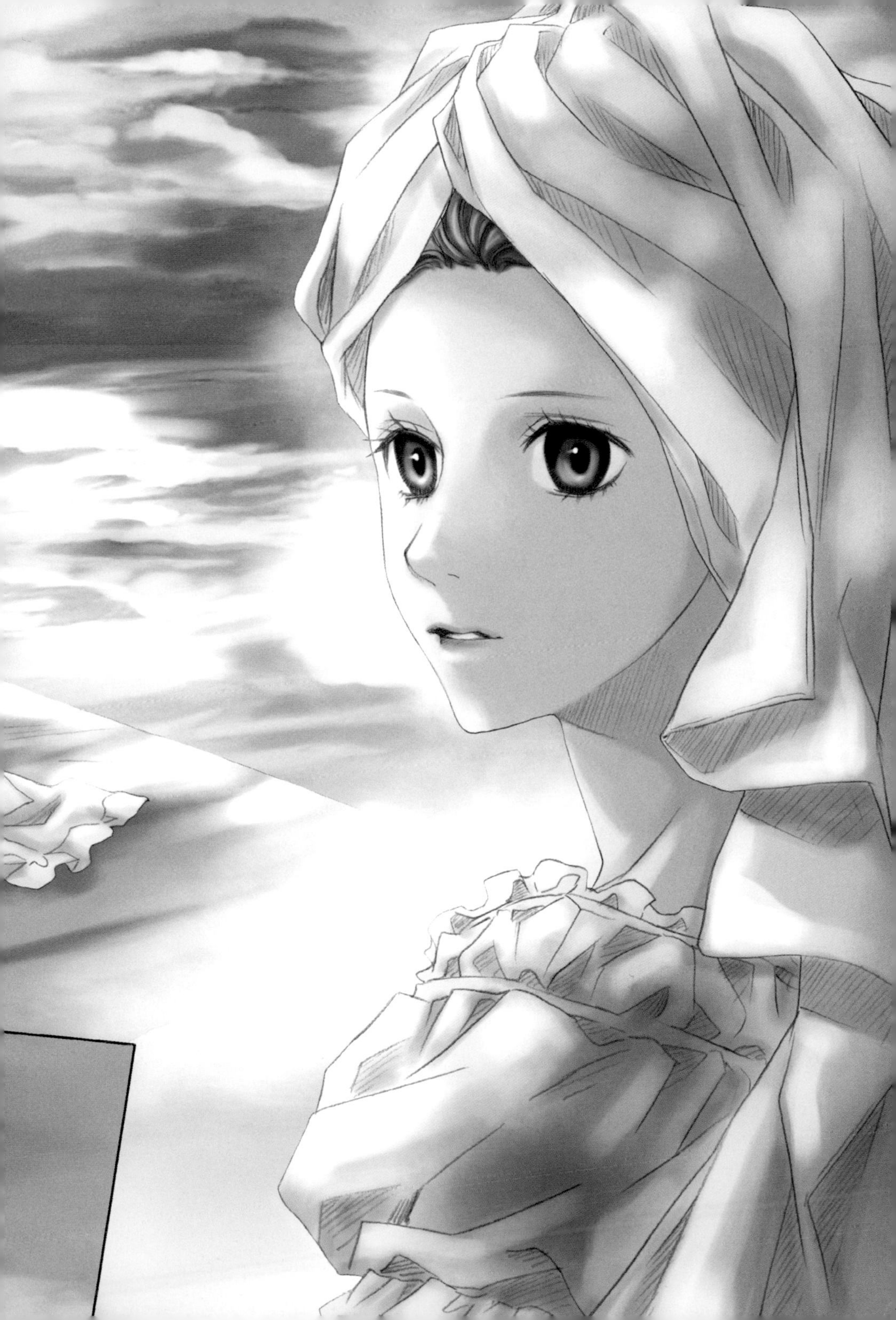

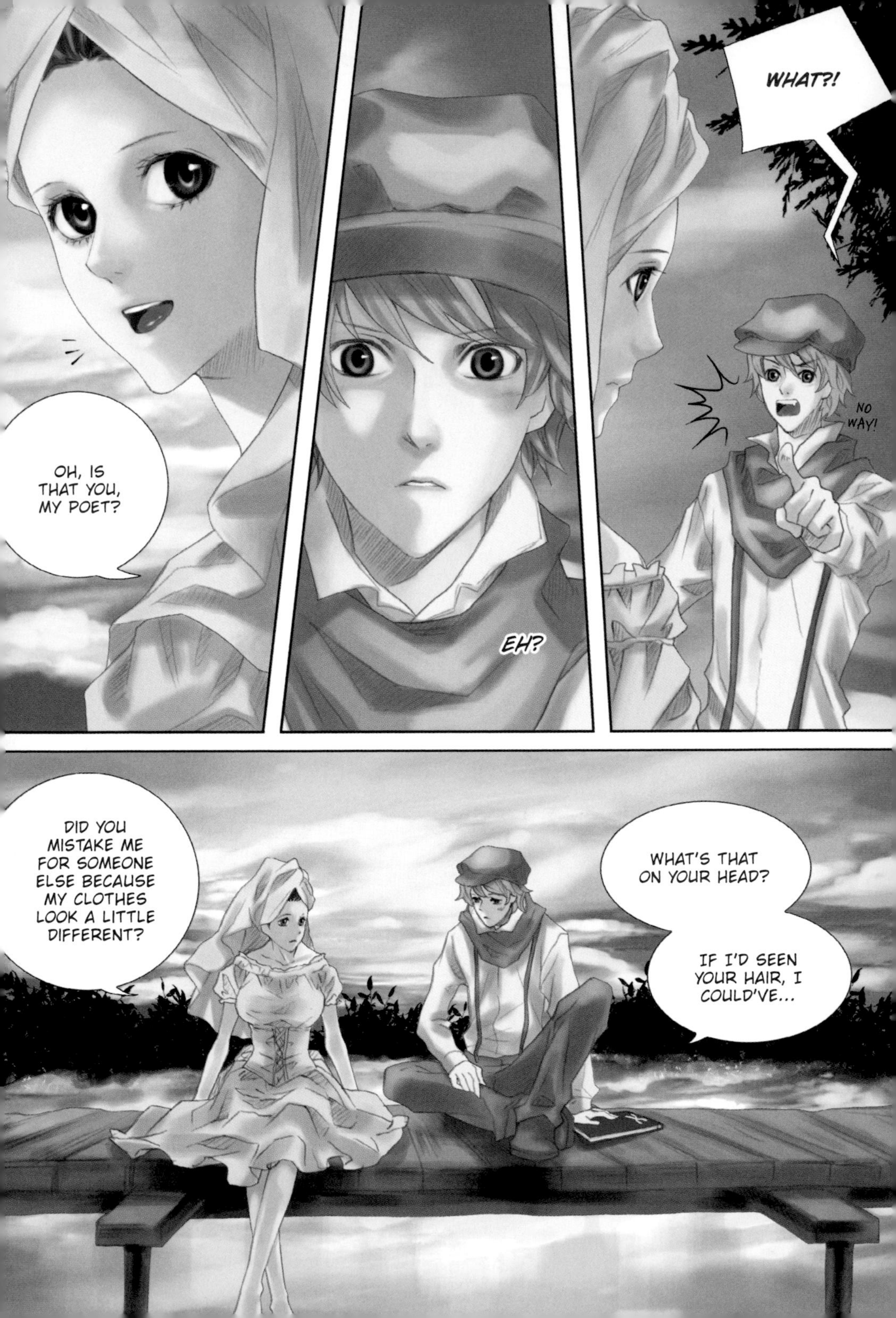
OH, IS THAT YOU, MY POET?
EH?
WHAT?!
NO WAY!
DID YOU MISTAKE ME FOR SOMEONE ELSE BECAUSE MY CLOTHES LOOK A LITTLE DIFFERENT?
WHAT'S THAT ON YOUR HEAD?
IF I'D SEEN YOUR HAIR, I COULD'VE...

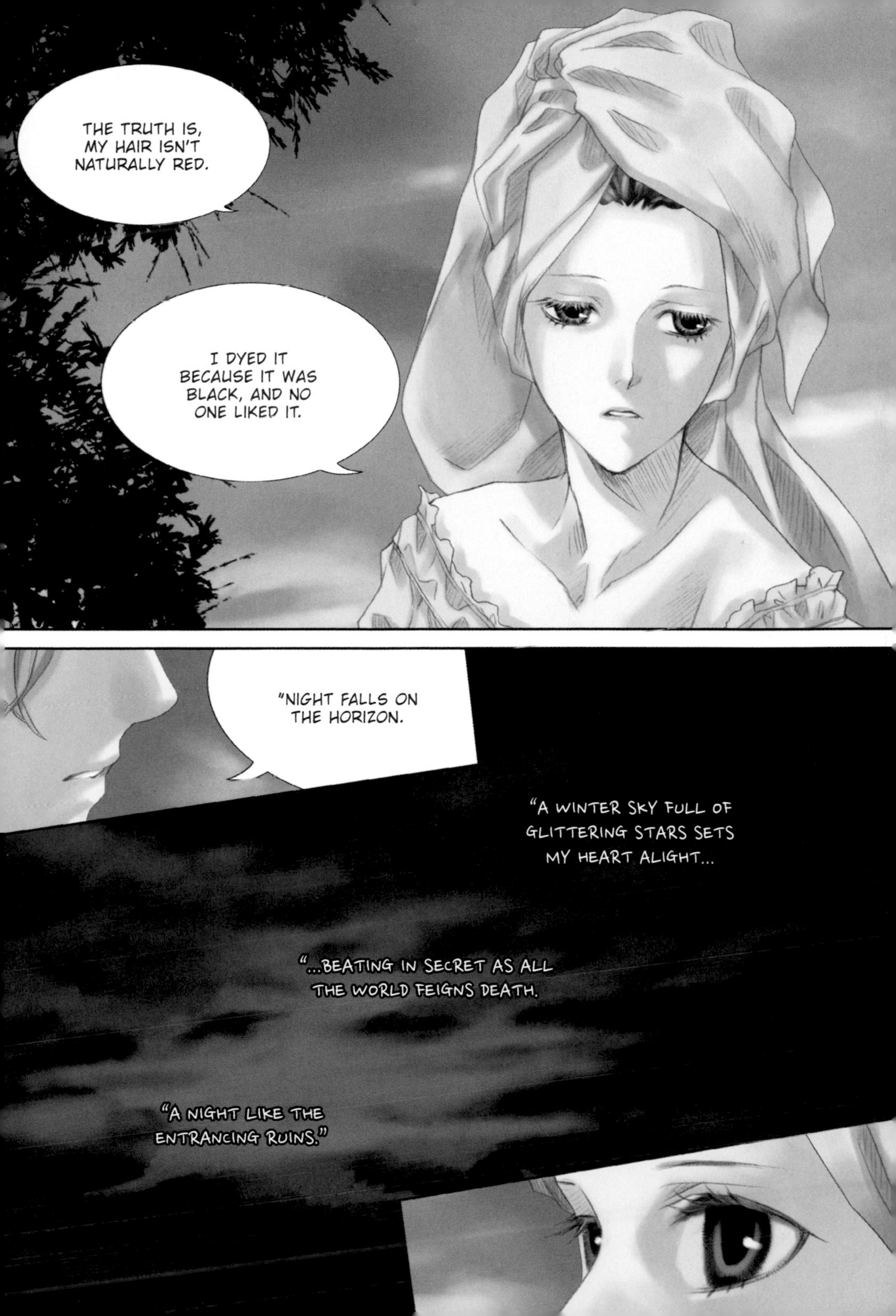
THE TRUTH IS, MY HAIR ISN'T NATURALLY RED.
I DYED IT BECAUSE IT WAS BLACK, AND NO ONE LIKED IT.
"NIGHT FALLS ON THE HORIZON.
"A WINTER SKY FULL OF GLITTERING STARS SETS MY HEART ALIGHT...
"...BEATING IN SECRET AS ALL THE WORLD FEIGNS DEATH.
"A NIGHT LIKE THE ENTRANCING RUINS."

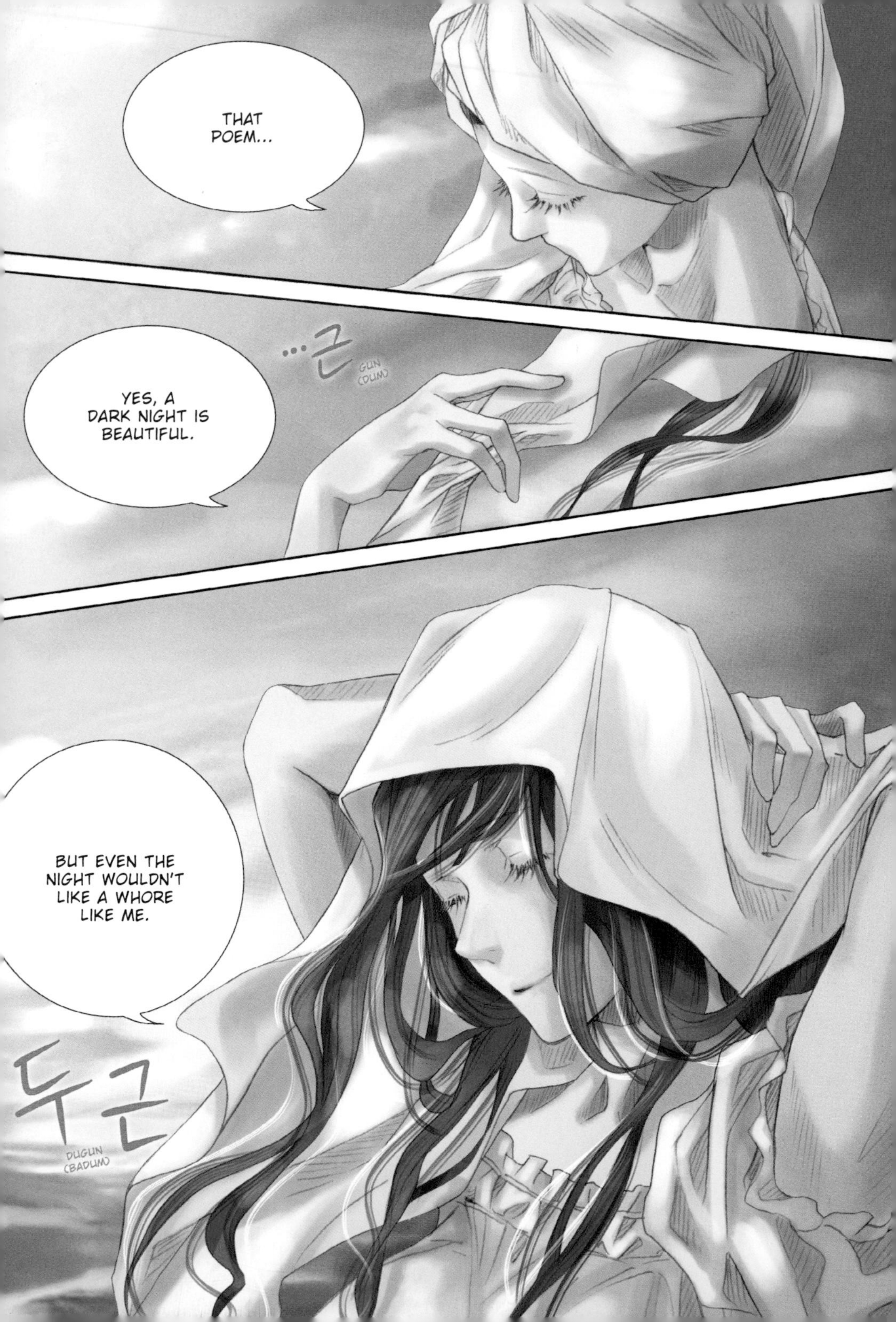
THAT POEM...
YES, A DARK NIGHT IS BEAUTIFUL.
...근
GUN (DUM)
BUT EVEN THE NIGHT WOULDN'T LIKE A WHORE LIKE ME.
두근
DUGUN (BADUM)

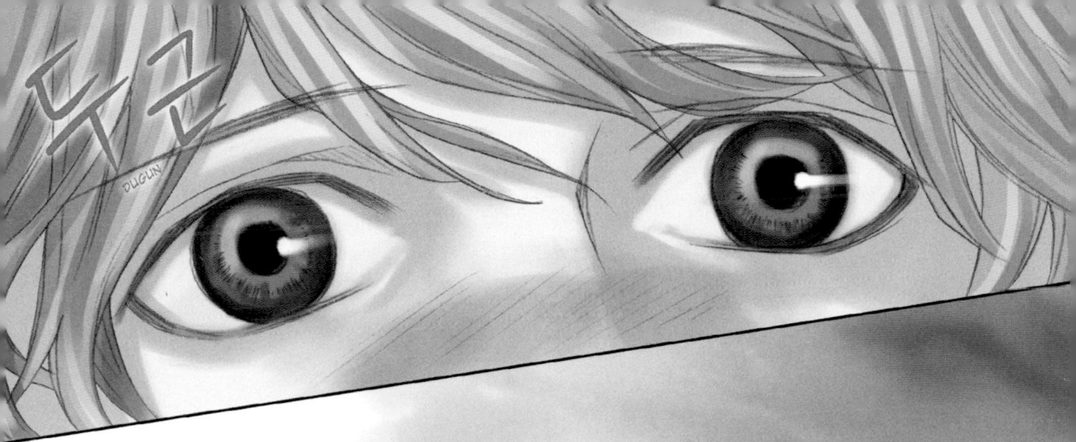
두군
DUGUN

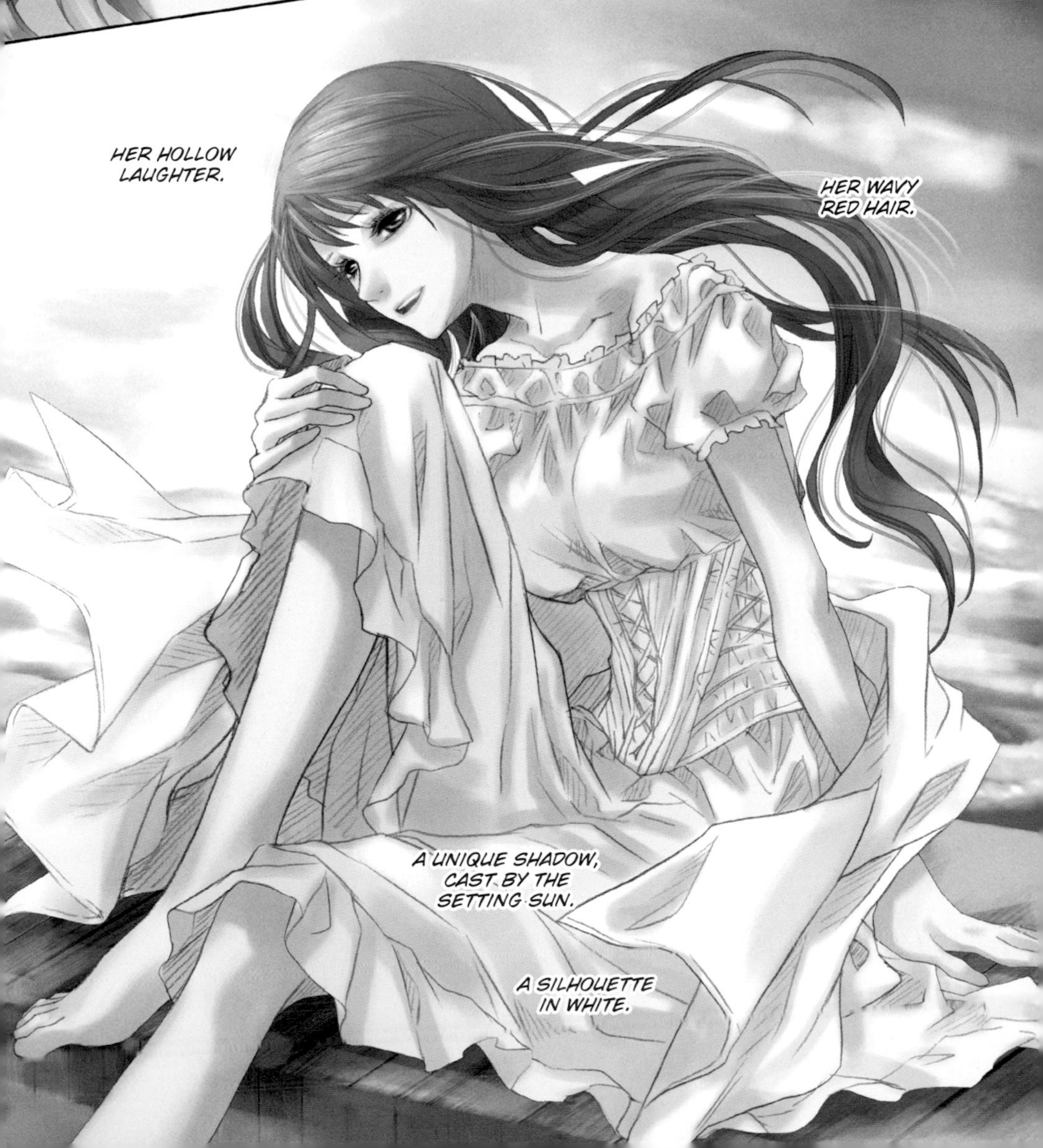
HER HOLLOW LAUGHTER.
HER WAVY RED HAIR.
A UNIQUE SHADOW, CAST BY THE SETTING SUN.
A SILHOUETTE IN WHITE.

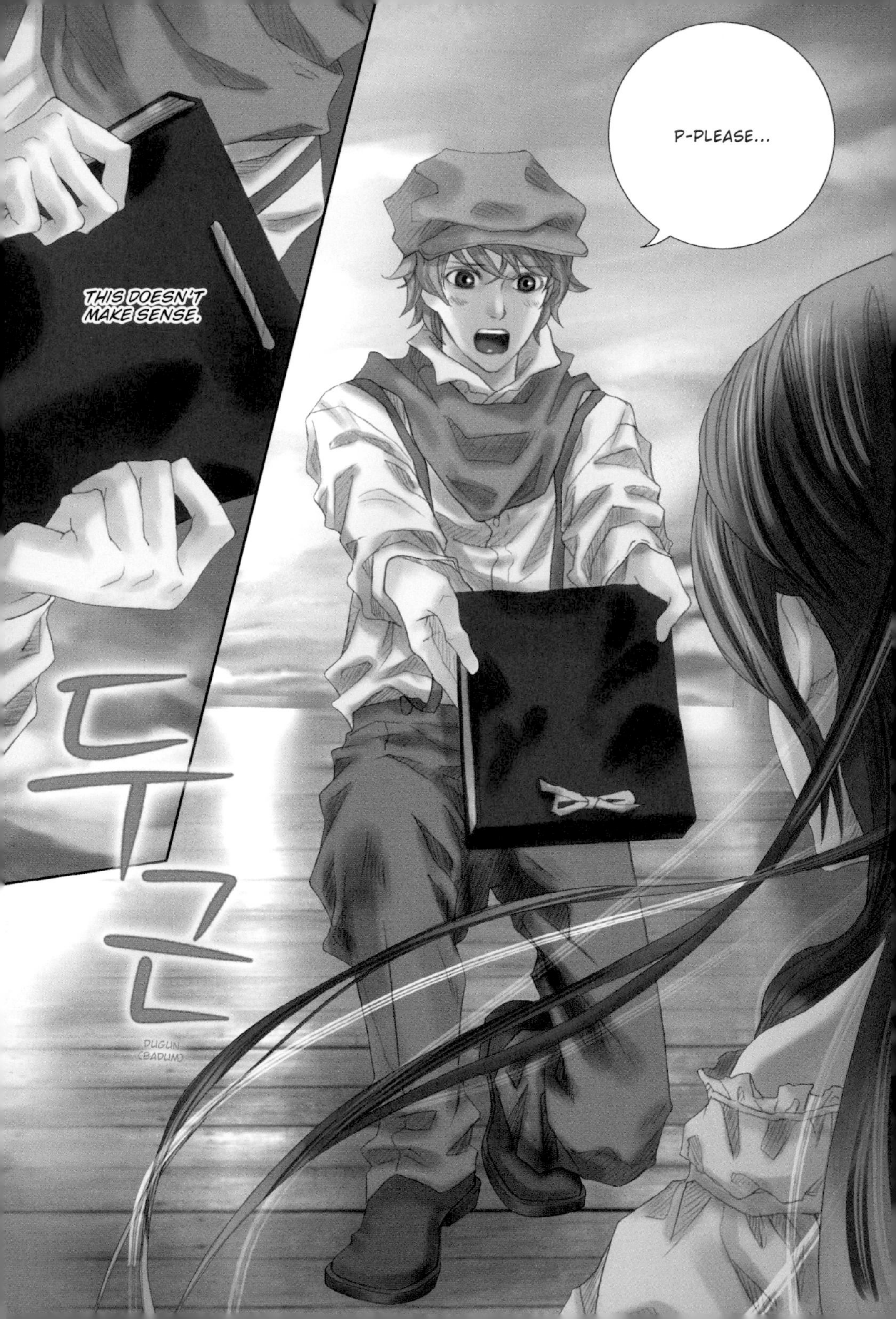
THIS DOESN'T MAKE SENSE.
두근
DUGUN (BADUM)
P-PLEASE...

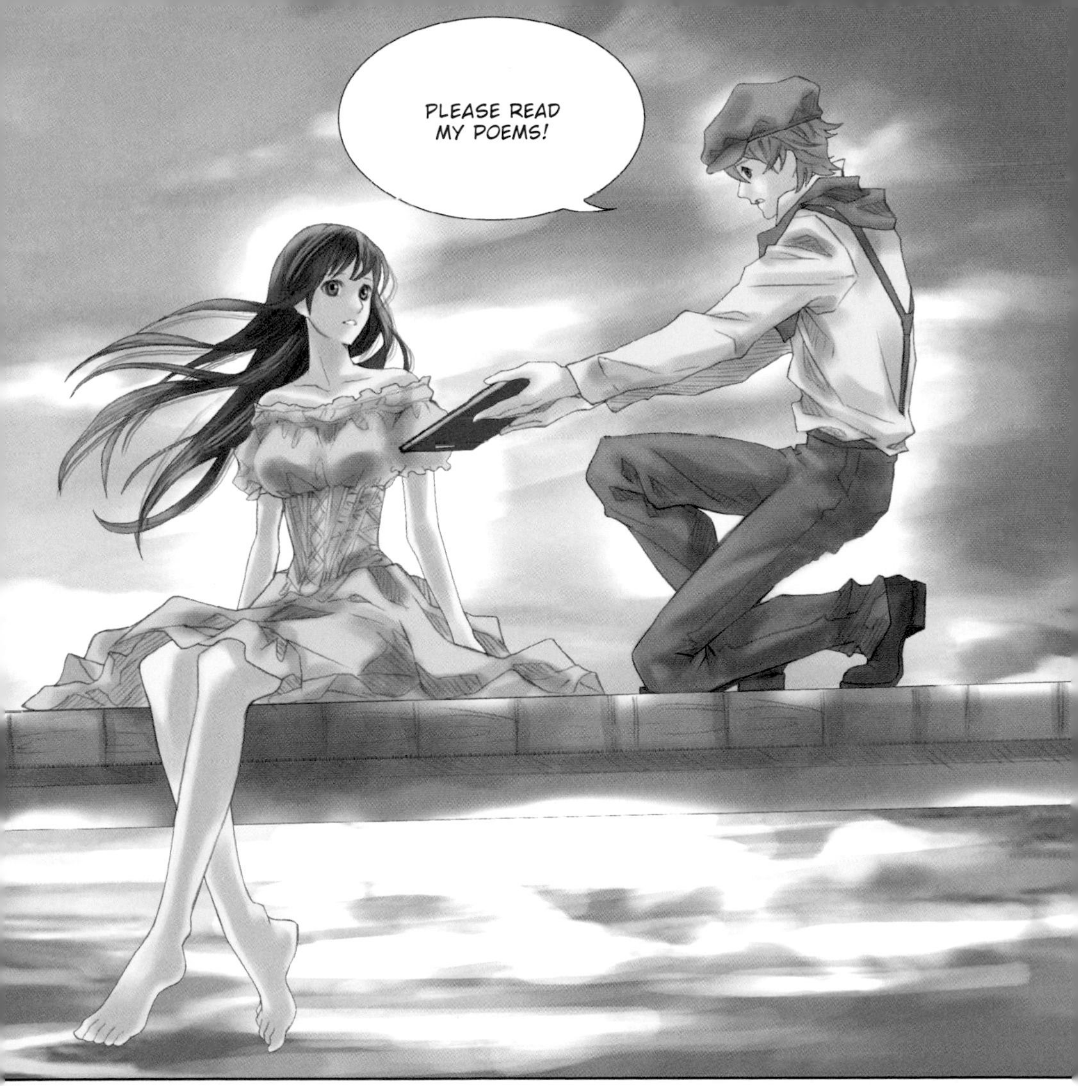
PLEASE READ MY POEMS!
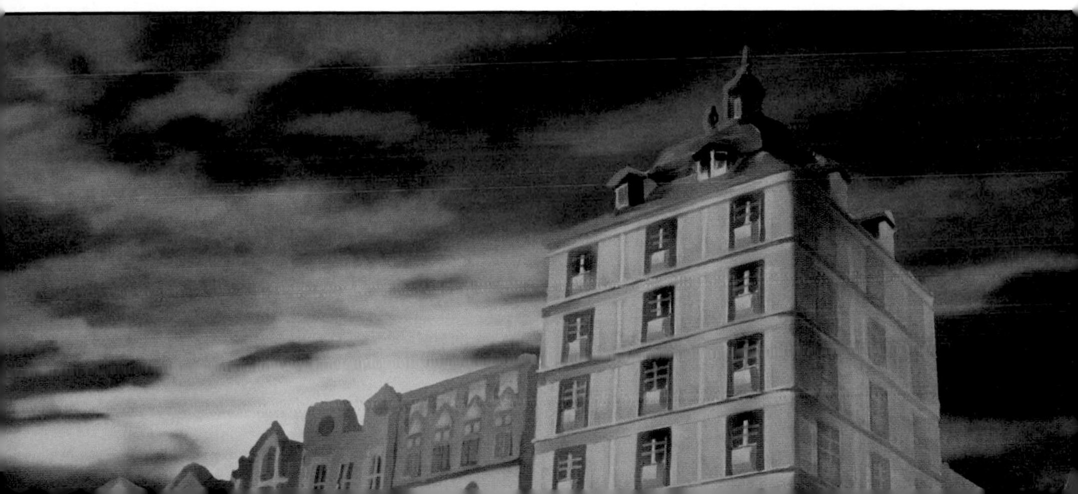

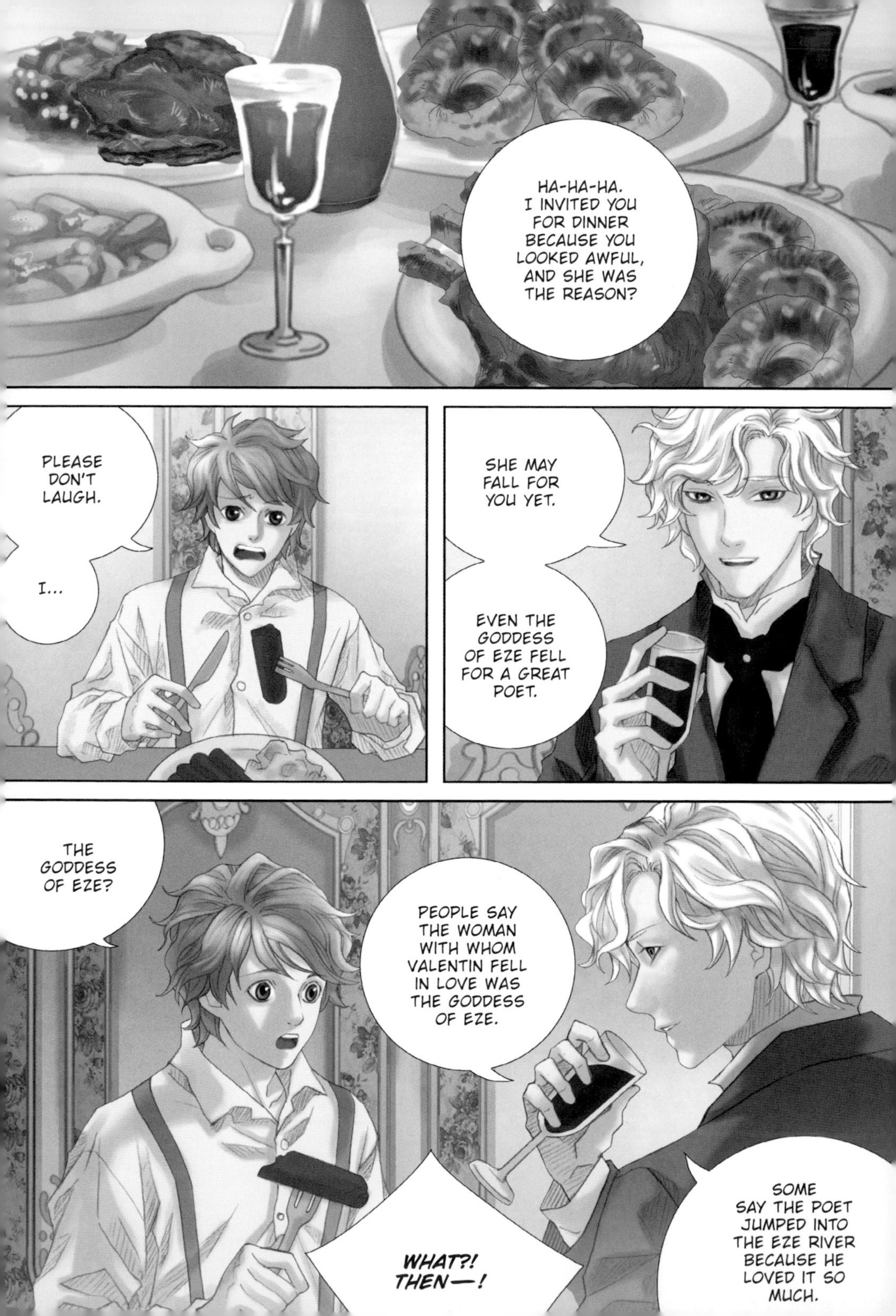
HA-HA-HA. I INVITED YOU FOR DINNER BECAUSE YOU LOOKED AWFUL, AND SHE WAS THE REASON?
PLEASE DON'T LAUGH.
I...
SHE MAY FALL FOR YOU YET.
EVEN THE GODDESS OF EZE FELL FOR A GREAT POET.
THE GODDESS OF EZE?
PEOPLE SAY THE WOMAN WITH WHOM VALENTIN FELL IN LOVE WAS THE GODDESS OF EZE.
WHAT?! THEN—!
SOME SAY THE POET JUMPED INTO THE EZE RIVER BECAUSE HE LOVED IT SO MUCH.

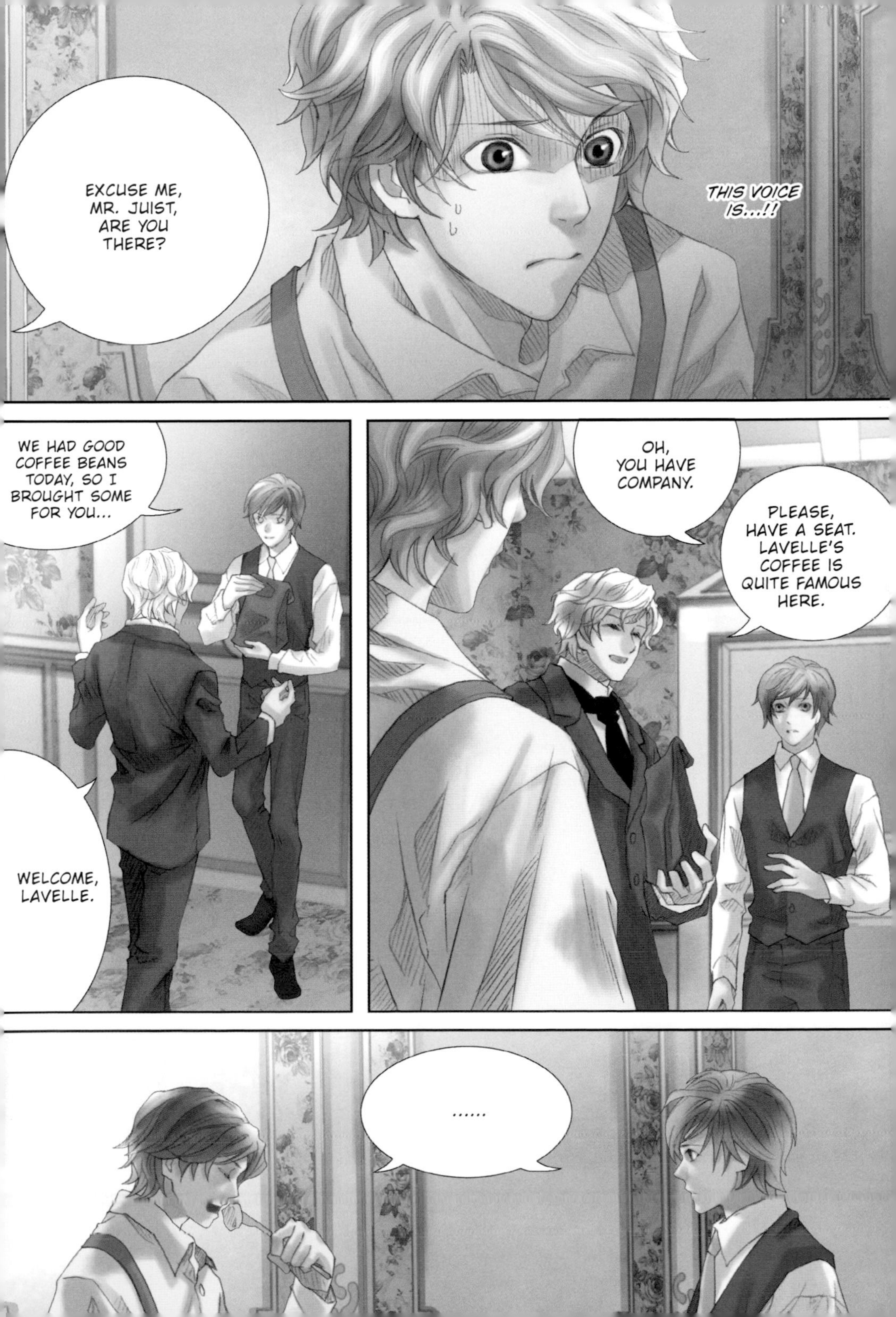
EXCUSE ME, MR. JUIST, ARE YOU THERE?
THIS VOICE IS...!!
WE HAD GOOD COFFEE BEANS TODAY, SO I BROUGHT SOME FOR YOU...
WELCOME, LAVELLE.
OH, YOU HAVE COMPANY.
PLEASE, HAVE A SEAT. LAVELLE'S COFFEE IS QUITE FAMOUS HERE.
......

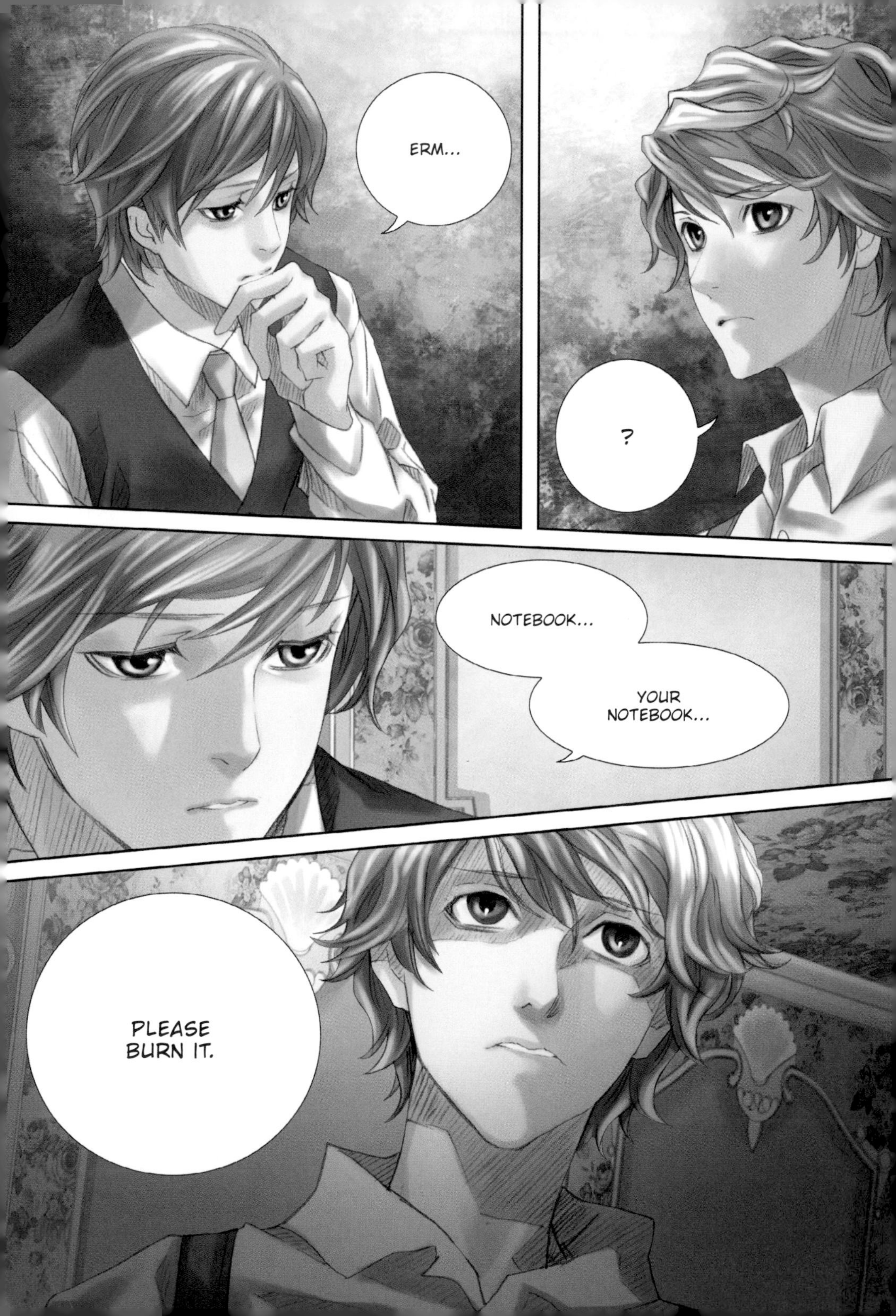
ERM...
?
NOTEBOOK...
YOUR NOTEBOOK...
PLEASE BURN IT.

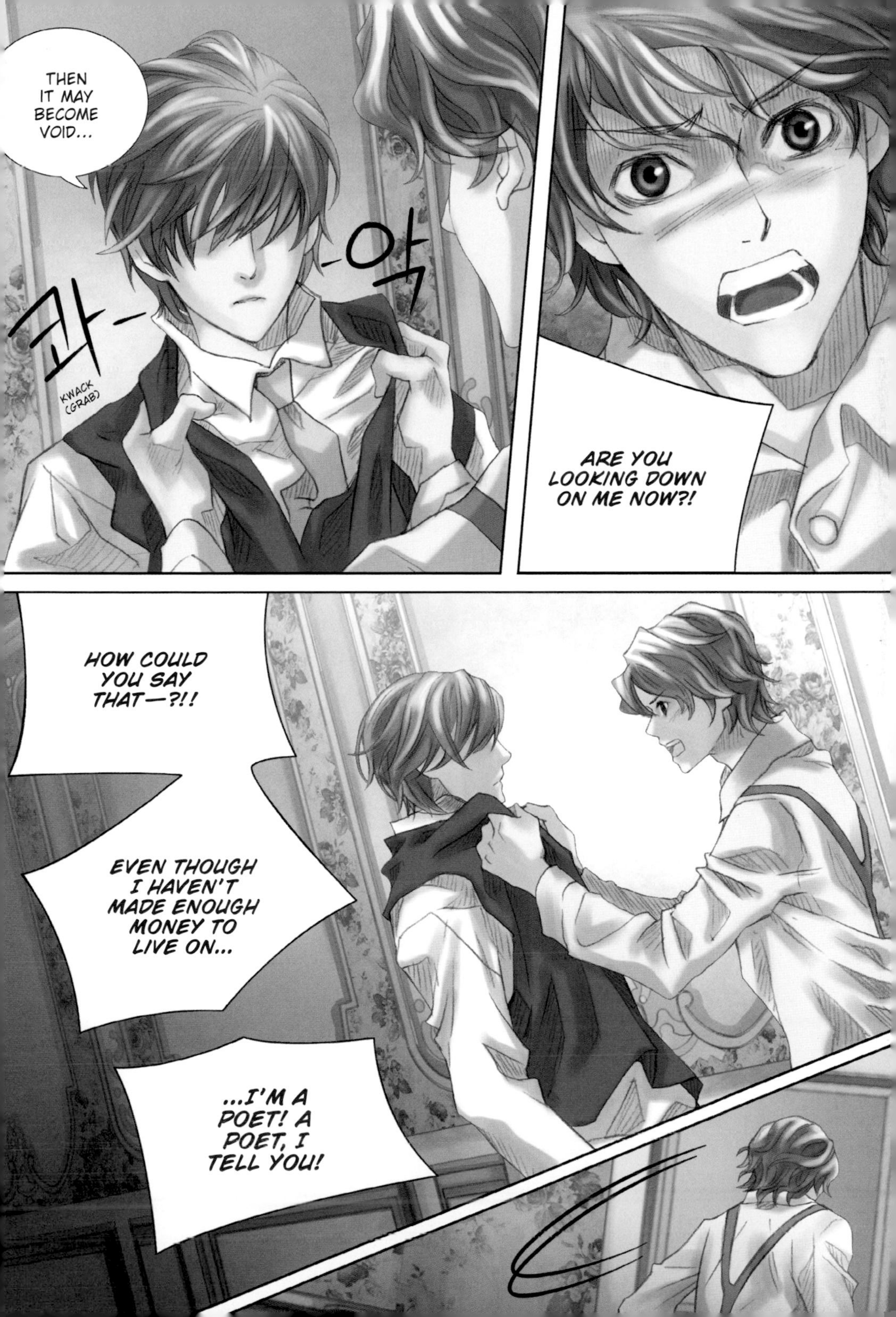
THEN IT MAY BECOME VOID...
콱-악
KWACK (GRAB)
ARE YOU LOOKING DOWN ON ME NOW?!
HOW COULD YOU SAY THAT—?!!
EVEN THOUGH I HAVEN'T MADE ENOUGH MONEY TO LIVE ON...
...I'M A POET! A POET, I TELL YOU!

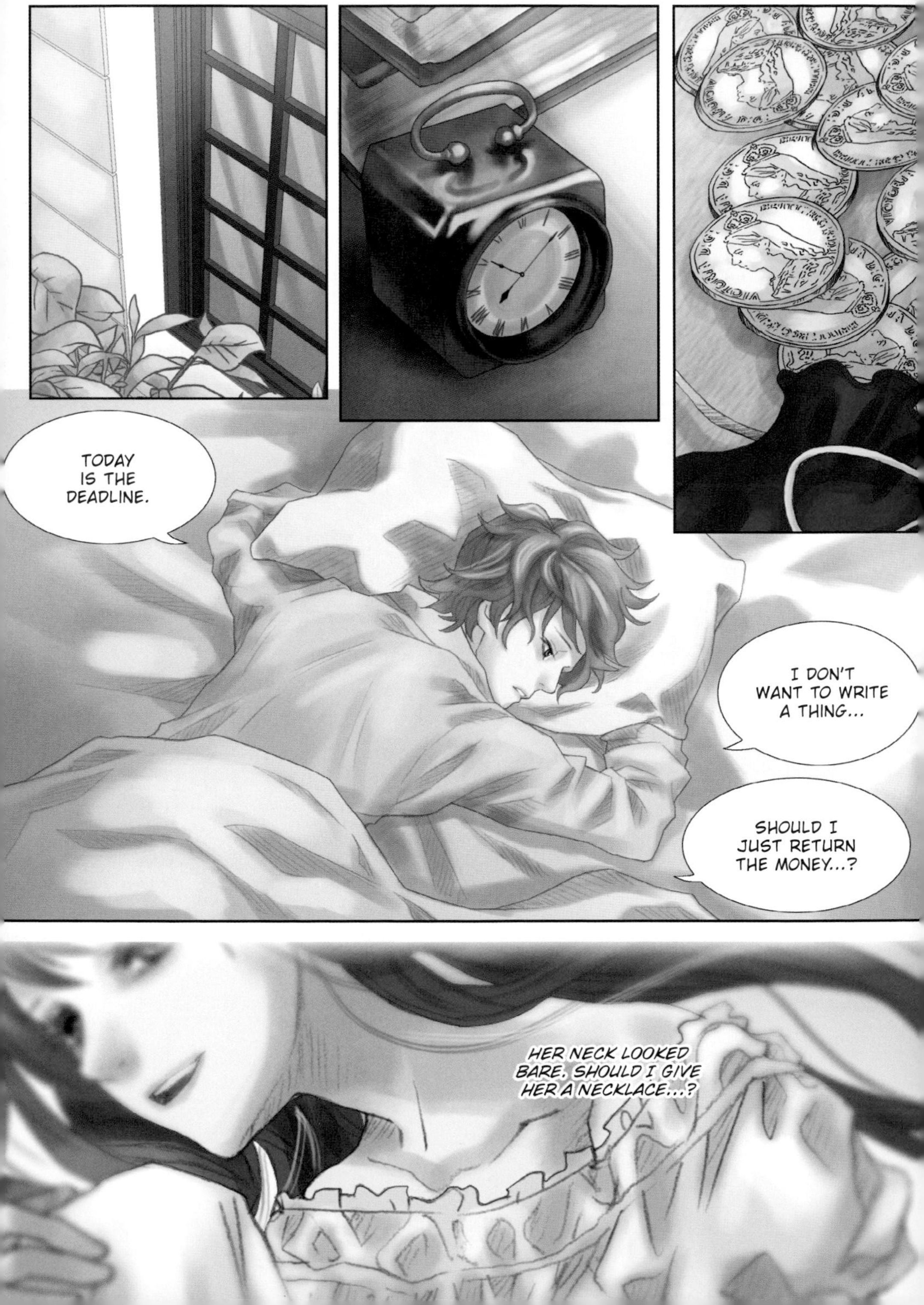
TODAY IS THE DEADLINE.
I DON'T WANT TO WRITE A THING...
SHOULD I JUST RETURN THE MONEY...?
HER NECK LOOKED BARE. SHOULD I GIVE HER A NECKLACE...?

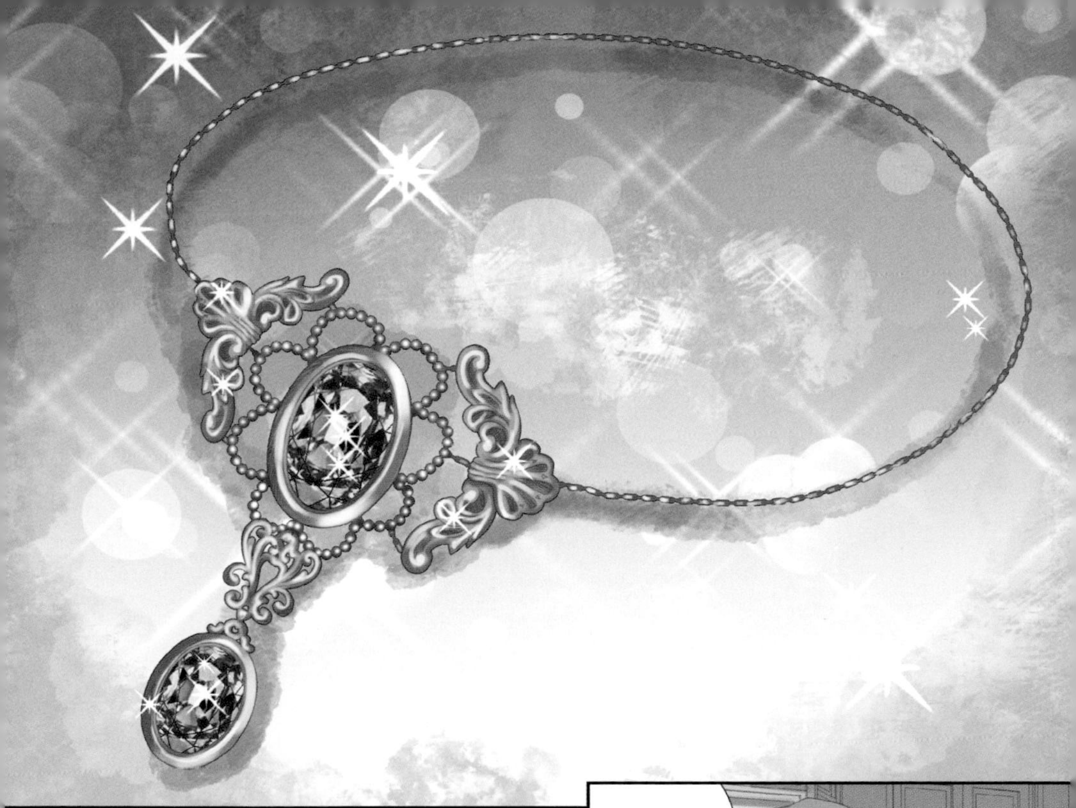

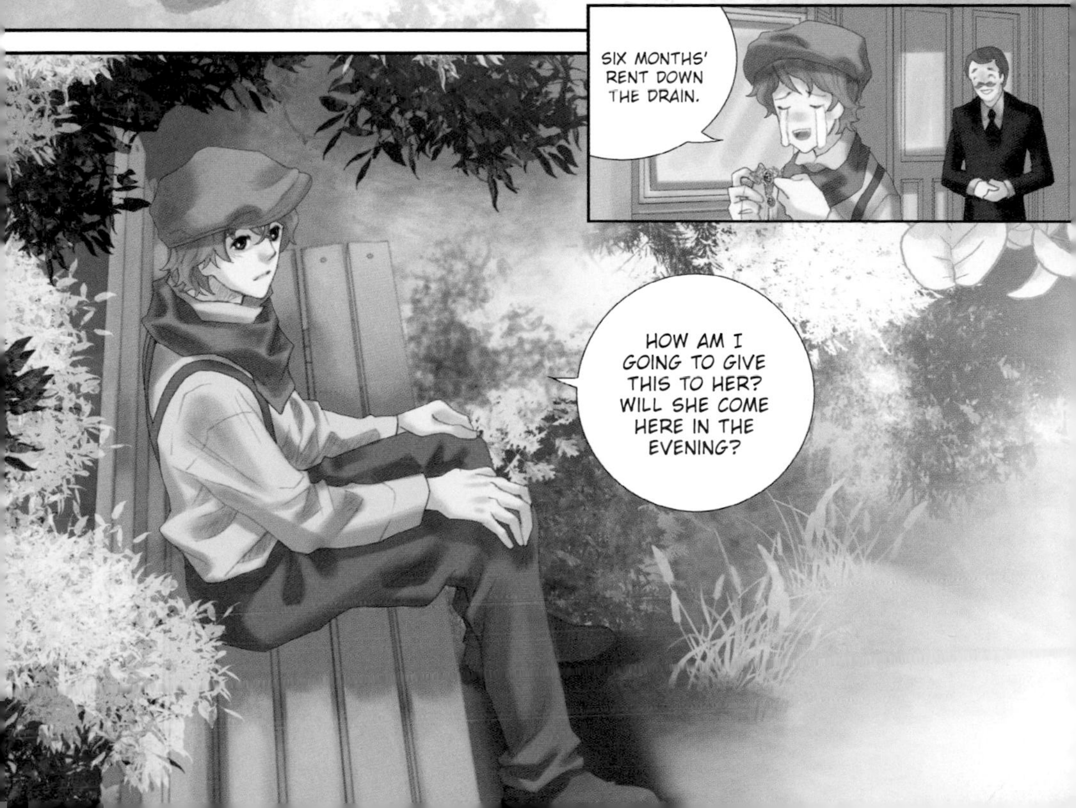
SIX MONTHS' RENT DOWN THE DRAIN.
HOW AM I GOING TO GIVE THIS TO HER? WILL SHE COME HERE IN THE EVENING?

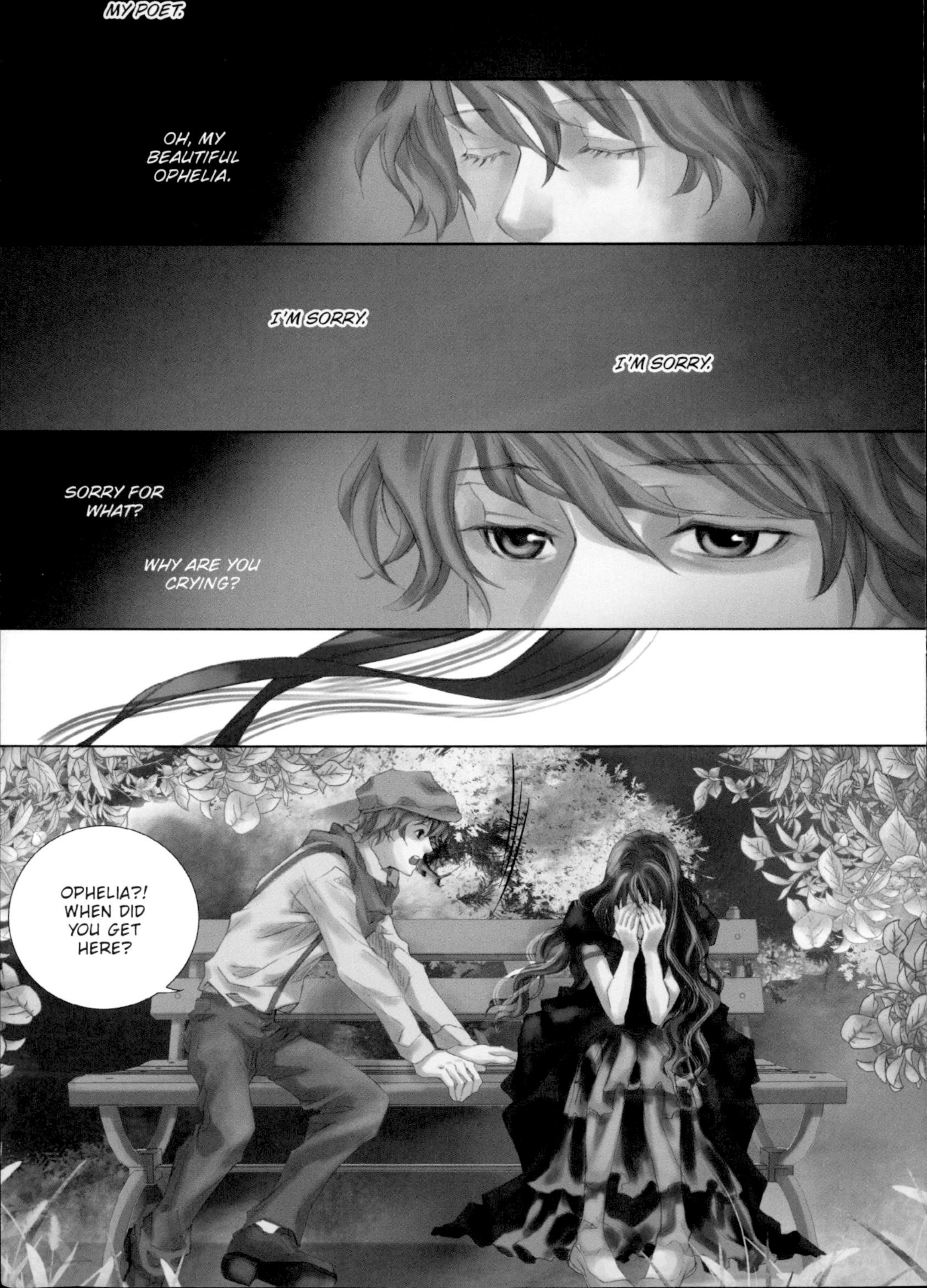
MY POET.
OH, MY BEAUTIFUL OPHELIA.
I'M SORRY.
I'M SORRY.
SORRY FOR WHAT?
WHY ARE YOU CRYING?
OPHELIA?! WHEN DID YOU GET HERE?

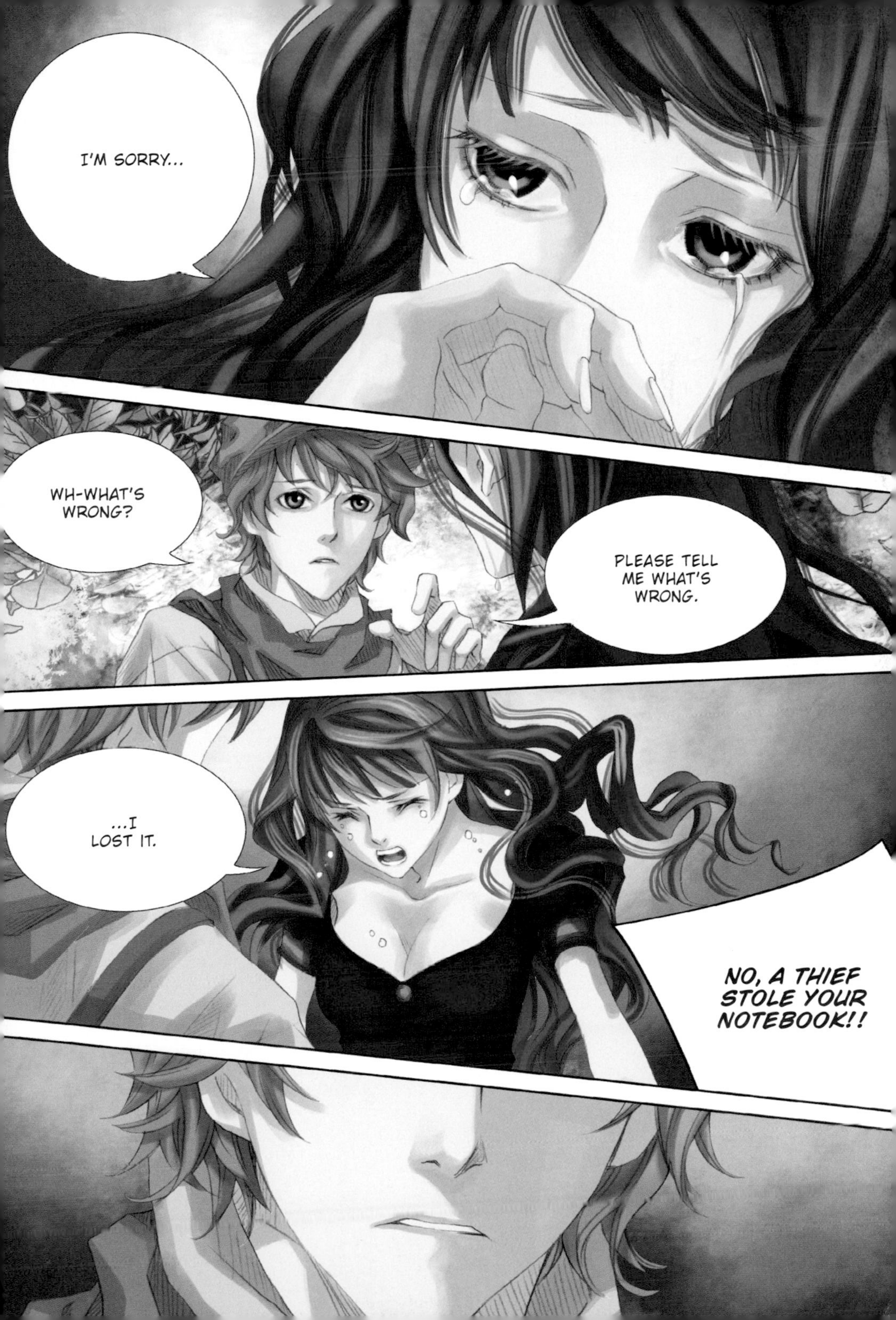
I'M SORRY...
WH-WHAT'S WRONG?
PLEASE TELL ME WHAT'S WRONG.
...I LOST IT.
NO, A THIEF STOLE YOUR NOTEBOOK!!

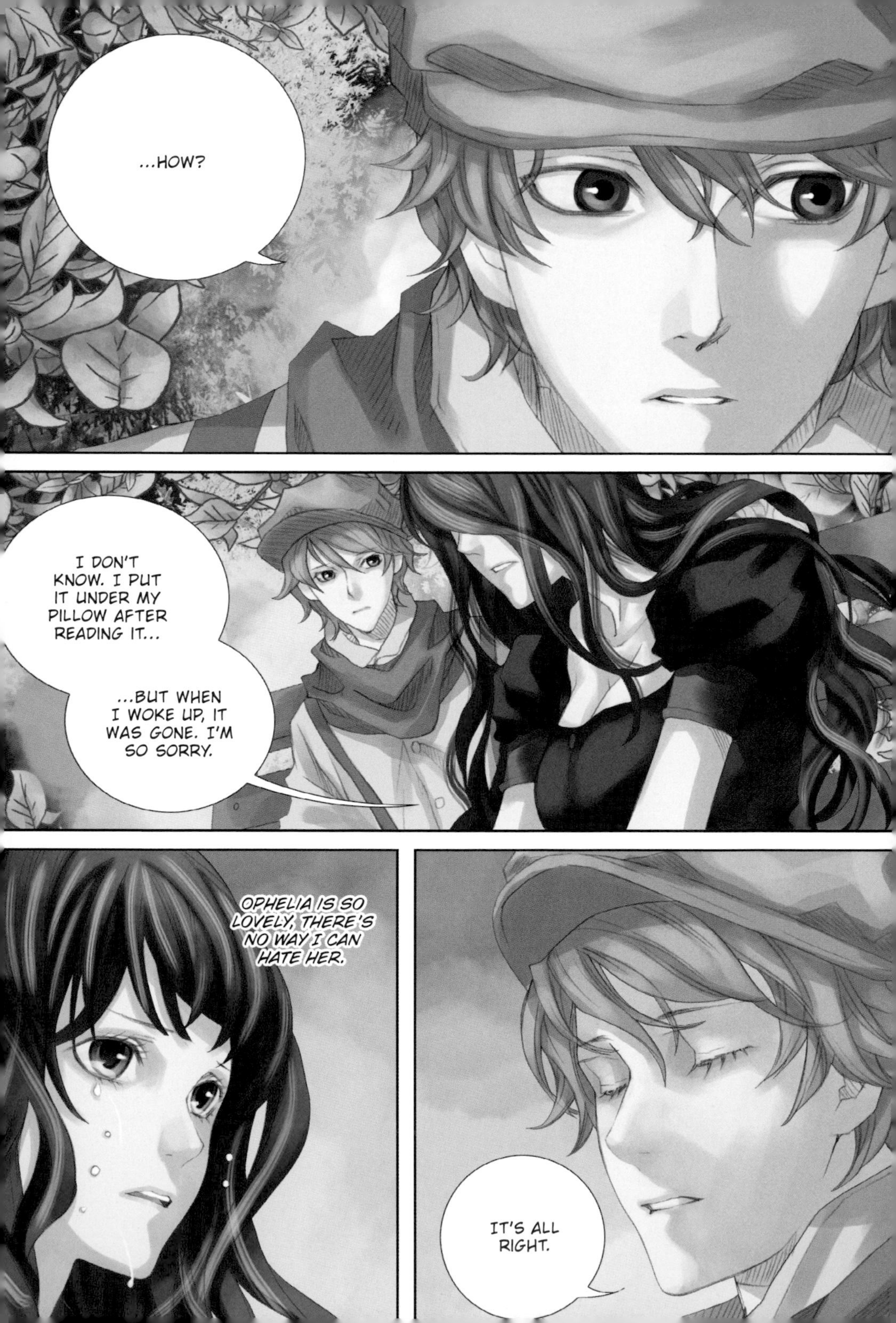

...HOW?
I DON'T KNOW. I PUT IT UNDER MY PILLOW AFTER READING IT...
...BUT WHEN I WOKE UP, IT WAS GONE. I'M SO SORRY.
OPHELIA IS SO LOVELY, THERE'S NO WAY I CAN HATE HER.
IT'S ALL RIGHT.

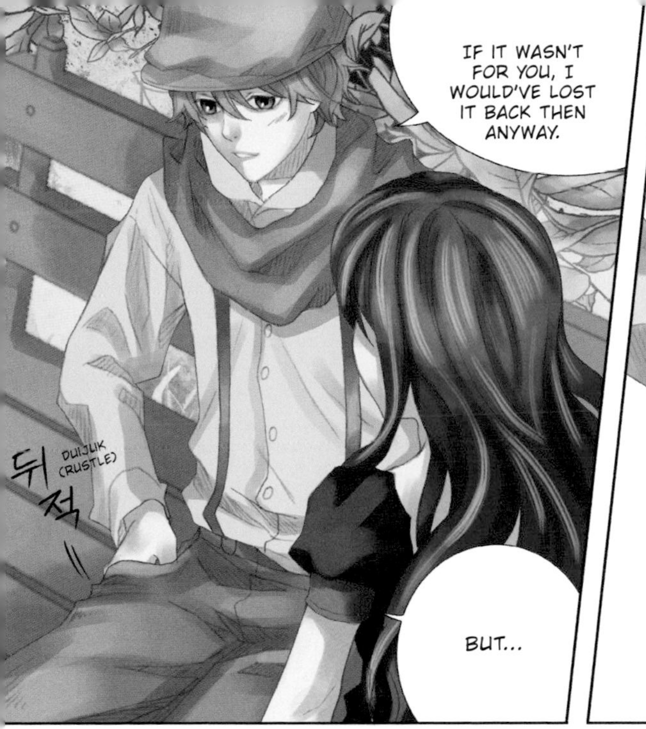
IF IT WASN'T FOR YOU, I WOULD'VE LOST IT BACK THEN ANYWAY.
뒤적
DUIJUK (RUSTLE)
BUT...
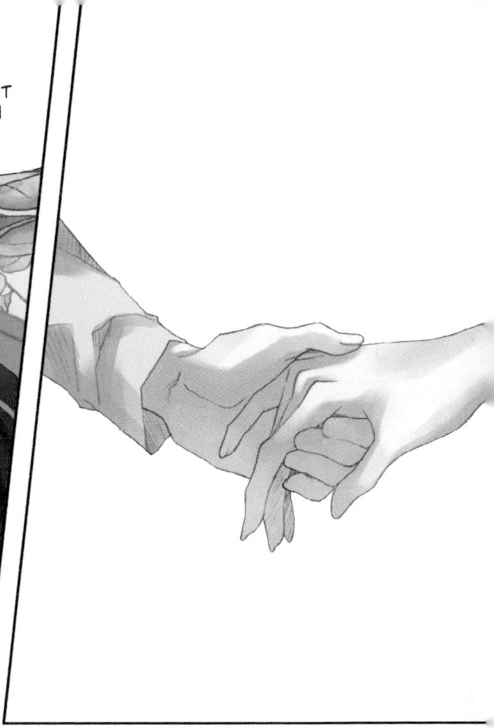
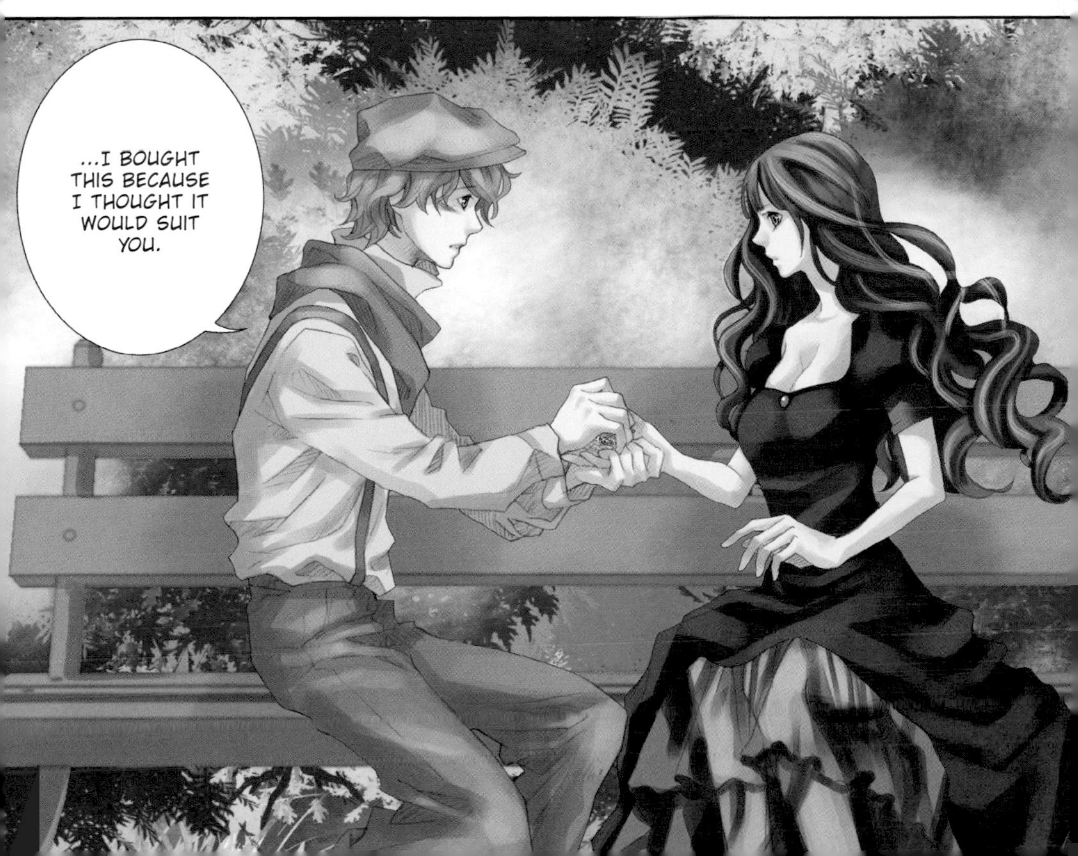
...I BOUGHT THIS BECAUSE I THOUGHT IT WOULD SUIT YOU.

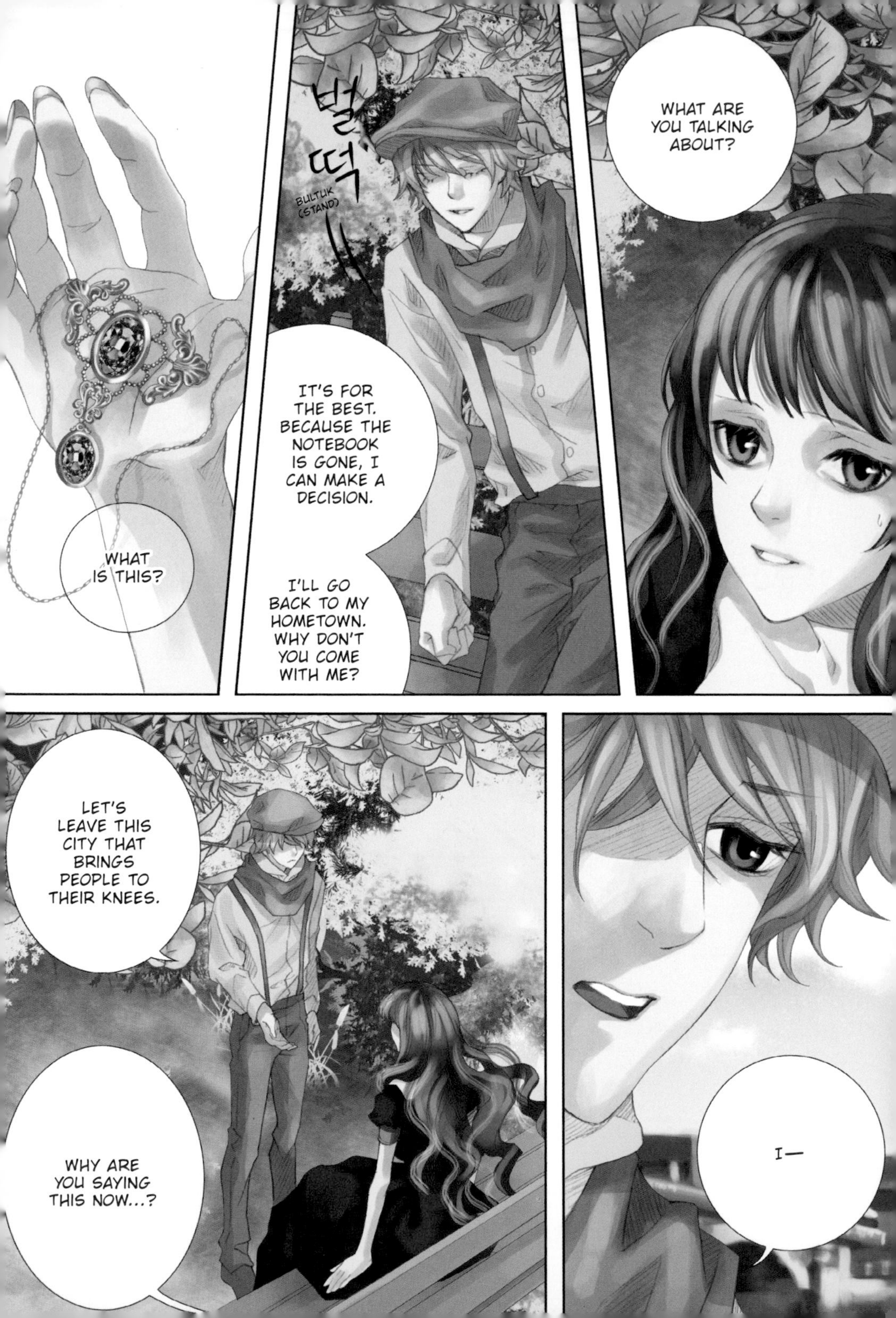
WHAT IS THIS?
벌떡
BULTUK (STAND)
IT'S FOR THE BEST. BECAUSE THE NOTEBOOK IS GONE, I CAN MAKE A DECISION.
I'LL GO BACK TO MY HOMETOWN. WHY DON'T YOU COME WITH ME?
WHAT ARE YOU TALKING ABOUT?
LET'S LEAVE THIS CITY THAT BRINGS PEOPLE TO THEIR KNEES.
WHY ARE YOU SAYING THIS NOW...?
I—

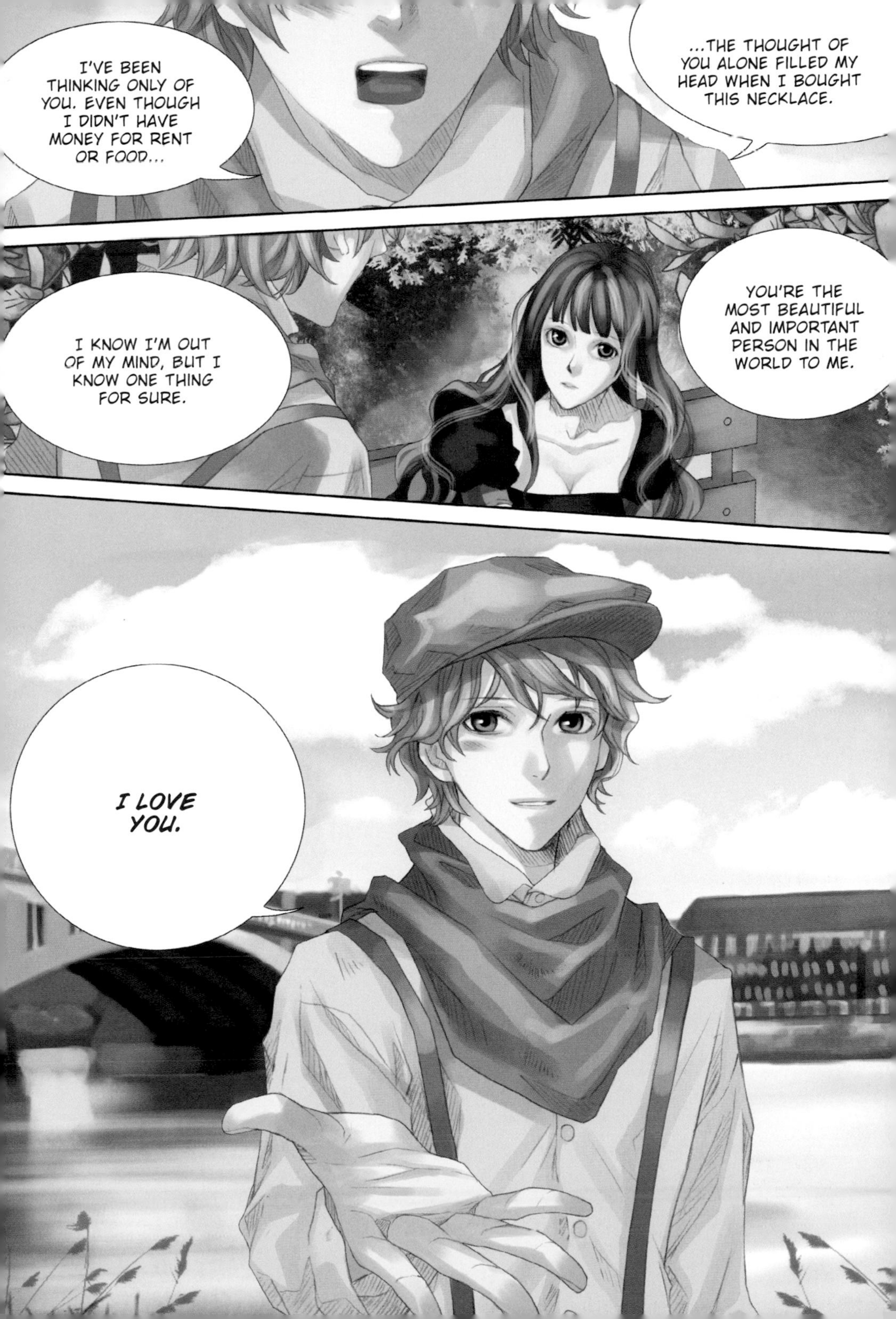
I'VE BEEN THINKING ONLY OF YOU. EVEN THOUGH I DIDN'T HAVE MONEY FOR RENT OR FOOD...
...THE THOUGHT OF YOU ALONE FILLED MY HEAD WHEN I BOUGHT THIS NECKLACE.
I KNOW I'M OUT OF MY MIND, BUT I KNOW ONE THING FOR SURE.
YOU'RE THE MOST BEAUTIFUL AND IMPORTANT PERSON IN THE WORLD TO ME.
I LOVE YOU.

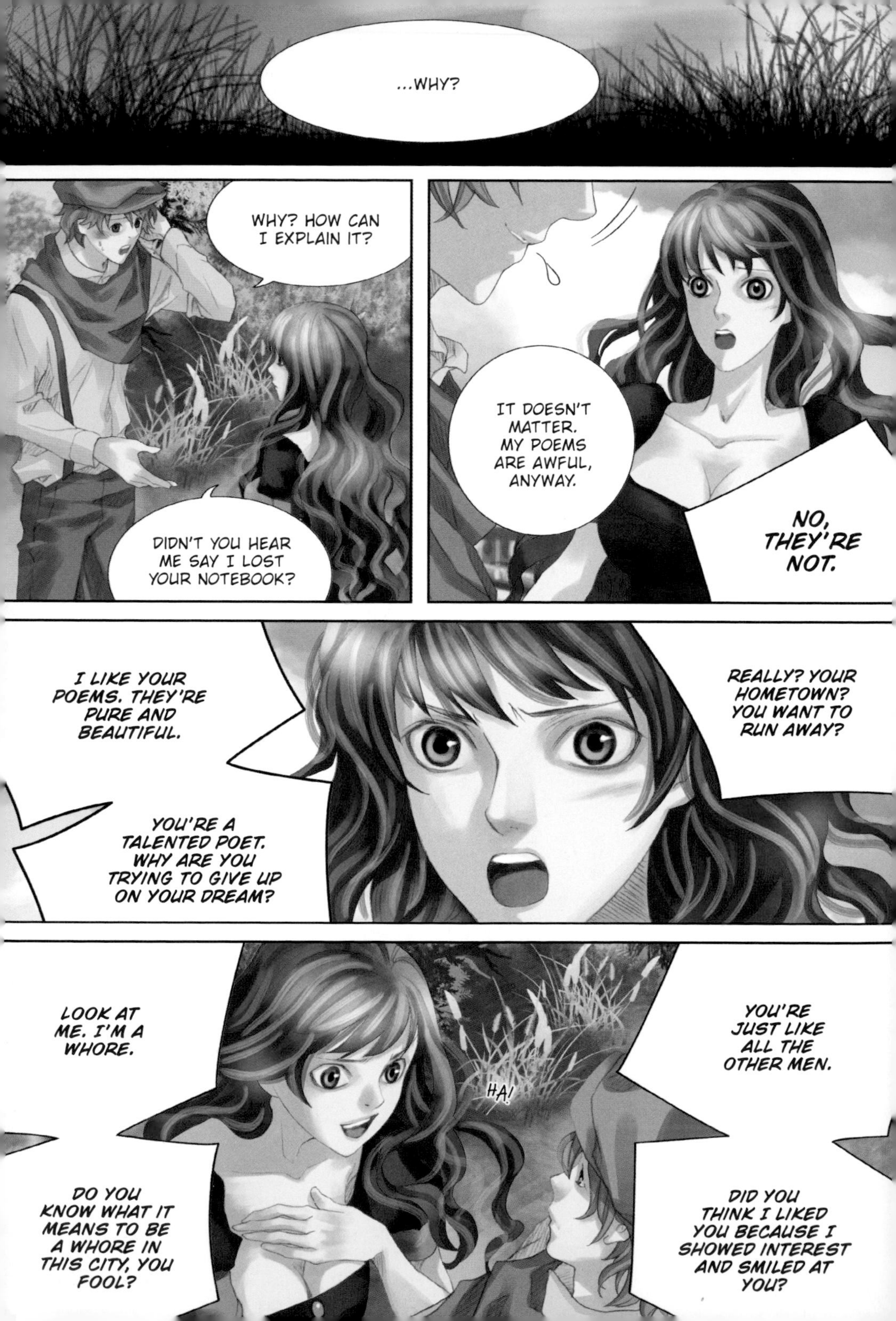
...WHY?
WHY? HOW CAN I EXPLAIN IT?
DIDN'T YOU HEAR ME SAY I LOST YOUR NOTEBOOK?
IT DOESN'T MATTER. MY POEMS ARE AWFUL, ANYWAY.
NO, THEY'RE NOT.
I LIKE YOUR POEMS. THEY'RE PURE AND BEAUTIFUL.
YOU'RE A TALENTED POET. WHY ARE YOU TRYING TO GIVE UP ON YOUR DREAM?
REALLY? YOUR HOMETOWN? YOU WANT TO RUN AWAY?
LOOK AT ME. I'M A WHORE.
DO YOU KNOW WHAT IT MEANS TO BE A WHORE IN THIS CITY, YOU FOOL?
HA!
YOU'RE JUST LIKE ALL THE OTHER MEN.
DID YOU THINK I LIKED YOU BECAUSE I SHOWED INTEREST AND SMILED AT YOU?

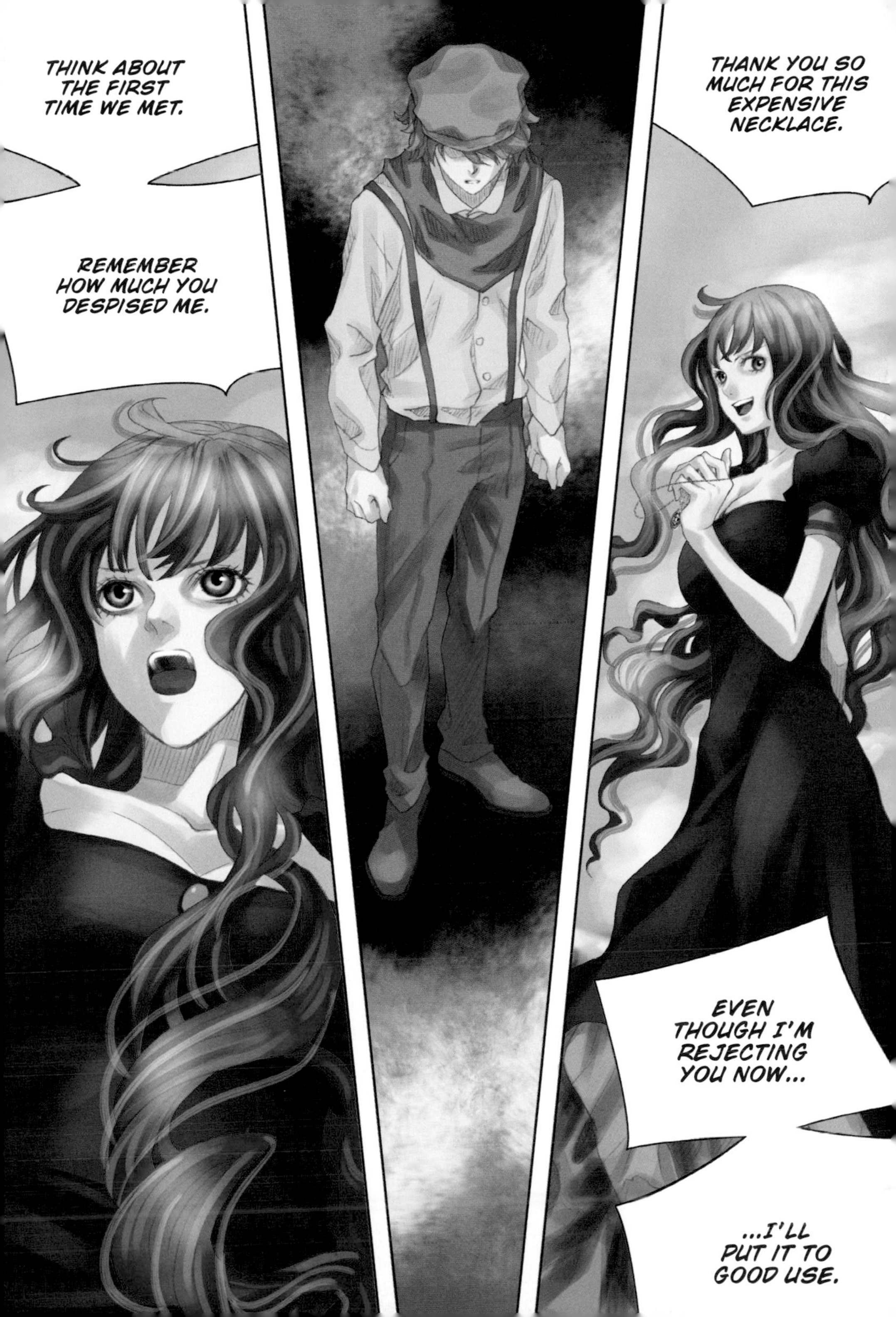
THINK ABOUT THE FIRST TIME WE MET.
REMEMBER HOW MUCH YOU DESPISED ME.
THANK YOU SO MUCH FOR THIS EXPENSIVE NECKLACE.
EVEN THOUGH I'M REJECTING YOU NOW...
...I'LL PUT IT TO GOOD USE.

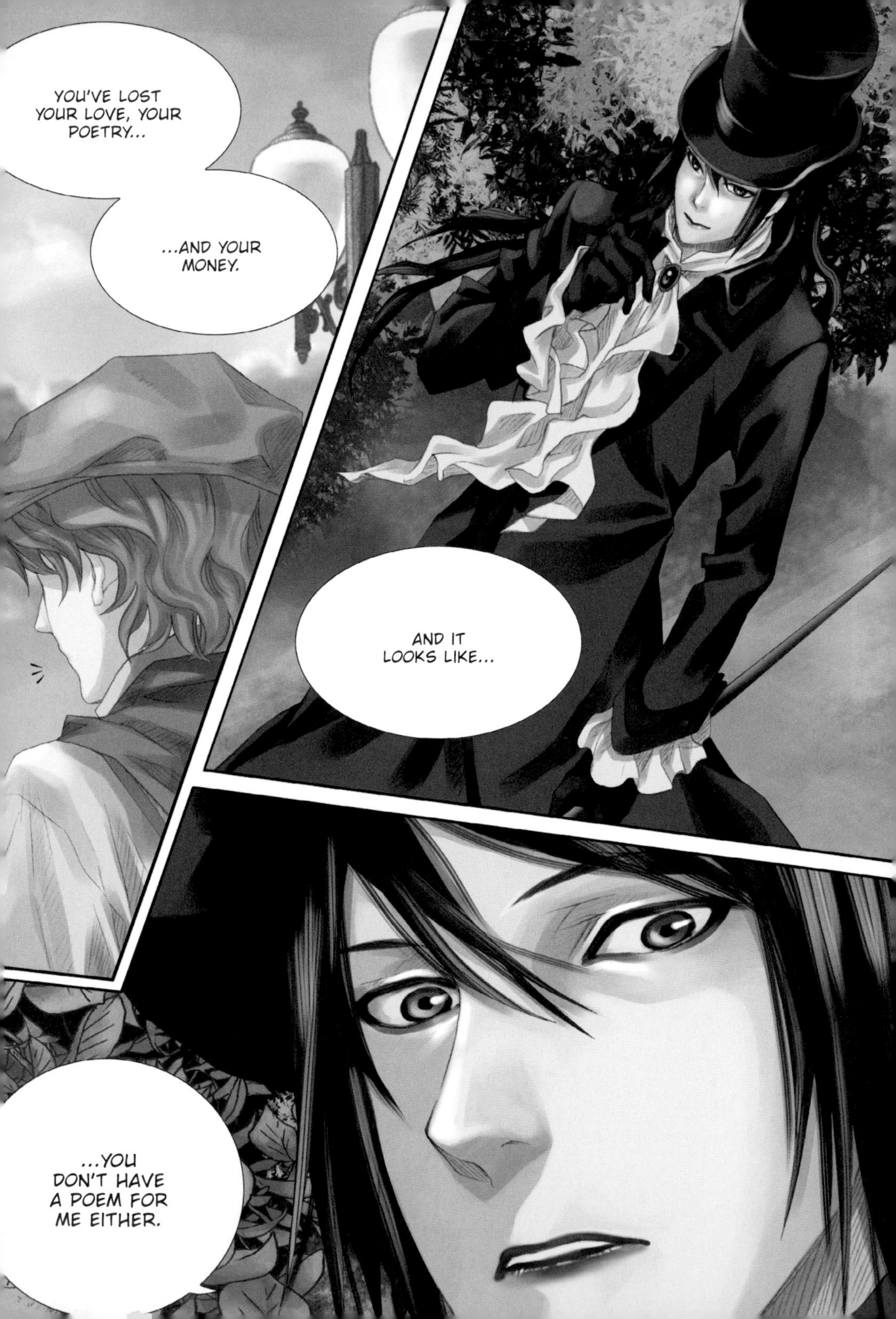
YOU'VE LOST YOUR LOVE, YOUR POETRY...
...AND YOUR MONEY.
AND IT LOOKS LIKE...
...YOU DON'T HAVE A POEM FOR ME EITHER.

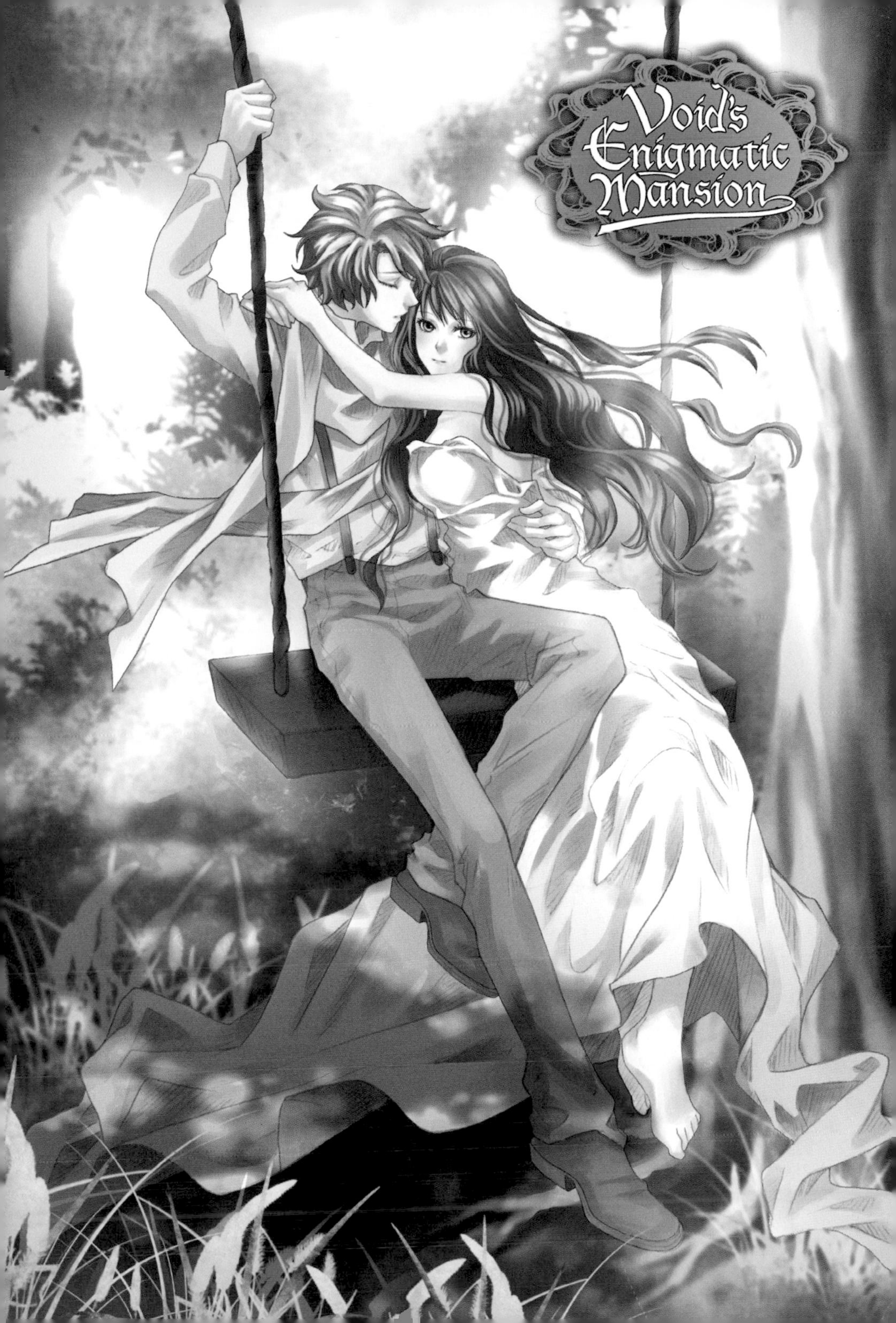
Void's
Enigmatic
Mansion

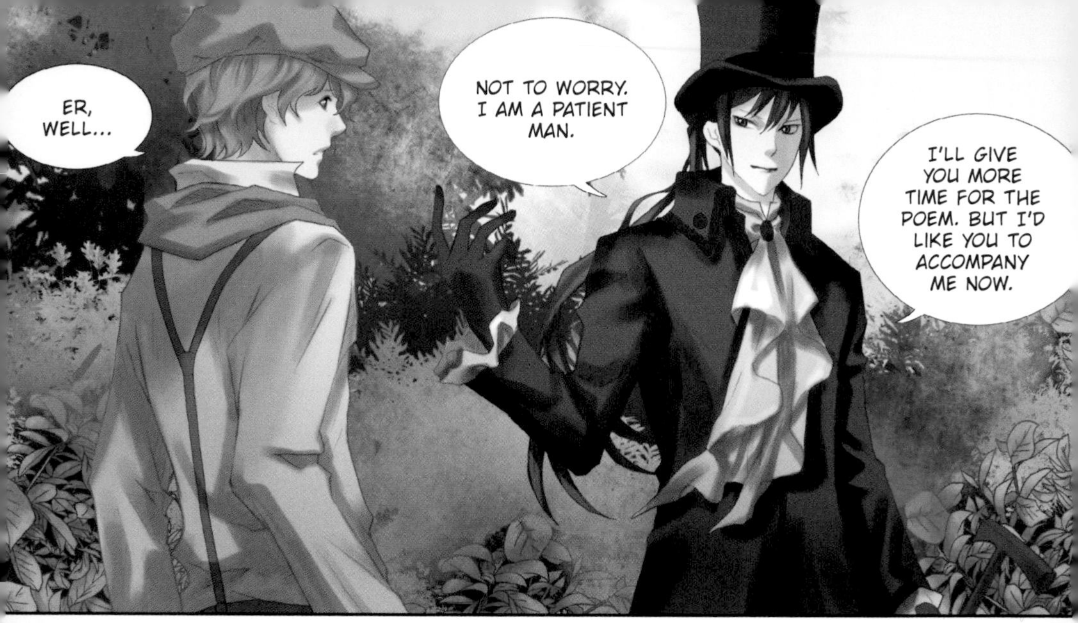
ER, WELL...
NOT TO WORRY. I AM A PATIENT MAN.
I'LL GIVE YOU MORE TIME FOR THE POEM. BUT I'D LIKE YOU TO ACCOMPANY ME NOW.
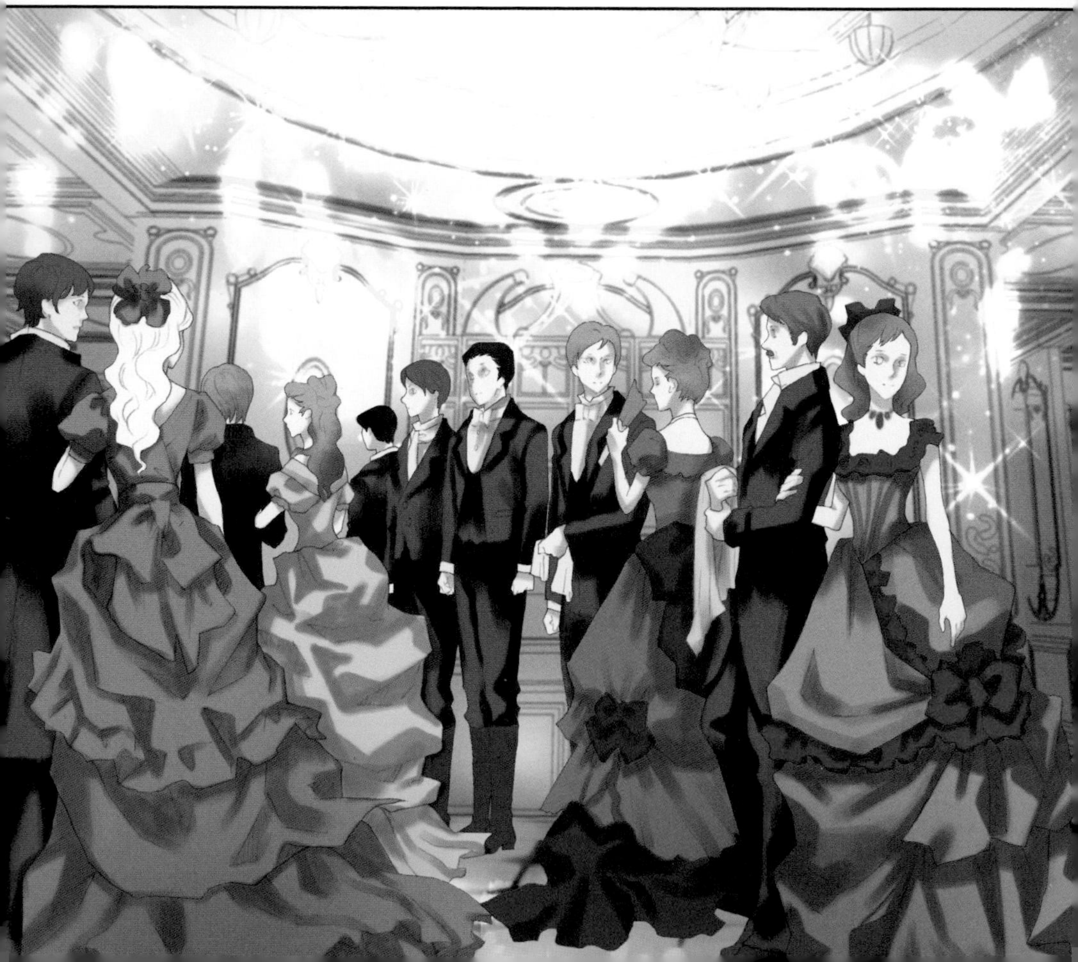

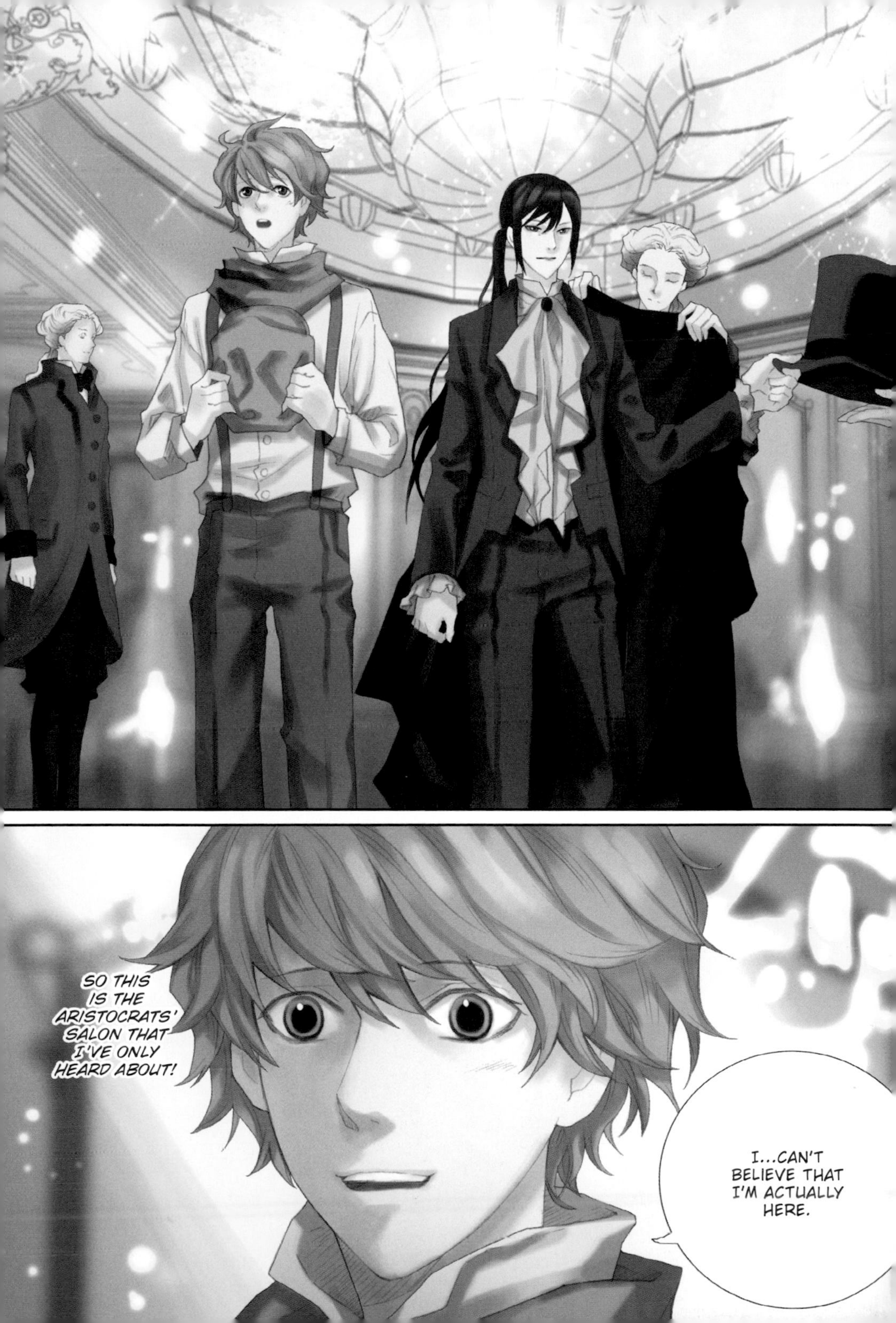
SO THIS IS THE ARISTOCRATS' SALON THAT I'VE ONLY HEARD ABOUT!
I...CAN'T BELIEVE THAT I'M ACTUALLY HERE.

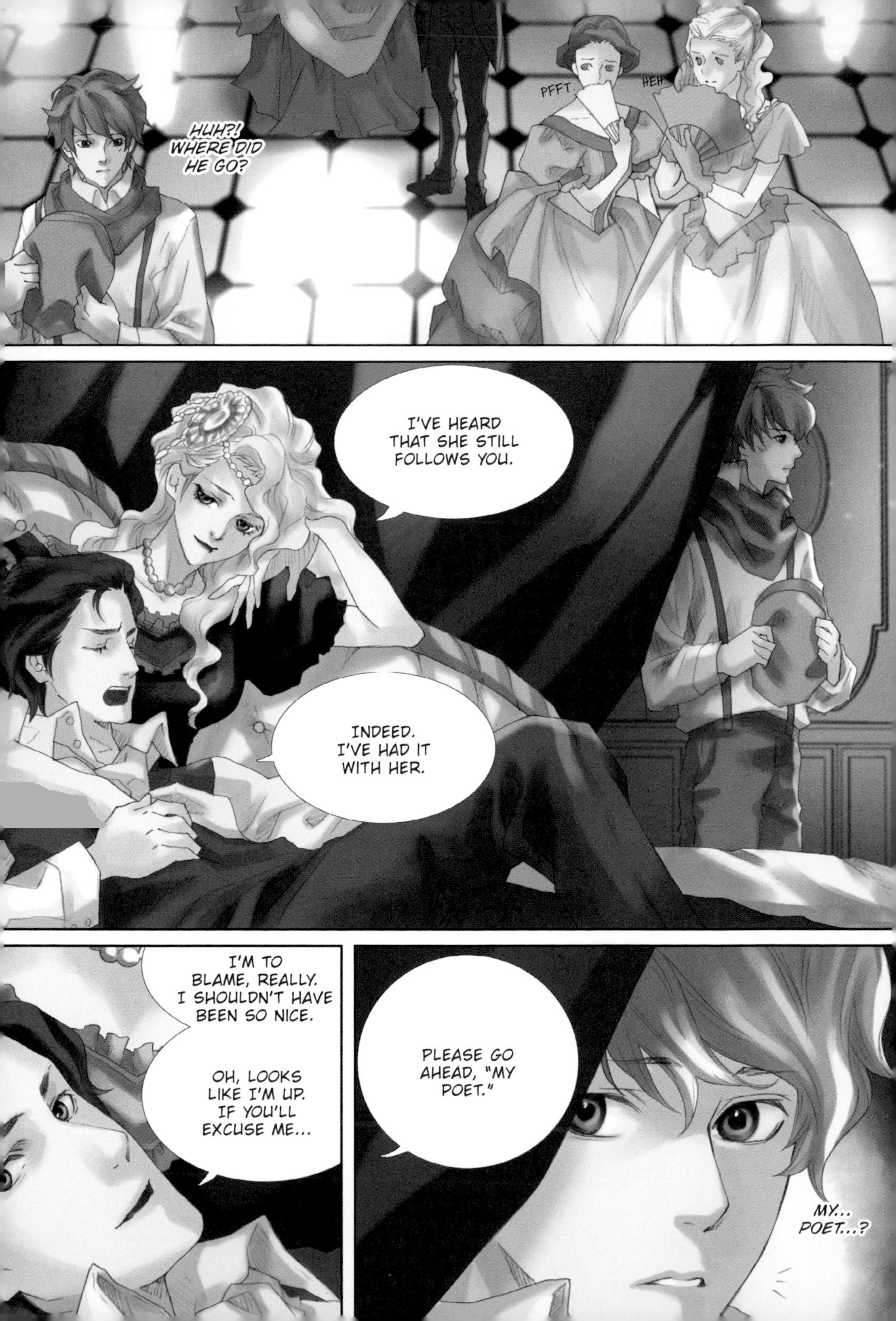
HUH?! WHERE DID HE GO?
PFFT.
HEH.
I'VE HEARD THAT SHE STILL FOLLOWS YOU.
INDEED. I'VE HAD IT WITH HER.
I'M TO BLAME, REALLY. I SHOULDN'T HAVE BEEN SO NICE.
OH, LOOKS LIKE I'M UP. IF YOU'LL EXCUSE ME...
PLEASE GO AHEAD, "MY POET."
MY... POET...?

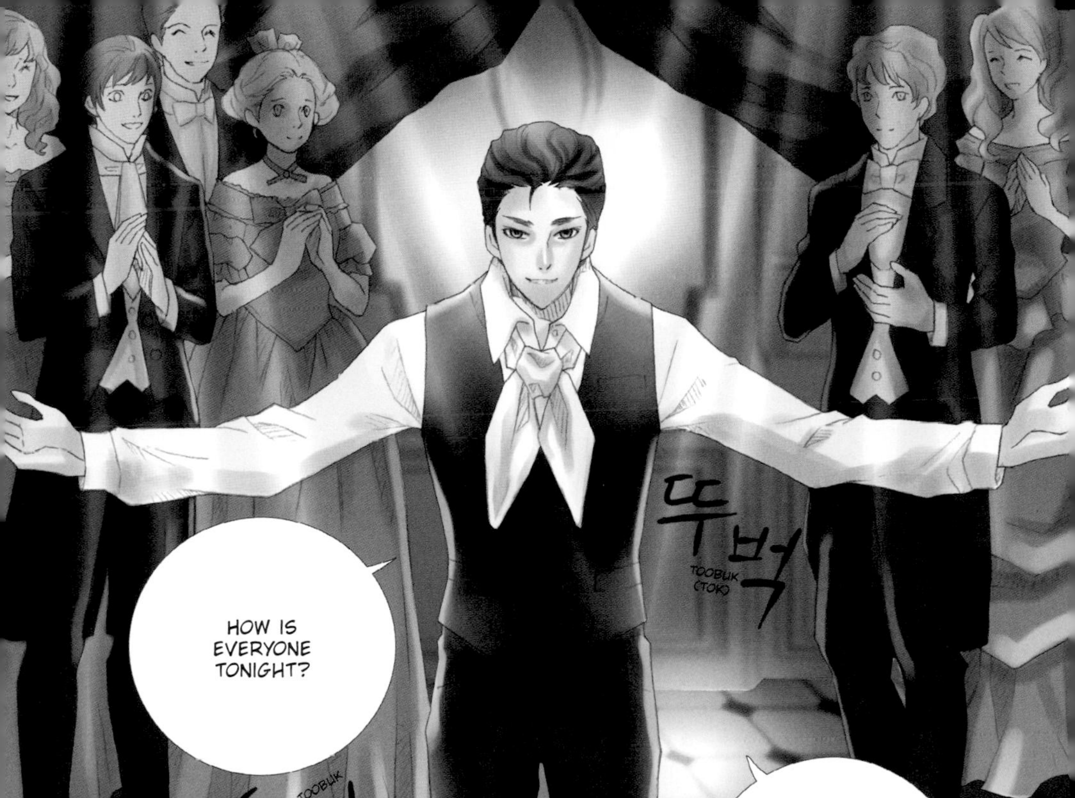
뚜벅
TOOBUK (TOK)
HOW IS EVERYONE TONIGHT?
뚜벅
TOOBUK
I AM RONKINS, THE POET.

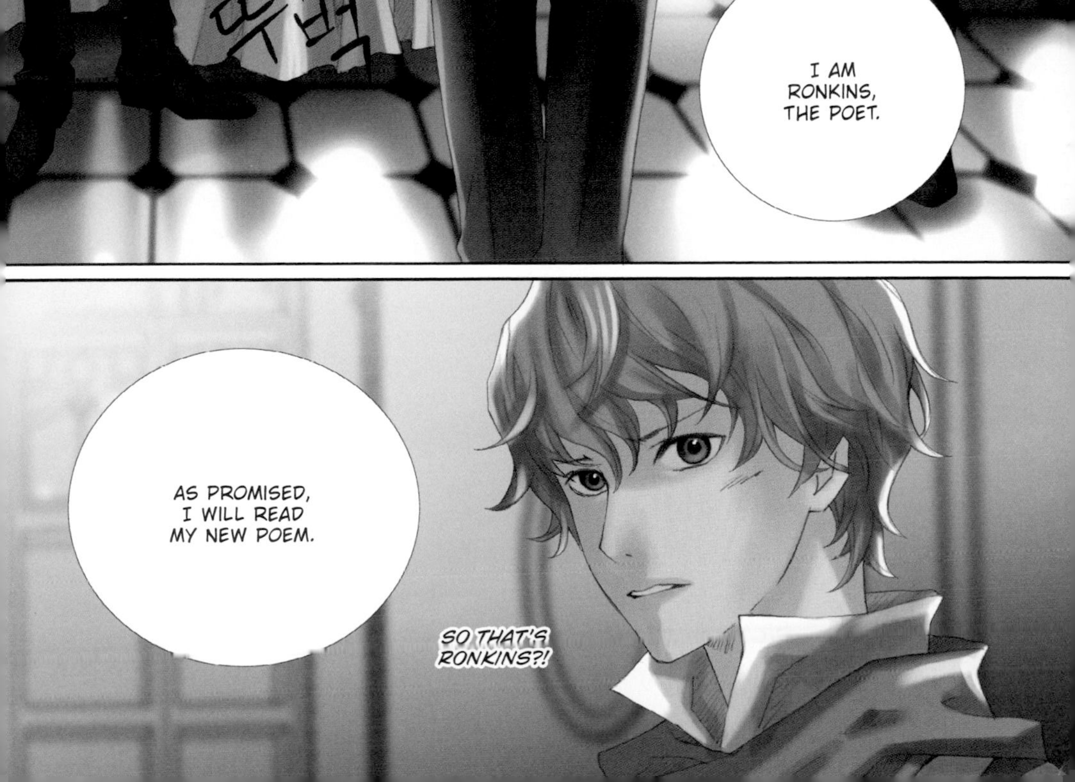
AS PROMISED, I WILL READ MY NEW POEM.
SO THAT'S RONKINS?!

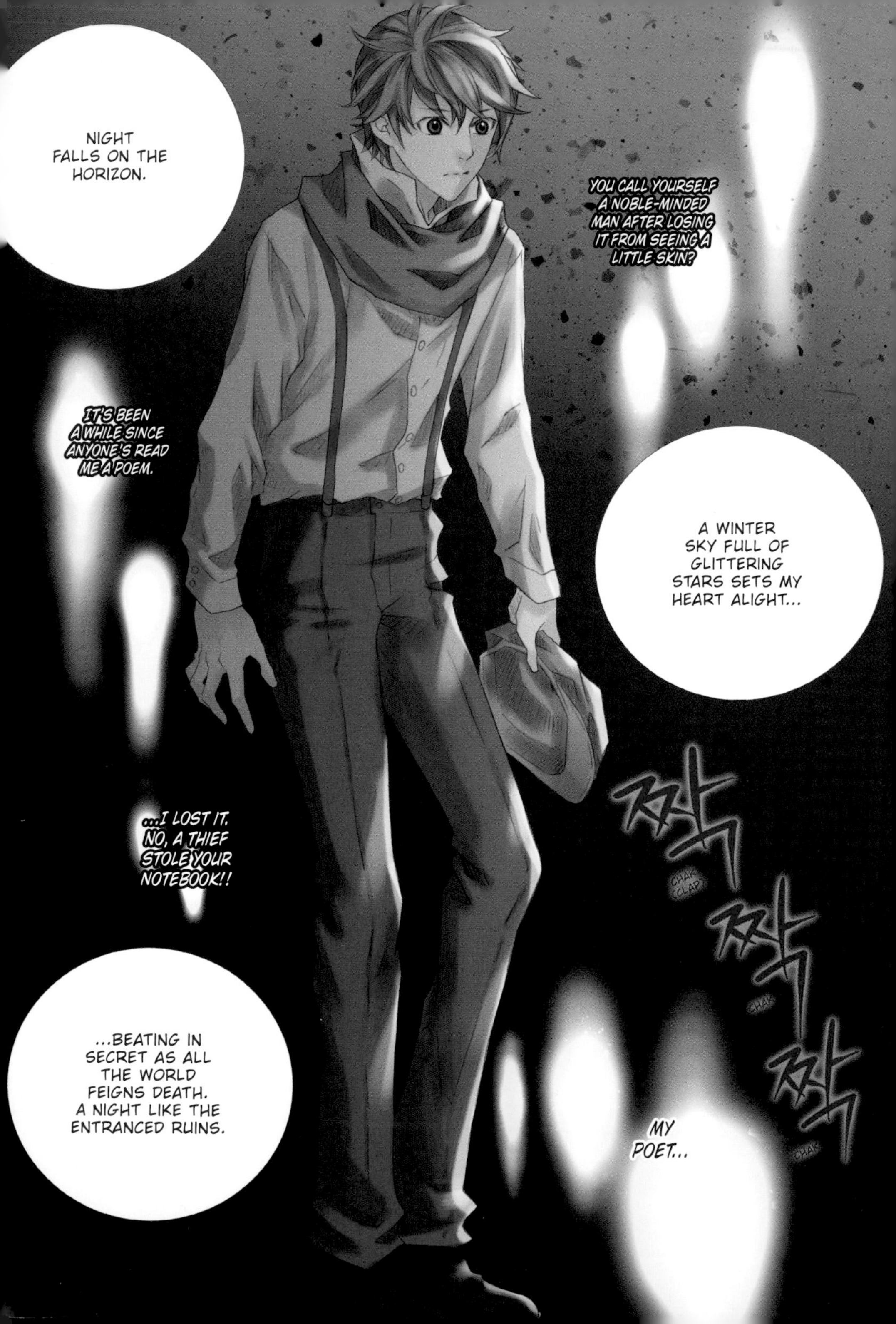
NIGHT FALLS ON THE HORIZON.
YOU CALL YOURSELF A NOBLE-MINDED MAN AFTER LOSING IT FROM SEEING A LITTLE SKIN?
IT'S BEEN A WHILE SINCE ANYONE'S READ ME A POEM.
A WINTER SKY FULL OF GLITTERING STARS SETS MY HEART ALIGHT...
...I LOST IT. NO, A THIEF STOLE YOUR NOTEBOOK!!
짝
CHAK (CLAP)
짝
CHAK
짝
CHAK
...BEATING IN SECRET AS ALL THE WORLD FEIGNS DEATH. A NIGHT LIKE THE ENTRANCED RUINS.
MY POET...

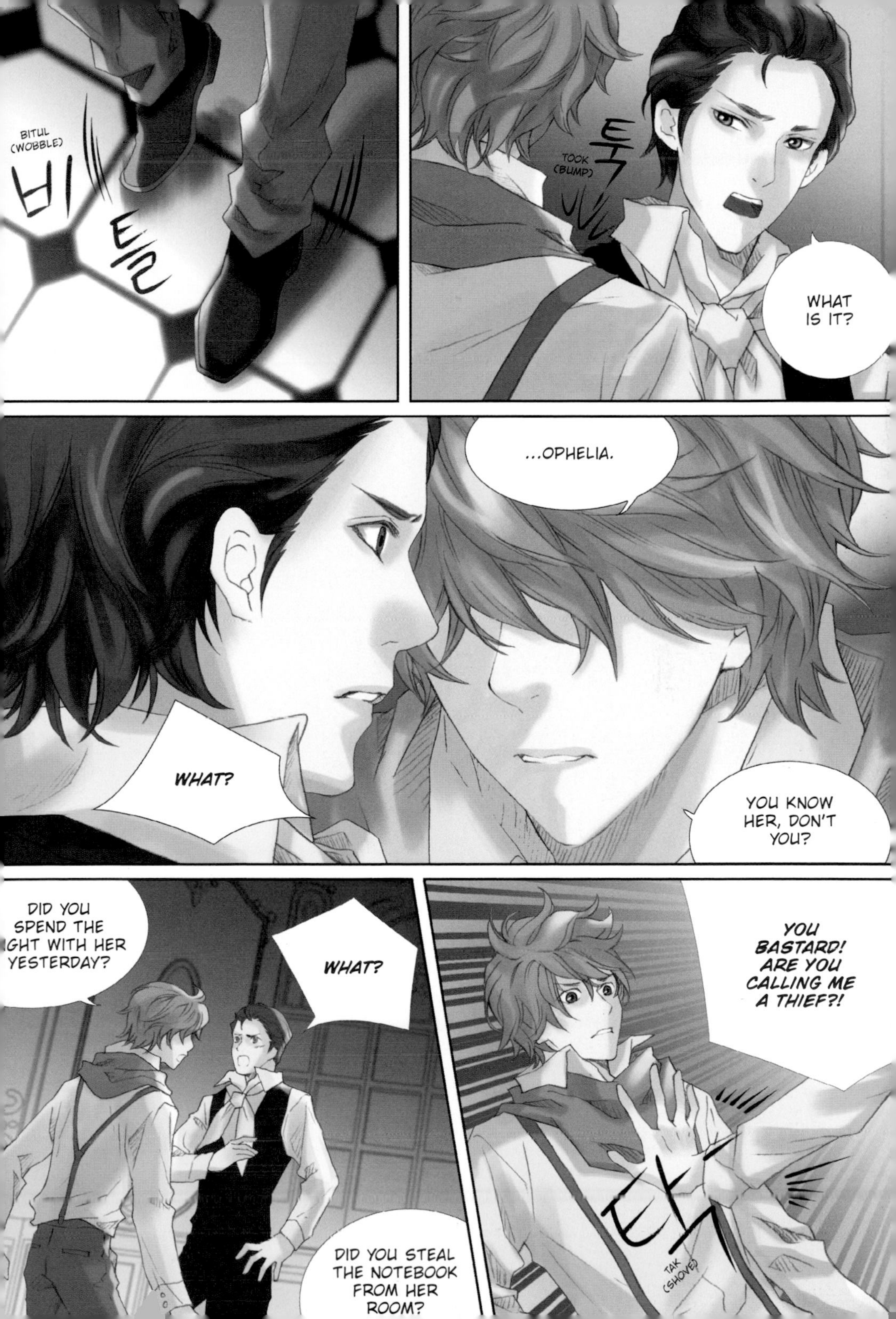

BITUL (WOBBLE)
비틀
TOOK (BUMP)
툭
WHAT IS IT?
...OPHELIA.
WHAT?
YOU KNOW HER, DON'T YOU?
DID YOU SPEND THE GHT WITH HER YESTERDAY?
WHAT?
DID YOU STEAL THE NOTEBOOK FROM HER ROOM?
YOU BASTARD! ARE YOU CALLING ME A THIEF?!
탁
TAK (SHOVE)

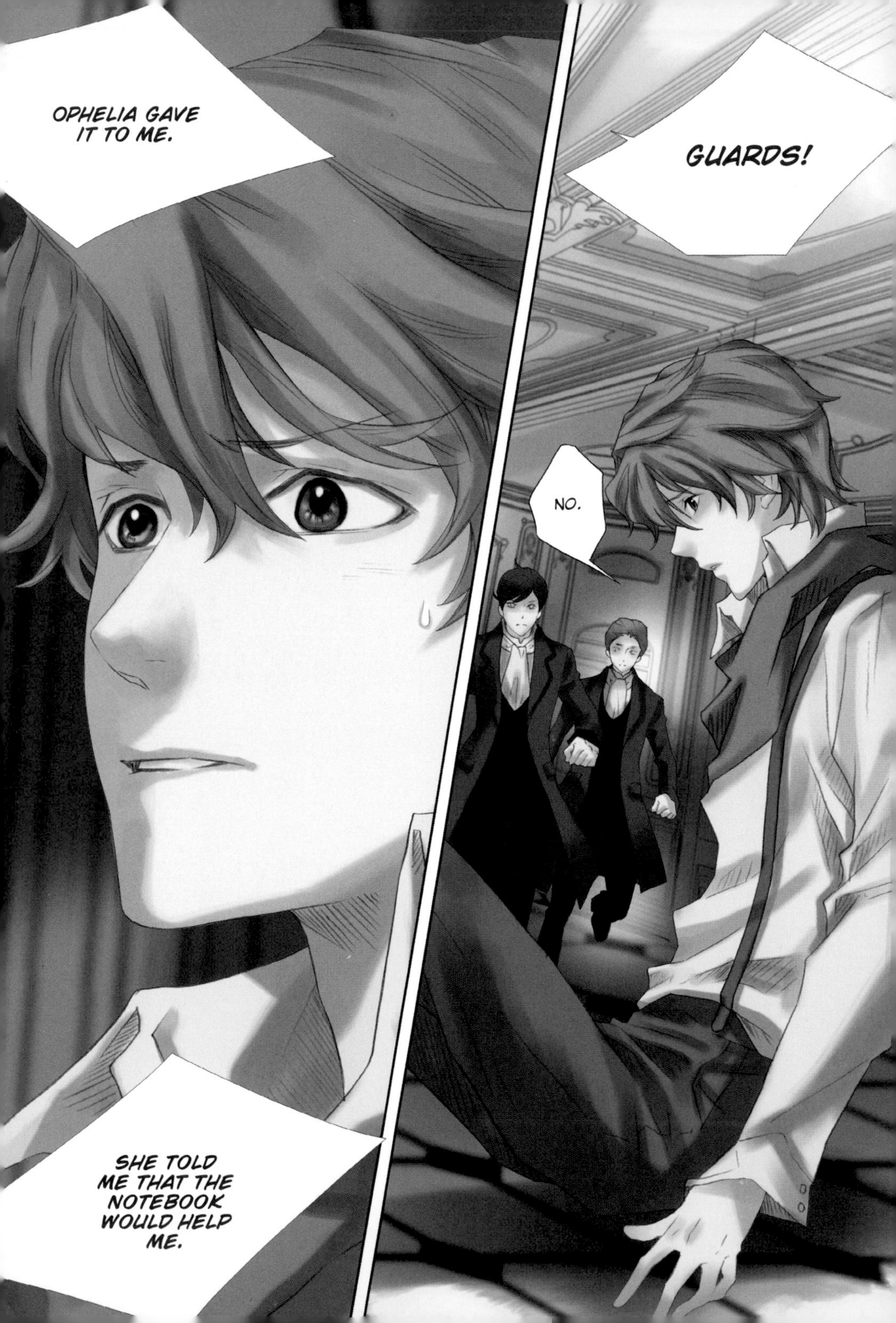
OPHELIA GAVE IT TO ME.
SHE TOLD ME THAT THE NOTEBOOK WOULD HELP ME.
GUARDS!
NO.

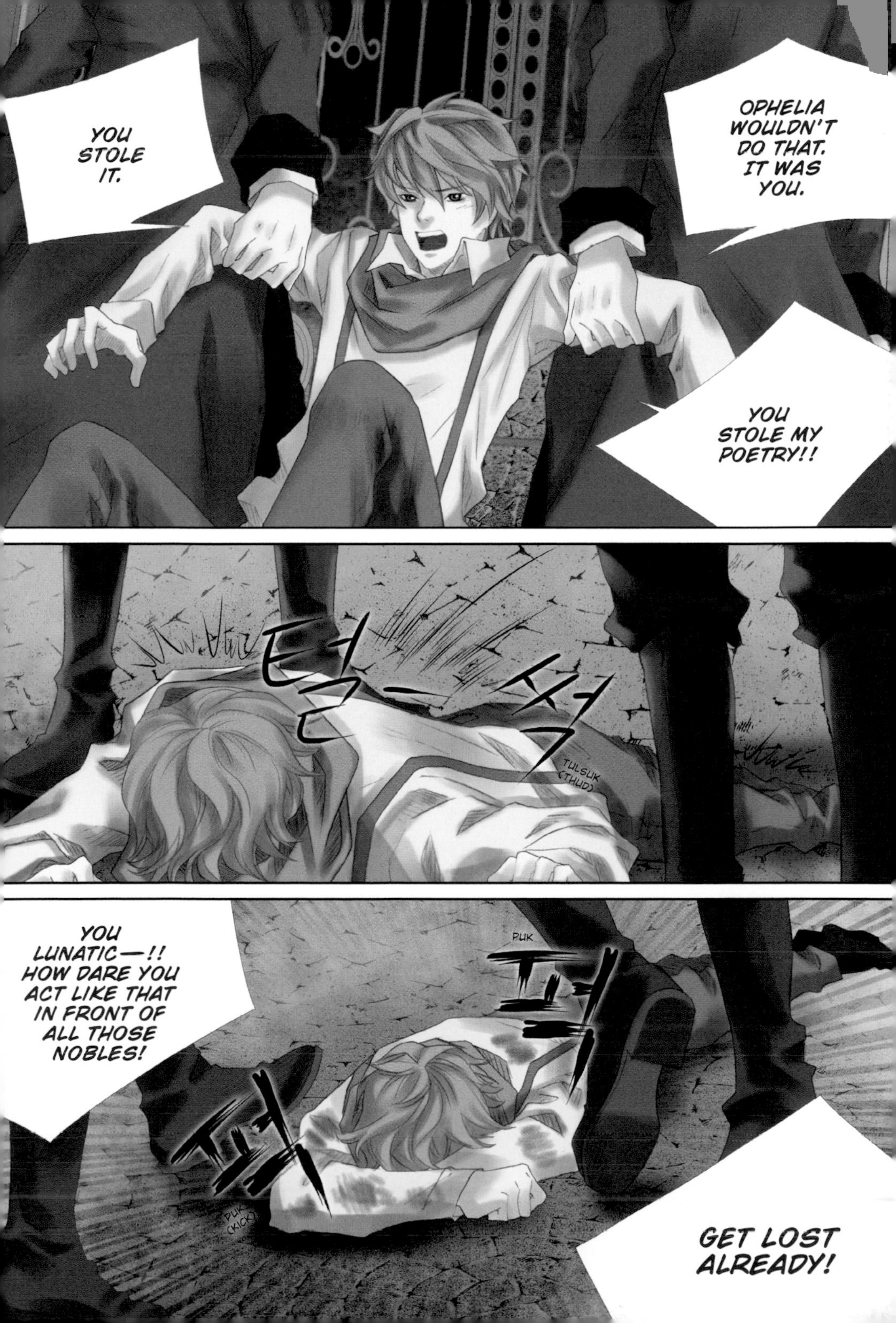
YOU STOLE IT.
OPHELIA WOULDN'T DO THAT. IT WAS YOU.
YOU STOLE MY POETRY!!
TULSUK (THUD)
YOU LUNATIC—!! HOW DARE YOU ACT LIKE THAT IN FRONT OF ALL THOSE NOBLES!
PUK
PUK (KICK)
GET LOST ALREADY!

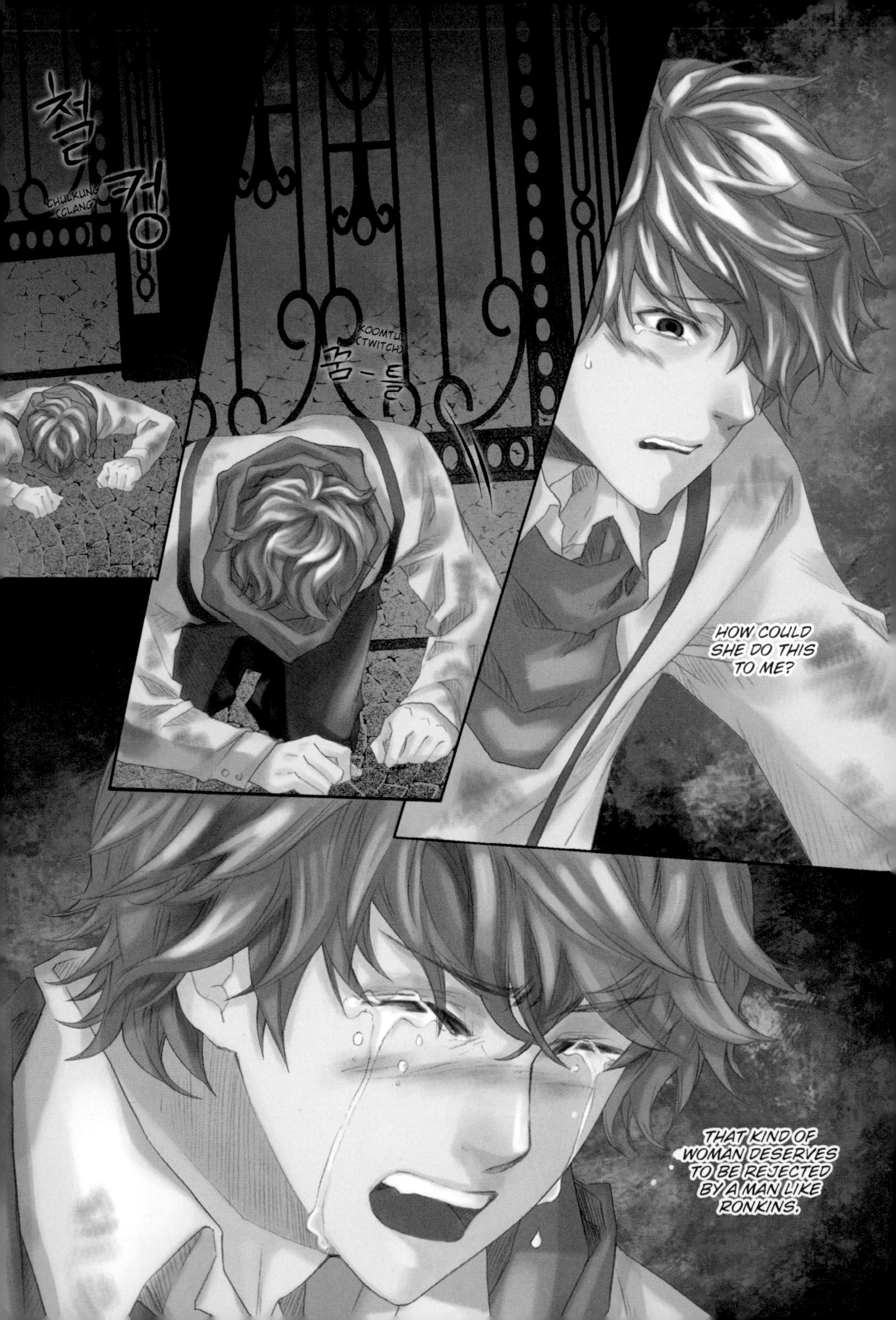

철컹
CHULKUNG (CLANG)
KOOMTUL (TWITCH)
꿈-틀
HOW COULD SHE DO THIS TO ME?
THAT KIND OF WOMAN DESERVES TO BE REJECTED BY A MAN LIKE RONKINS.

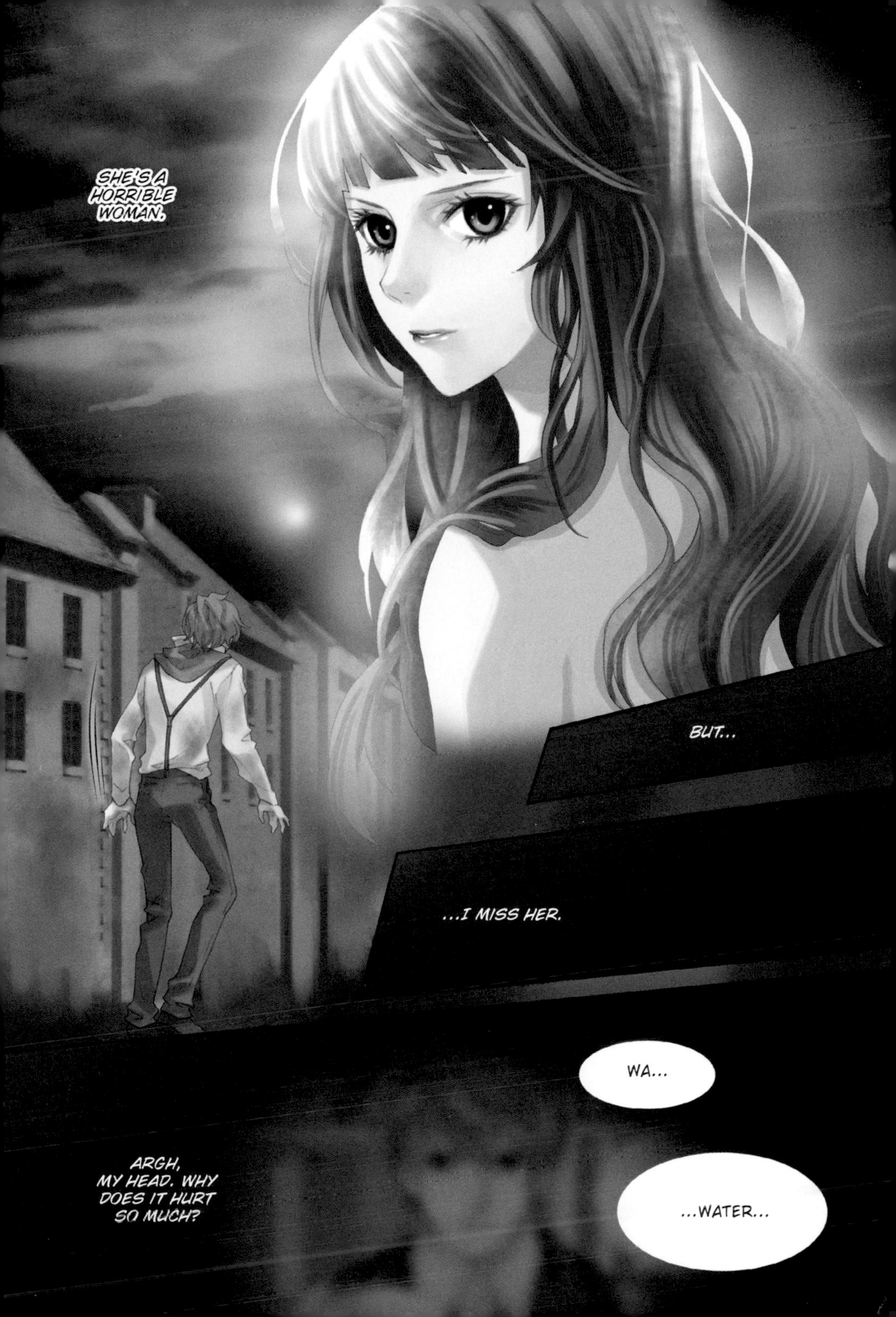
SHE'S A HORRIBLE WOMAN.
BUT...
...I MISS HER.
WA...
ARGH, MY HEAD. WHY DOES IT HURT SO MUCH?
...WATER...

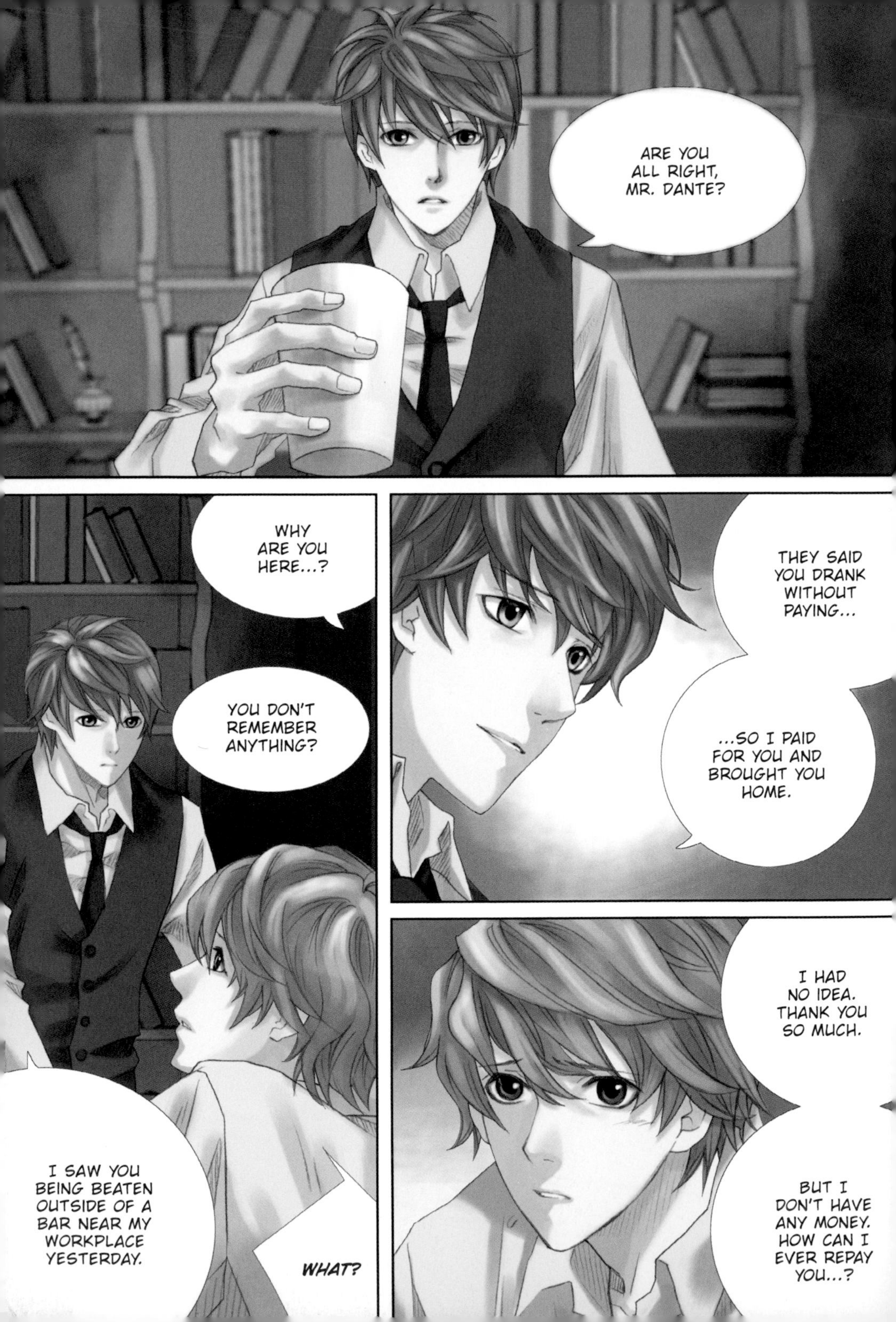
ARE YOU ALL RIGHT, MR. DANTE?
WHY ARE YOU HERE...?
YOU DON'T REMEMBER ANYTHING?
I SAW YOU BEING BEATEN OUTSIDE OF A BAR NEAR MY WORKPLACE YESTERDAY.
WHAT?
THEY SAID YOU DRANK WITHOUT PAYING...
...SO I PAID FOR YOU AND BROUGHT YOU HOME.
I HAD NO IDEA. THANK YOU SO MUCH.
BUT I DON'T HAVE ANY MONEY. HOW CAN I EVER REPAY YOU...?

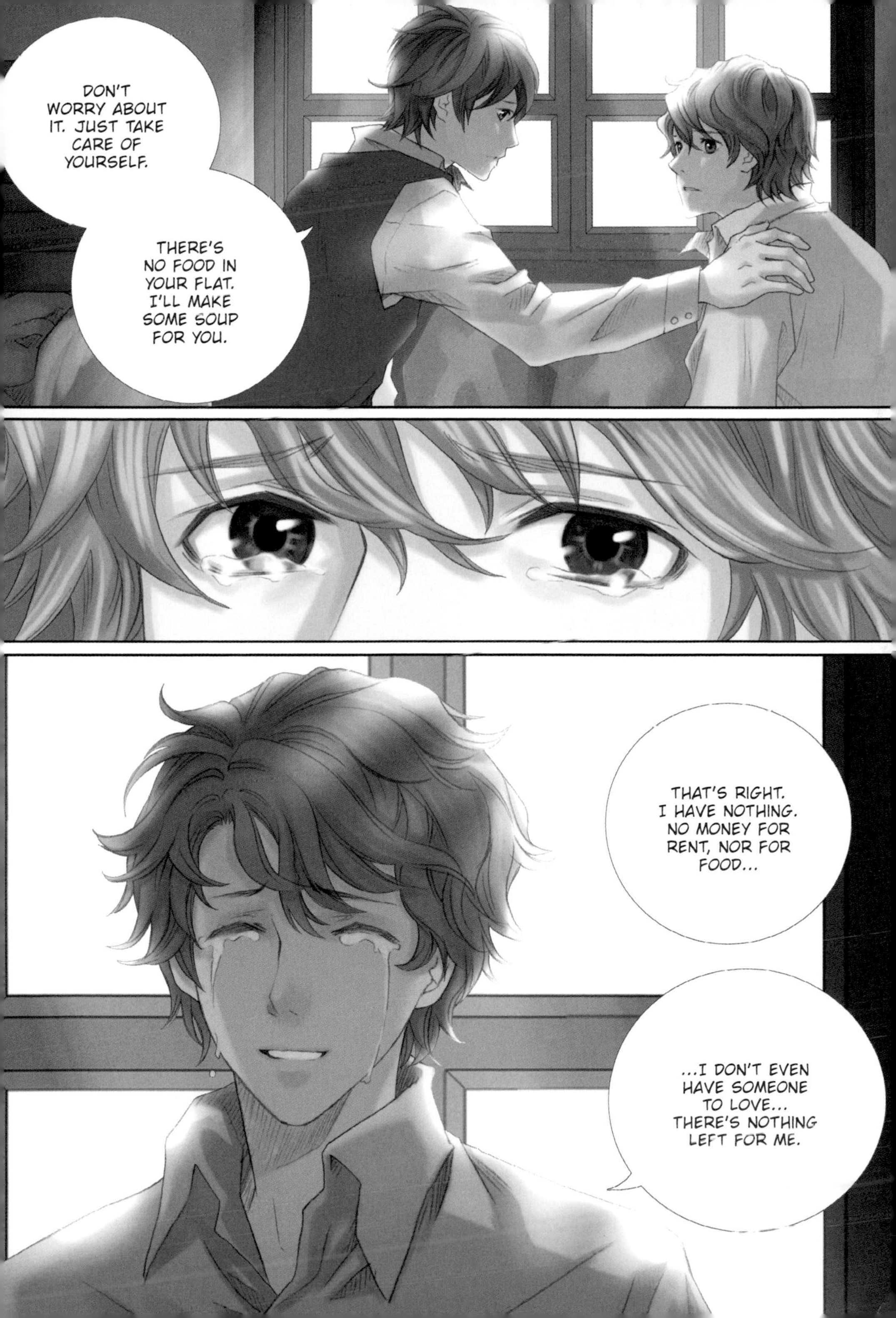
DON'T WORRY ABOUT IT. JUST TAKE CARE OF YOURSELF.
THERE'S NO FOOD IN YOUR FLAT. I'LL MAKE SOME SOUP FOR YOU.
THAT'S RIGHT. I HAVE NOTHING. NO MONEY FOR RENT, NOR FOR FOOD...
...I DON'T EVEN HAVE SOMEONE TO LOVE... THERE'S NOTHING LEFT FOR ME.

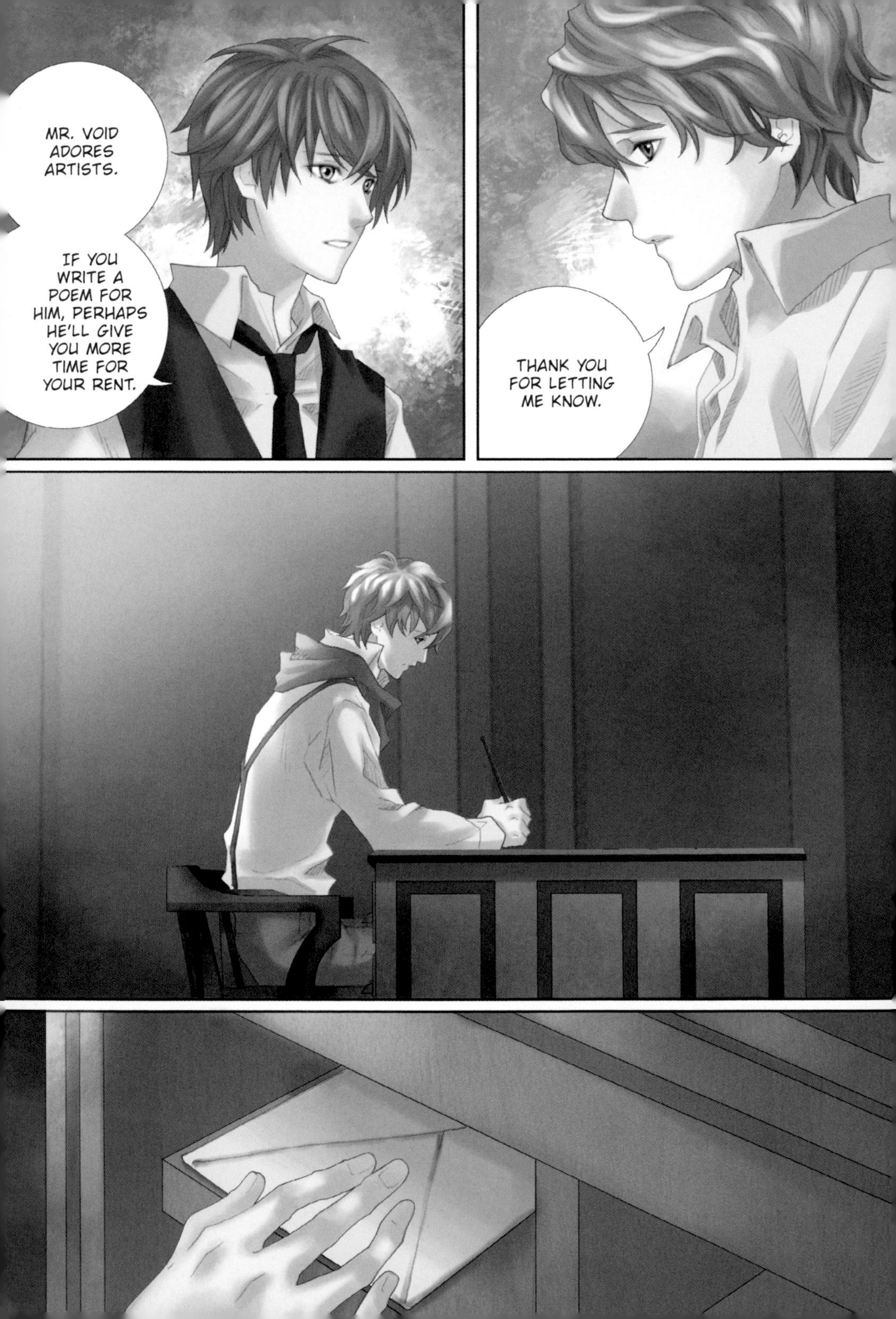
MR. VOID ADORES ARTISTS.
IF YOU WRITE A POEM FOR HIM, PERHAPS HE'LL GIVE YOU MORE TIME FOR YOUR RENT.
THANK YOU FOR LETTING ME KNOW.

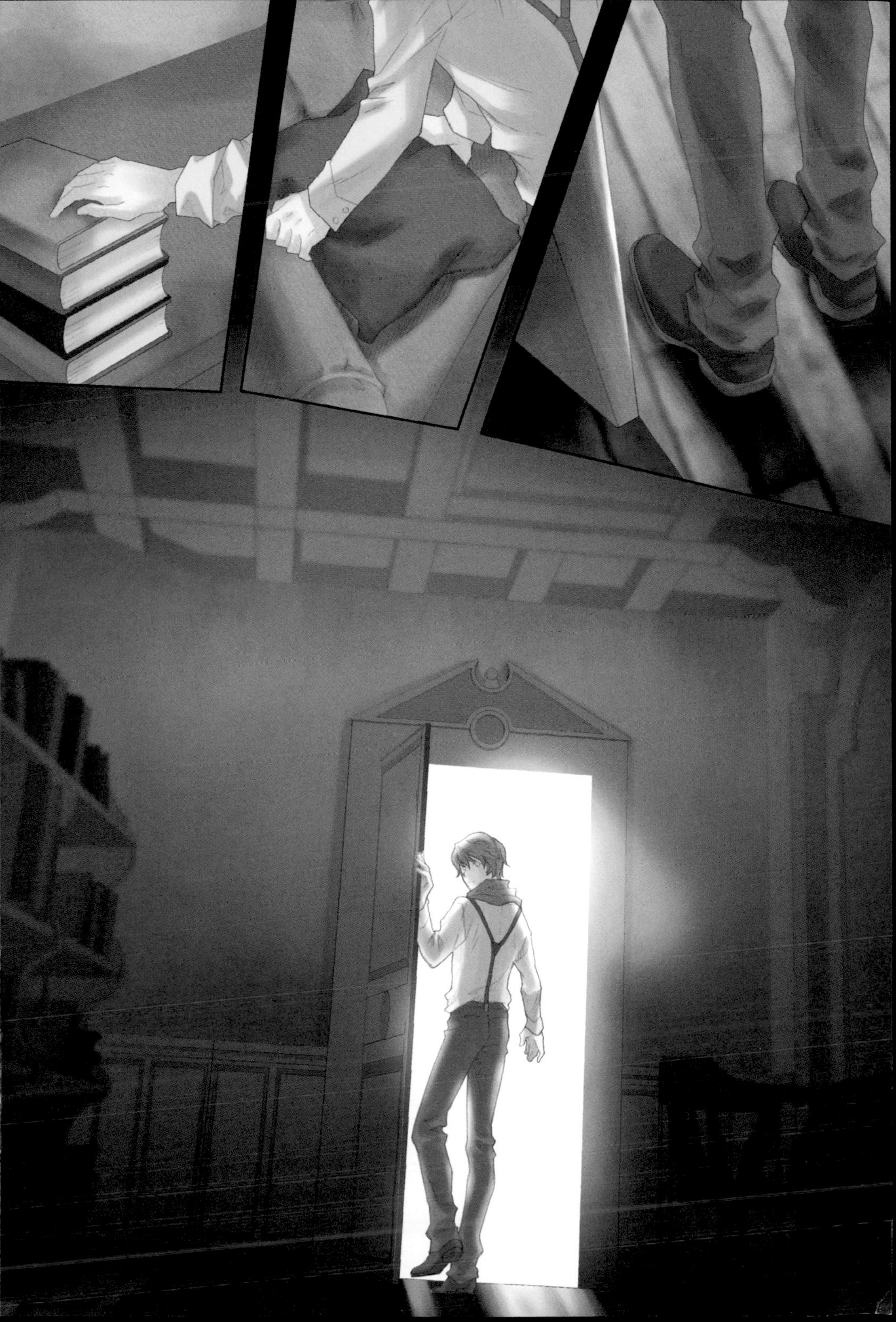

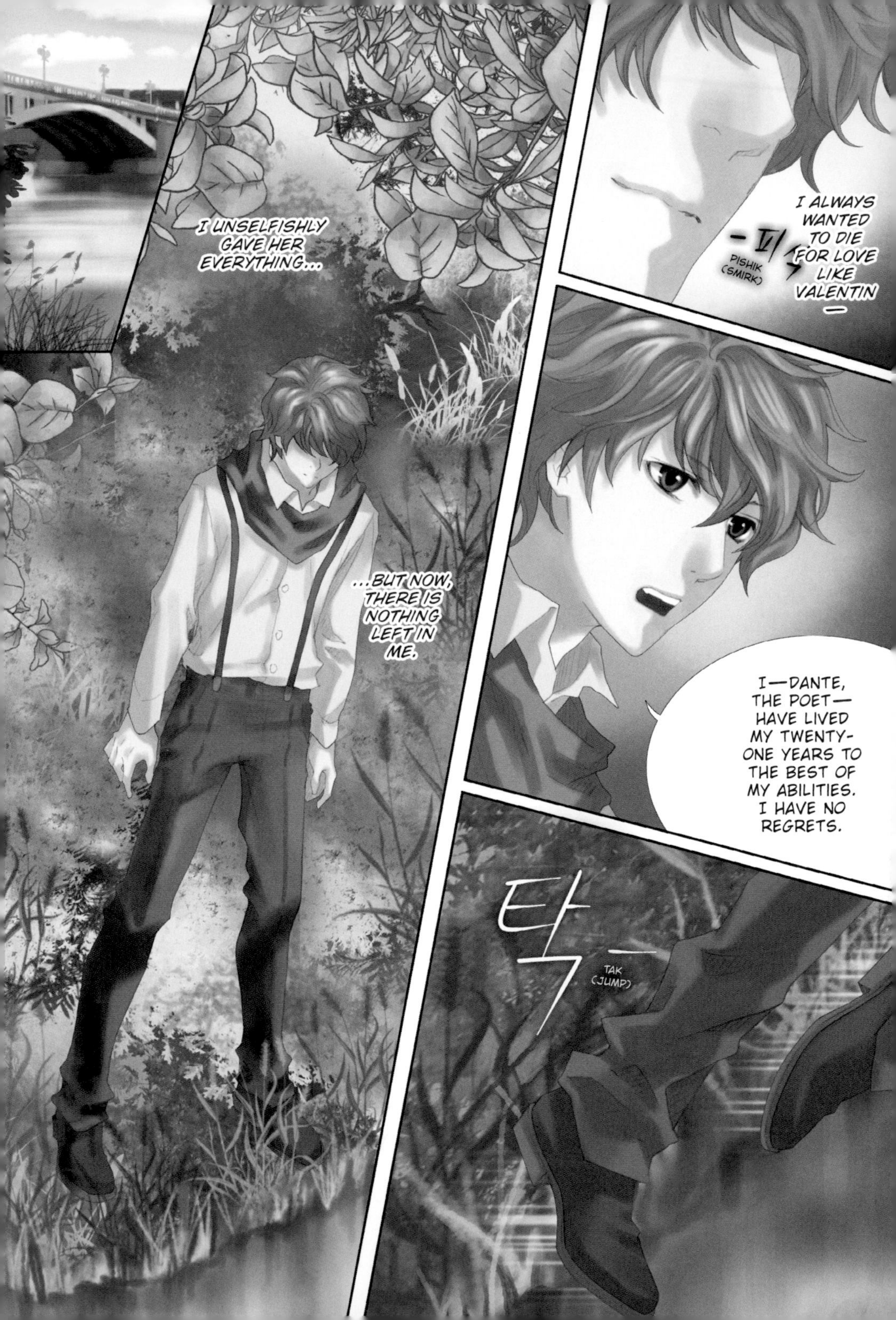
I UNSELFISHLY GAVE HER EVERYTHING...
...BUT NOW, THERE IS NOTHING LEFT IN ME.
I ALWAYS WANTED TO DIE FOR LOVE LIKE VALENTIN—
PISHIK (SMIRK)
I—DANTE, THE POET—HAVE LIVED MY TWENTY-ONE YEARS TO THE BEST OF MY ABILITIES. I HAVE NO REGRETS.
탁
TAK (JUMP)

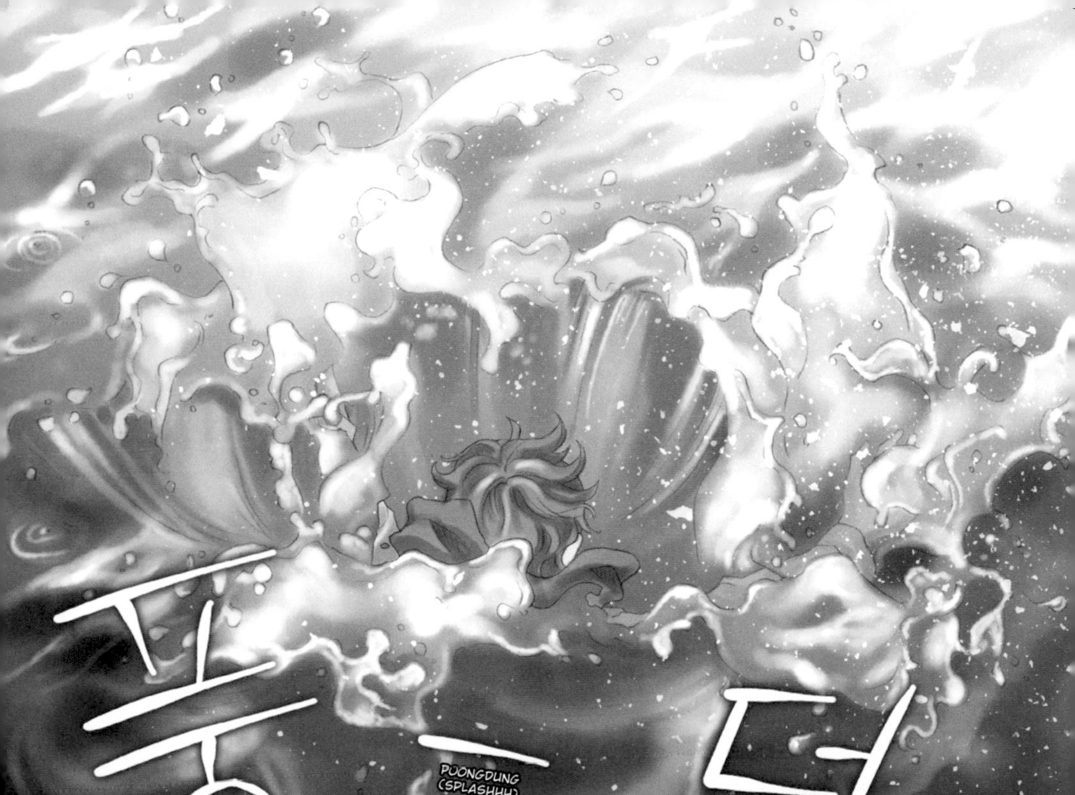
풍덩
POONGDUNG
(SPLASHHH)
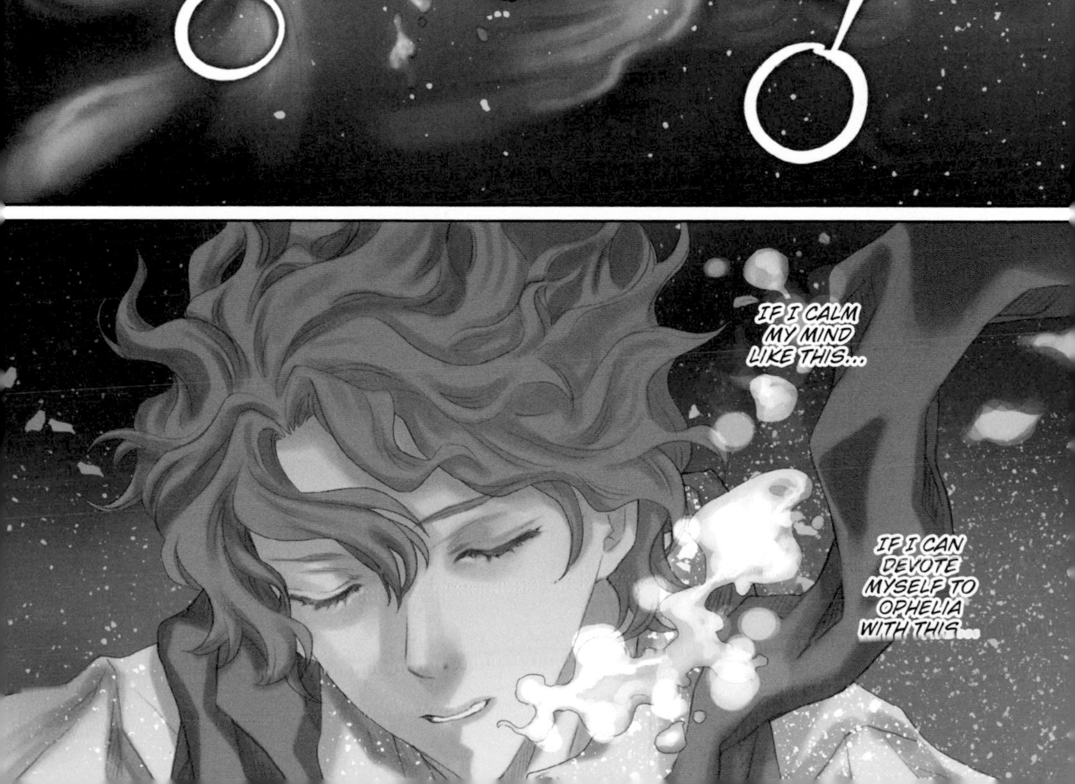
IF I CALM MY MIND LIKE THIS...
IF I CAN DEVOTE MYSELF TO OPHELIA WITH THIS...

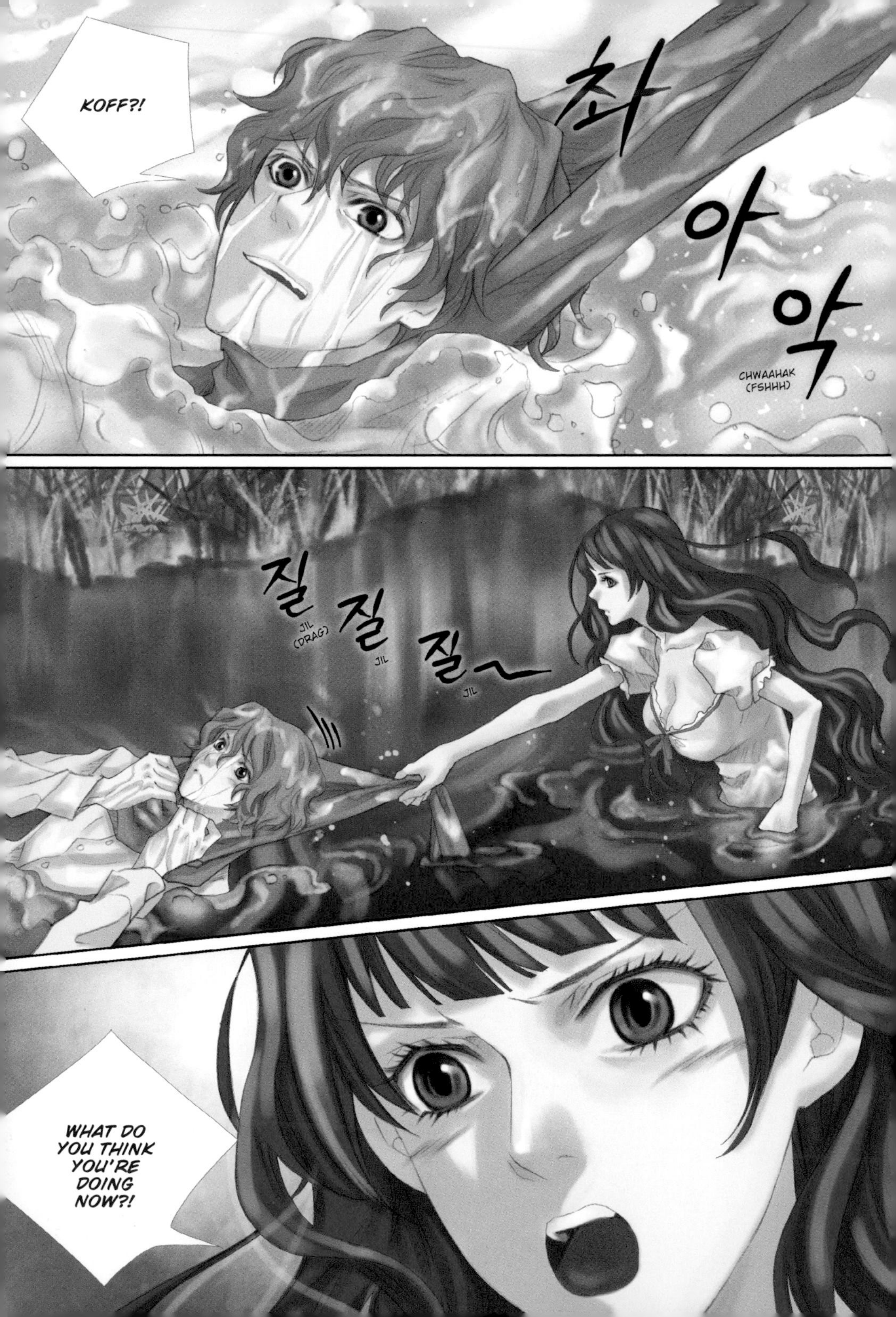
KOFF?!
촤아악
CHWAAHAK (FSHHH)
질 질 질~
JIL (DRAG)
JIL
JIL
WHAT DO YOU THINK YOU'RE DOING NOW?!

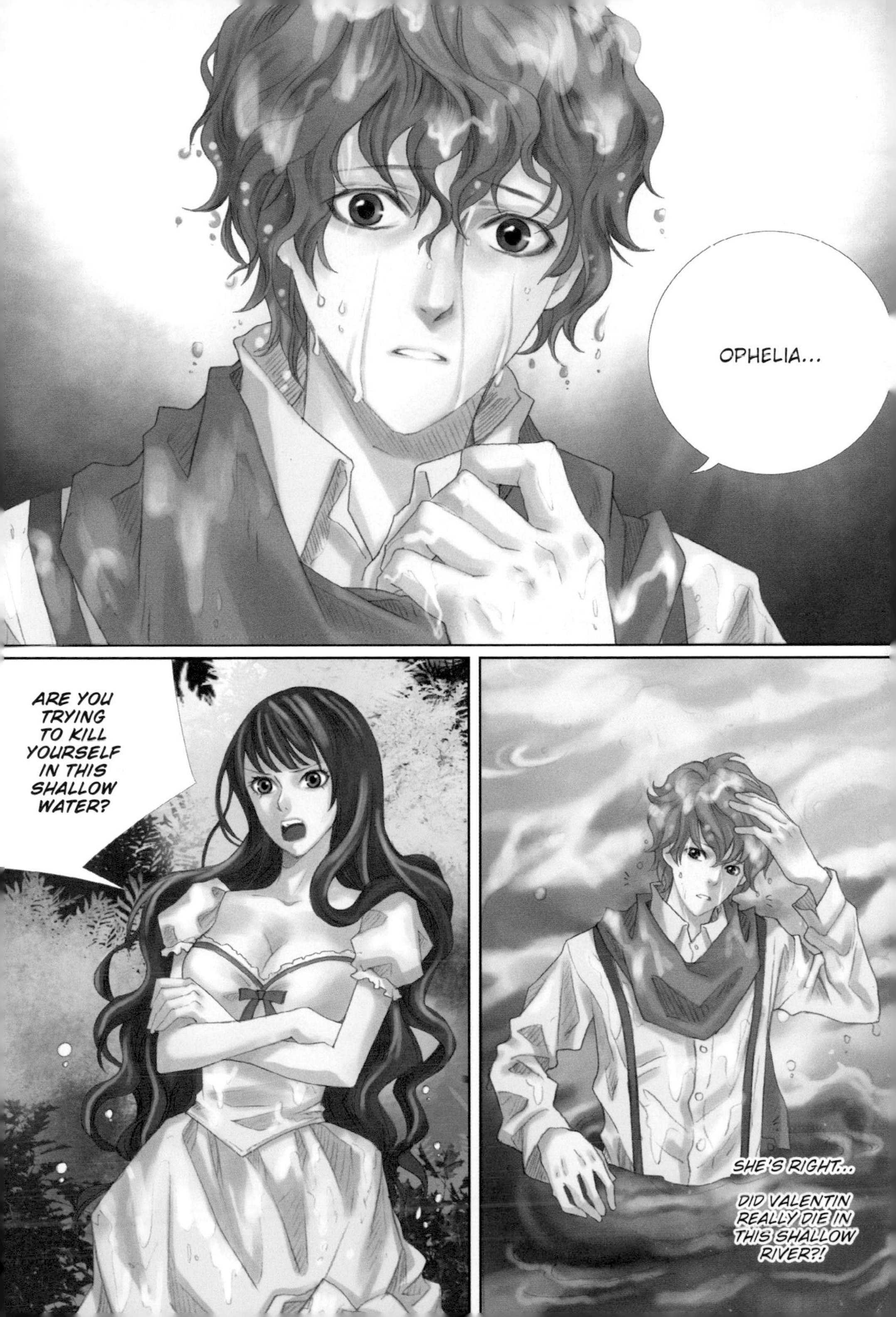
OPHELIA...
ARE YOU TRYING TO KILL YOURSELF IN THIS SHALLOW WATER?
SHE'S RIGHT...
DID VALENTIN REALLY DIE IN THIS SHALLOW RIVER?!

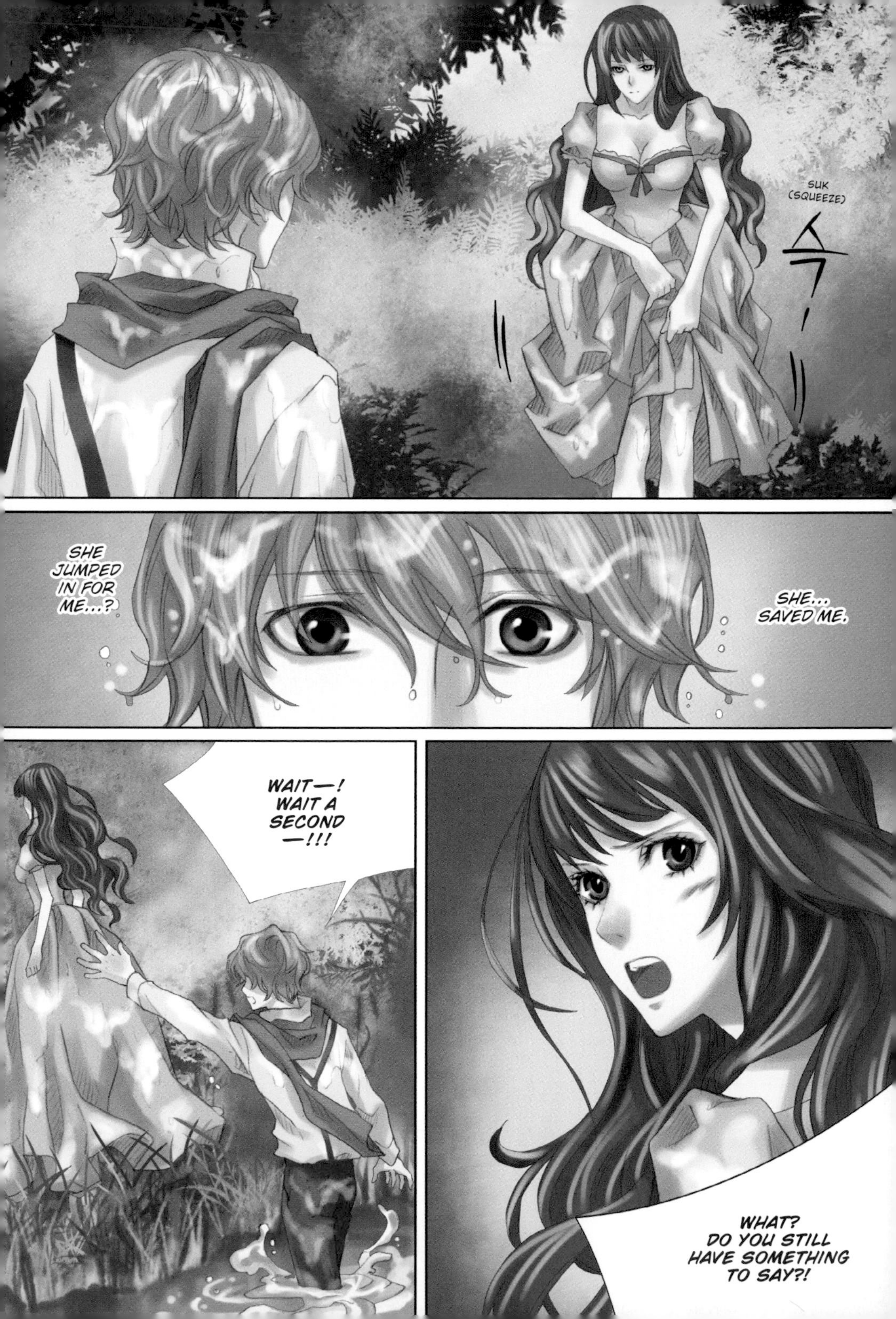
SUK (SQUEEZE)
SHE JUMPED IN FOR ME...?
SHE... SAVED ME.
WAIT—! WAIT A SECOND —!!!
WHAT? DO YOU STILL HAVE SOMETHING TO SAY?!

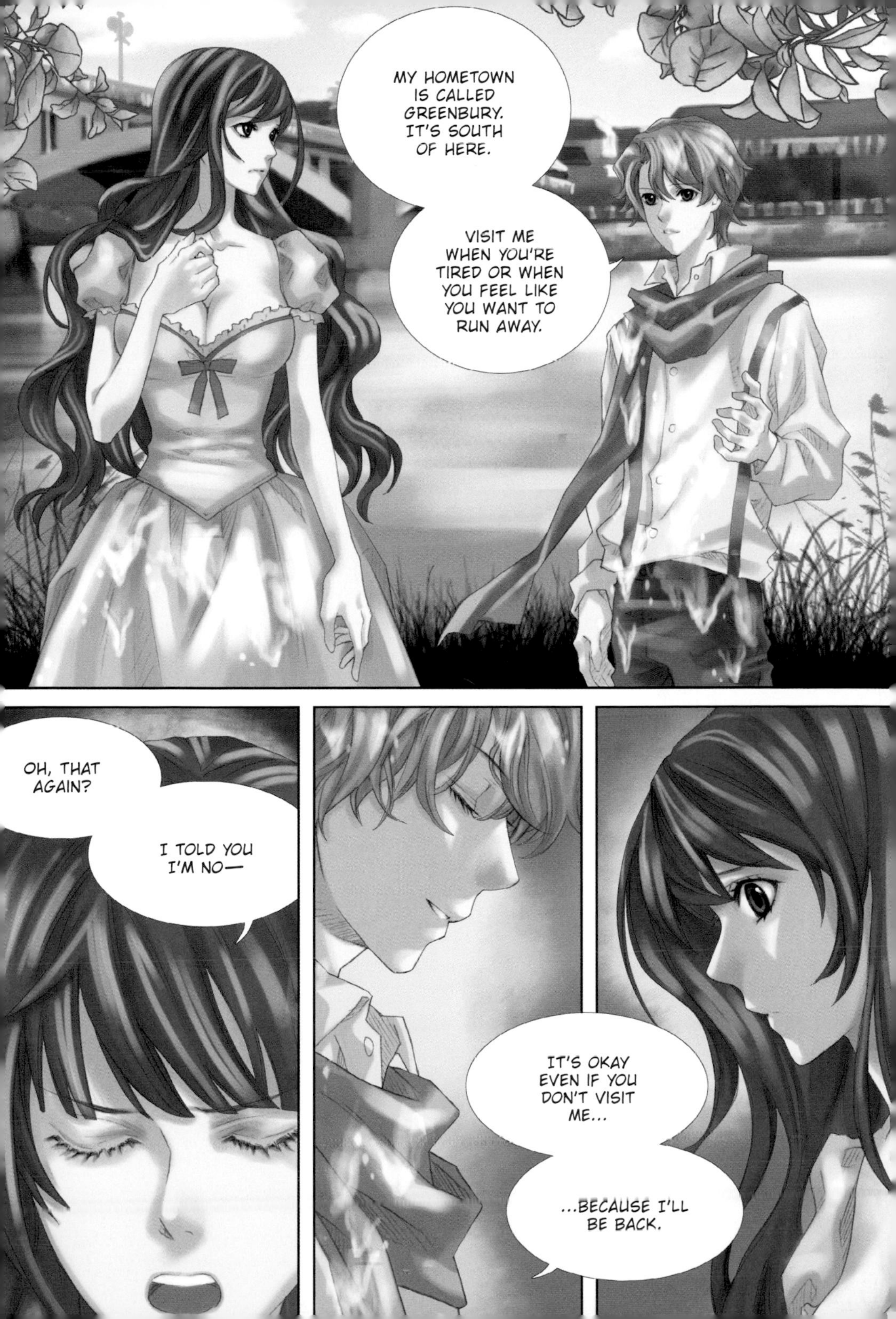
MY HOMETOWN IS CALLED GREENBURY. IT'S SOUTH OF HERE.
VISIT ME WHEN YOU'RE TIRED OR WHEN YOU FEEL LIKE YOU WANT TO RUN AWAY.
OH, THAT AGAIN?
I TOLD YOU I'M NO—
IT'S OKAY EVEN IF YOU DON'T VISIT ME...
...BECAUSE I'LL BE BACK.

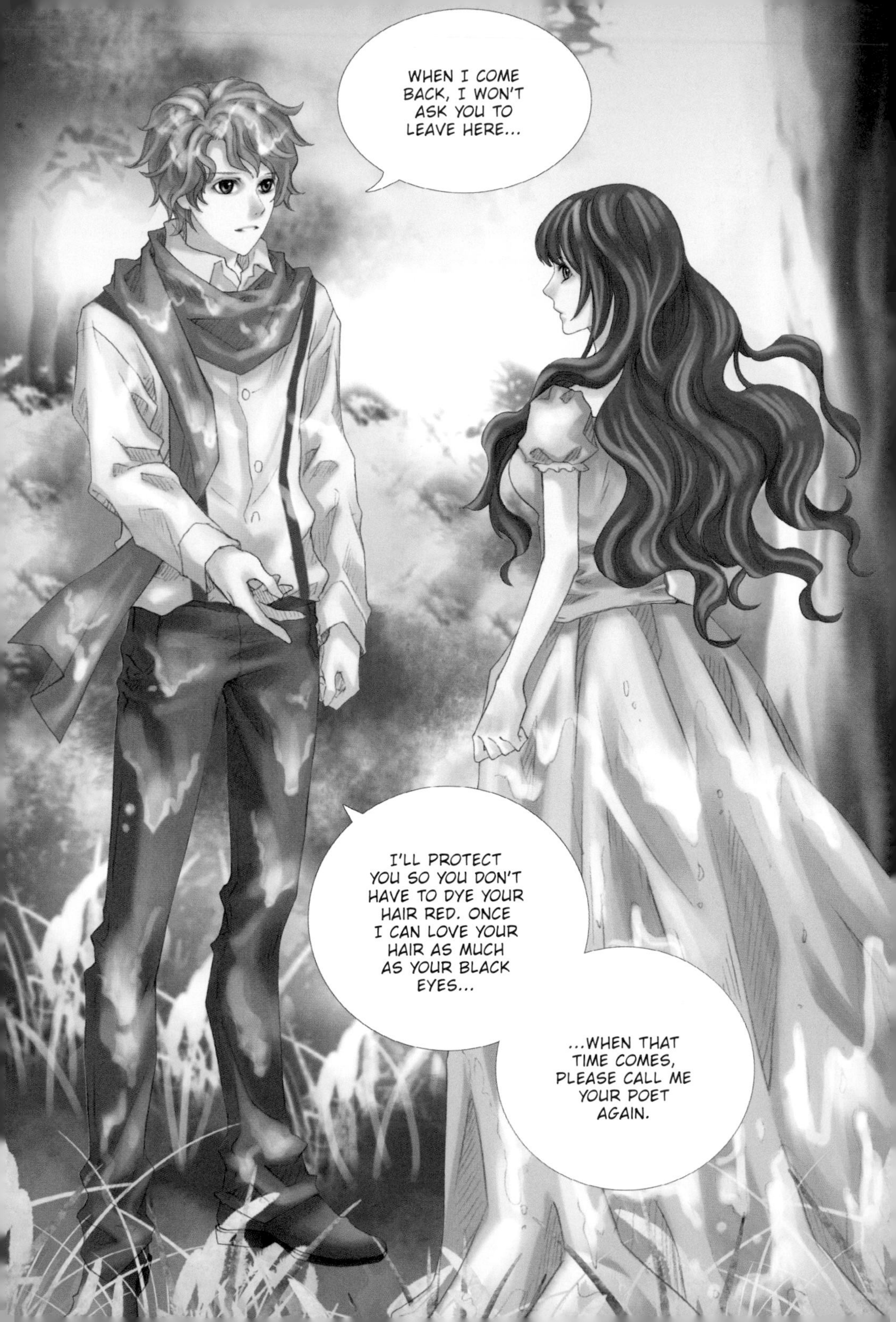
WHEN I COME BACK, I WON'T ASK YOU TO LEAVE HERE...
I'LL PROTECT YOU SO YOU DON'T HAVE TO DYE YOUR HAIR RED. ONCE I CAN LOVE YOUR HAIR AS MUCH AS YOUR BLACK EYES...
...WHEN THAT TIME COMES, PLEASE CALL ME YOUR POET AGAIN.

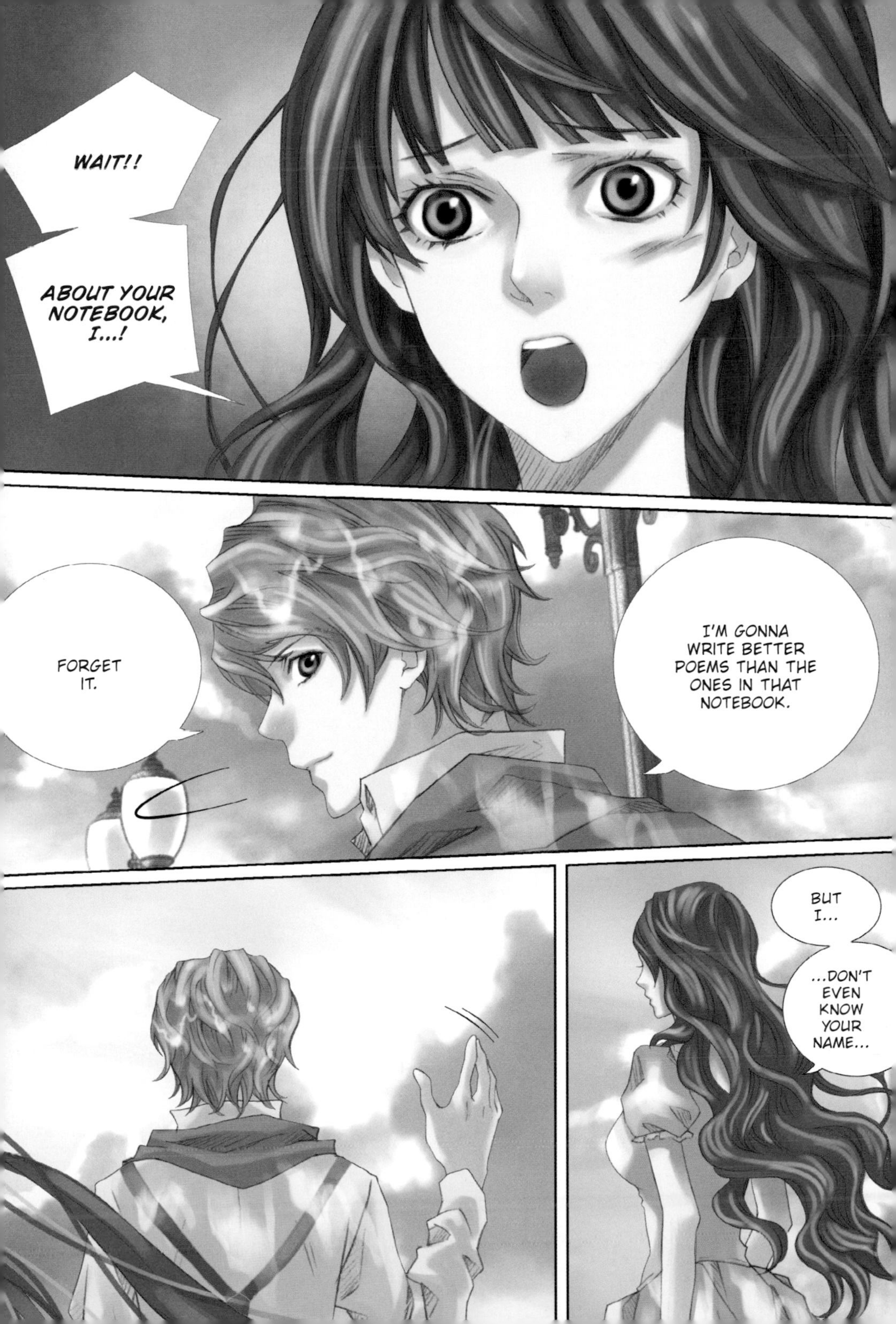
WAIT!!
ABOUT YOUR NOTEBOOK, I...!
FORGET IT.
I'M GONNA WRITE BETTER POEMS THAN THE ONES IN THAT NOTEBOOK.
BUT I...
...DON'T EVEN KNOW YOUR NAME...

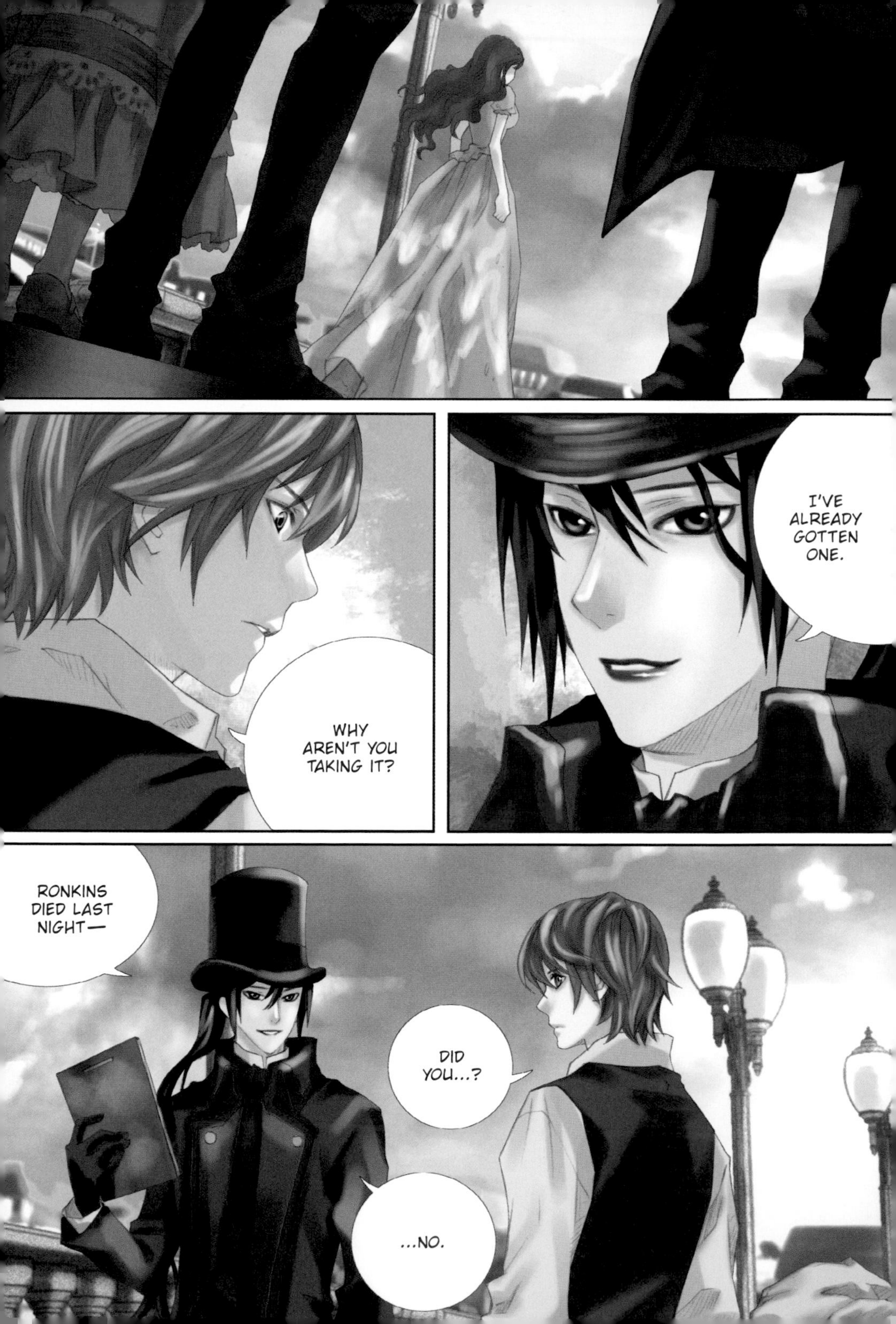
WHY AREN'T YOU TAKING IT?
I'VE ALREADY GOTTEN ONE.
RONKINS DIED LAST NIGHT—
DID YOU...?
...NO.

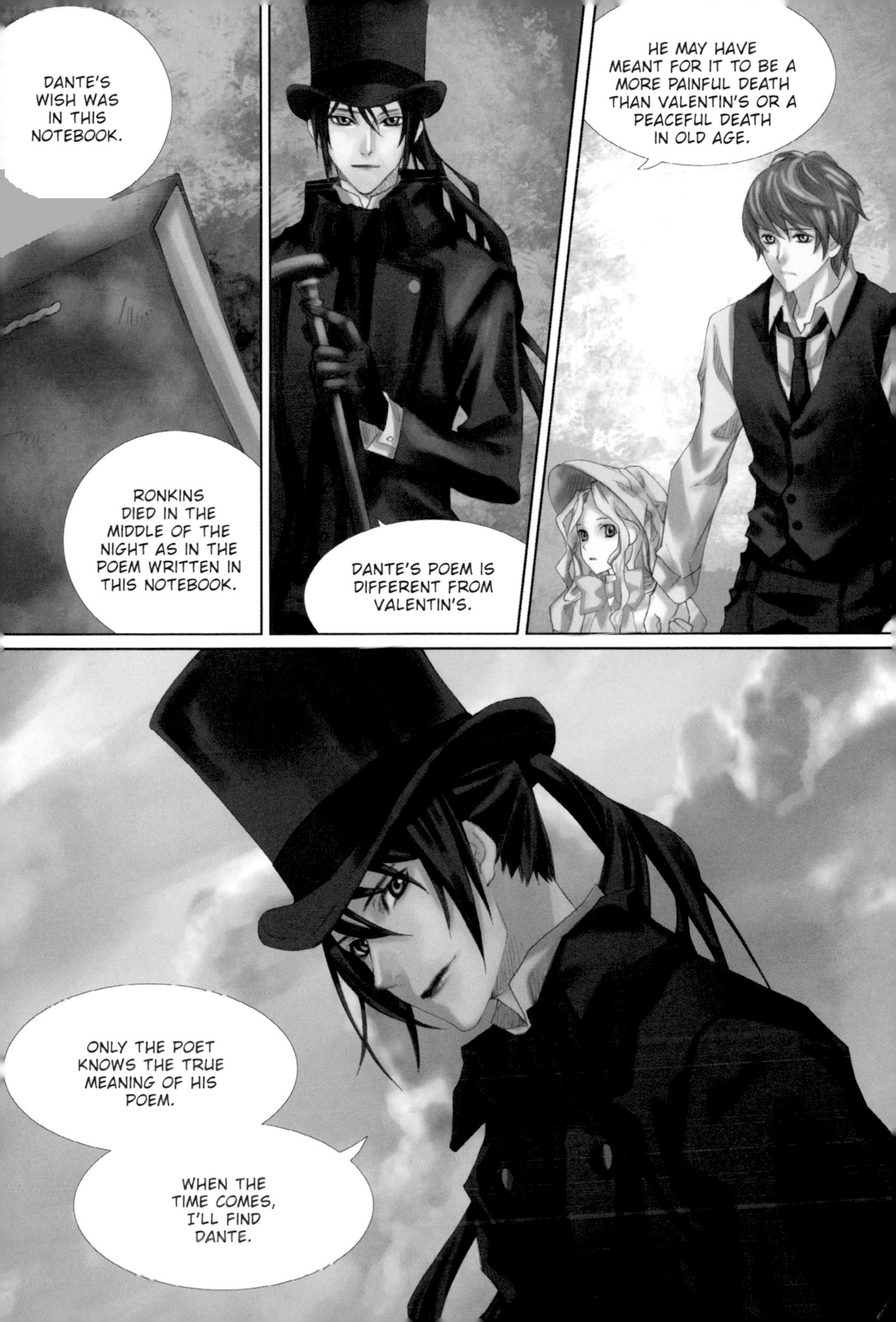
DANTE'S WISH WAS IN THIS NOTEBOOK.
RONKINS DIED IN THE MIDDLE OF THE NIGHT AS IN THE POEM WRITTEN IN THIS NOTEBOOK.
DANTE'S POEM IS DIFFERENT FROM VALENTIN'S.
HE MAY HAVE MEANT FOR IT TO BE A MORE PAINFUL DEATH THAN VALENTIN'S OR A PEACEFUL DEATH IN OLD AGE.
ONLY THE POET KNOWS THE TRUE MEANING OF HIS POEM.
WHEN THE TIME COMES, I'LL FIND DANTE.

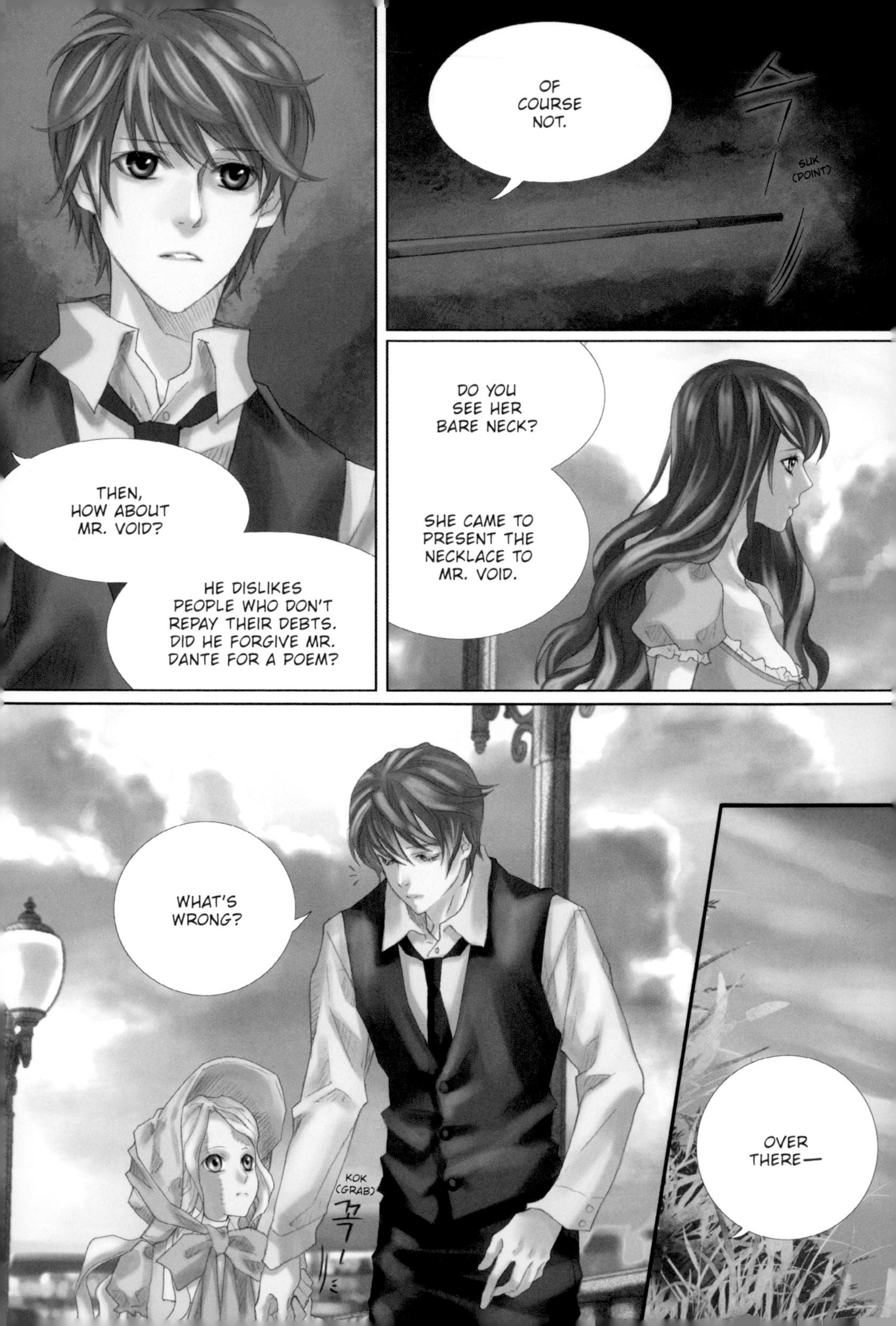
THEN, HOW ABOUT MR. VOID?
HE DISLIKES PEOPLE WHO DON'T REPAY THEIR DEBTS. DID HE FORGIVE MR. DANTE FOR A POEM?
OF COURSE NOT.
SUK (POINT)
DO YOU SEE HER BARE NECK?
SHE CAME TO PRESENT THE NECKLACE TO MR. VOID.
WHAT'S WRONG?
KOK (GRAB)
OVER THERE—

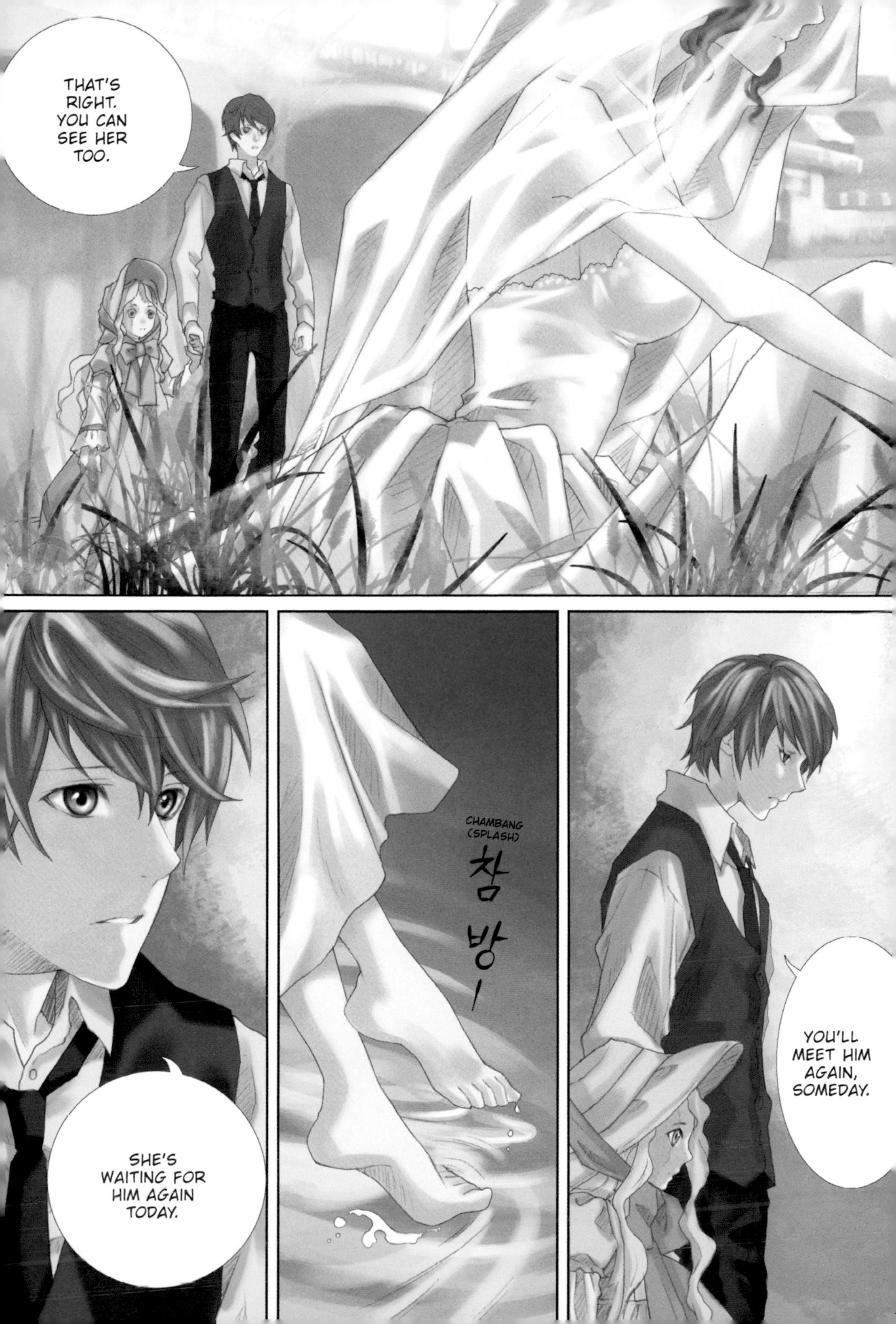
THAT'S RIGHT. YOU CAN SEE HER TOO.
SHE'S WAITING FOR HIM AGAIN TODAY.
CHAMBANG (SPLASH)
참방
YOU'LL MEET HIM AGAIN, SOMEDAY.

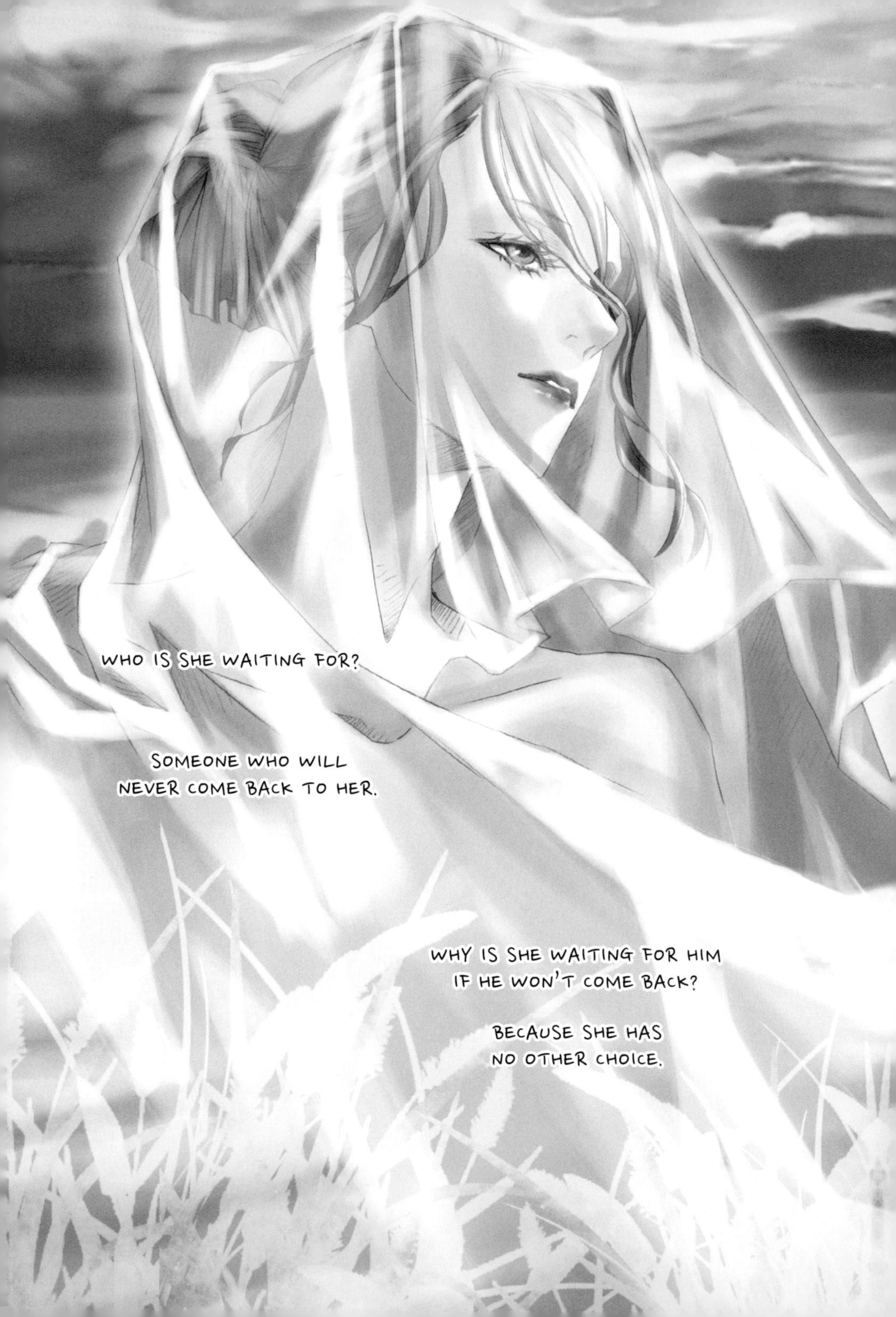
WHO IS SHE WAITING FOR?
SOMEONE WHO WILL NEVER COME BACK TO HER.
WHY IS SHE WAITING FOR HIM IF HE WON'T COME BACK?
BECAUSE SHE HAS NO OTHER CHOICE.

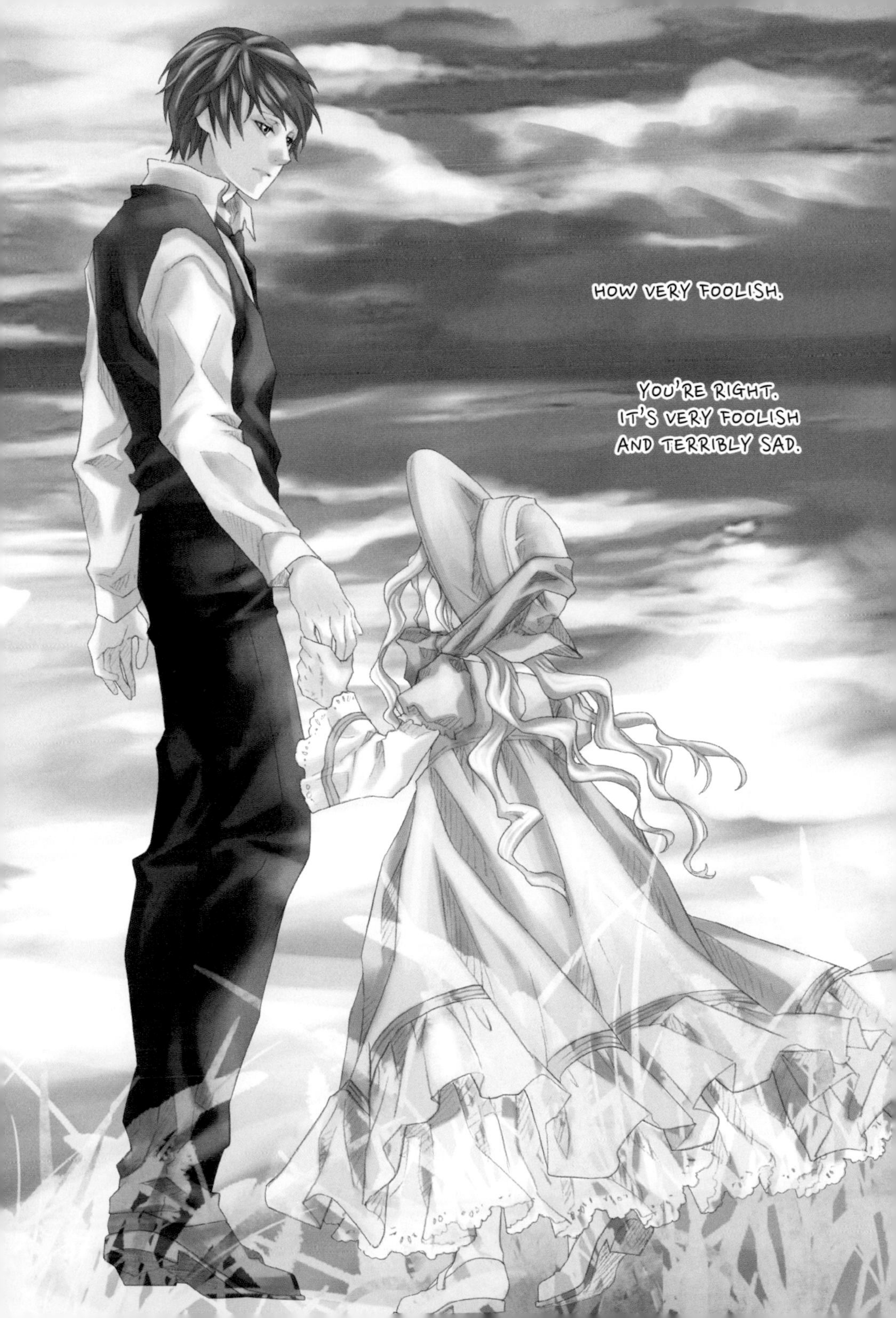
HOW VERY FOOLISH.
YOU'RE RIGHT. IT'S VERY FOOLISH AND TERRIBLY SAD.

Void's Enigmatic Mansion

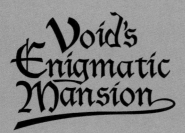

"

"He can make
other people's
wishes come true,
but not his own."

"

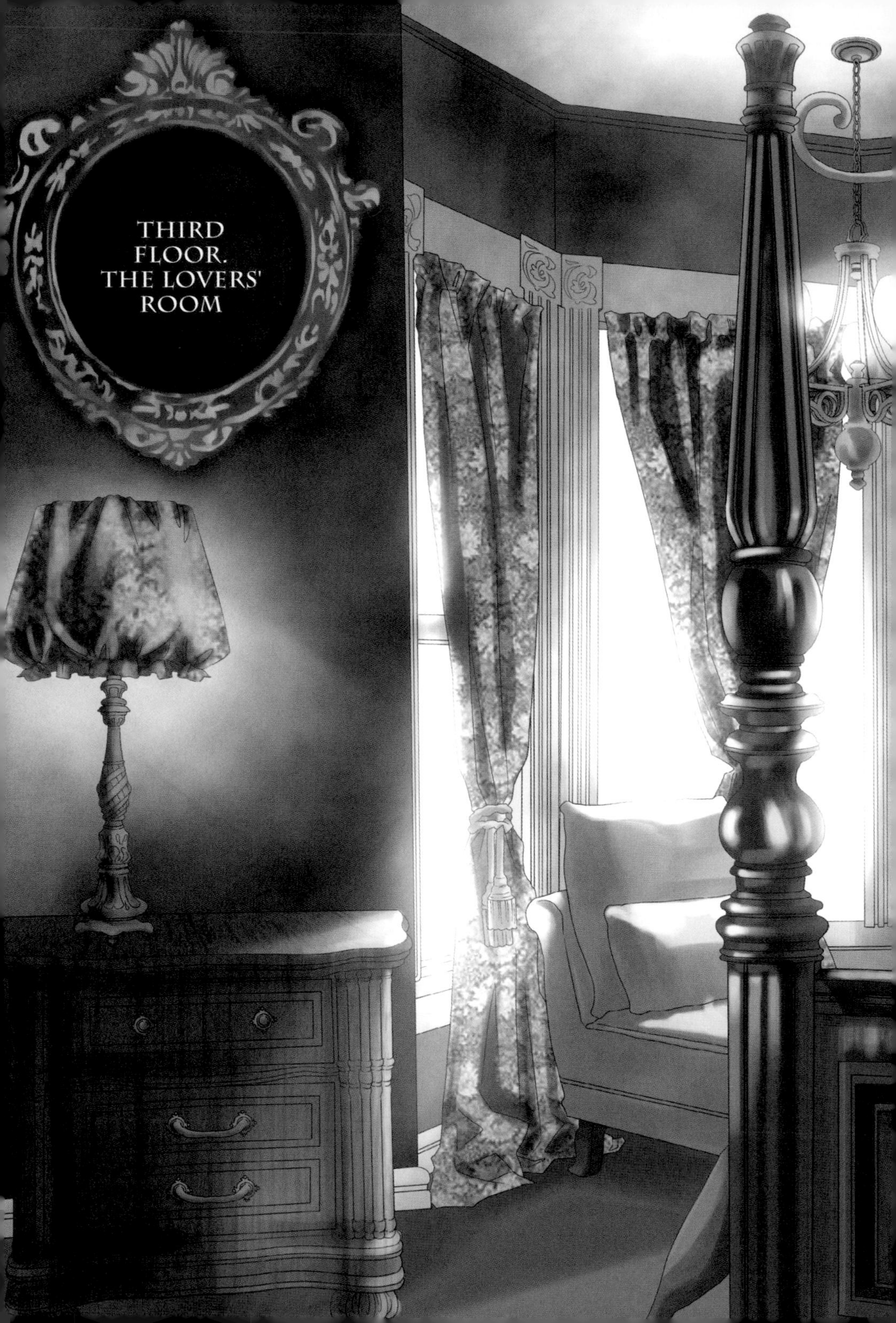
THIRD FLOOR. THE LOVERS' ROOM

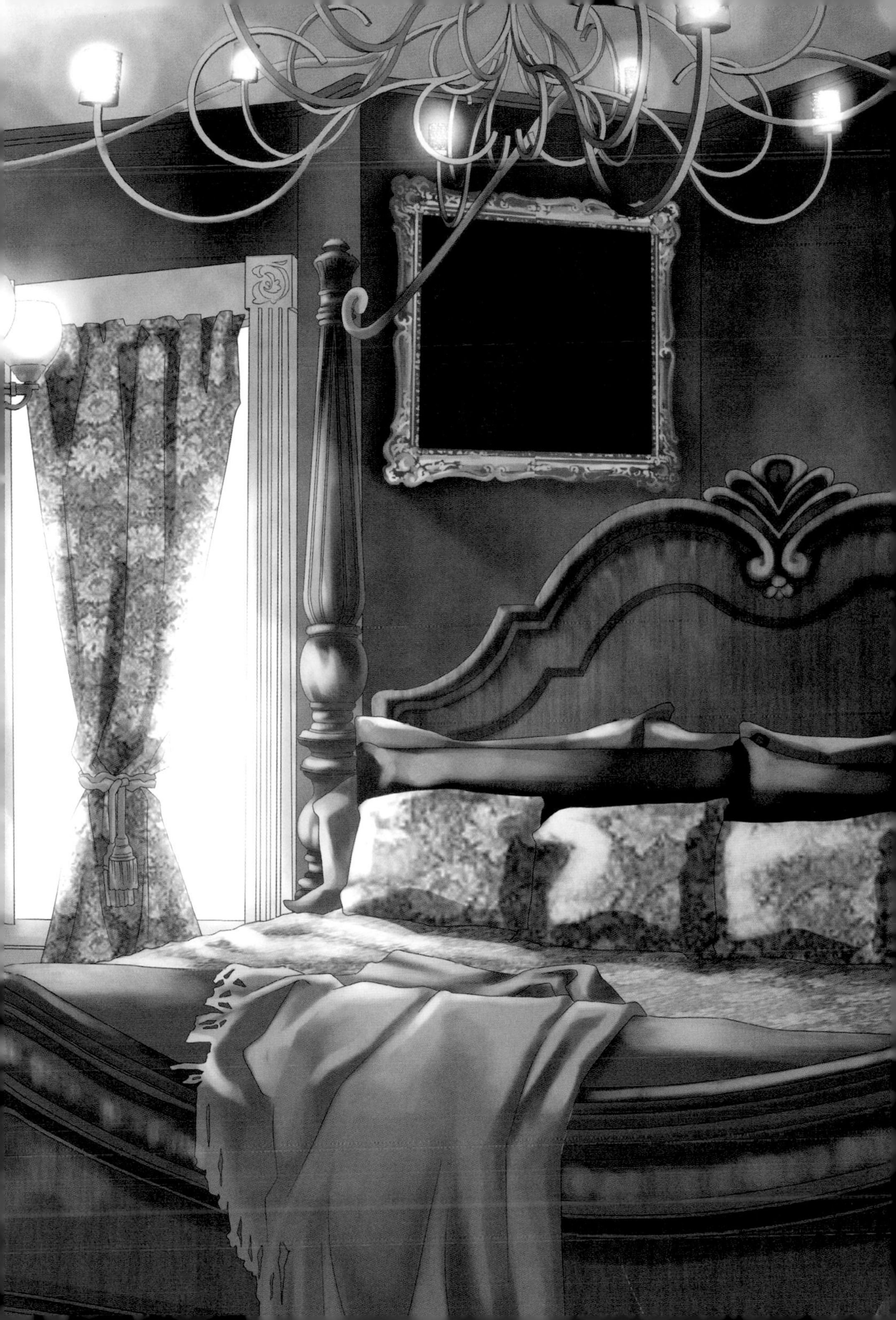

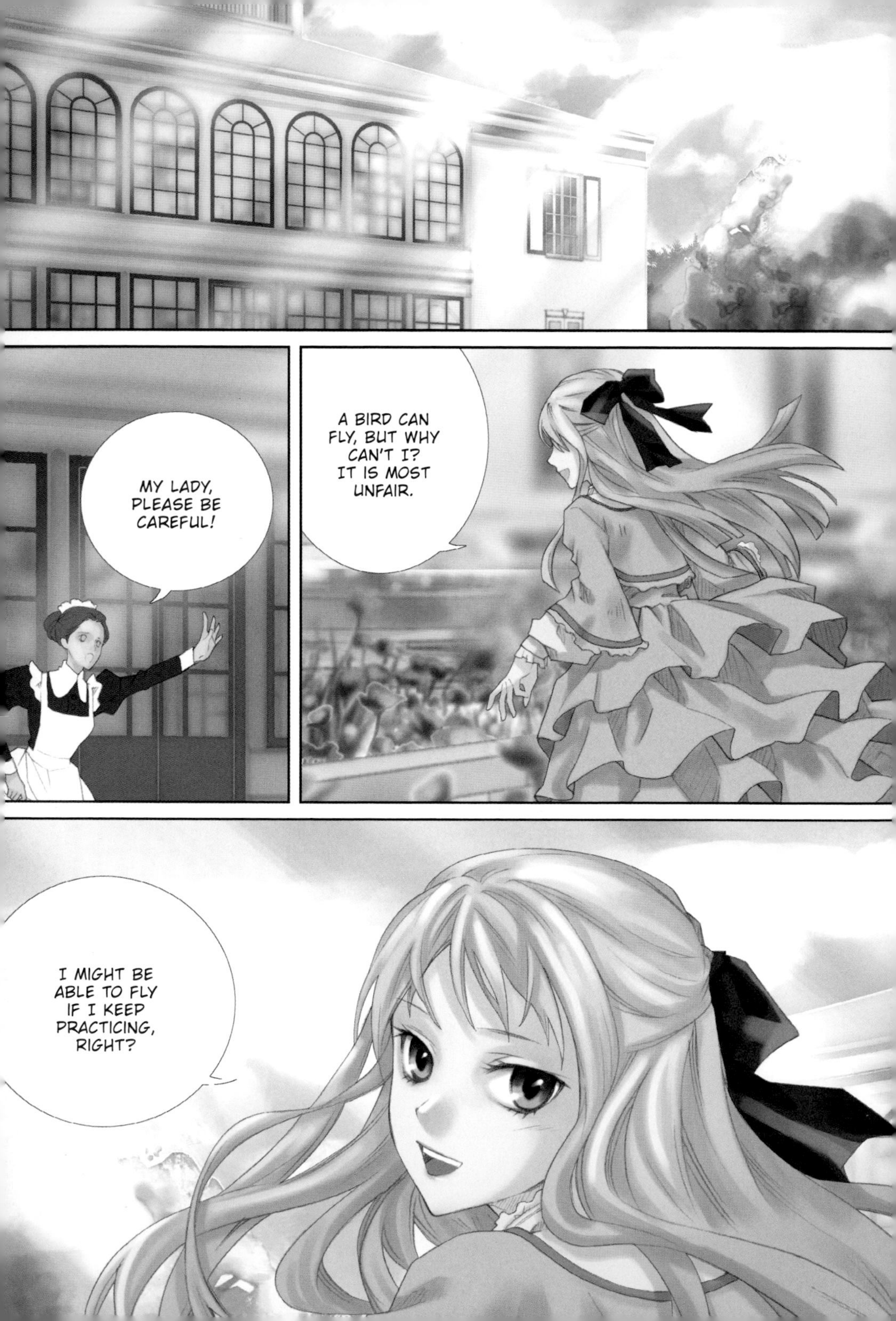
MY LADY, PLEASE BE CAREFUL!
A BIRD CAN FLY, BUT WHY CAN'T I? IT IS MOST UNFAIR.
I MIGHT BE ABLE TO FLY IF I KEEP PRACTICING, RIGHT?

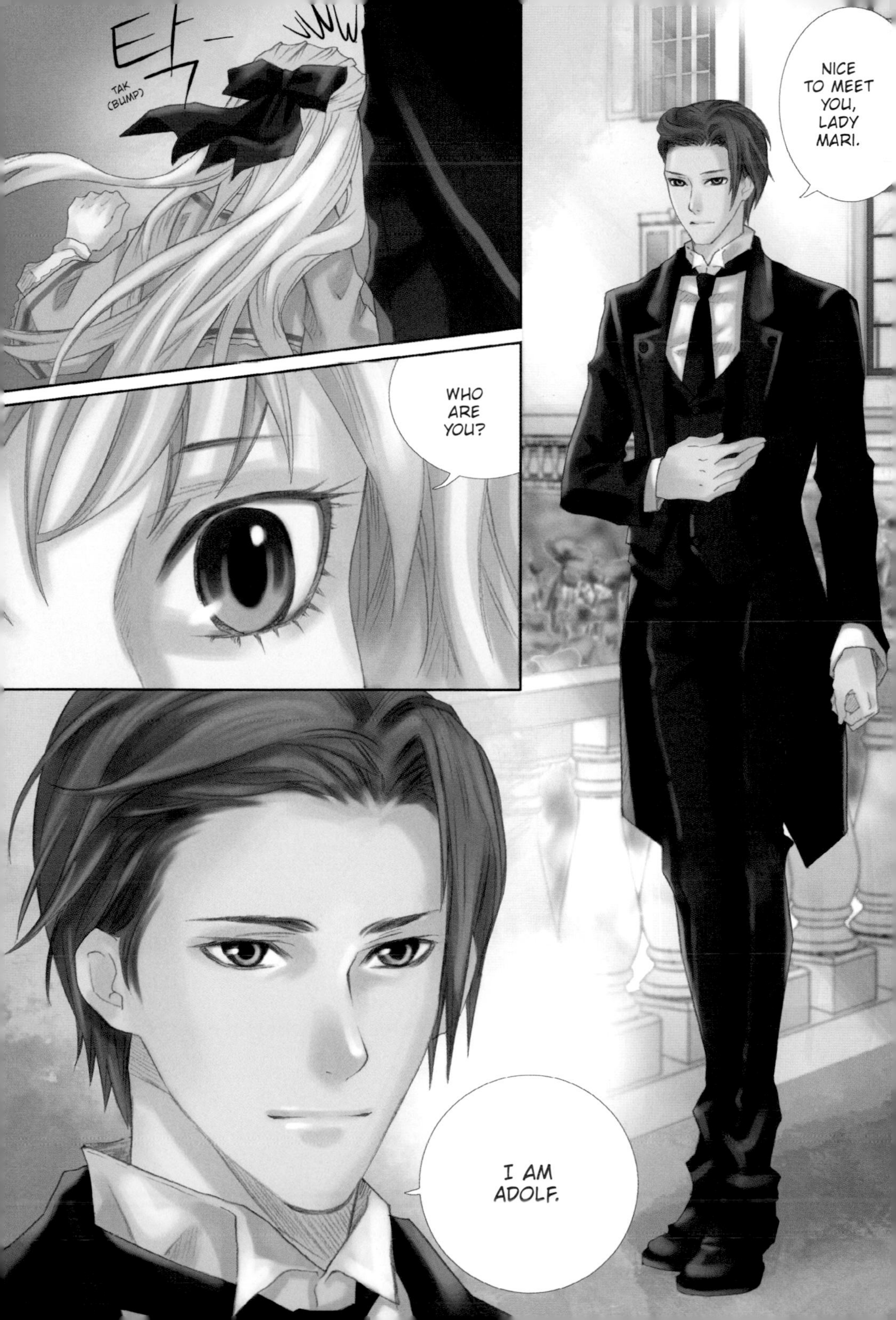
TAK (BUMP)
WHO ARE YOU?
I AM ADOLF.
NICE TO MEET YOU, LADY MARI.

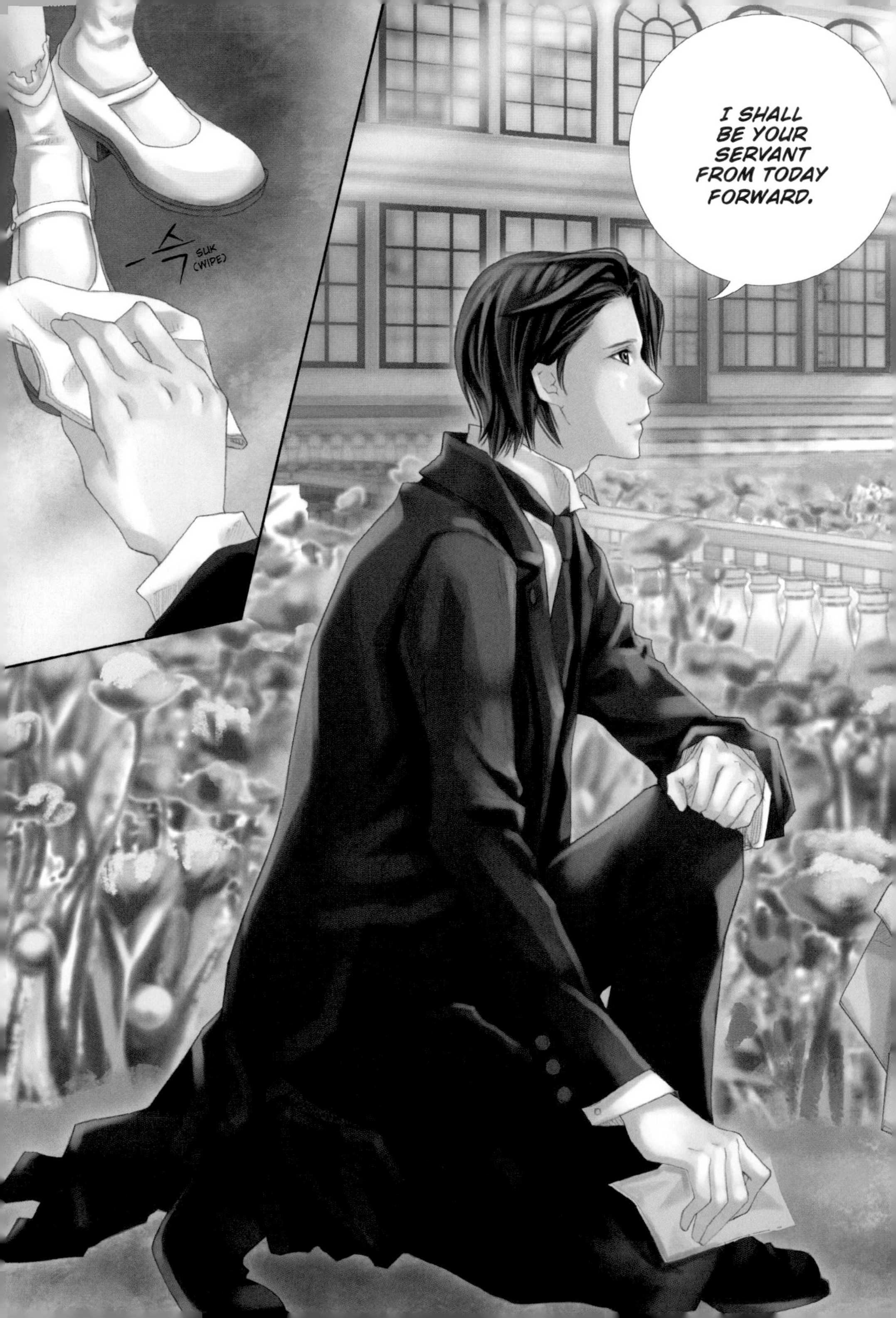

스윽
SUK (WIPE)
I SHALL BE YOUR SERVANT FROM TODAY FORWARD.

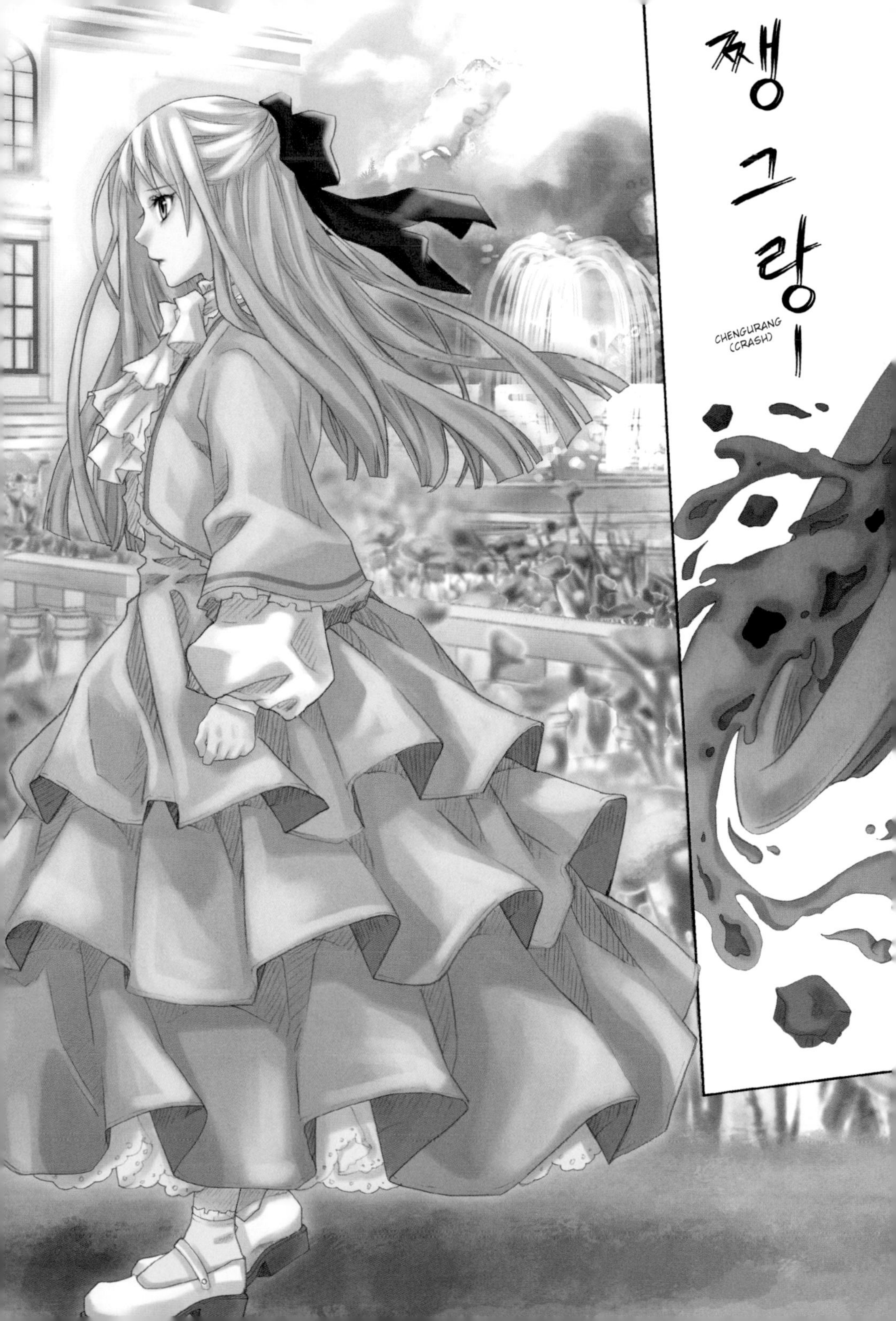
쨍그랑!
CHENGURANG
(CRASH)

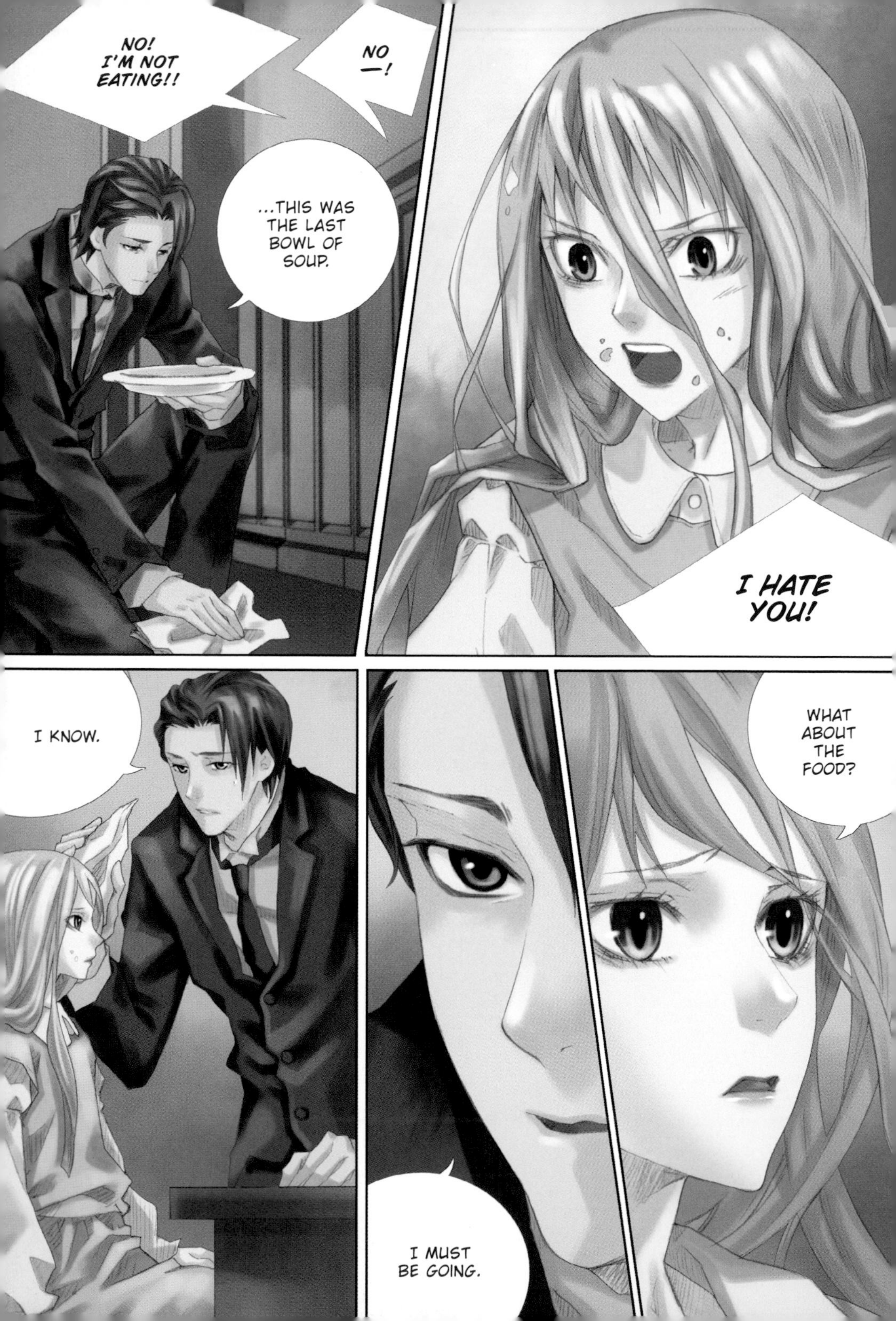
NO! I'M NOT EATING!!
NO —!
...THIS WAS THE LAST BOWL OF SOUP.
I HATE YOU!
I KNOW.
I MUST BE GOING.
WHAT ABOUT THE FOOD?

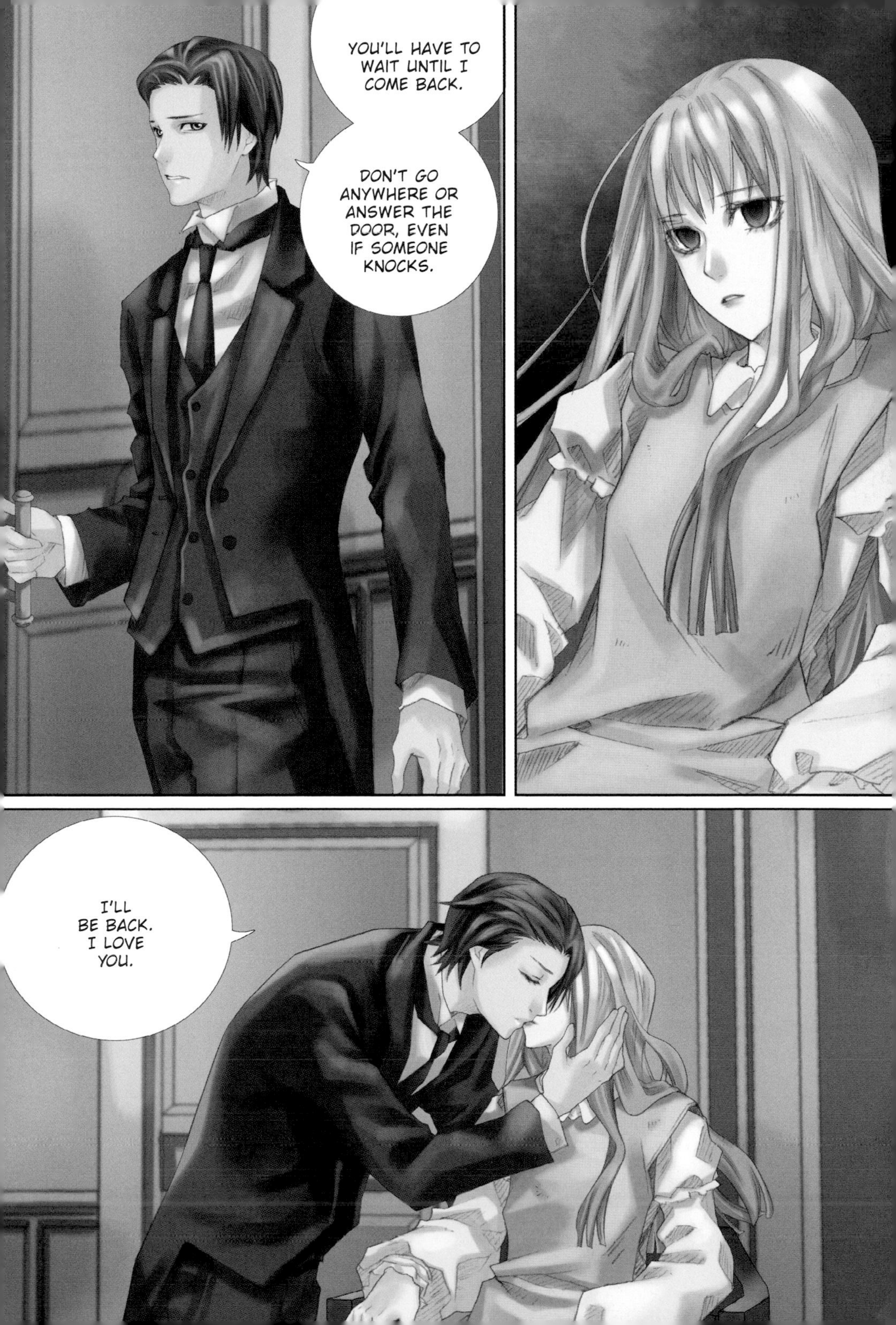
YOU'LL HAVE TO WAIT UNTIL I COME BACK.
DON'T GO ANYWHERE OR ANSWER THE DOOR, EVEN IF SOMEONE KNOCKS.
I'LL BE BACK. I LOVE YOU.

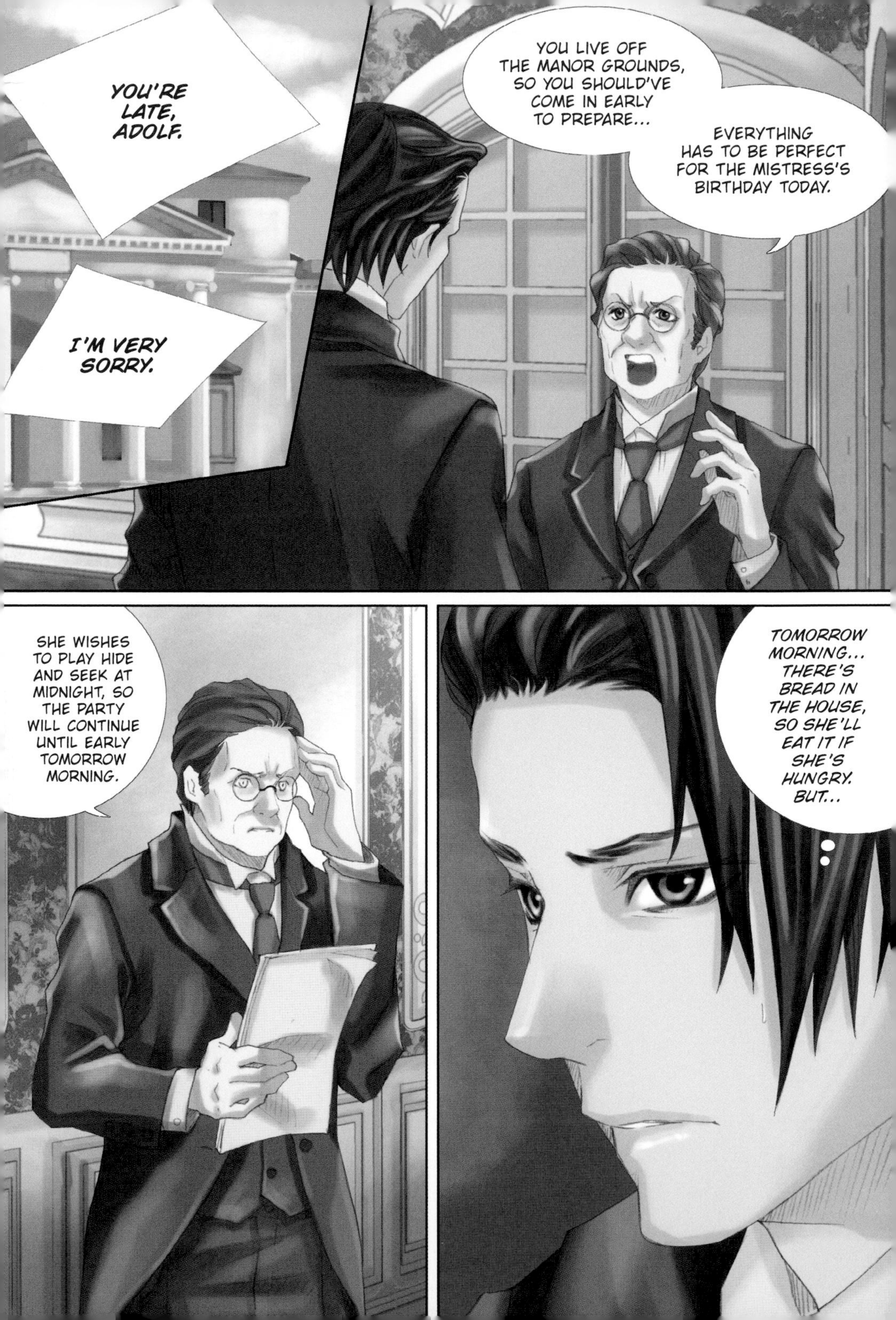
YOU'RE LATE, ADOLF.
I'M VERY SORRY.
YOU LIVE OFF THE MANOR GROUNDS, SO YOU SHOULD'VE COME IN EARLY TO PREPARE...
EVERYTHING HAS TO BE PERFECT FOR THE MISTRESS'S BIRTHDAY TODAY.
SHE WISHES TO PLAY HIDE AND SEEK AT MIDNIGHT, SO THE PARTY WILL CONTINUE UNTIL EARLY TOMORROW MORNING.
TOMORROW MORNING... THERE'S BREAD IN THE HOUSE, SO SHE'LL EAT IT IF SHE'S HUNGRY. BUT...

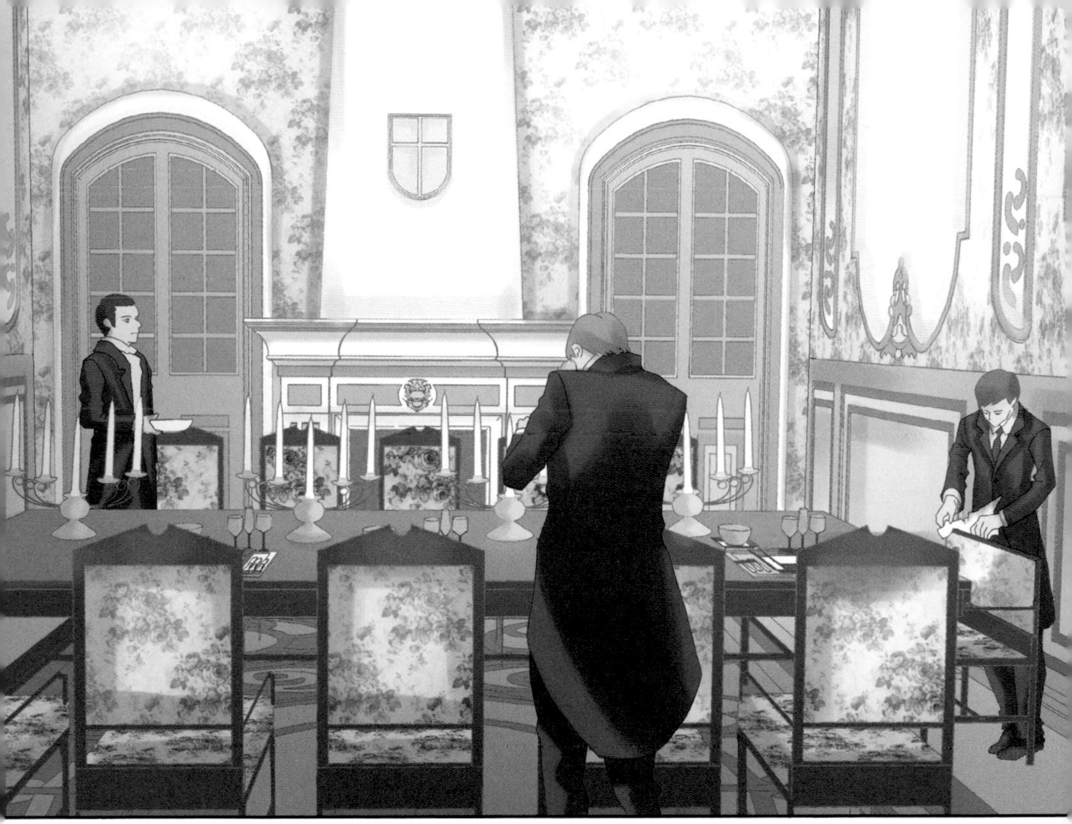
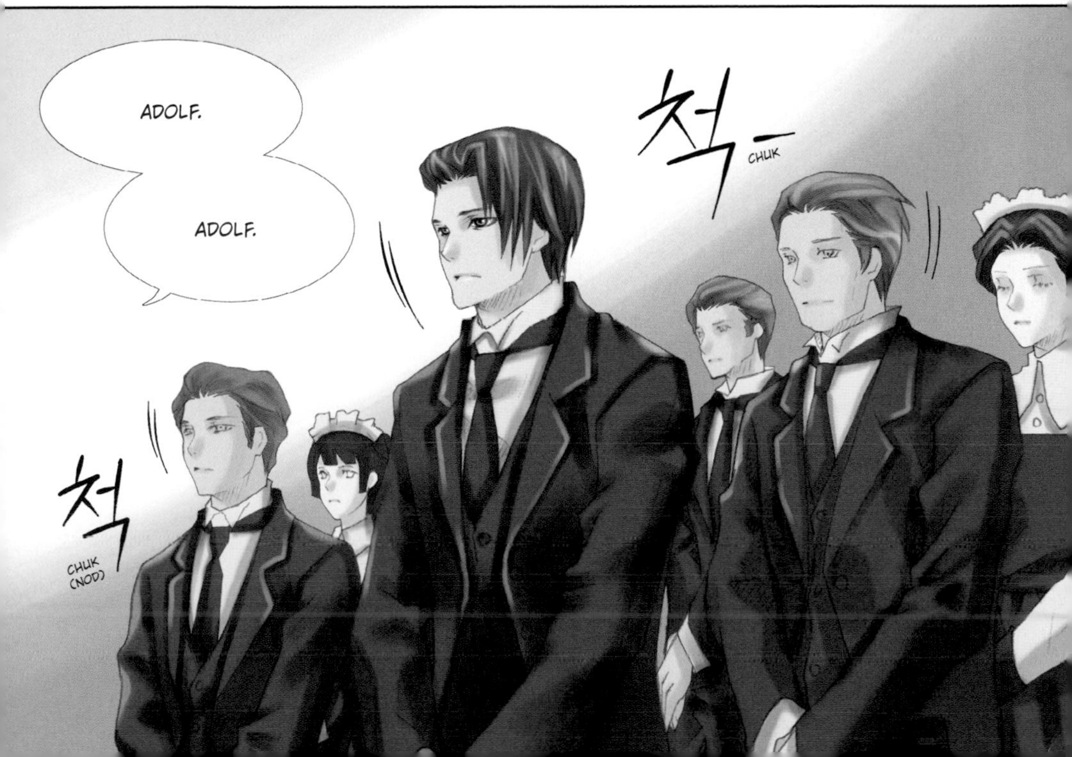
ADOLF.
ADOLF.
척
CHUK
척
CHUK (NOD)

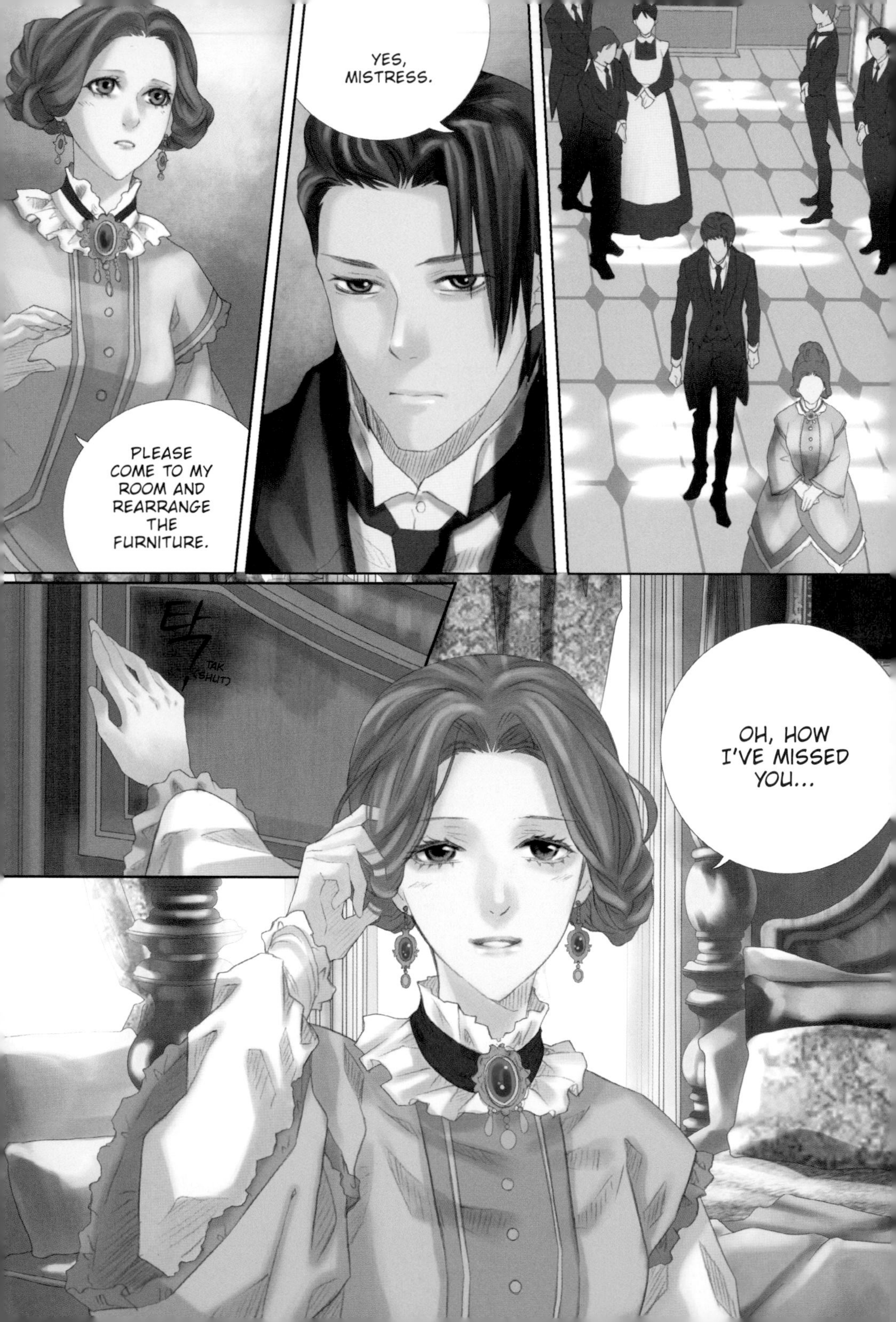
PLEASE COME TO MY ROOM AND REARRANGE THE FURNITURE.
YES, MISTRESS.
탁
TAK (SHUT)
OH, HOW I'VE MISSED YOU...

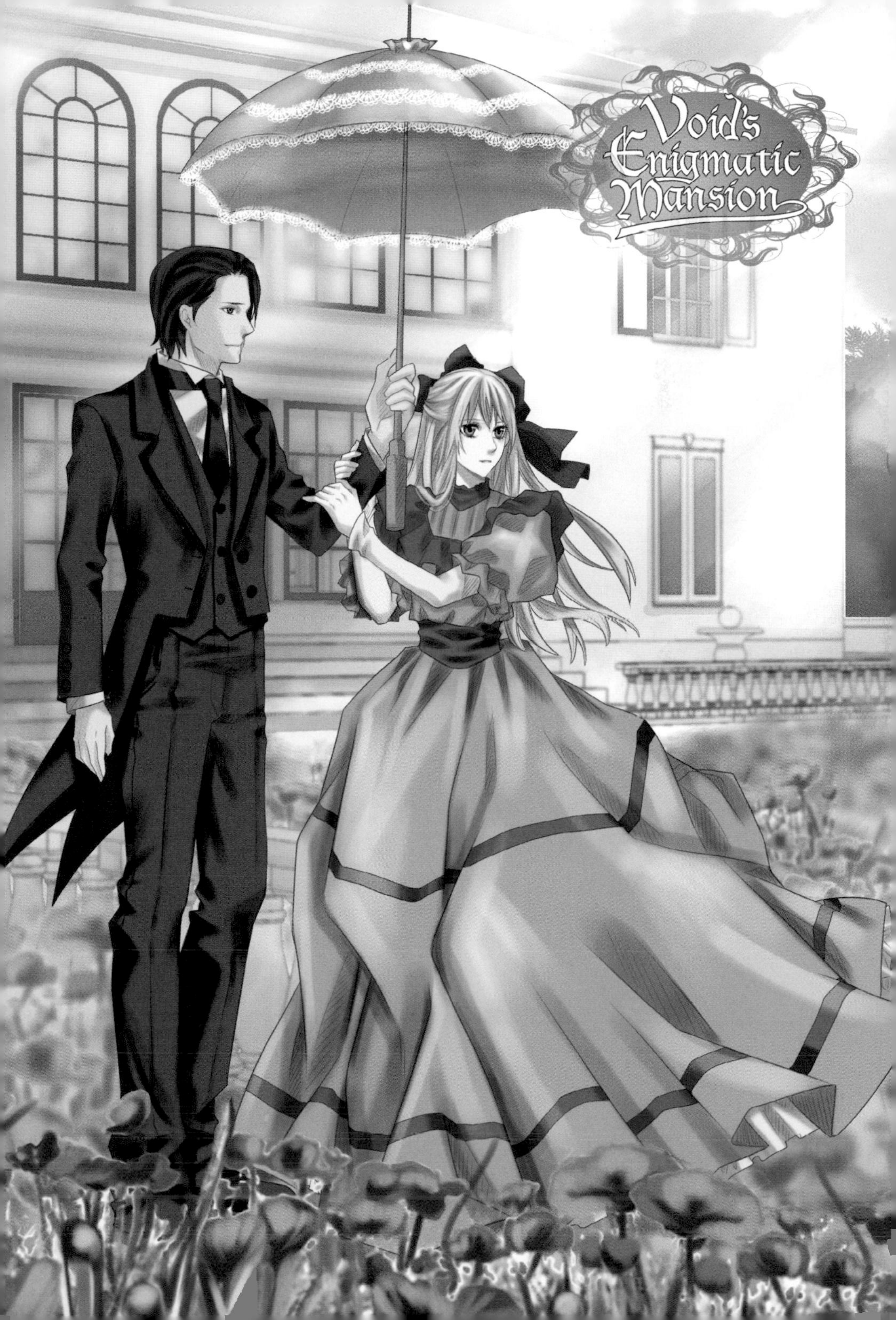
Void's Enigmatic Mansion

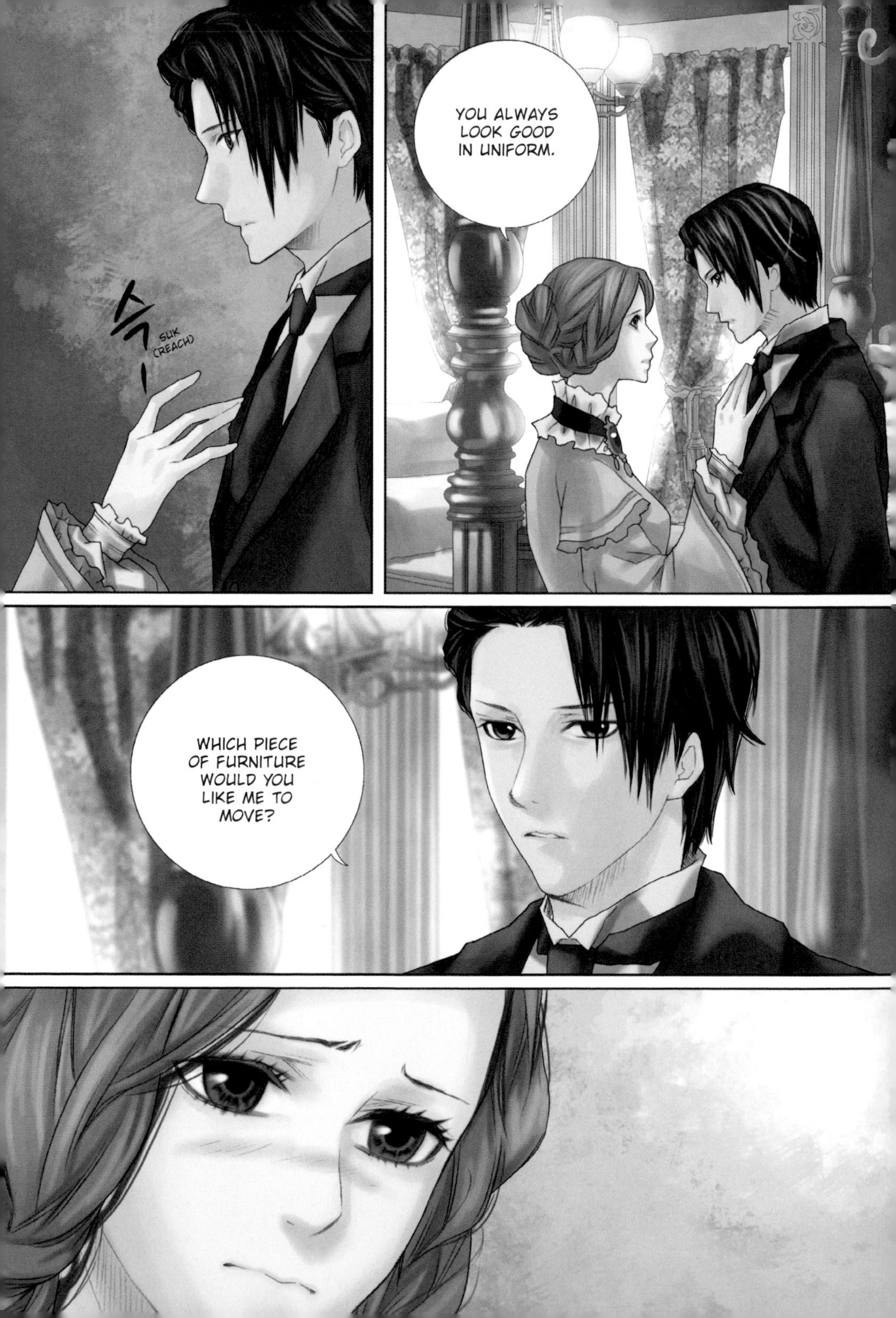
스-
SUK (REACH)
YOU ALWAYS LOOK GOOD IN UNIFORM.
WHICH PIECE OF FURNITURE WOULD YOU LIKE ME TO MOVE?

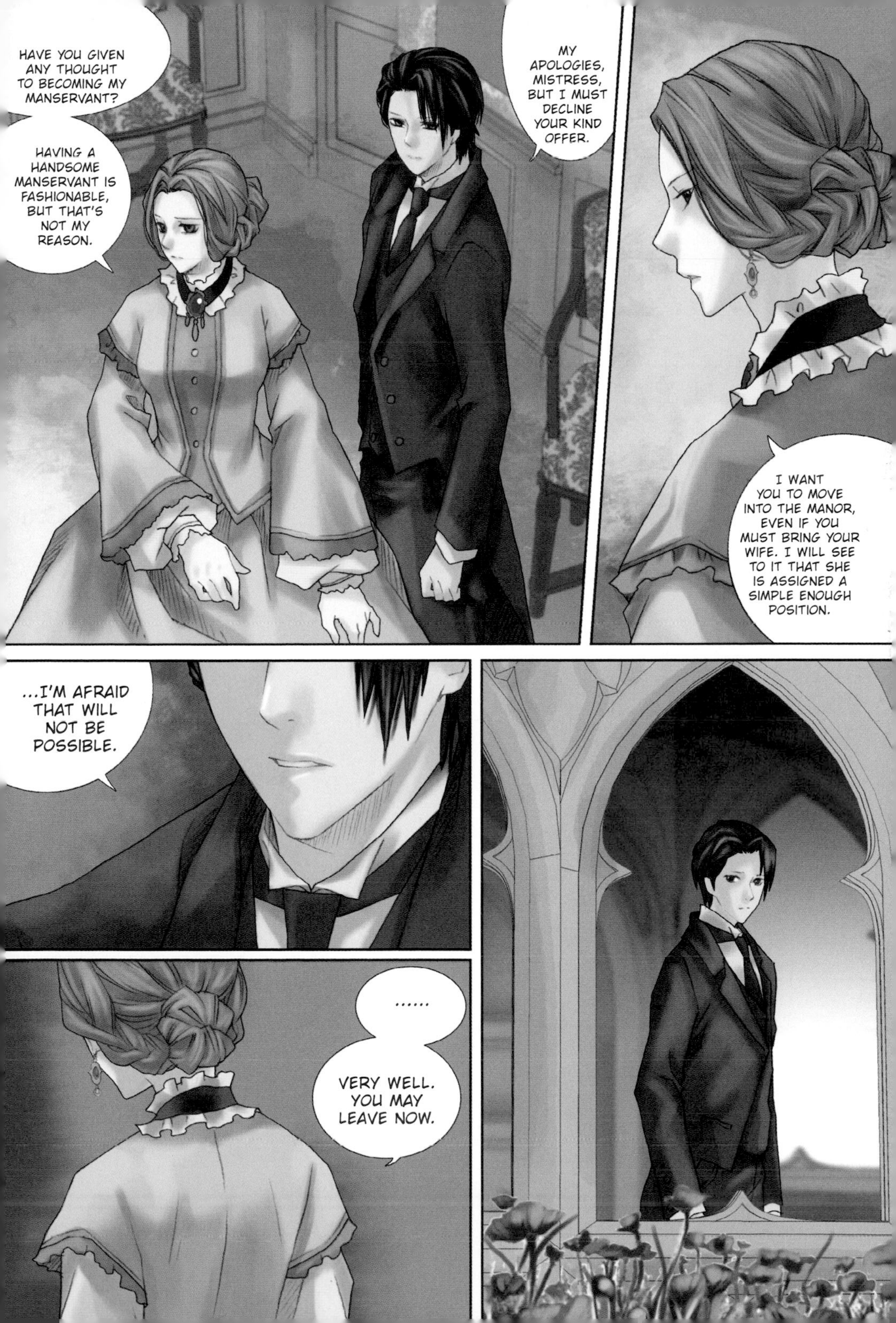
HAVE YOU GIVEN ANY THOUGHT TO BECOMING MY MANSERVANT?
HAVING A HANDSOME MANSERVANT IS FASHIONABLE, BUT THAT'S NOT MY REASON.
MY APOLOGIES, MISTRESS, BUT I MUST DECLINE YOUR KIND OFFER.
I WANT YOU TO MOVE INTO THE MANOR, EVEN IF YOU MUST BRING YOUR WIFE. I WILL SEE TO IT THAT SHE IS ASSIGNED A SIMPLE ENOUGH POSITION.
...I'M AFRAID THAT WILL NOT BE POSSIBLE.
......
VERY WELL. YOU MAY LEAVE NOW.

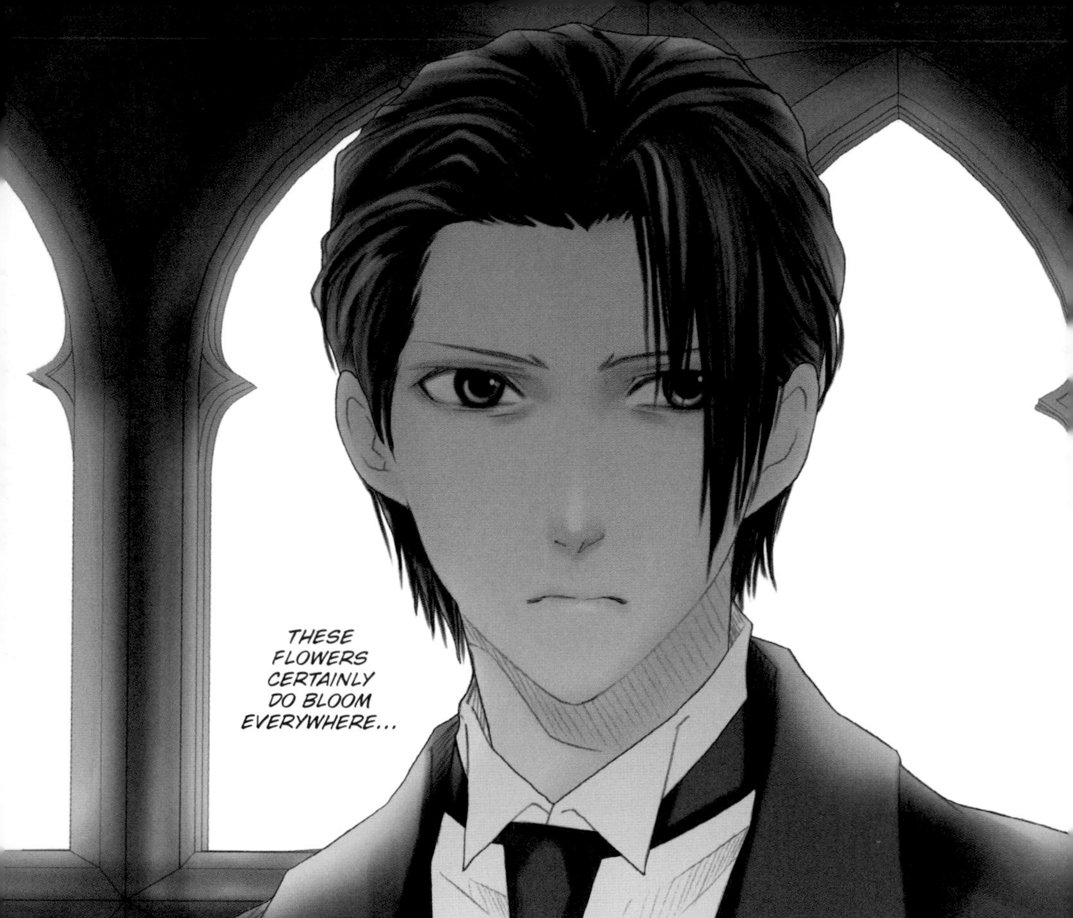
THESE FLOWERS CERTAINLY DO BLOOM EVERYWHERE...
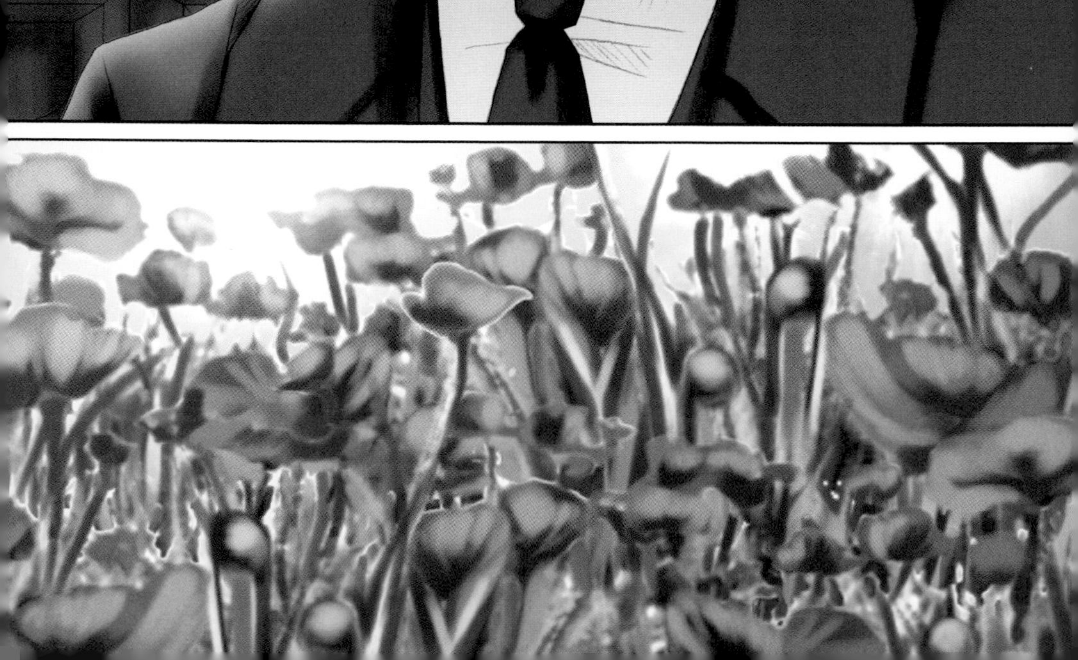

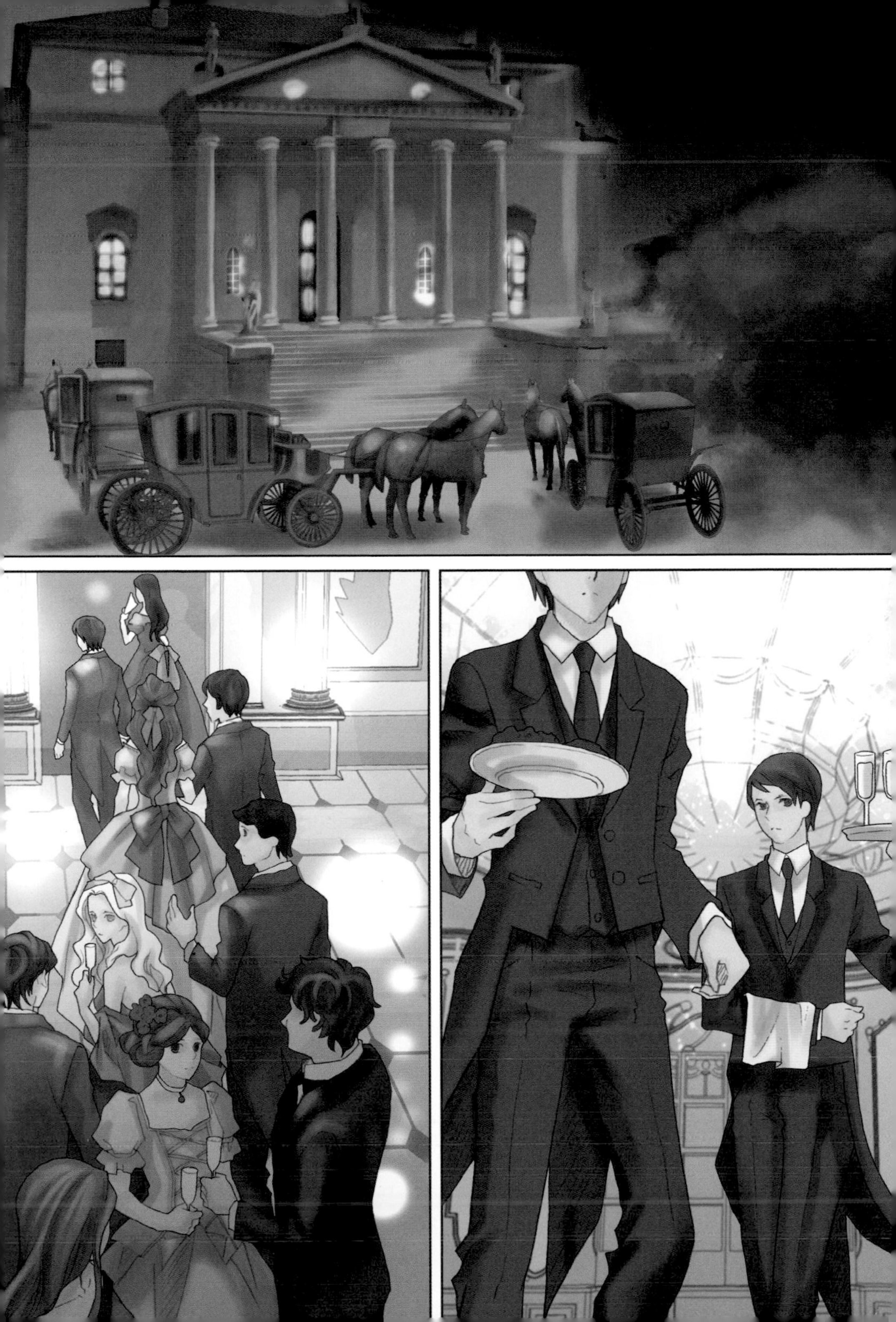

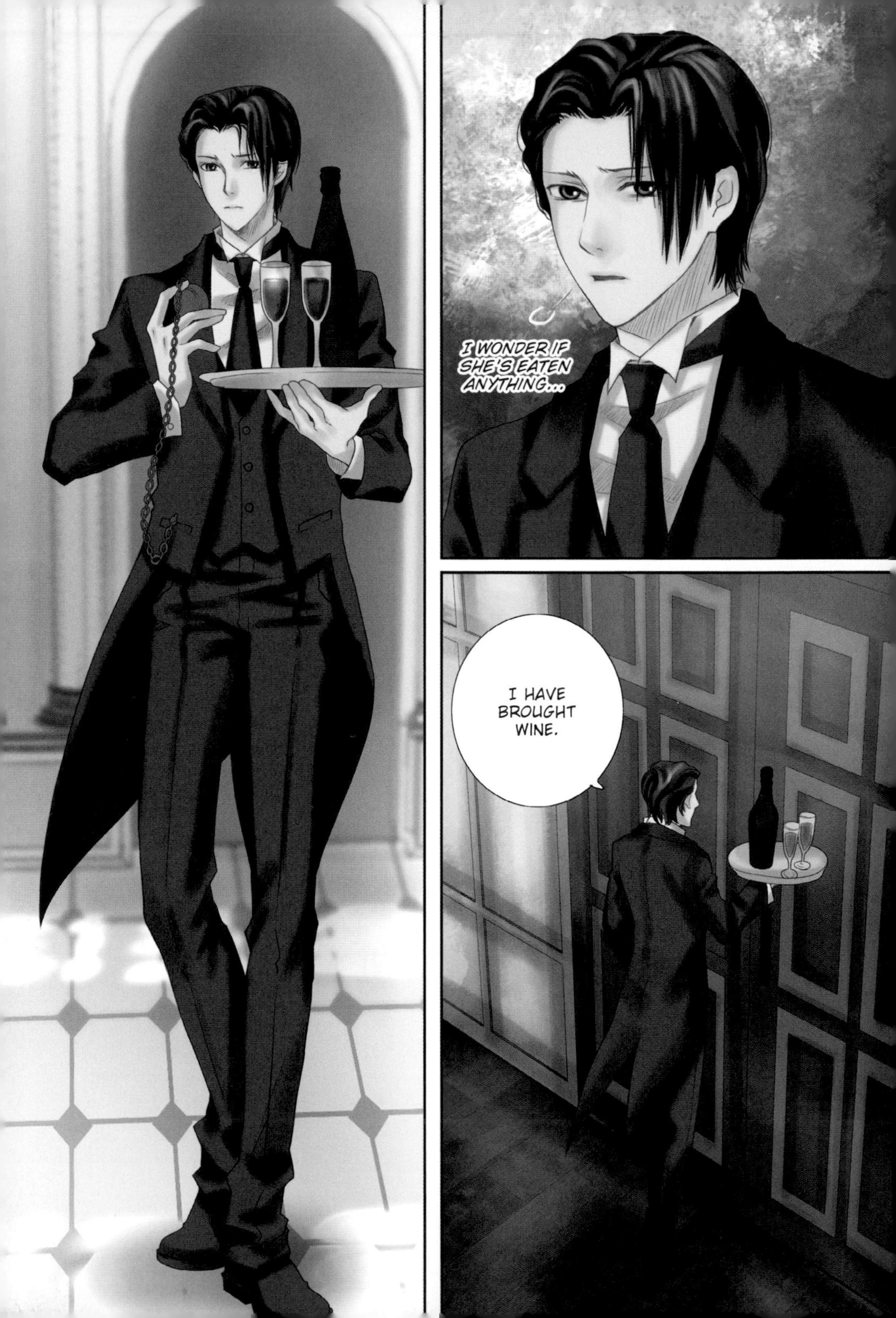
I WONDER IF SHE'S EATEN ANYTHING...
I HAVE BROUGHT WINE.

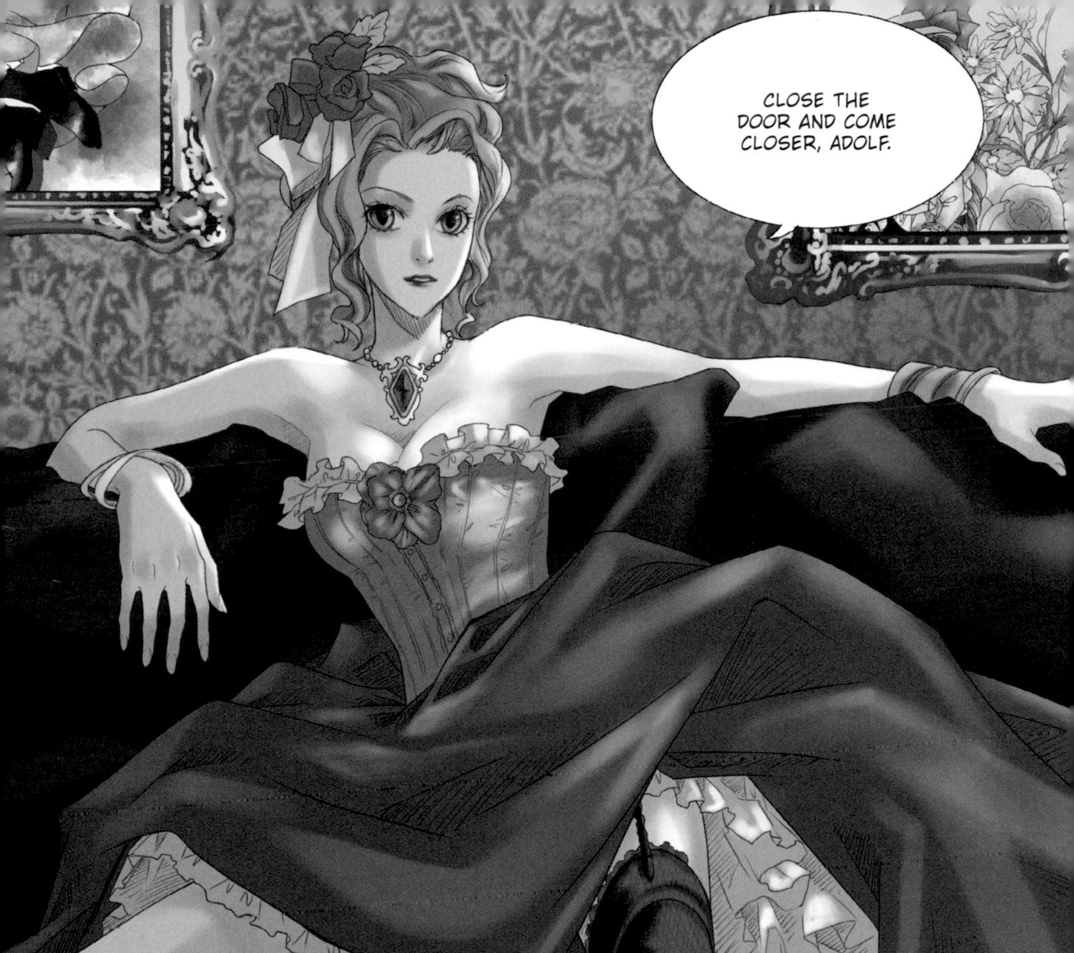
CLOSE THE
DOOR AND COME
CLOSER, ADOLF.
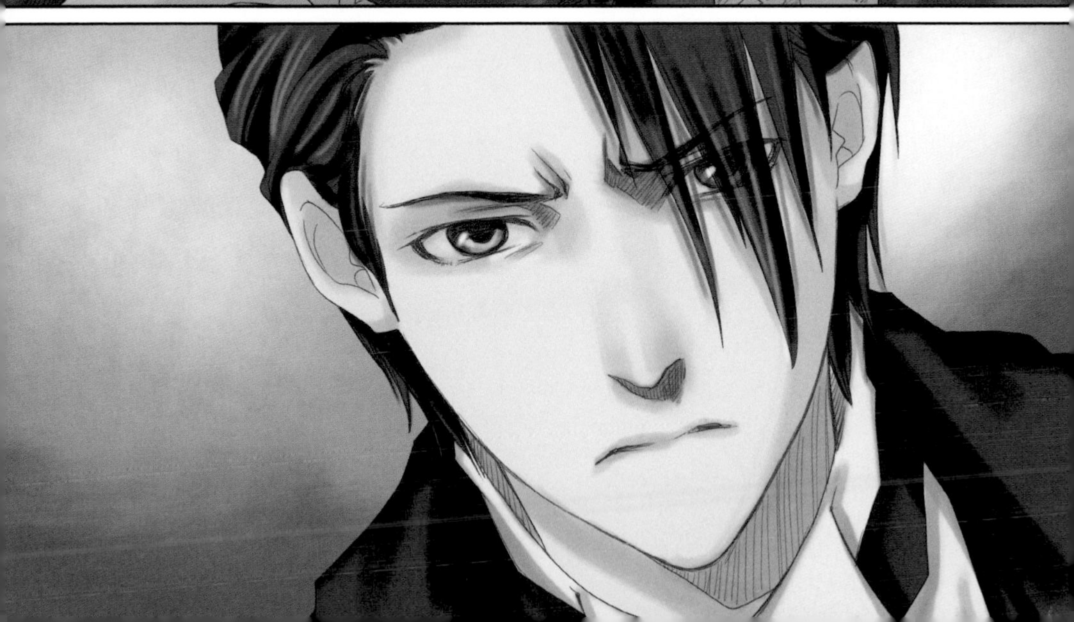

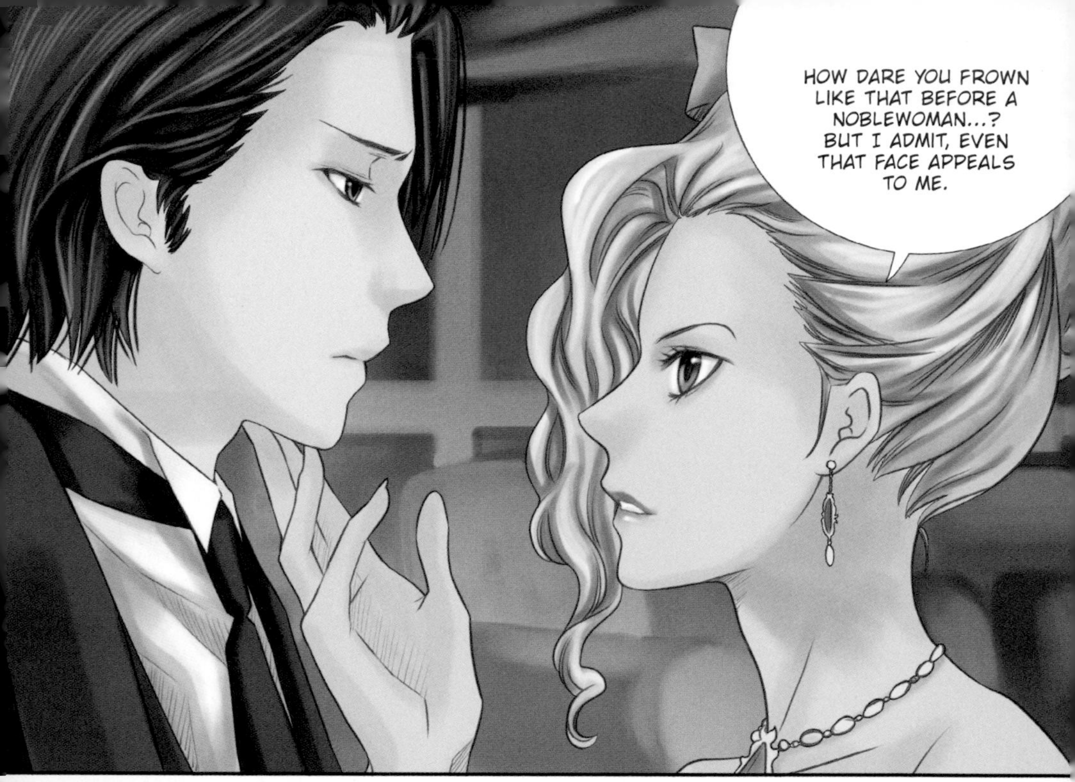
HOW DARE YOU FROWN LIKE THAT BEFORE A NOBLEWOMAN...? BUT I ADMIT, EVEN THAT FACE APPEALS TO ME.

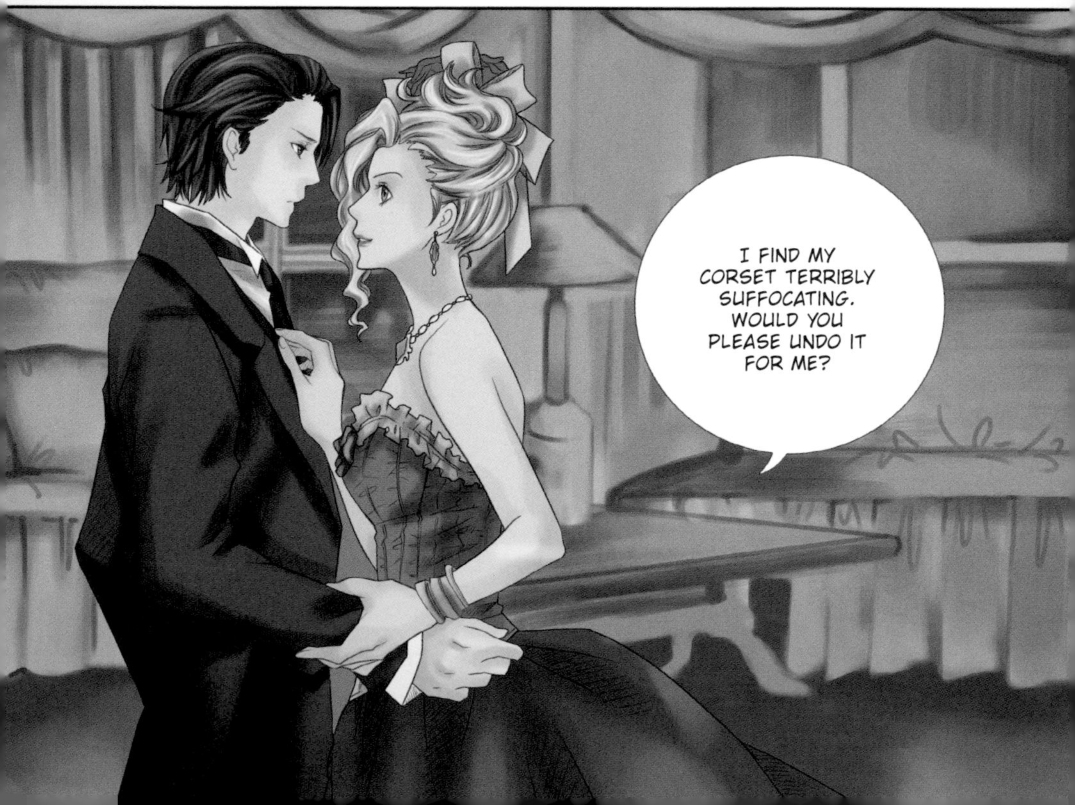
I FIND MY CORSET TERRIBLY SUFFOCATING. WOULD YOU PLEASE UNDO IT FOR ME?

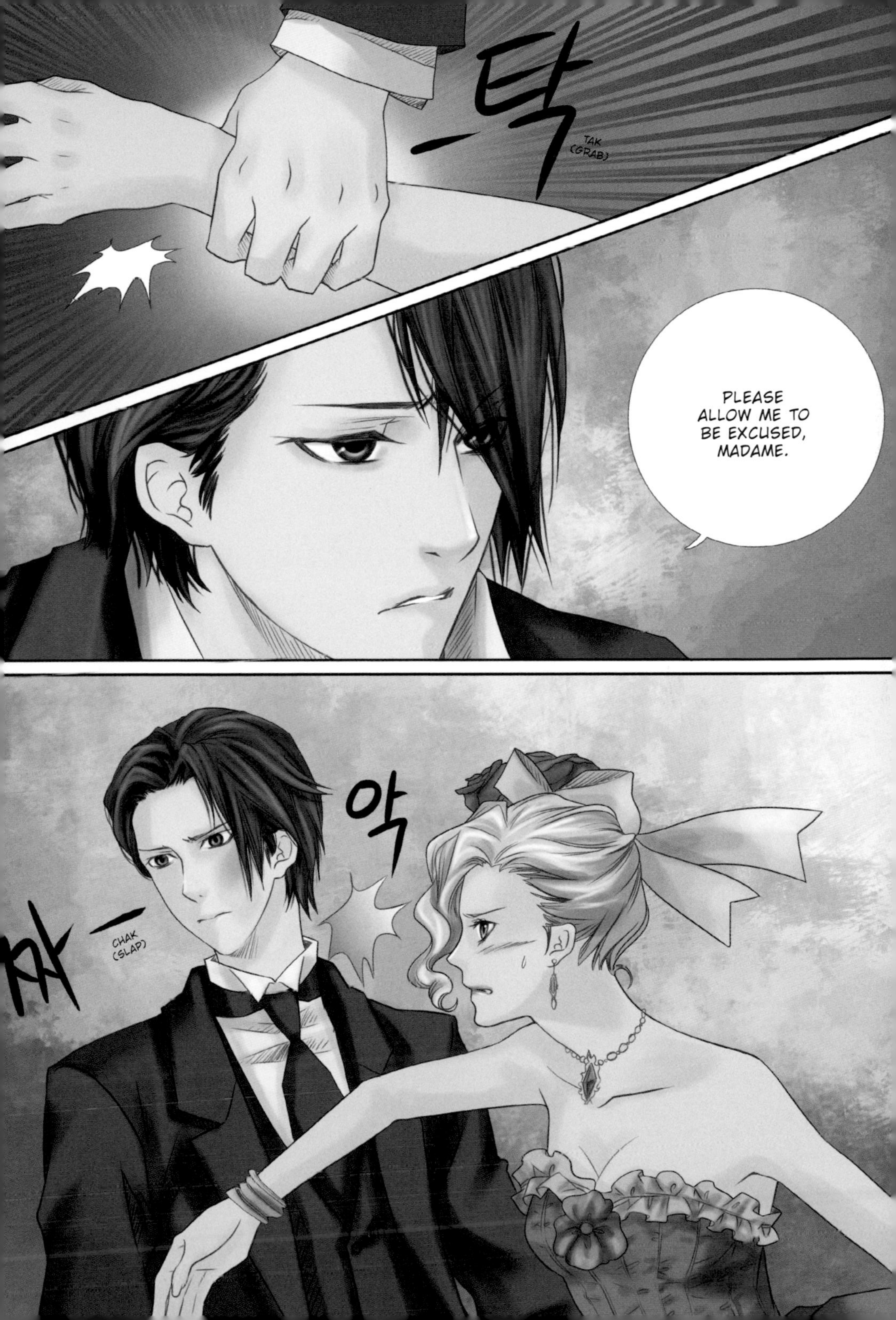
탁
TAK (GRAB)
PLEASE ALLOW ME TO BE EXCUSED, MADAME.
짜
CHAK (SLAP)
악

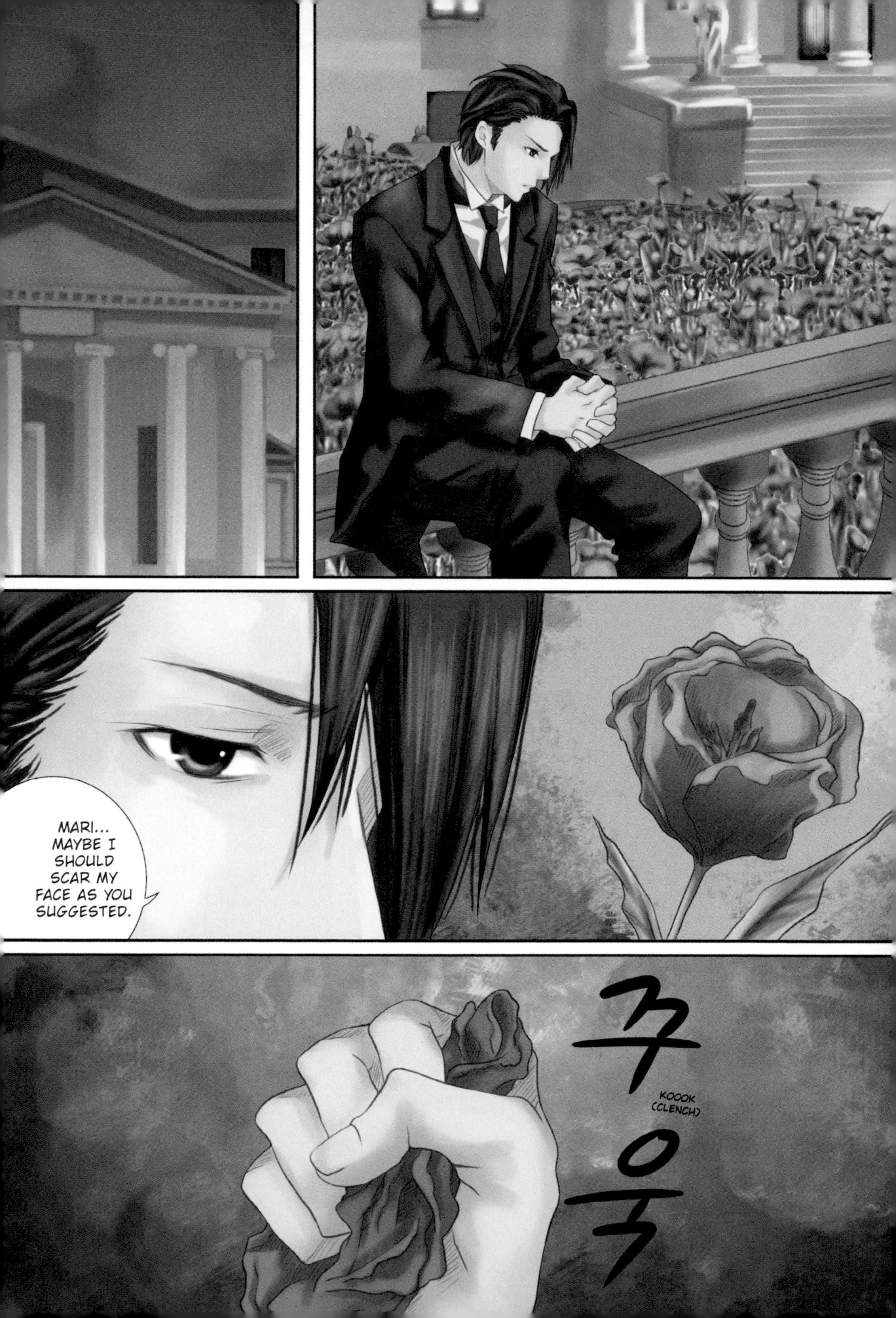
MARI... MAYBE I SHOULD SCAR MY FACE AS YOU SUGGESTED.
KOOOK (CLENCH)

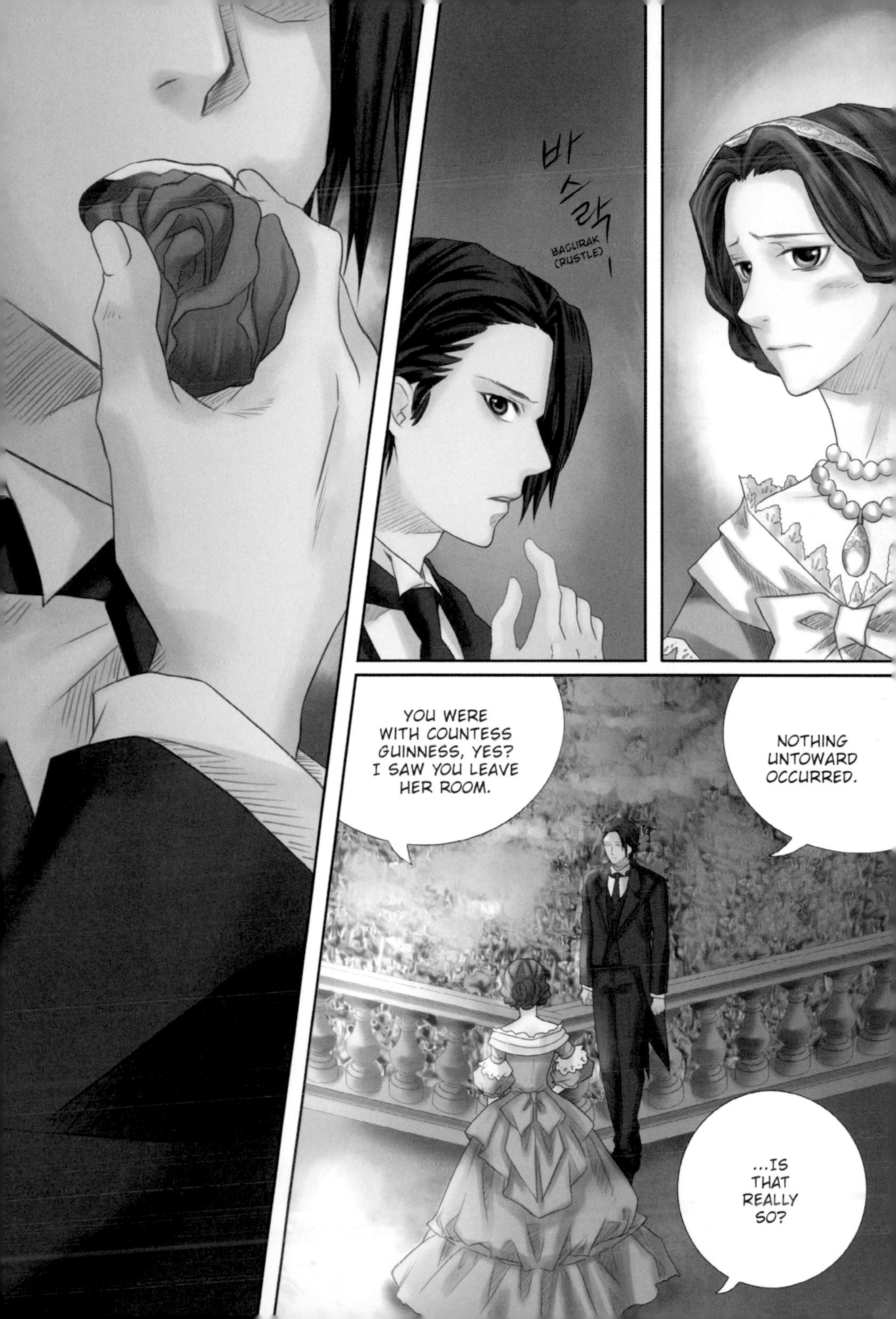
바스락!
BASURAK (RUSTLE)
YOU WERE WITH COUNTESS GUINNESS, YES? I SAW YOU LEAVE HER ROOM.
NOTHING UNTOWARD OCCURRED.
...IS THAT REALLY SO?

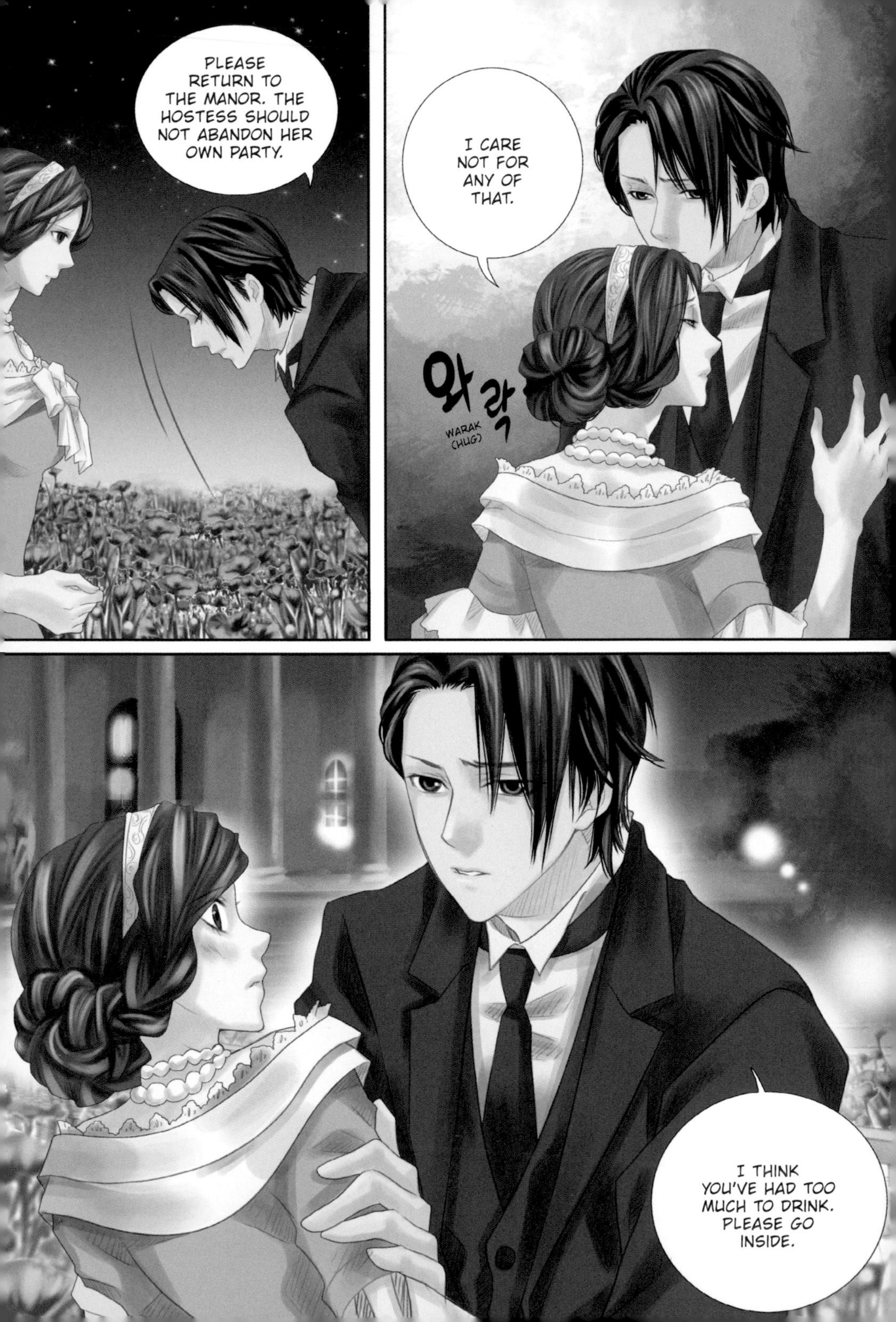
PLEASE RETURN TO THE MANOR. THE HOSTESS SHOULD NOT ABANDON HER OWN PARTY.
I CARE NOT FOR ANY OF THAT.
와락
WARAK (HUG)
I THINK YOU'VE HAD TOO MUCH TO DRINK. PLEASE GO INSIDE.

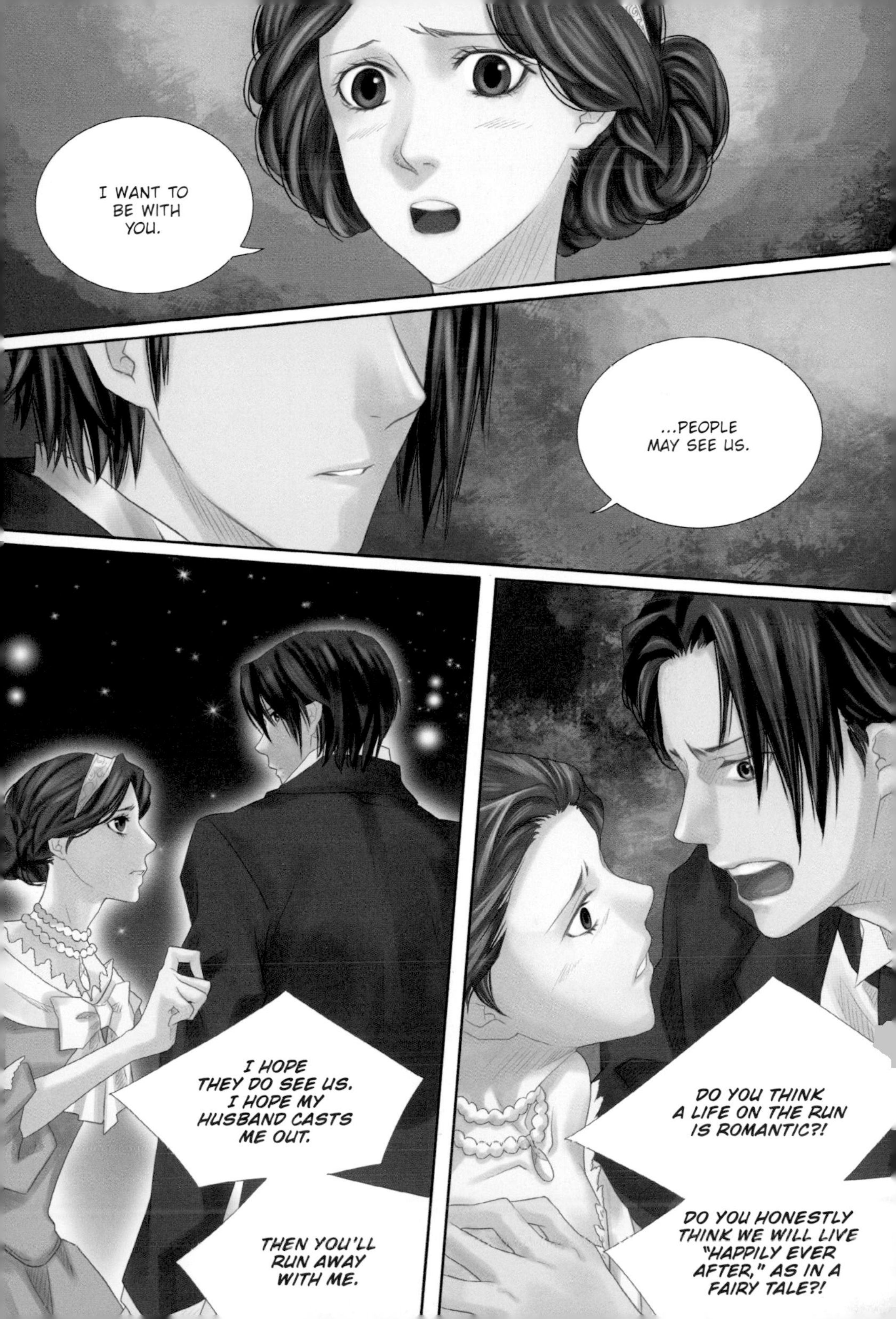
I WANT TO BE WITH YOU.
...PEOPLE MAY SEE US.
I HOPE THEY DO SEE US. I HOPE MY HUSBAND CASTS ME OUT.
THEN YOU'LL RUN AWAY WITH ME.
DO YOU THINK A LIFE ON THE RUN IS ROMANTIC?!
DO YOU HONESTLY THINK WE WILL LIVE "HAPPILY EVER AFTER," AS IN A FAIRY TALE?!

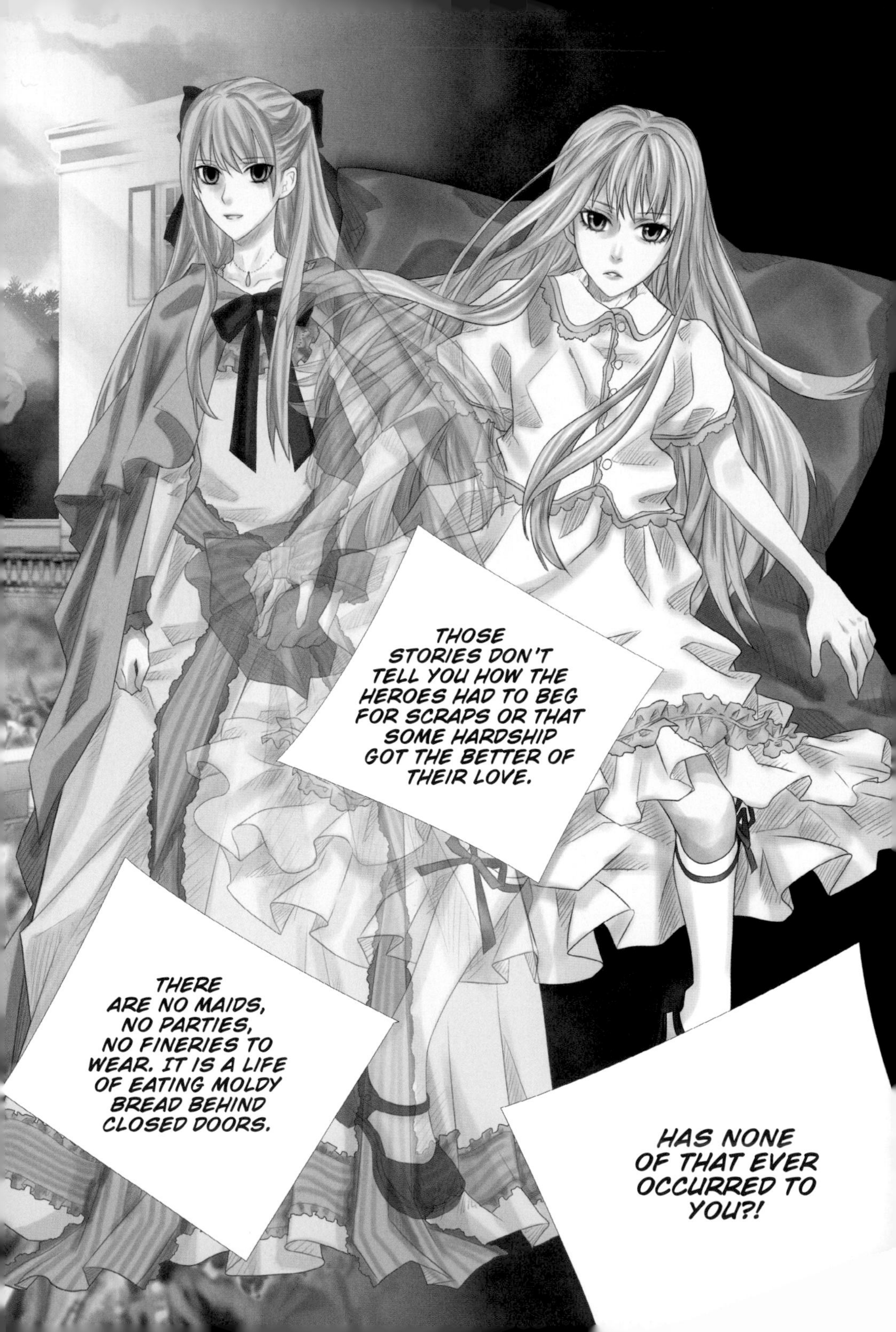
THOSE STORIES DON'T TELL YOU HOW THE HEROES HAD TO BEG FOR SCRAPS OR THAT SOME HARDSHIP GOT THE BETTER OF THEIR LOVE.
THERE ARE NO MAIDS, NO PARTIES, NO FINERIES TO WEAR. IT IS A LIFE OF EATING MOLDY BREAD BEHIND CLOSED DOORS.
HAS NONE OF THAT EVER OCCURRED TO YOU?!

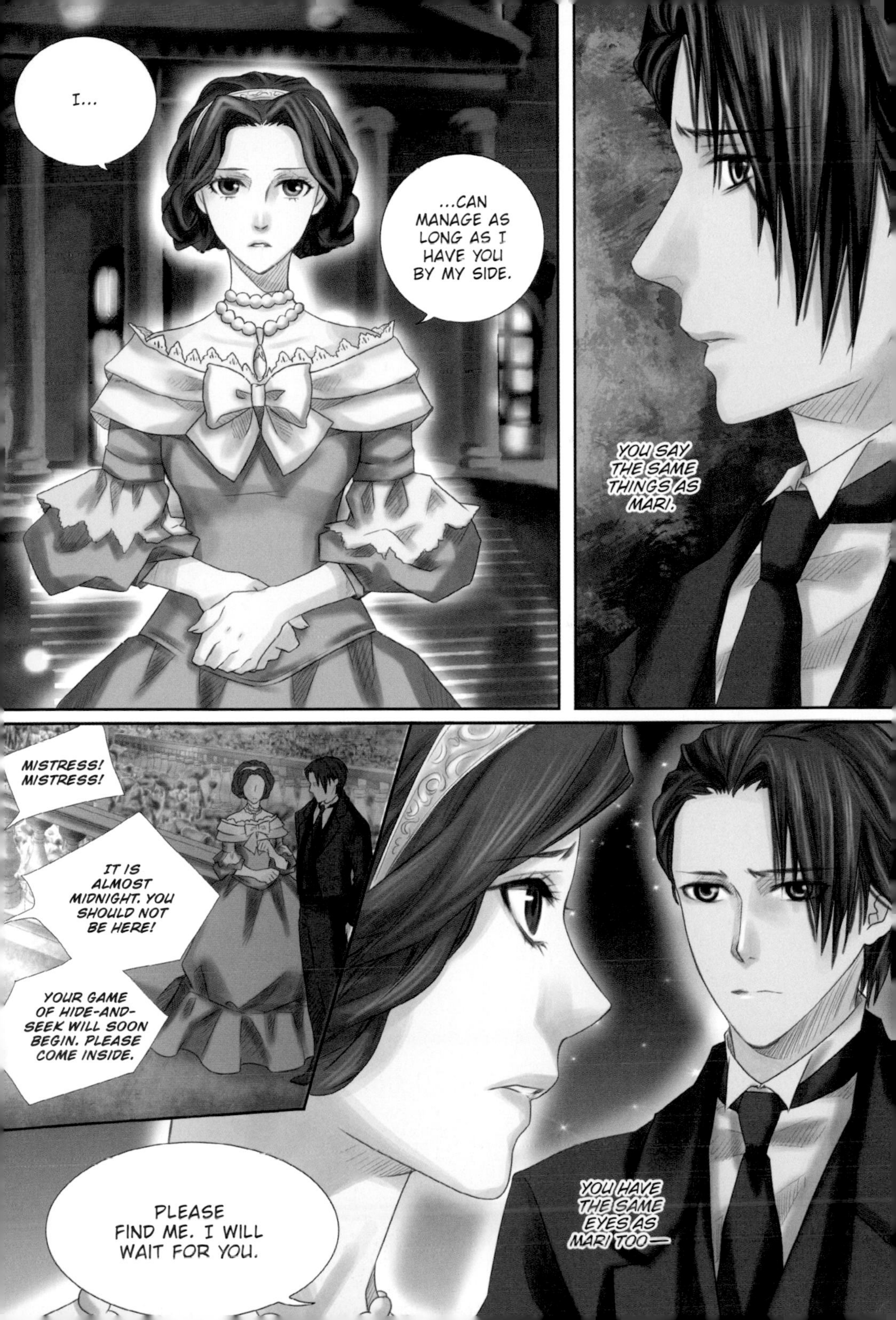

I...
...CAN MANAGE AS LONG AS I HAVE YOU BY MY SIDE.
YOU SAY THE SAME THINGS AS MARI.
MISTRESS! MISTRESS!
IT IS ALMOST MIDNIGHT. YOU SHOULD NOT BE HERE!
YOUR GAME OF HIDE-AND-SEEK WILL SOON BEGIN. PLEASE COME INSIDE.
PLEASE FIND ME. I WILL WAIT FOR YOU.
YOU HAVE THE SAME EYES AS MARI TOO—

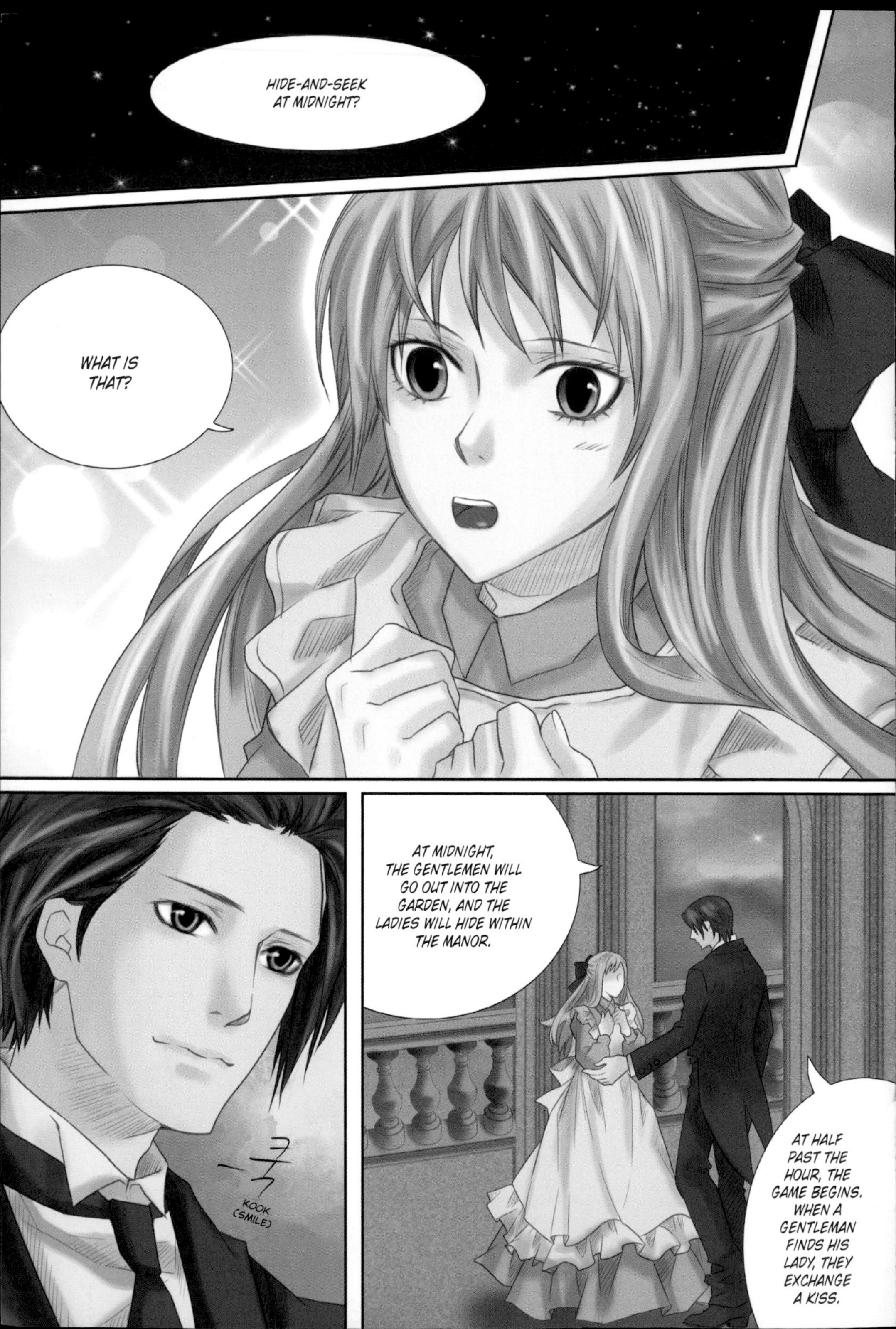
HIDE-AND-SEEK AT MIDNIGHT?
WHAT IS THAT?
KOOK (SMILE)
AT MIDNIGHT, THE GENTLEMEN WILL GO OUT INTO THE GARDEN, AND THE LADIES WILL HIDE WITHIN THE MANOR.
AT HALF PAST THE HOUR, THE GAME BEGINS. WHEN A GENTLEMAN FINDS HIS LADY, THEY EXCHANGE A KISS.

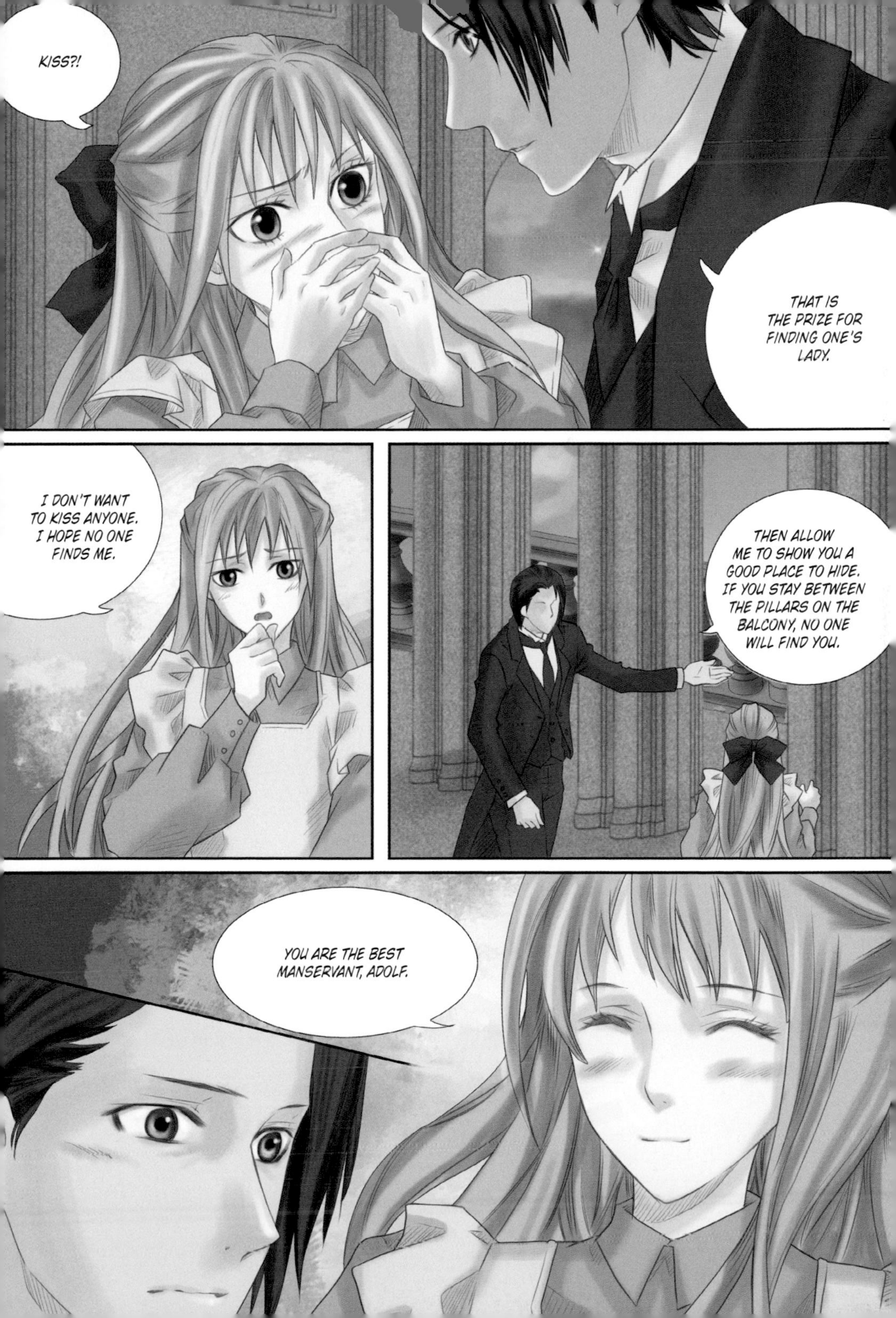
KISS?!
THAT IS THE PRIZE FOR FINDING ONE'S LADY.
I DON'T WANT TO KISS ANYONE. I HOPE NO ONE FINDS ME.
THEN ALLOW ME TO SHOW YOU A GOOD PLACE TO HIDE. IF YOU STAY BETWEEN THE PILLARS ON THE BALCONY, NO ONE WILL FIND YOU.
YOU ARE THE BEST MANSERVANT, ADOLF.

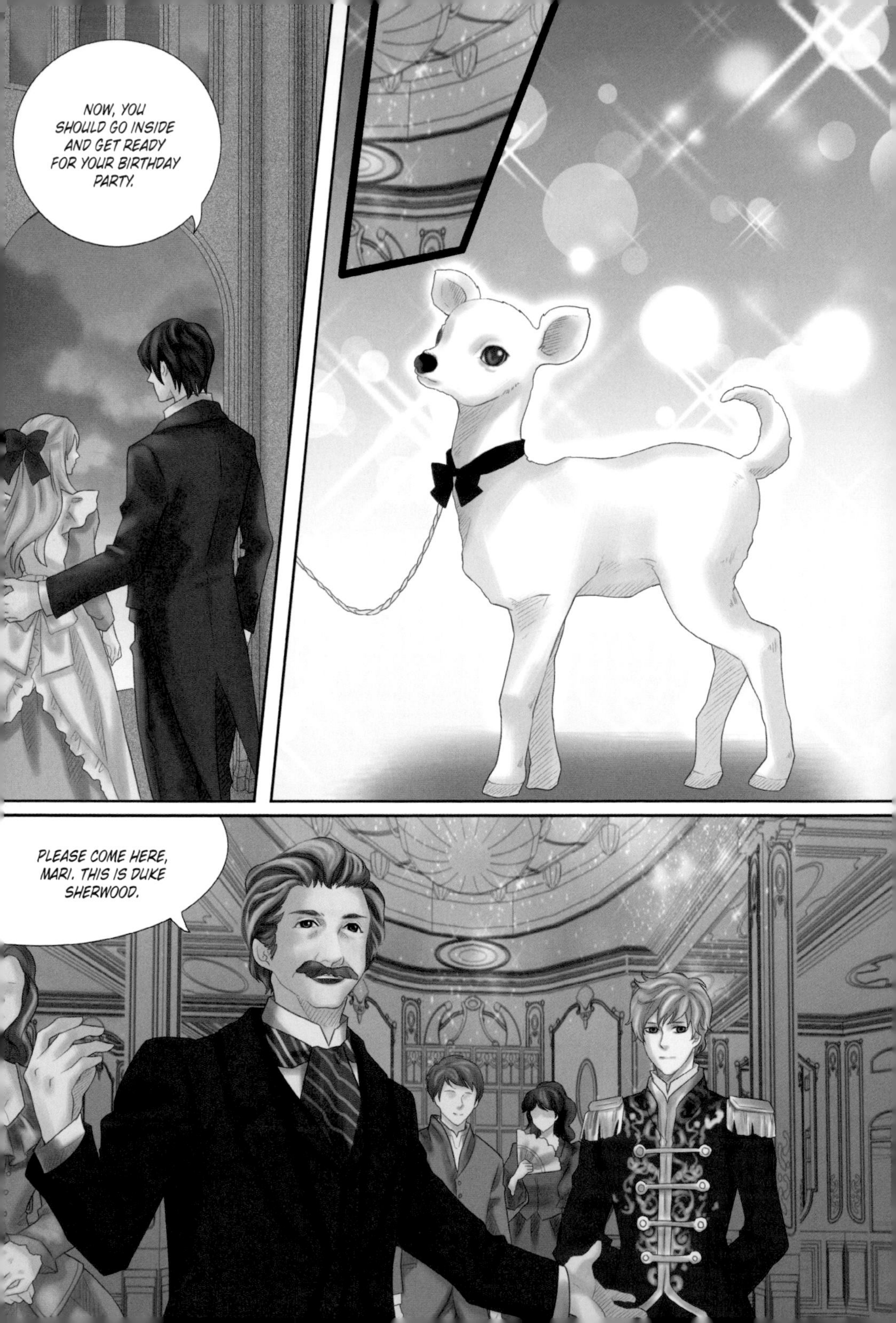
NOW, YOU SHOULD GO INSIDE AND GET READY FOR YOUR BIRTHDAY PARTY.
PLEASE COME HERE, MARI. THIS IS DUKE SHERWOOD.

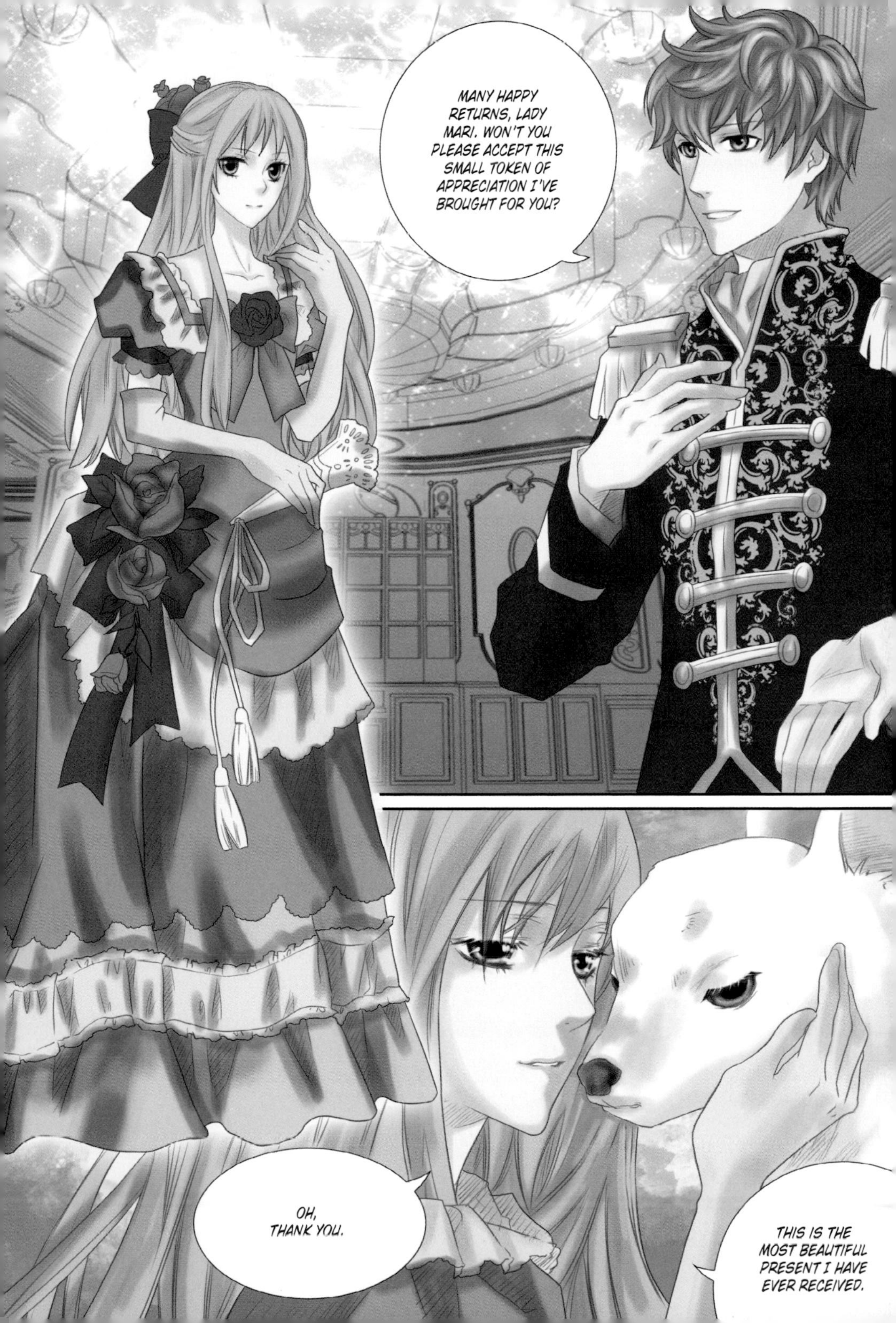
MANY HAPPY RETURNS, LADY MARI. WON'T YOU PLEASE ACCEPT THIS SMALL TOKEN OF APPRECIATION I'VE BROUGHT FOR YOU?
OH, THANK YOU.
THIS IS THE MOST BEAUTIFUL PRESENT I HAVE EVER RECEIVED.

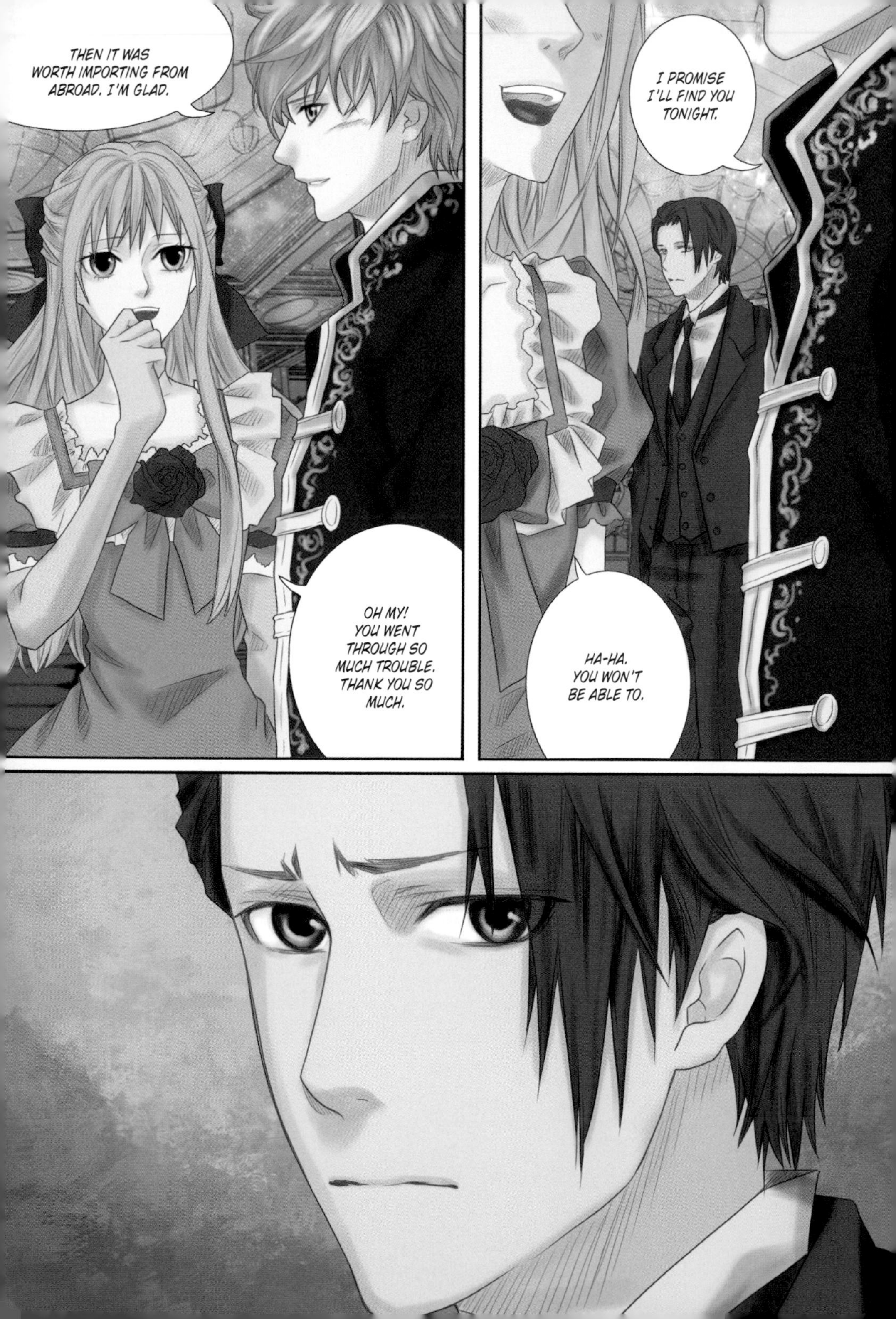
THEN IT WAS WORTH IMPORTING FROM ABROAD. I'M GLAD.
OH MY! YOU WENT THROUGH SO MUCH TROUBLE. THANK YOU SO MUCH.
I PROMISE I'LL FIND YOU TONIGHT.
HA-HA. YOU WON'T BE ABLE TO.

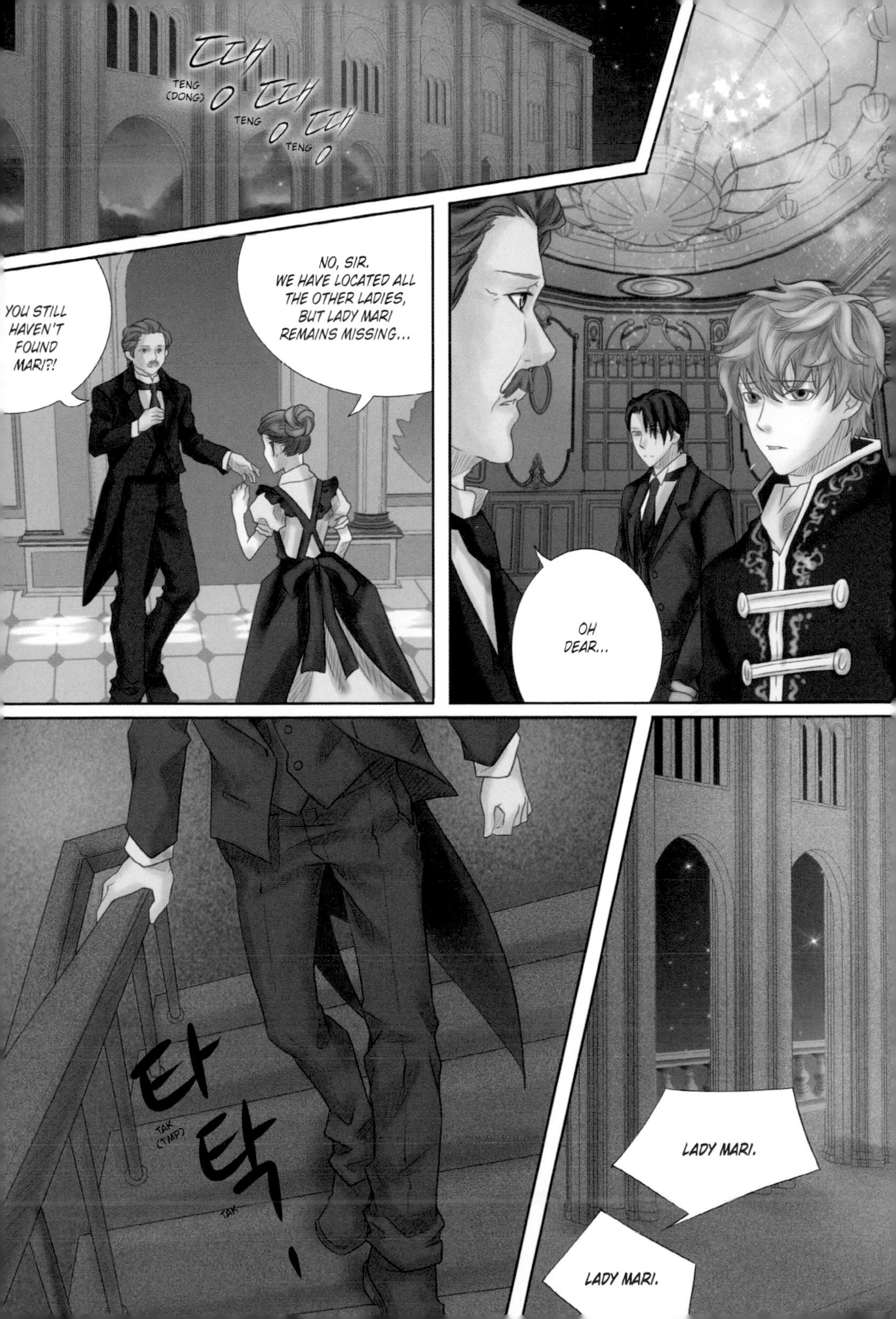
TENG (DONG)
TENG
TENG
YOU STILL HAVEN'T FOUND MARI?!
NO, SIR. WE HAVE LOCATED ALL THE OTHER LADIES, BUT LADY MARI REMAINS MISSING...
OH DEAR...
타
TAK (TMP)
탁
TAK
LADY MARI.
LADY MARI.

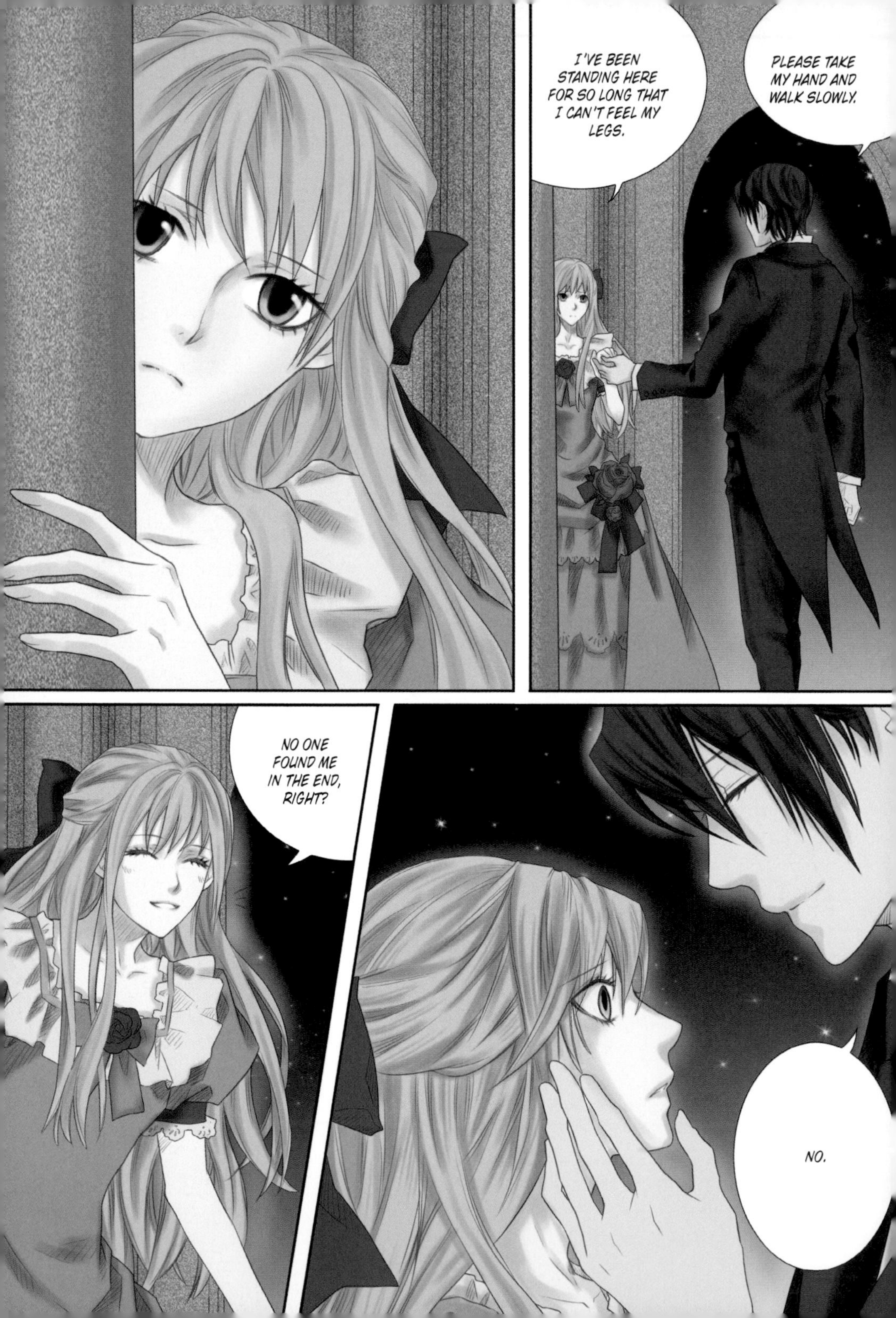
I'VE BEEN STANDING HERE FOR SO LONG THAT I CAN'T FEEL MY LEGS.
PLEASE TAKE MY HAND AND WALK SLOWLY.
NO ONE FOUND ME IN THE END, RIGHT?
NO.

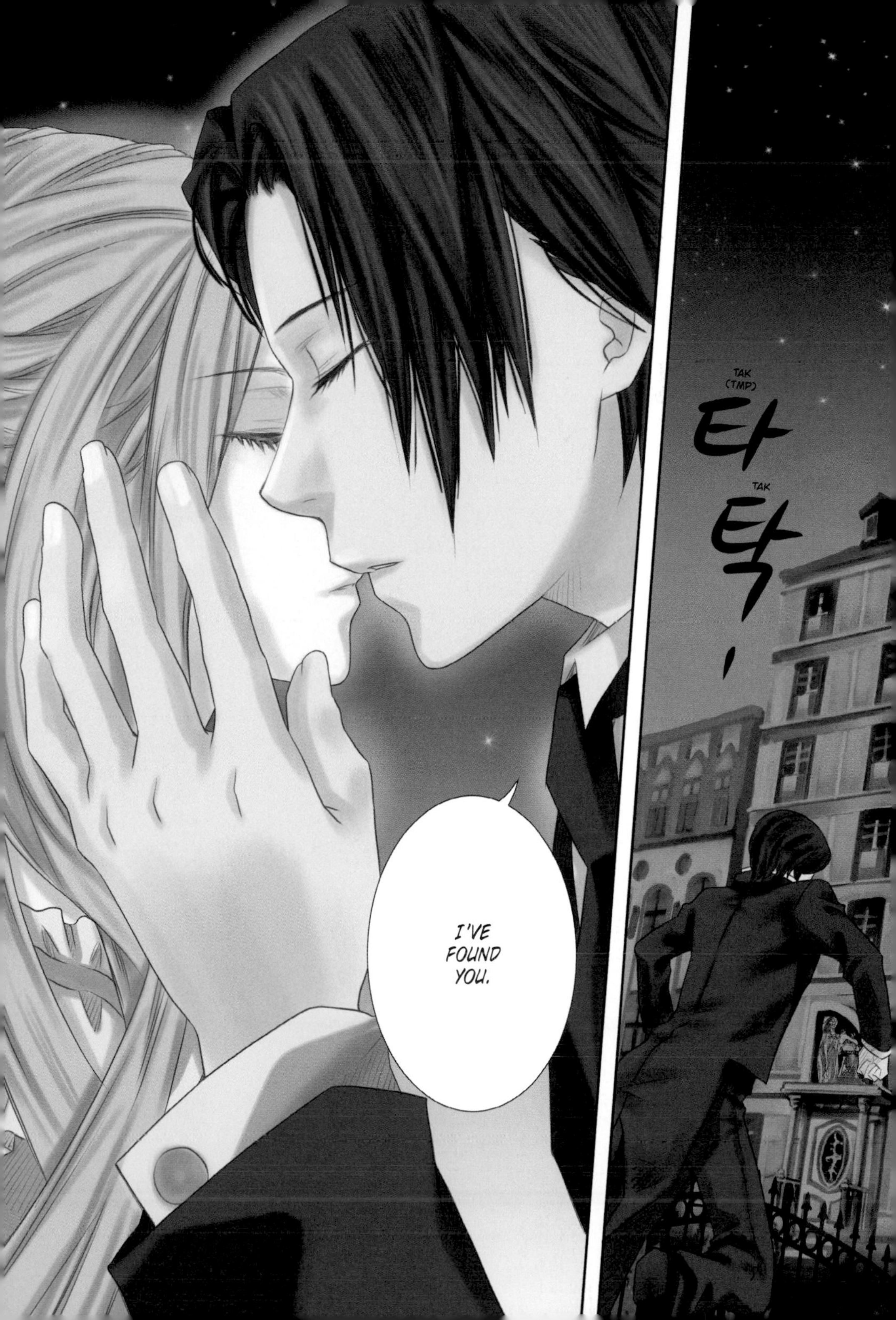
I'VE FOUND YOU.
TAK (TMP)
타
TAK
탁!

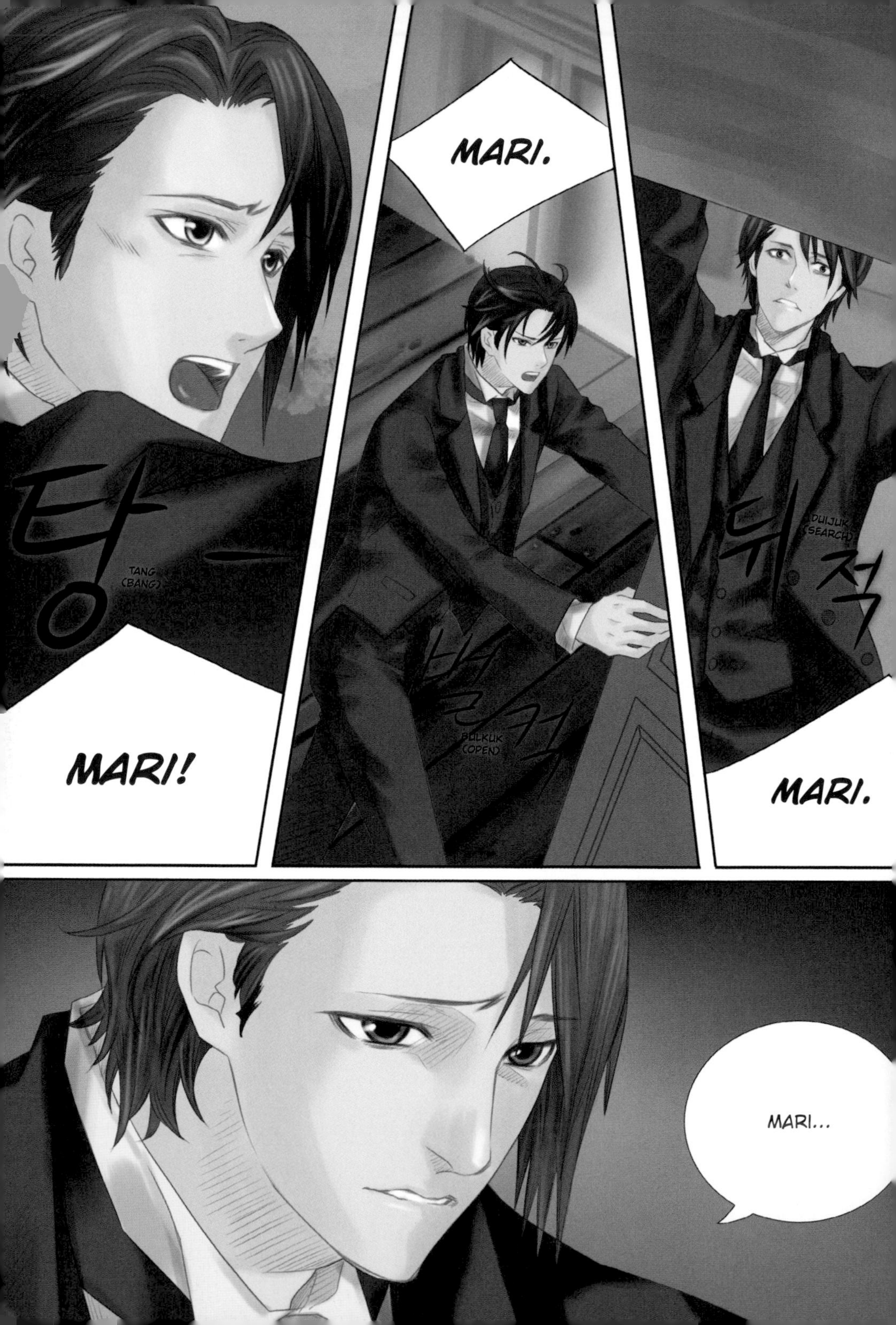
탕
TANG (BANG)
MARI!
MARI.
벌컥
BULKUK (OPEN)
뒤적
DUIJUK (SEARCH)
MARI.
MARI...

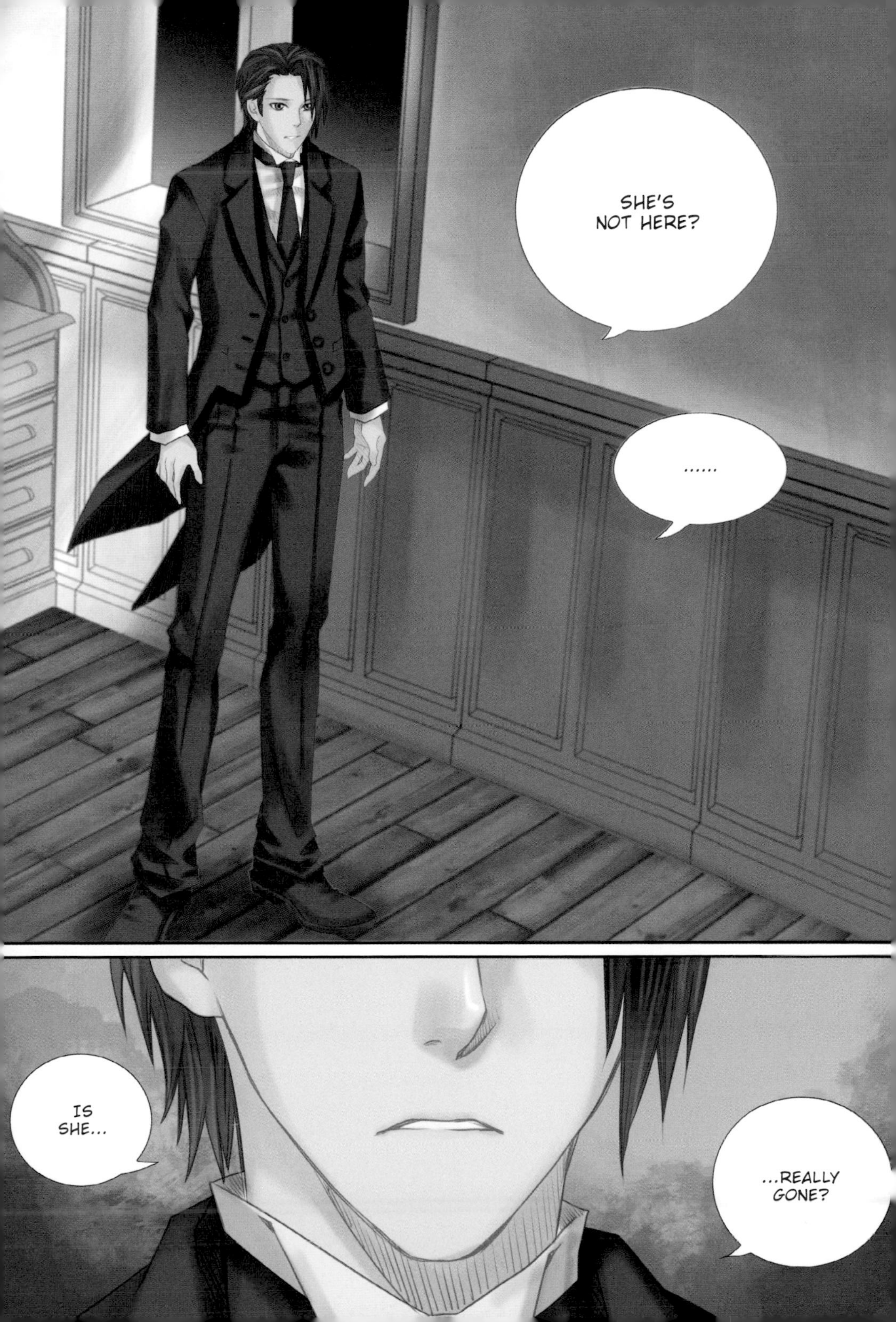
SHE'S NOT HERE?
......
IS SHE...
...REALLY GONE?

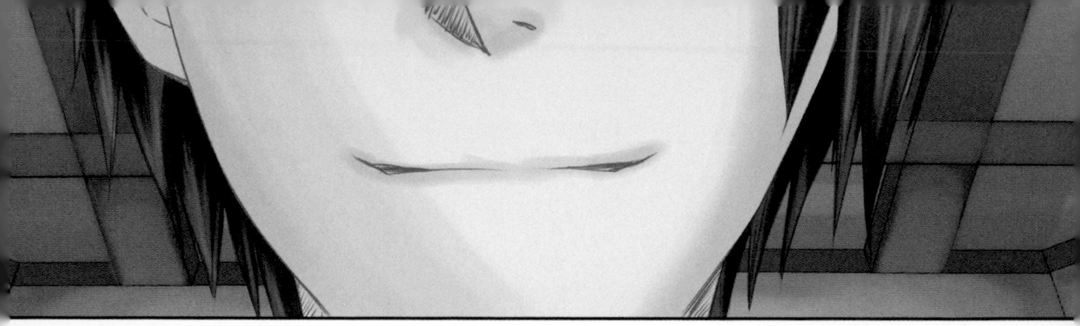

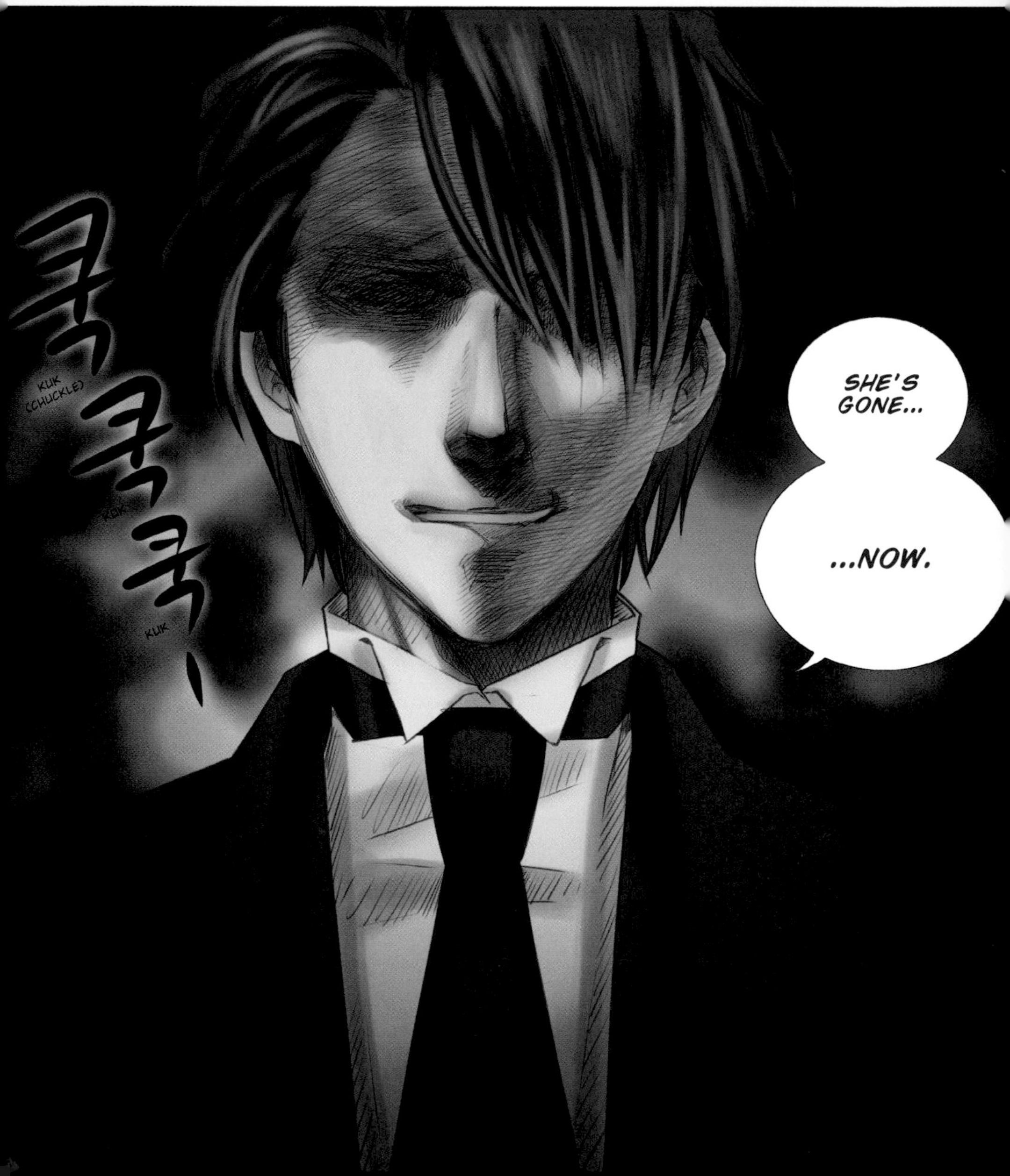
SHE'S GONE...
...NOW.
쿡
KUK (CHUCKLE)
쿡
KUK
쿡
KUK

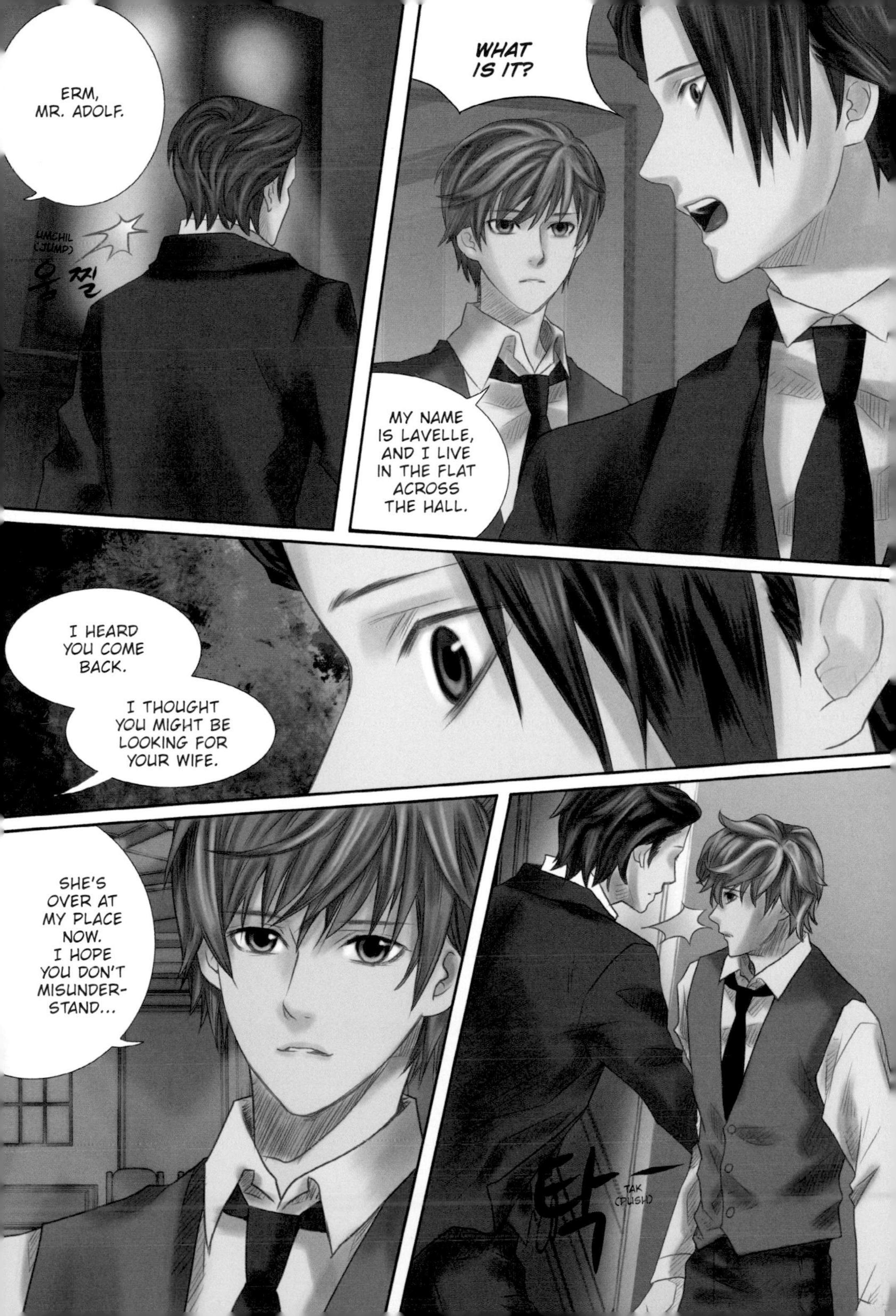
ERM, MR. ADOLF.
UMCHIL (JUMP)
움찔
WHAT IS IT?
MY NAME IS LAVELLE, AND I LIVE IN THE FLAT ACROSS THE HALL.
I HEARD YOU COME BACK.
I THOUGHT YOU MIGHT BE LOOKING FOR YOUR WIFE.
SHE'S OVER AT MY PLACE NOW. I HOPE YOU DON'T MISUNDER-STAND...
탁
TAK (PUSH)

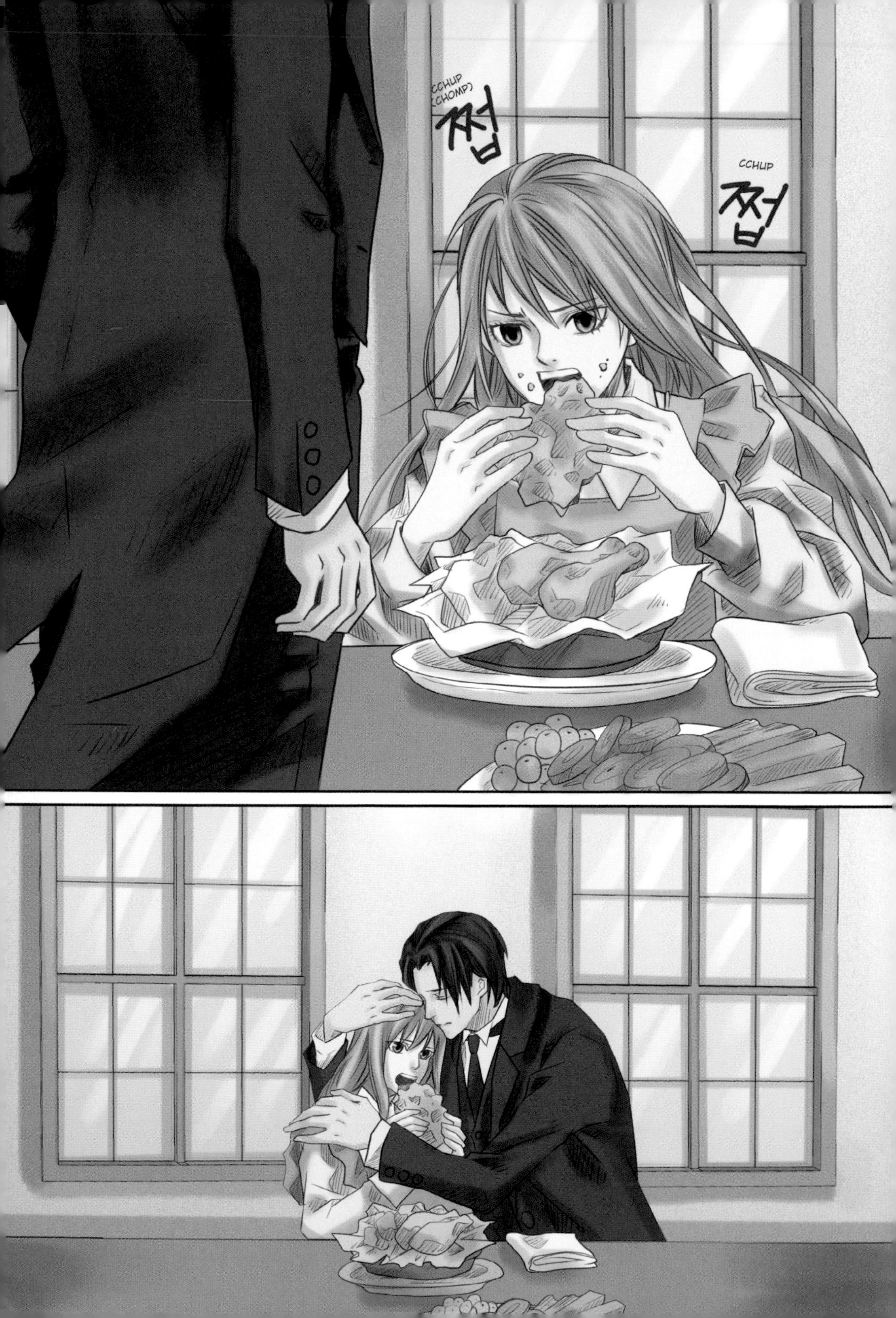
CCHUP
(CHOMP)
쩝
CCHUP
쩝

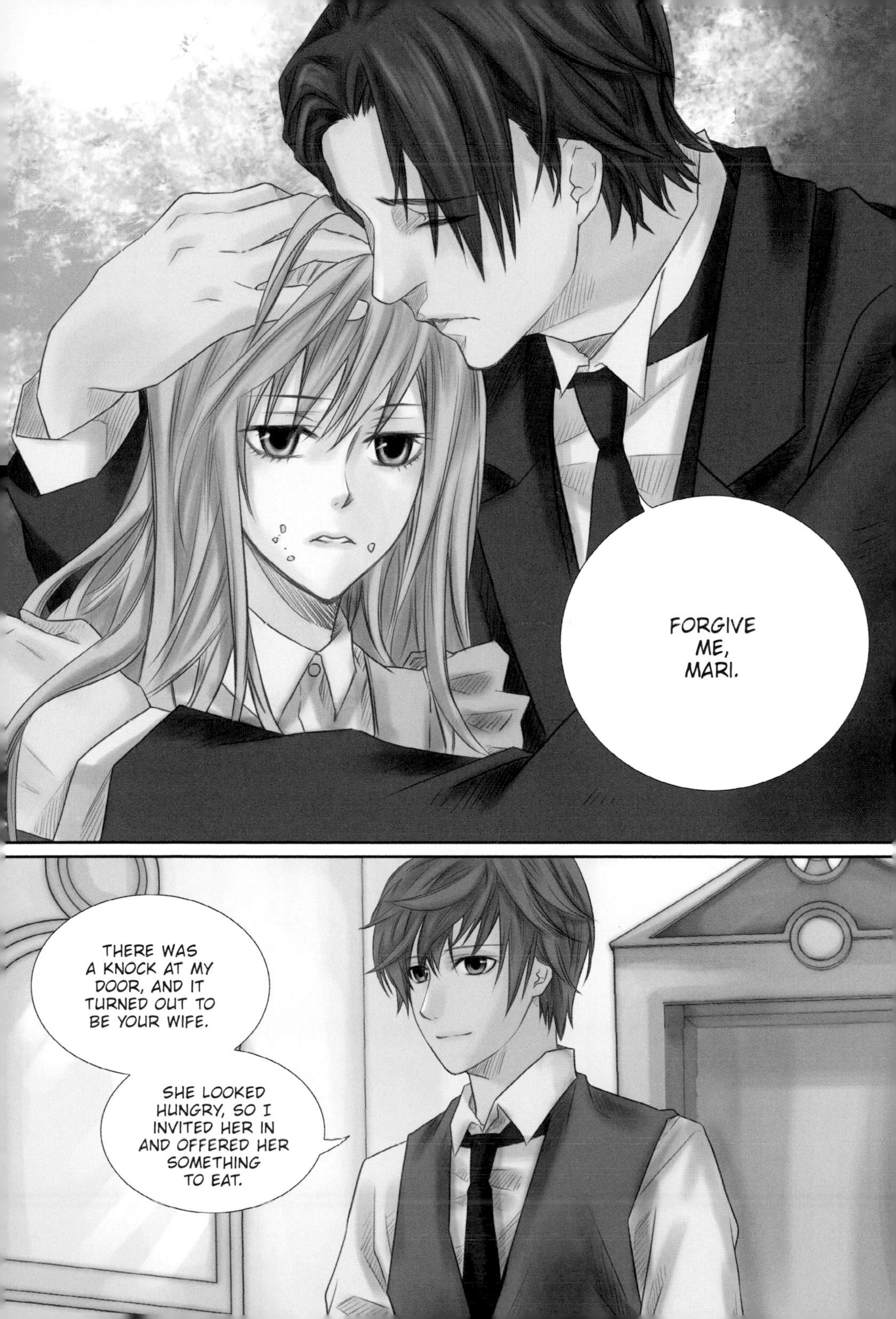
FORGIVE ME, MARI.
THERE WAS A KNOCK AT MY DOOR, AND IT TURNED OUT TO BE YOUR WIFE.
SHE LOOKED HUNGRY, SO I INVITED HER IN AND OFFERED HER SOMETHING TO EAT.

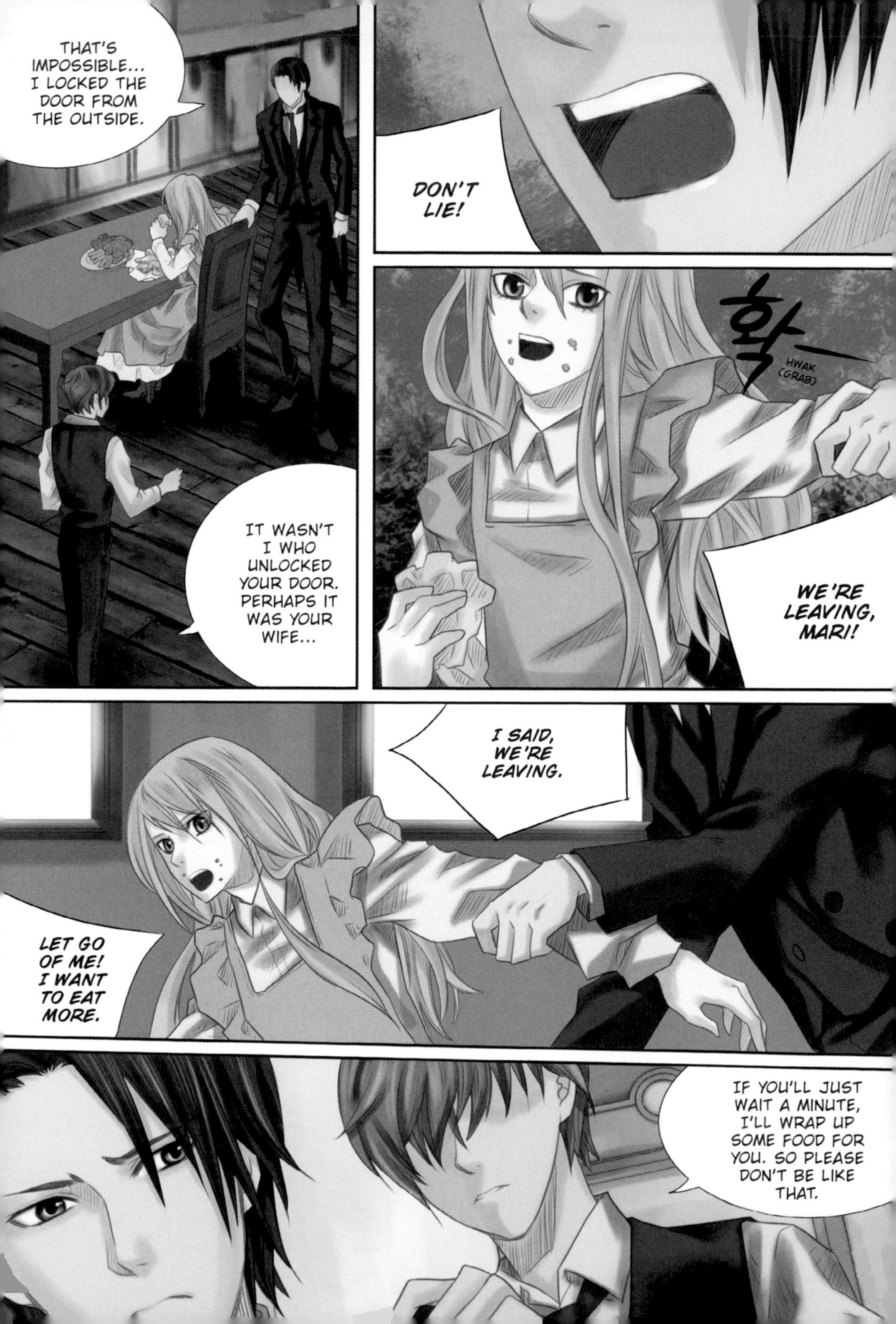
THAT'S IMPOSSIBLE... I LOCKED THE DOOR FROM THE OUTSIDE.
IT WASN'T I WHO UNLOCKED YOUR DOOR. PERHAPS IT WAS YOUR WIFE...
DON'T LIE!
확
HWAK (GRAB)
WE'RE LEAVING, MARI!
I SAID, WE'RE LEAVING.
LET GO OF ME! I WANT TO EAT MORE.
IF YOU'LL JUST WAIT A MINUTE, I'LL WRAP UP SOME FOOD FOR YOU. SO PLEASE DON'T BE LIKE THAT.

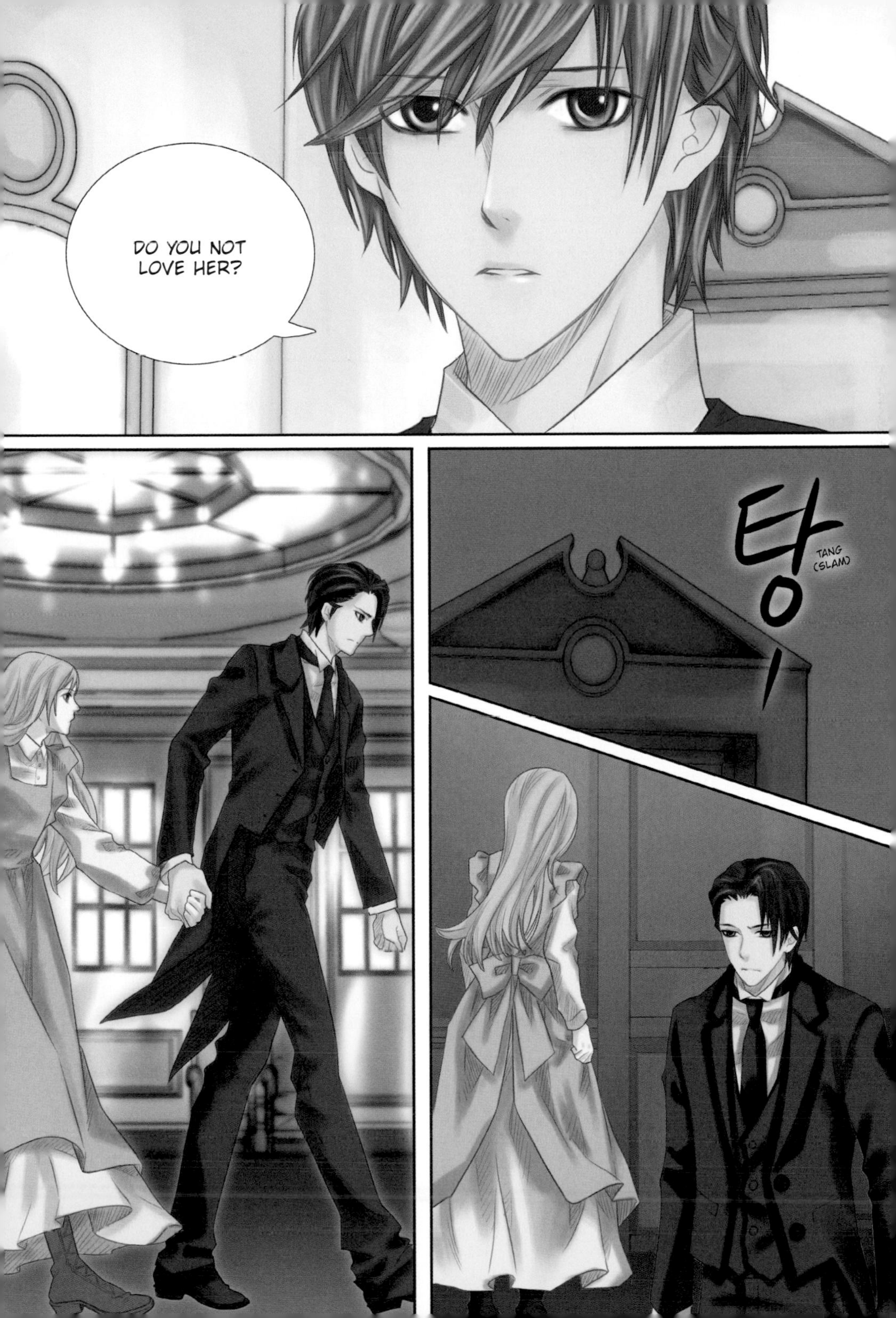
DO YOU NOT LOVE HER?
탕
TANG (SLAM)

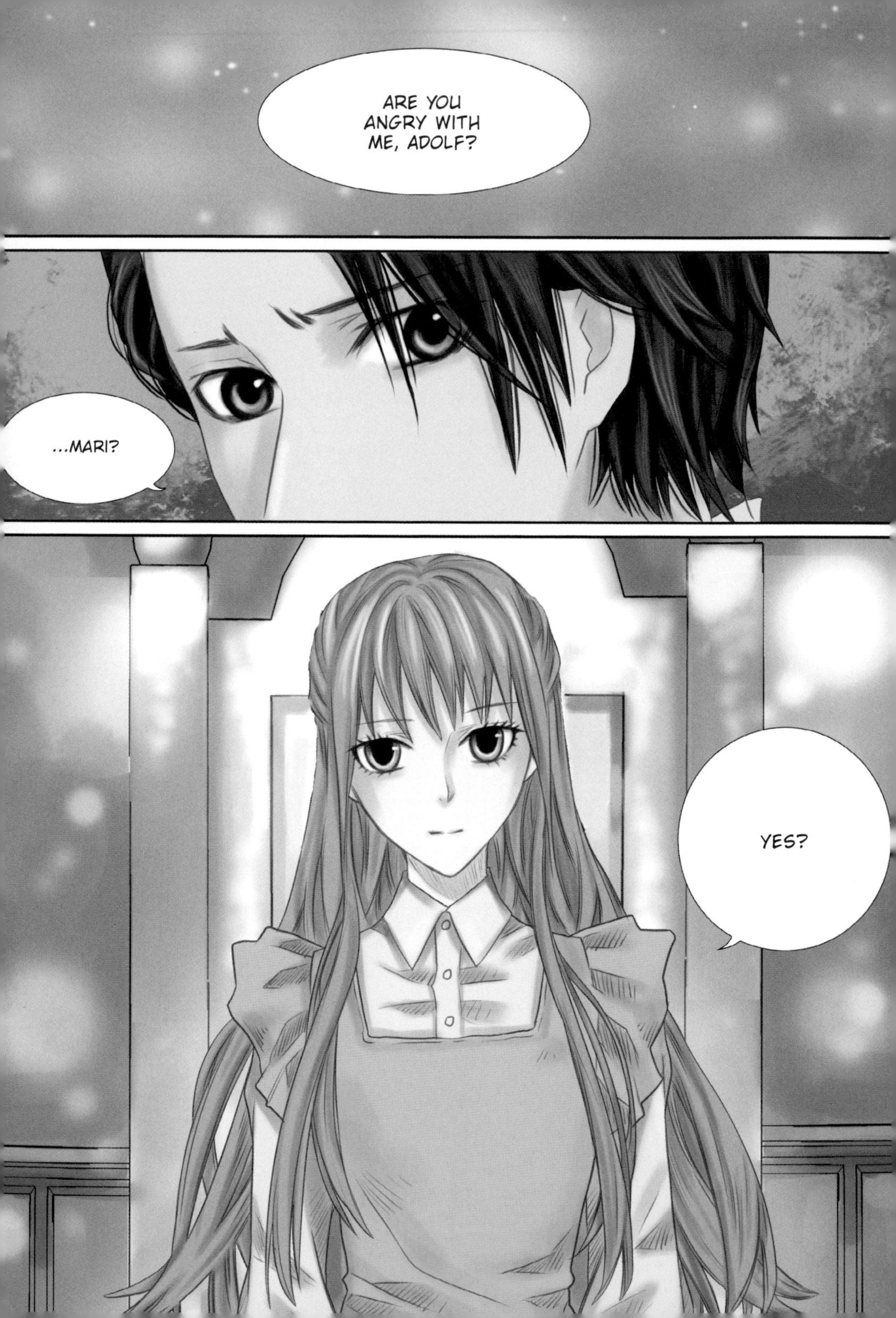
ARE YOU ANGRY WITH ME, ADOLF?
...MARI?
YES?

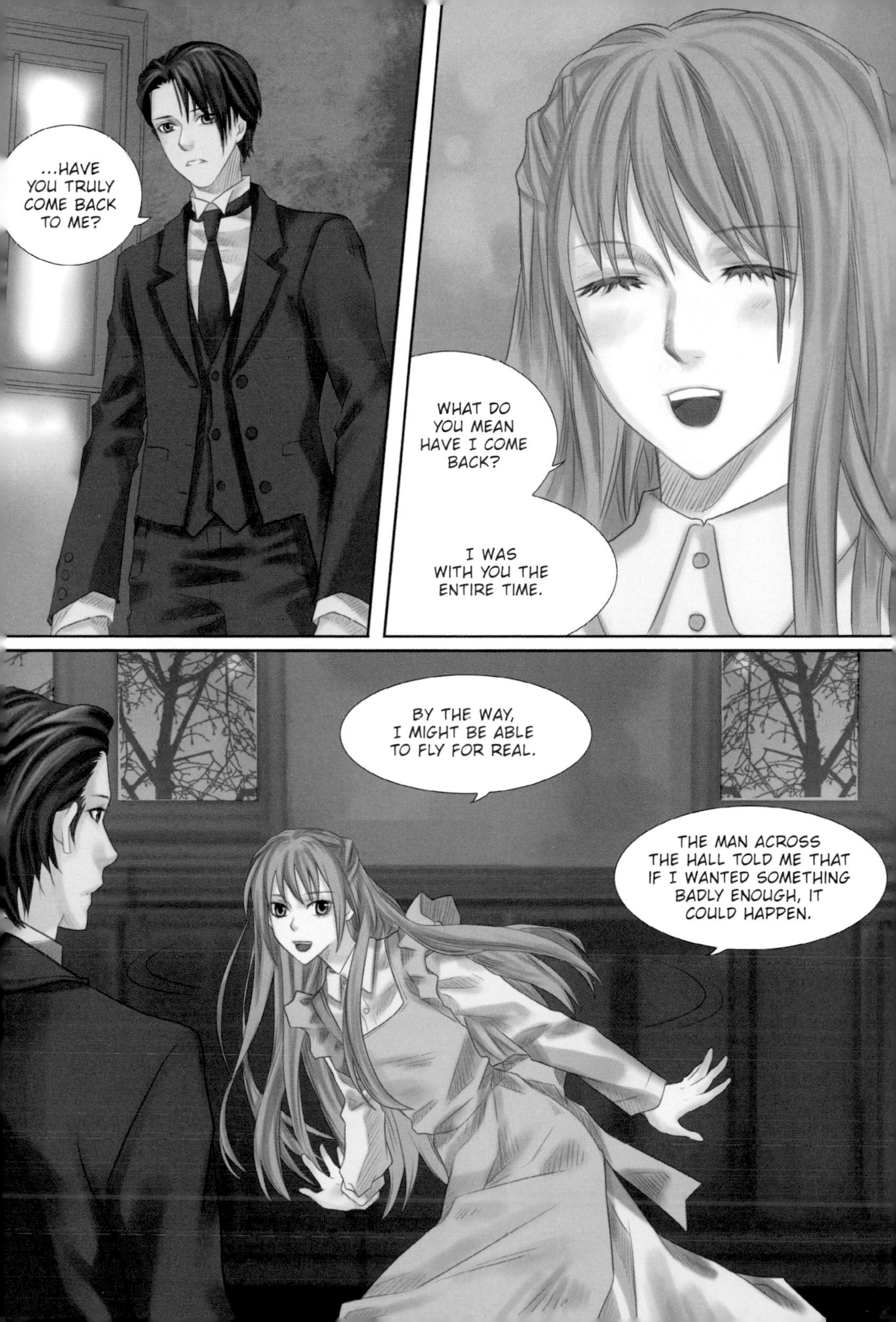
...HAVE YOU TRULY COME BACK TO ME?
WHAT DO YOU MEAN HAVE I COME BACK?
I WAS WITH YOU THE ENTIRE TIME.
BY THE WAY, I MIGHT BE ABLE TO FLY FOR REAL.
THE MAN ACROSS THE HALL TOLD ME THAT IF I WANTED SOMETHING BADLY ENOUGH, IT COULD HAPPEN.

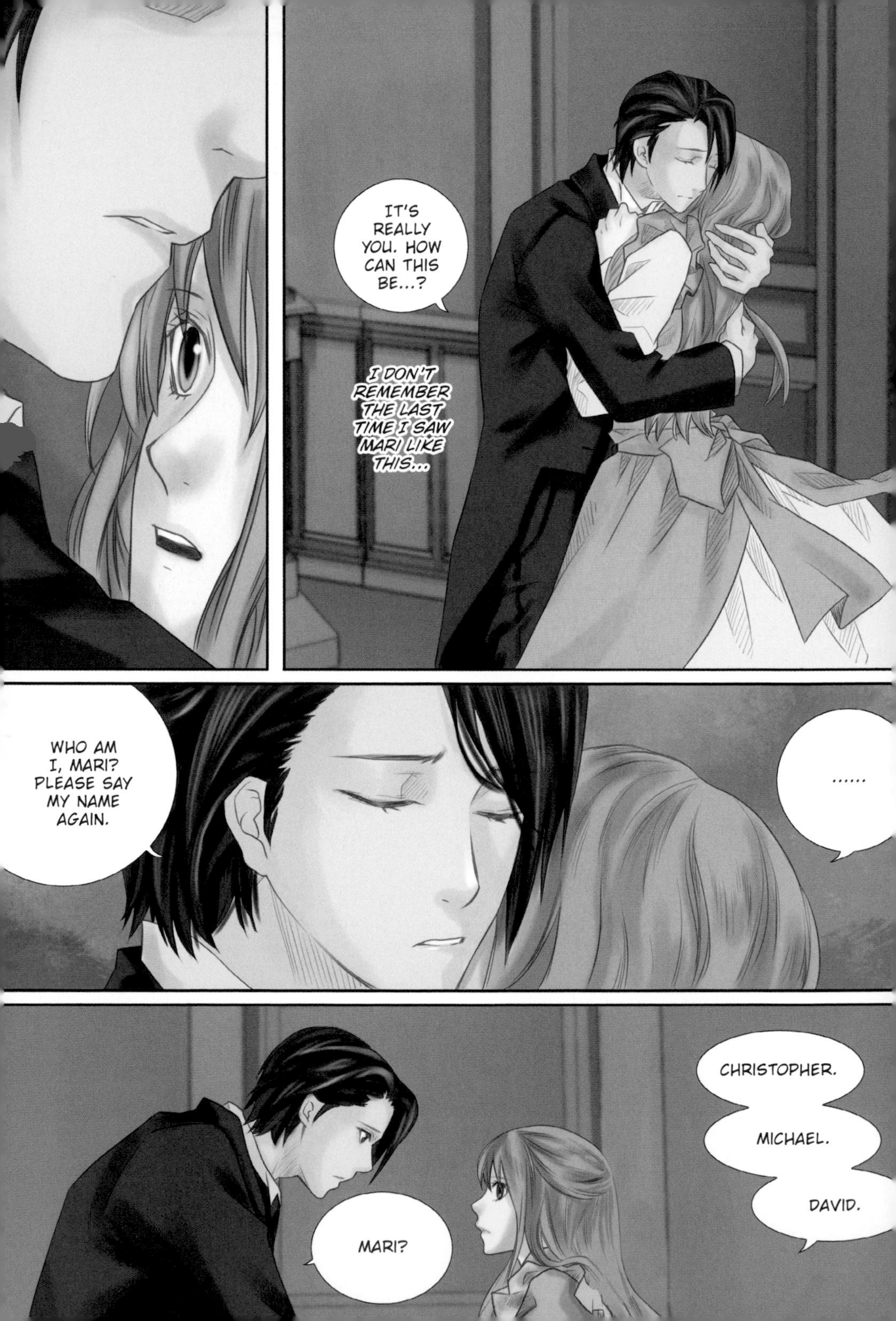
IT'S REALLY YOU. HOW CAN THIS BE...?
I DON'T REMEMBER THE LAST TIME I SAW MARI LIKE THIS...
WHO AM I, MARI? PLEASE SAY MY NAME AGAIN.
......
MARI?
CHRISTOPHER.
MICHAEL.
DAVID.

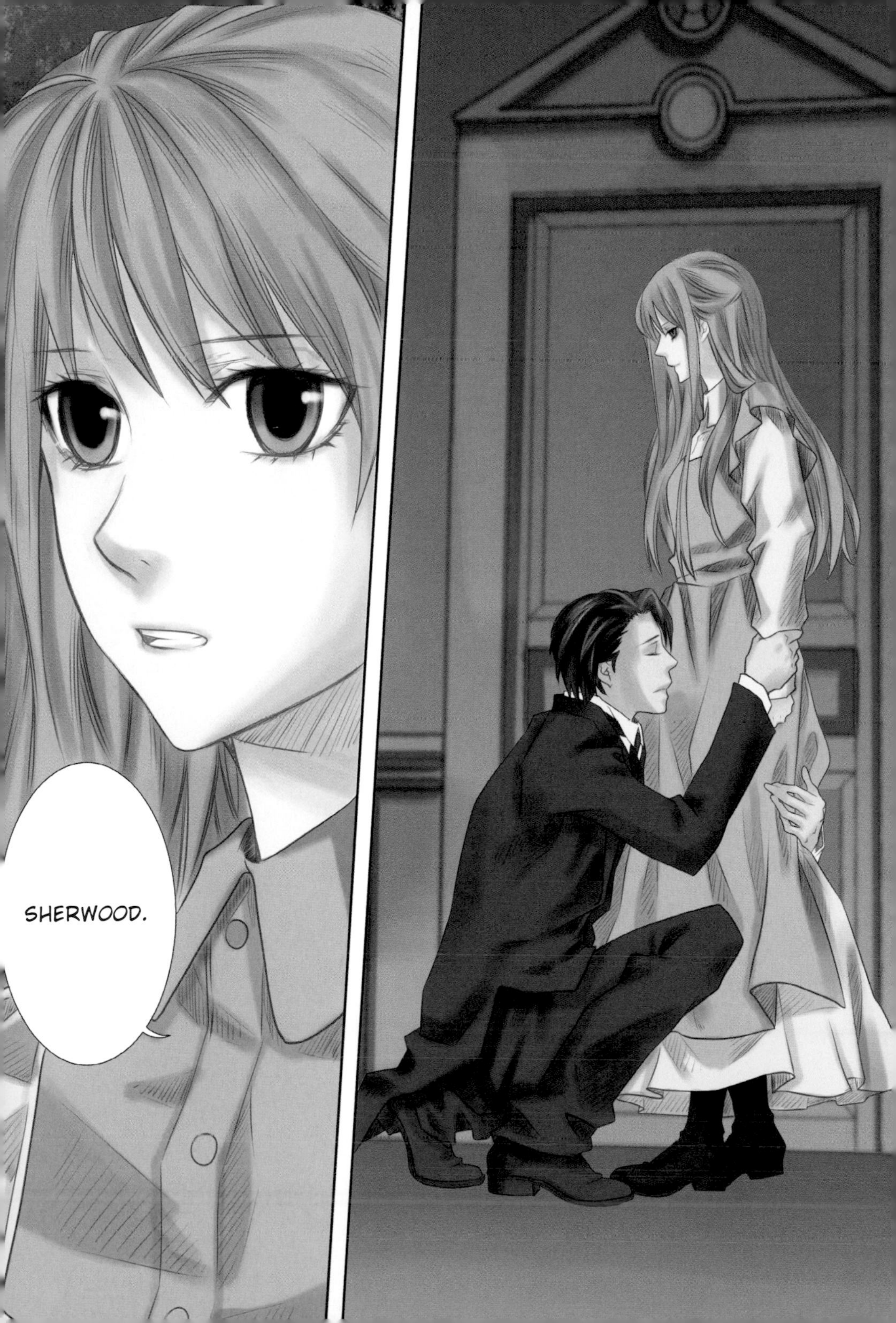
SHERWOOD.

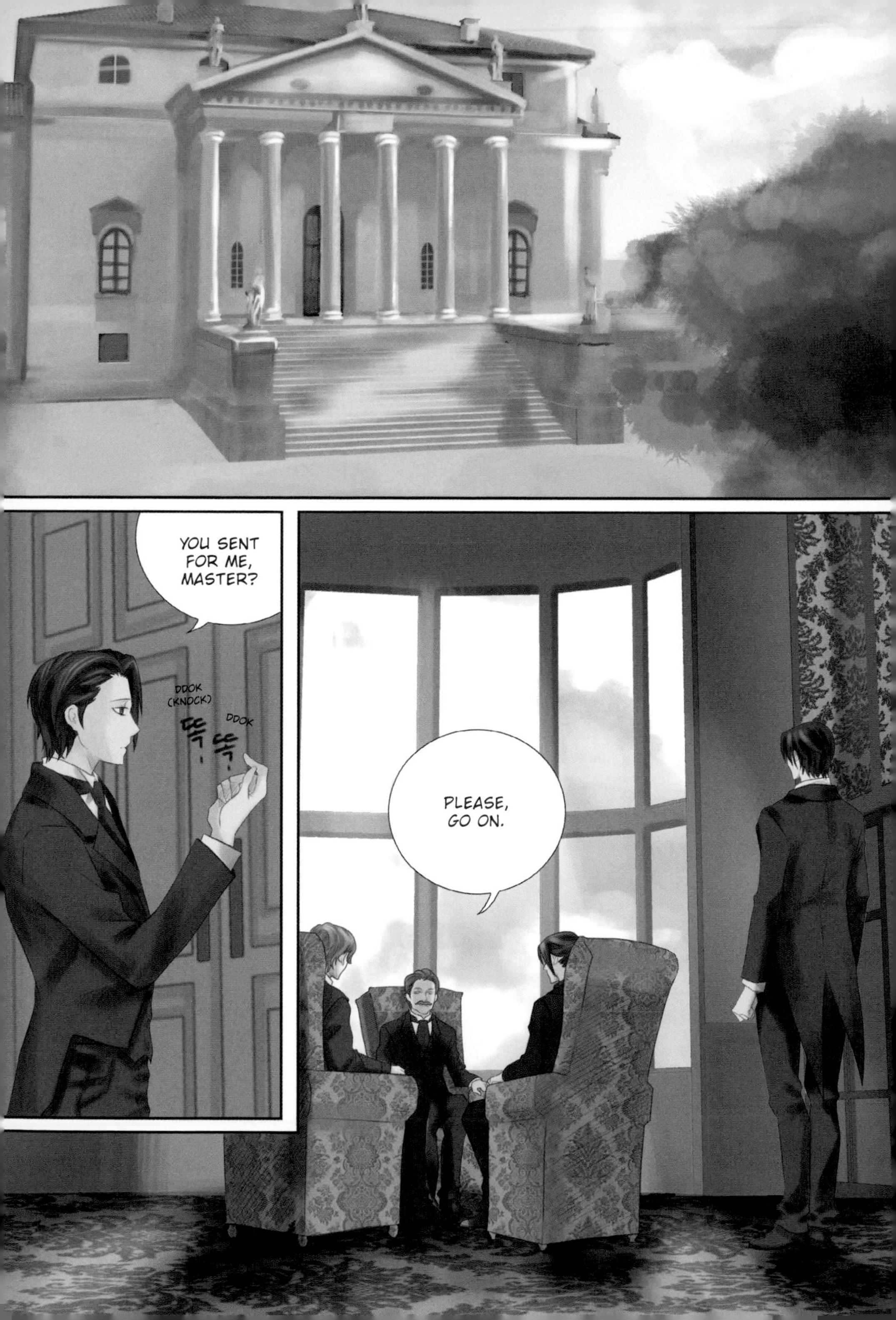
YOU SENT FOR ME, MASTER?
DDOK (KNOCK)
똑,
DDOK
똑,
PLEASE, GO ON.

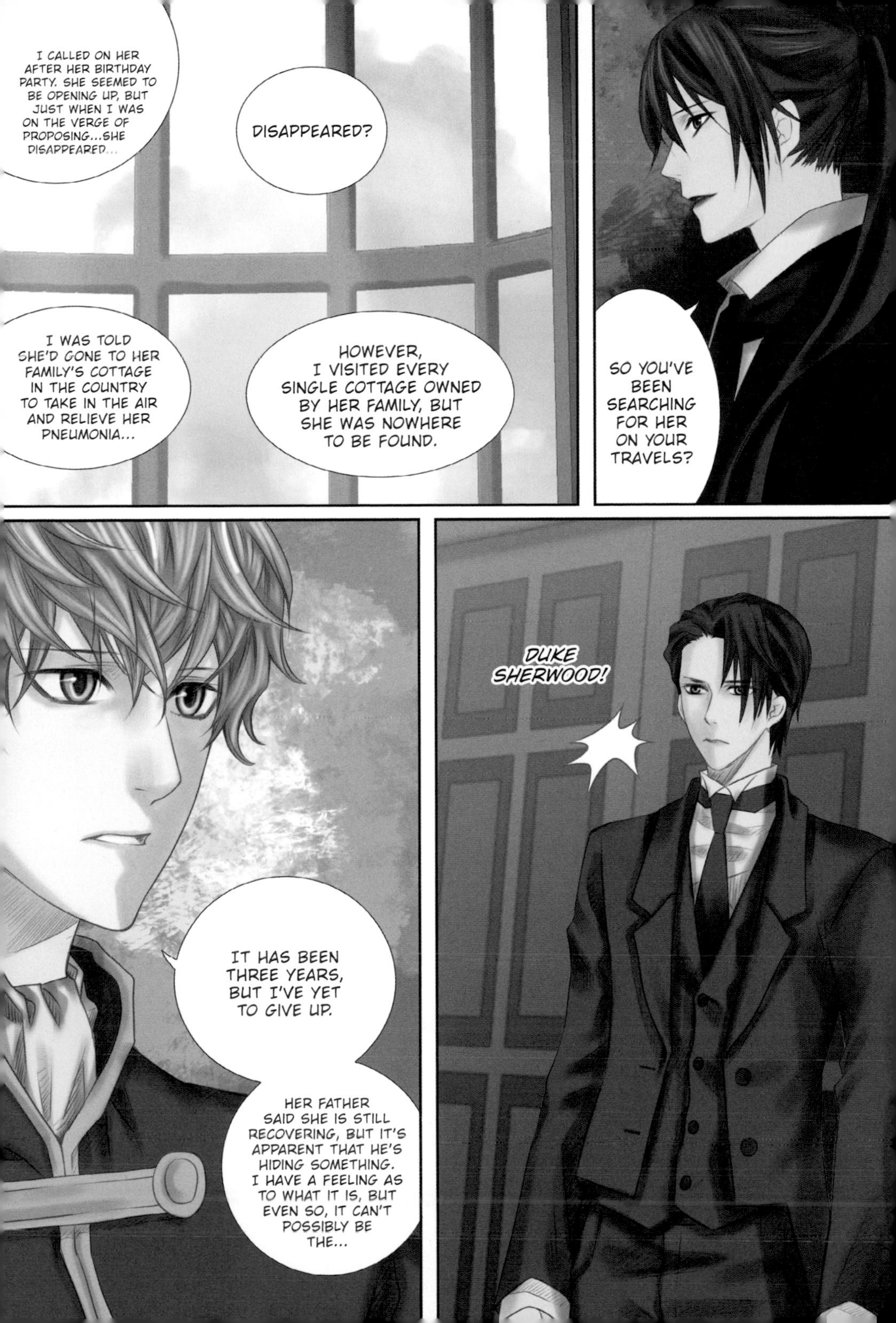
I CALLED ON HER AFTER HER BIRTHDAY PARTY. SHE SEEMED TO BE OPENING UP, BUT JUST WHEN I WAS ON THE VERGE OF PROPOSING...SHE DISAPPEARED...
DISAPPEARED?
I WAS TOLD SHE'D GONE TO HER FAMILY'S COTTAGE IN THE COUNTRY TO TAKE IN THE AIR AND RELIEVE HER PNEUMONIA...
HOWEVER, I VISITED EVERY SINGLE COTTAGE OWNED BY HER FAMILY, BUT SHE WAS NOWHERE TO BE FOUND.
SO YOU'VE BEEN SEARCHING FOR HER ON YOUR TRAVELS?
IT HAS BEEN THREE YEARS, BUT I'VE YET TO GIVE UP.
HER FATHER SAID SHE IS STILL RECOVERING, BUT IT'S APPARENT THAT HE'S HIDING SOMETHING. I HAVE A FEELING AS TO WHAT IT IS, BUT EVEN SO, IT CAN'T POSSIBLY BE THE...
DUKE SHERWOOD!

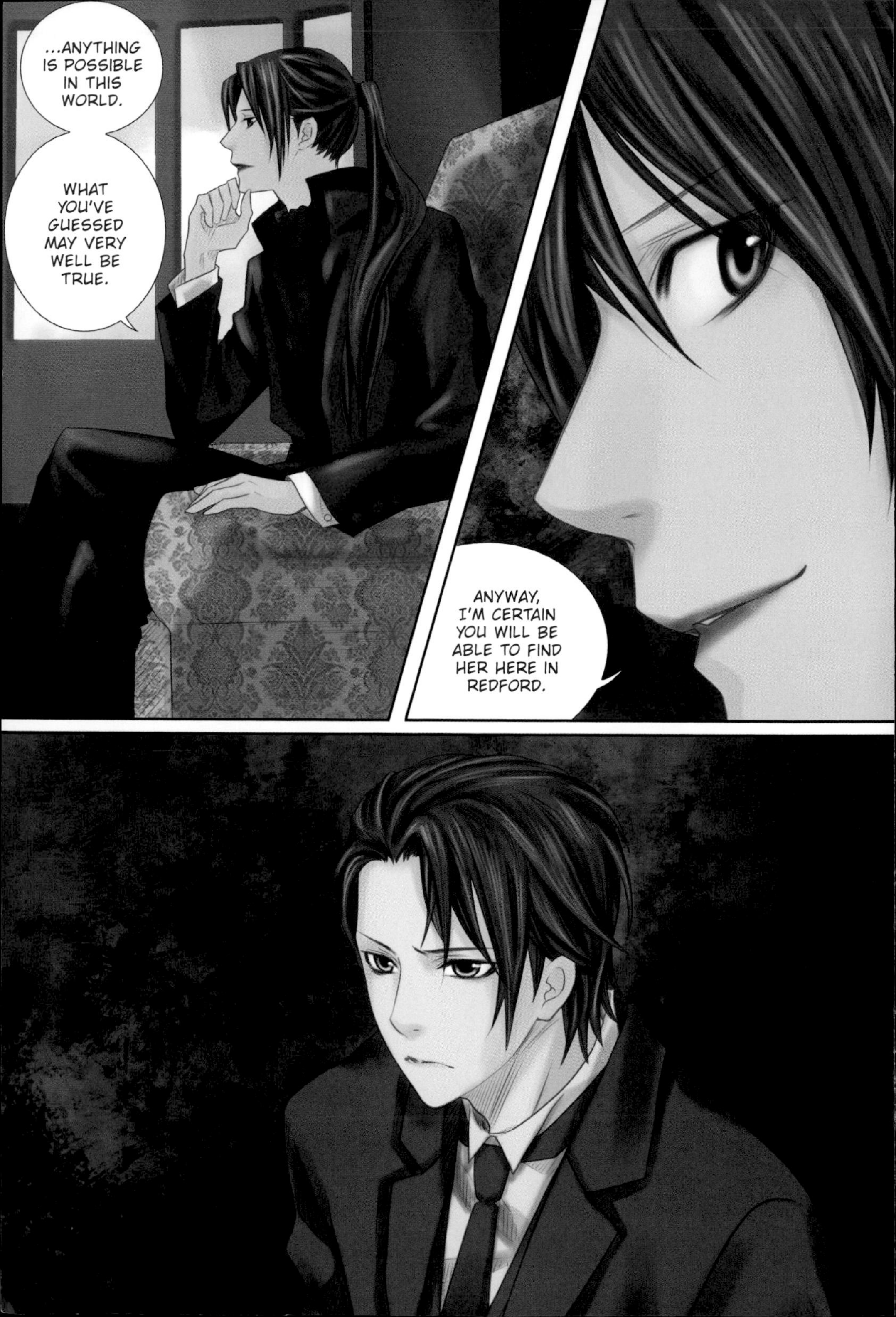
...ANYTHING IS POSSIBLE IN THIS WORLD.
WHAT YOU'VE GUESSED MAY VERY WELL BE TRUE.
ANYWAY, I'M CERTAIN YOU WILL BE ABLE TO FIND HER HERE IN REDFORD.

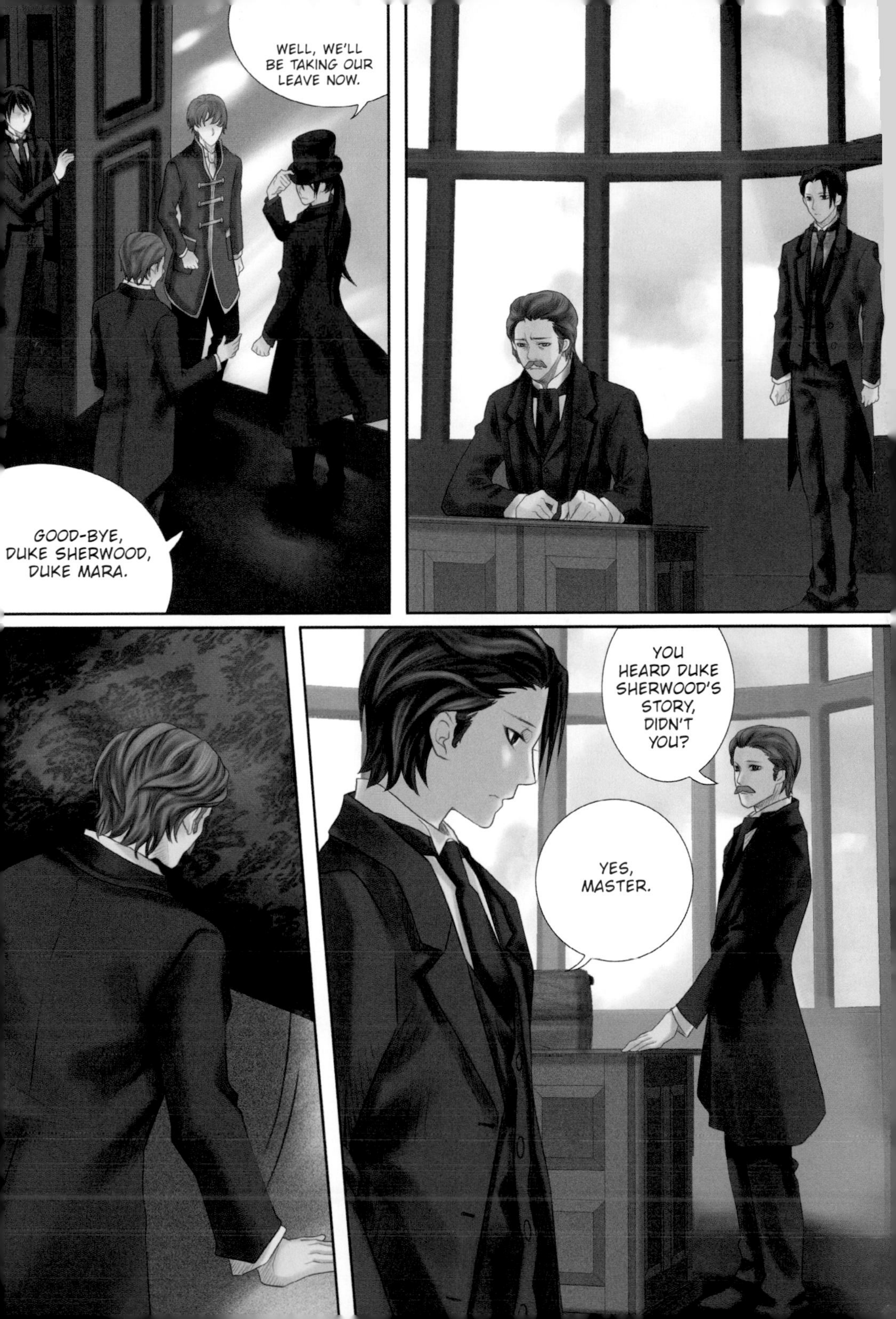
WELL, WE'LL BE TAKING OUR LEAVE NOW.
GOOD-BYE, DUKE SHERWOOD, DUKE MARA.
YOU HEARD DUKE SHERWOOD'S STORY, DIDN'T YOU?
YES, MASTER.

I AM NOT A FOOL, ADOLF. I'M JUST A MAN WHO LOVES HIS WIFE.
AND IF SOMETHING LIKE *THAT* WERE TO HAPPEN, I WOULD HUNT THEM BOTH DOWN AND KILL THEM.

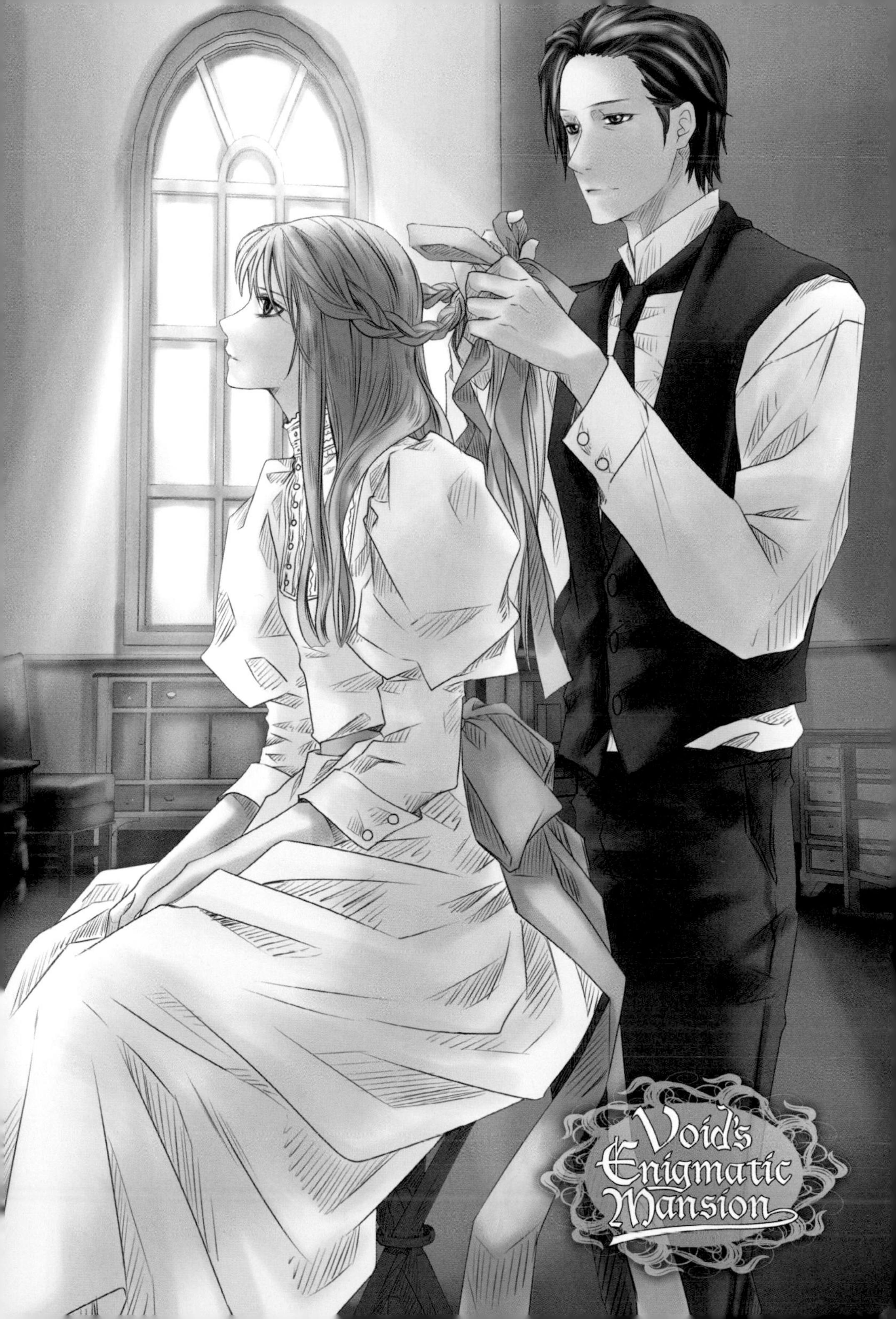
Void's Enigmatic Mansion

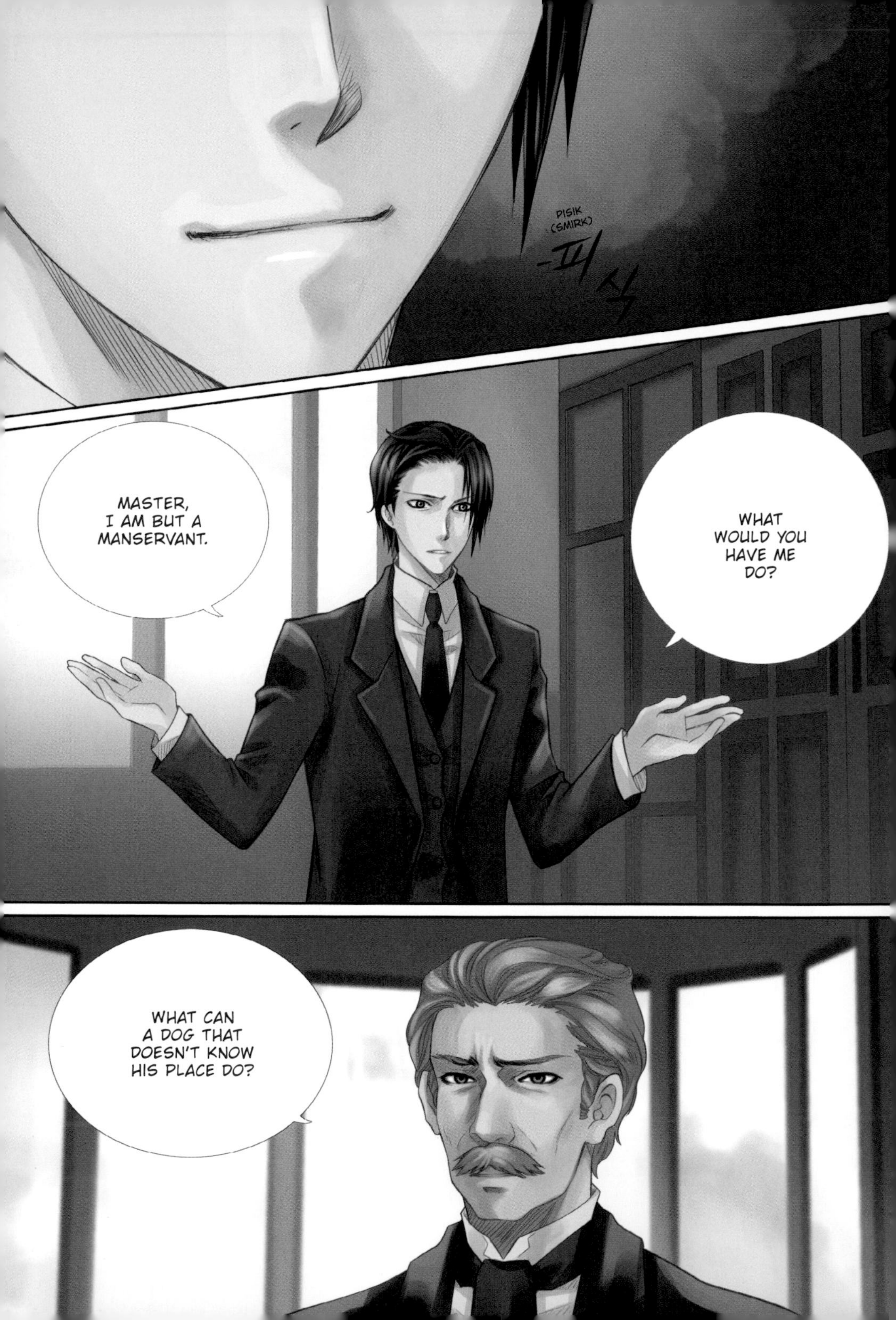
PISIK (SMIRK)
피식
MASTER, I AM BUT A MANSERVANT.
WHAT WOULD YOU HAVE ME DO?
WHAT CAN A DOG THAT DOESN'T KNOW HIS PLACE DO?

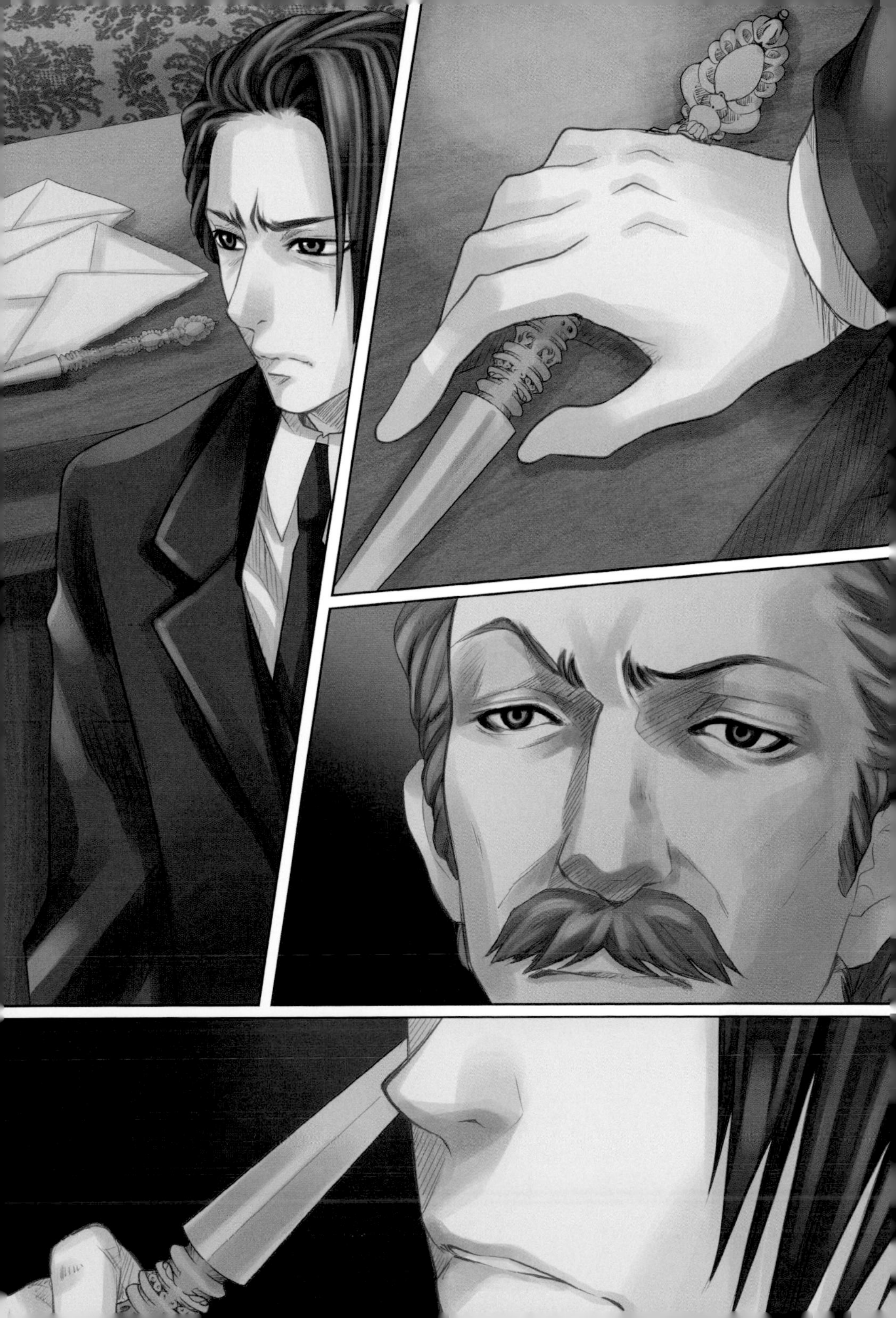

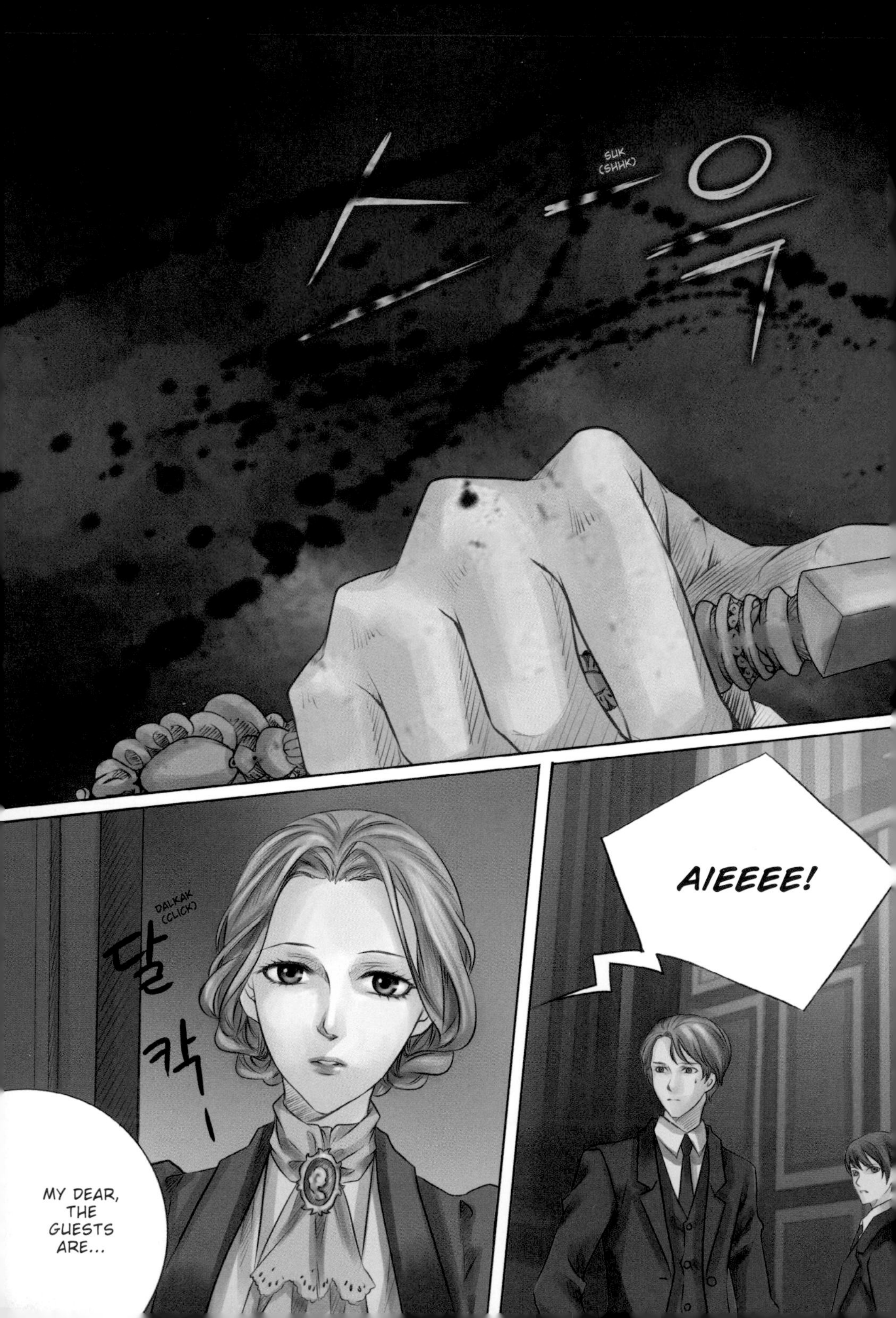
SUK (SHHK)
DALKAK (CLICK)
MY DEAR, THE GUESTS ARE...
AIEEEE!

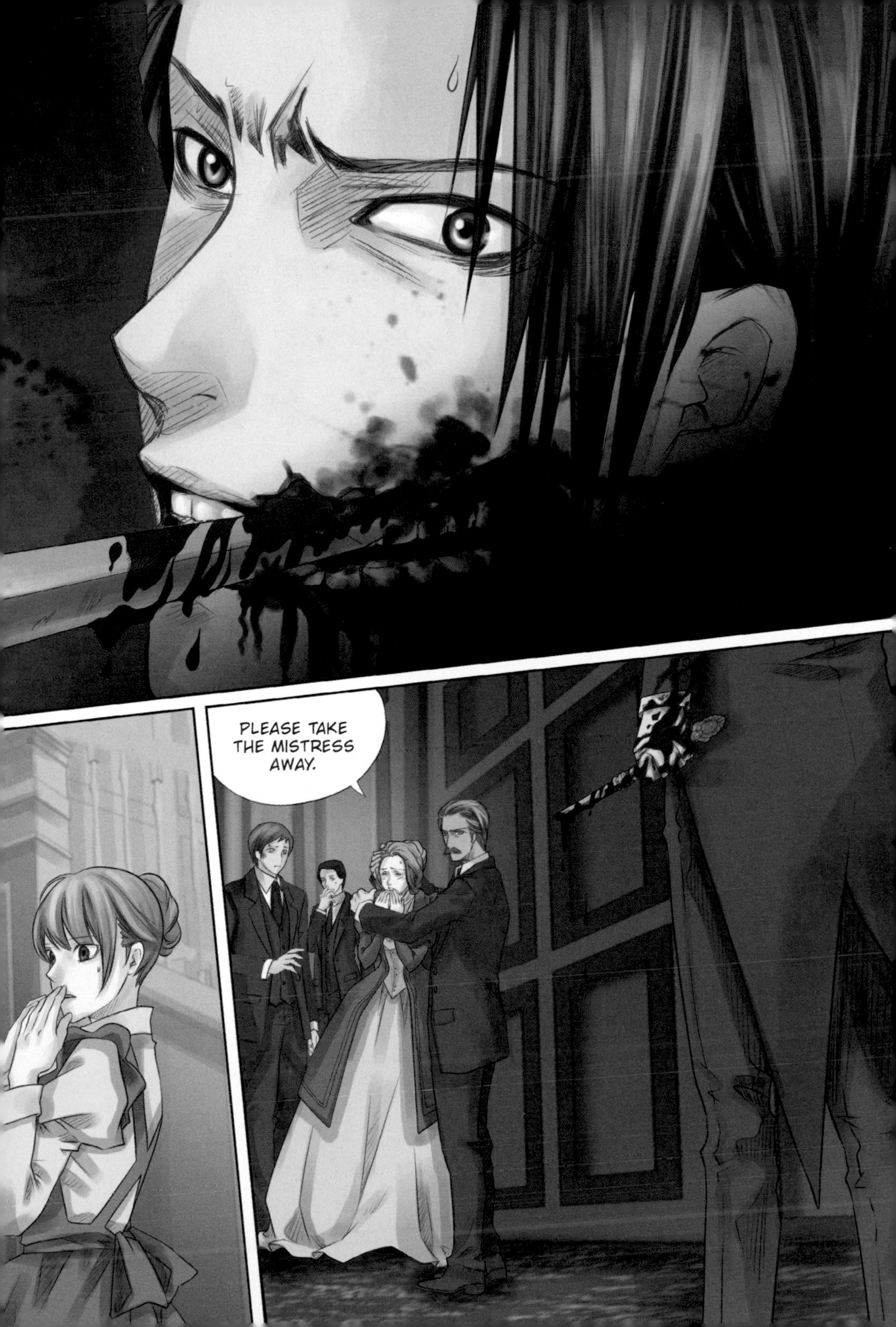
PLEASE TAKE THE MISTRESS AWAY.

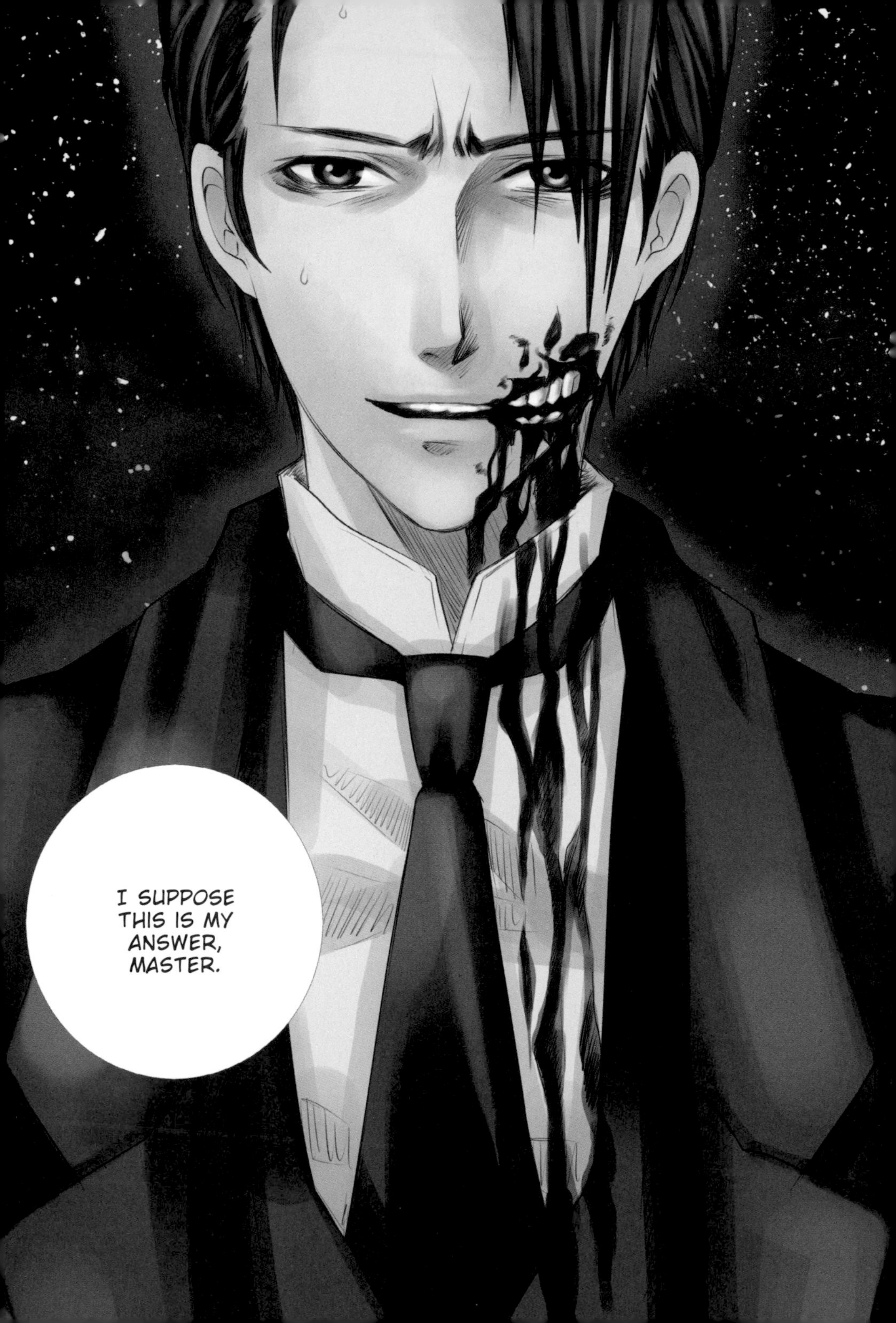
I SUPPOSE THIS IS MY ANSWER, MASTER.

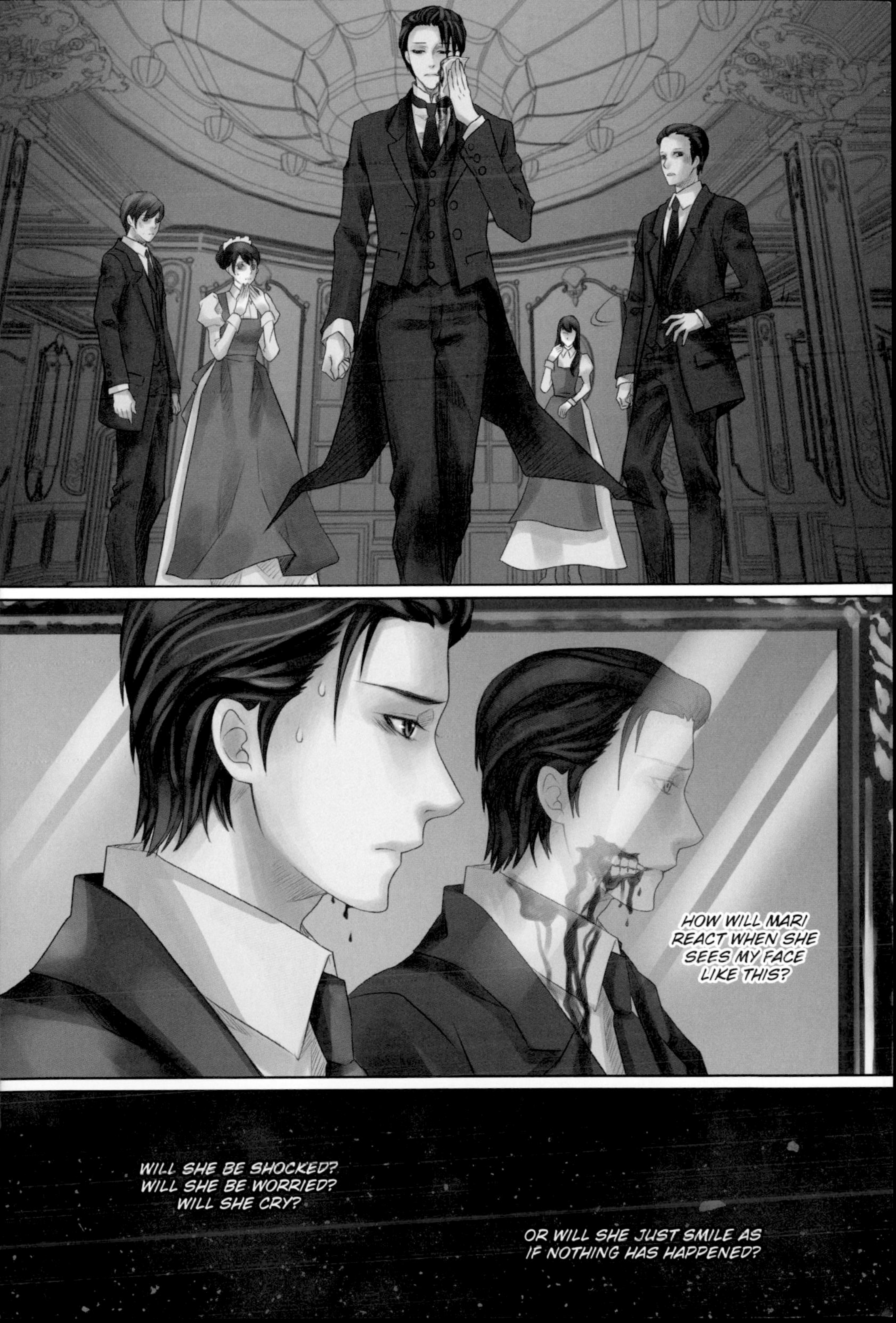
HOW WILL MARI REACT WHEN SHE SEES MY FACE LIKE THIS?
WILL SHE BE SHOCKED? WILL SHE BE WORRIED? WILL SHE CRY?
OR WILL SHE JUST SMILE AS IF NOTHING HAS HAPPENED?

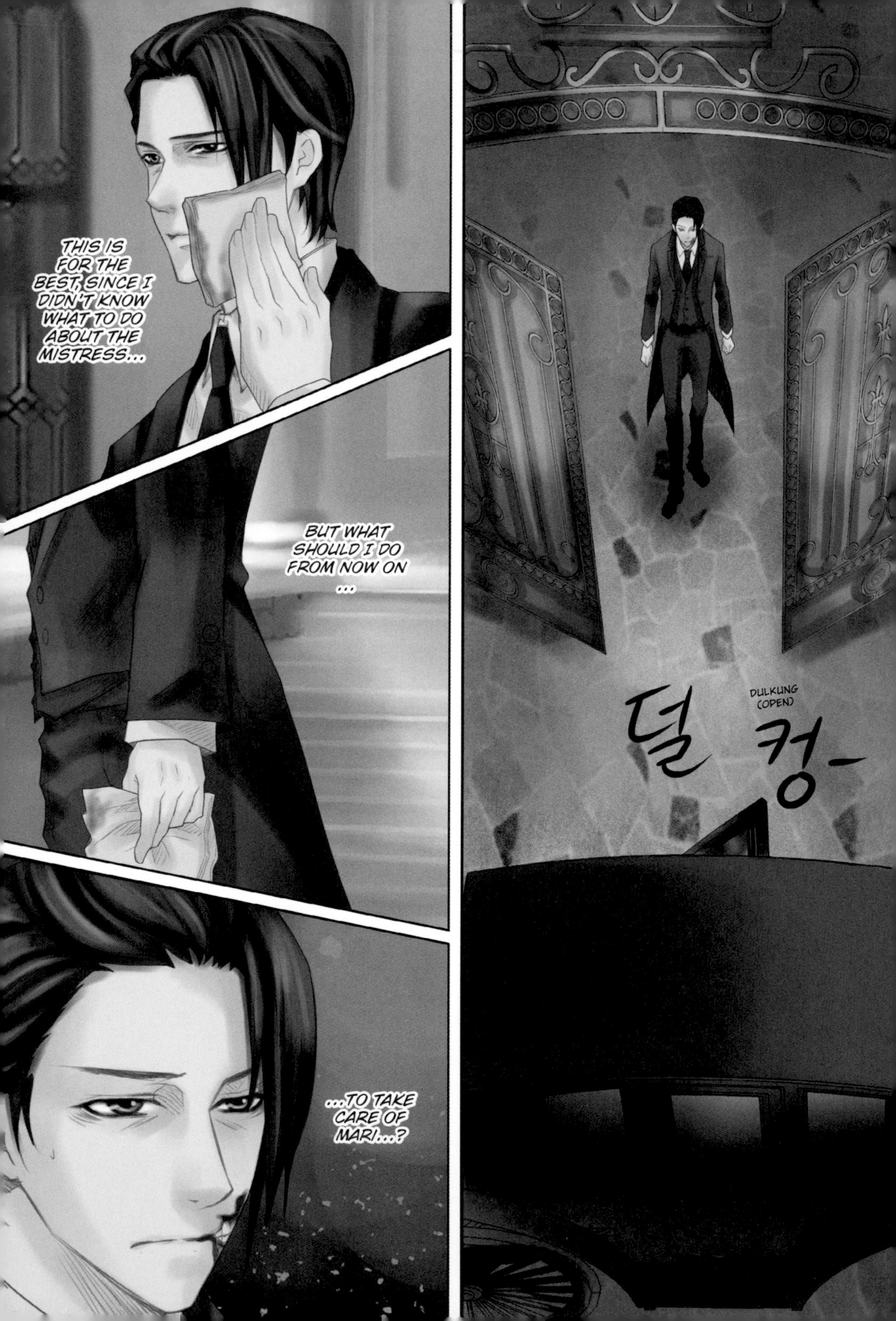
THIS IS FOR THE BEST, SINCE I DIDN'T KNOW WHAT TO DO ABOUT THE MISTRESS...
BUT WHAT SHOULD I DO FROM NOW ON ...
...TO TAKE CARE OF MARI...?
덜컹-
DULKUNG (OPEN)

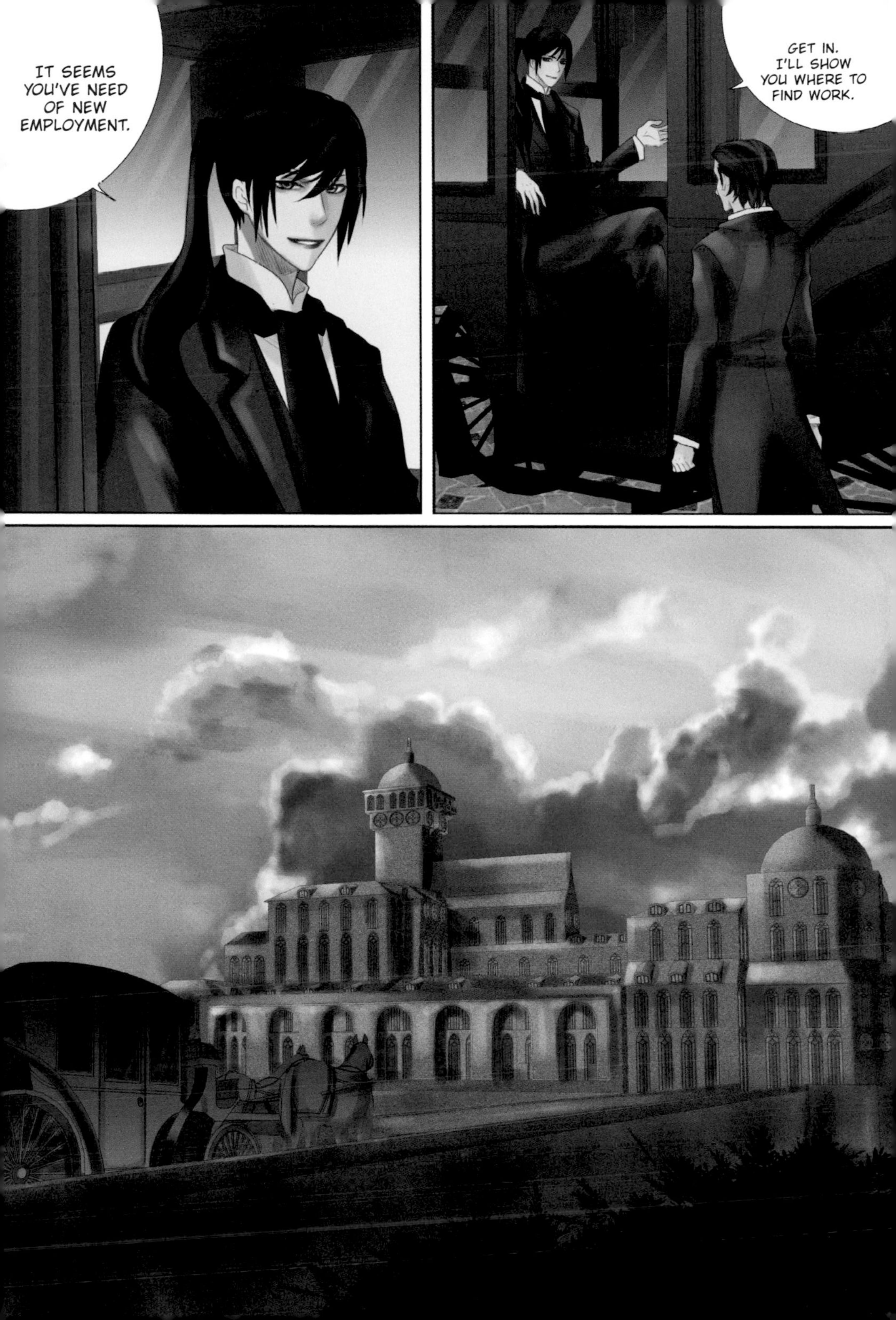
IT SEEMS YOU'VE NEED OF NEW EMPLOYMENT.
GET IN. I'LL SHOW YOU WHERE TO FIND WORK.

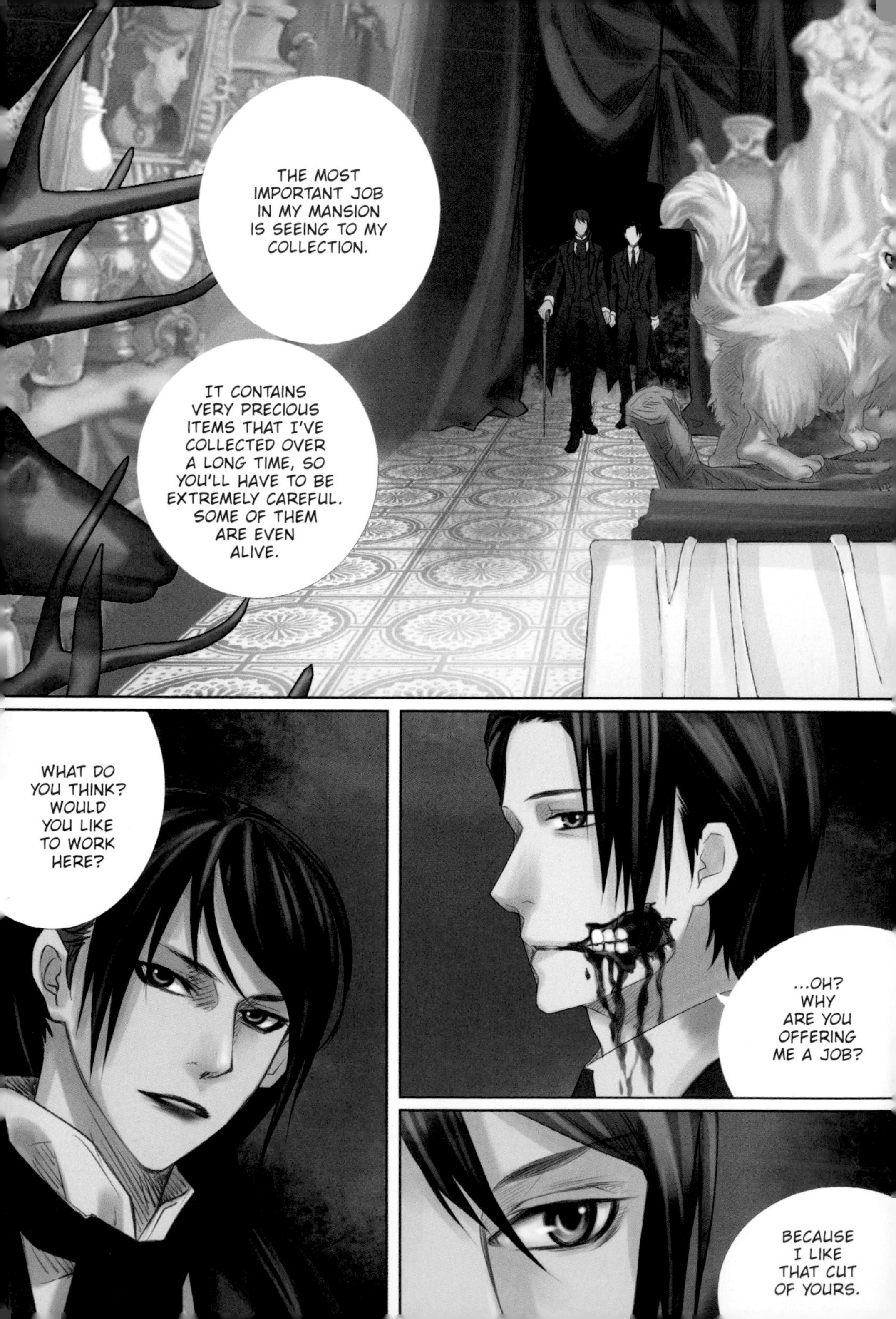
THE MOST IMPORTANT JOB IN MY MANSION IS SEEING TO MY COLLECTION.
IT CONTAINS VERY PRECIOUS ITEMS THAT I'VE COLLECTED OVER A LONG TIME, SO YOU'LL HAVE TO BE EXTREMELY CAREFUL. SOME OF THEM ARE EVEN ALIVE.
WHAT DO YOU THINK? WOULD YOU LIKE TO WORK HERE?
...OH? WHY ARE YOU OFFERING ME A JOB?
BECAUSE I LIKE THAT CUT OF YOURS.

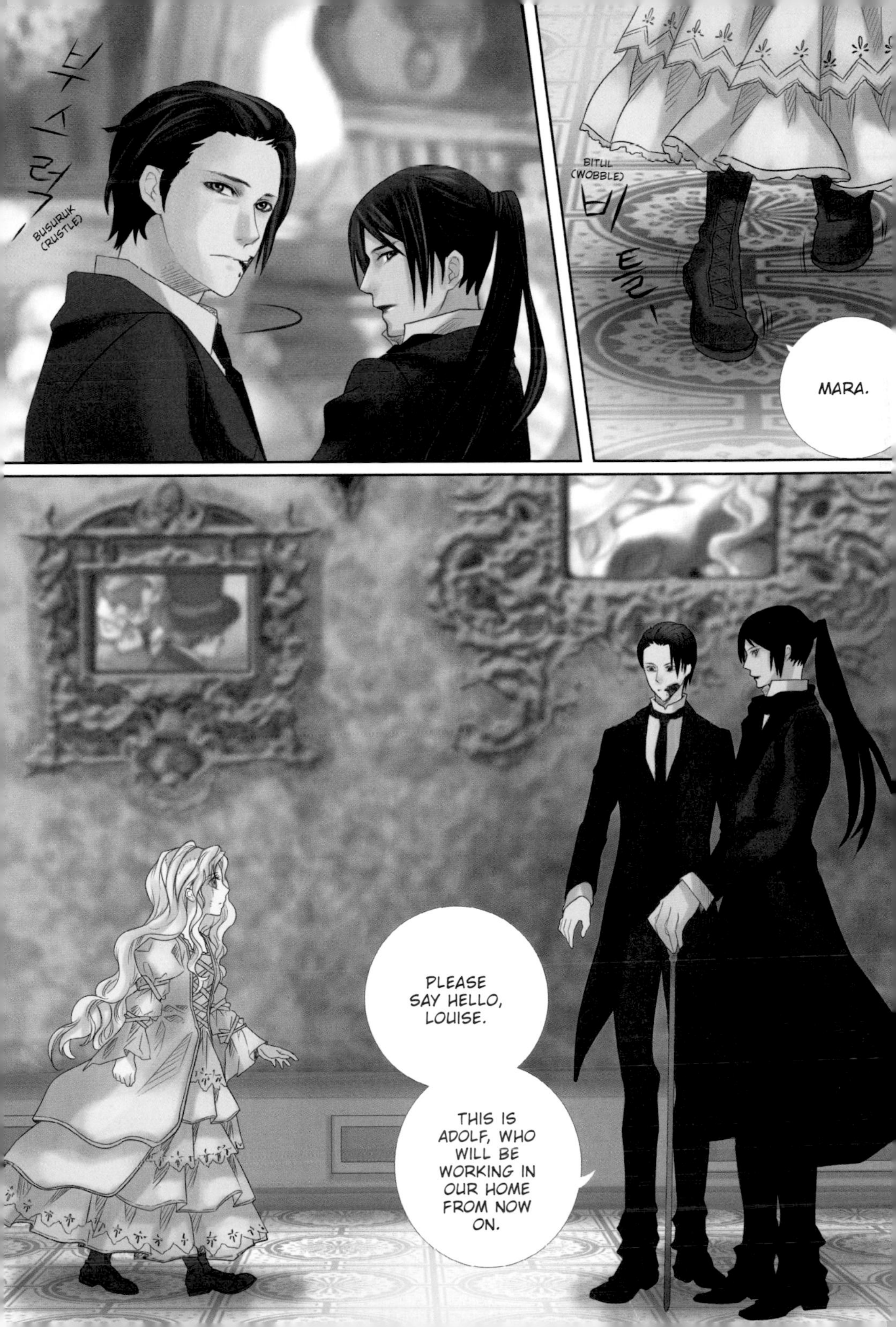
부스럭
BUSURUK (RUSTLE)
BITUL (WOBBLE)
비틀
MARA.
PLEASE SAY HELLO, LOUISE.
THIS IS ADOLF, WHO WILL BE WORKING IN OUR HOME FROM NOW ON.

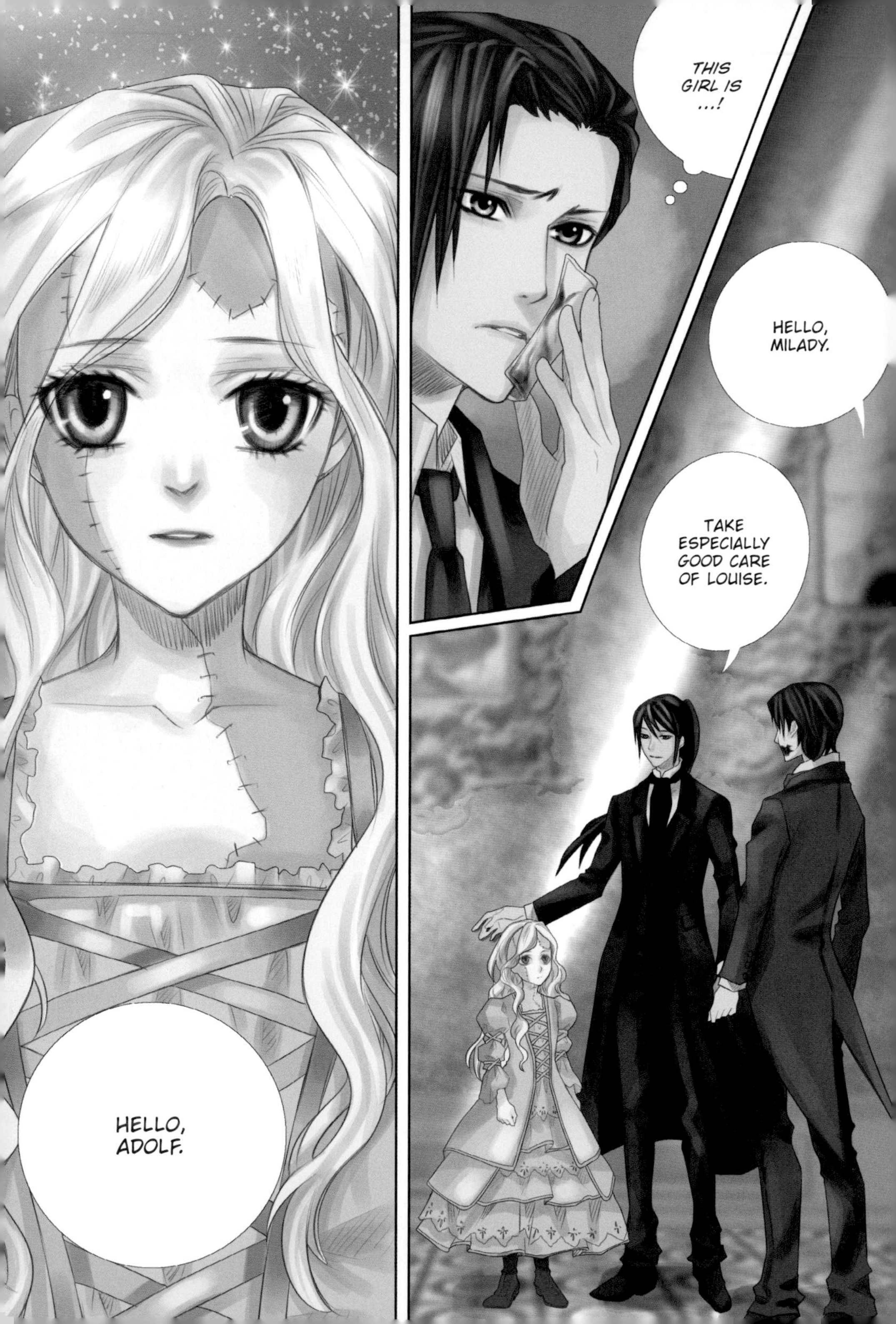
HELLO, ADOLF.
THIS GIRL IS ...!
HELLO, MILADY.
TAKE ESPECIALLY GOOD CARE OF LOUISE.

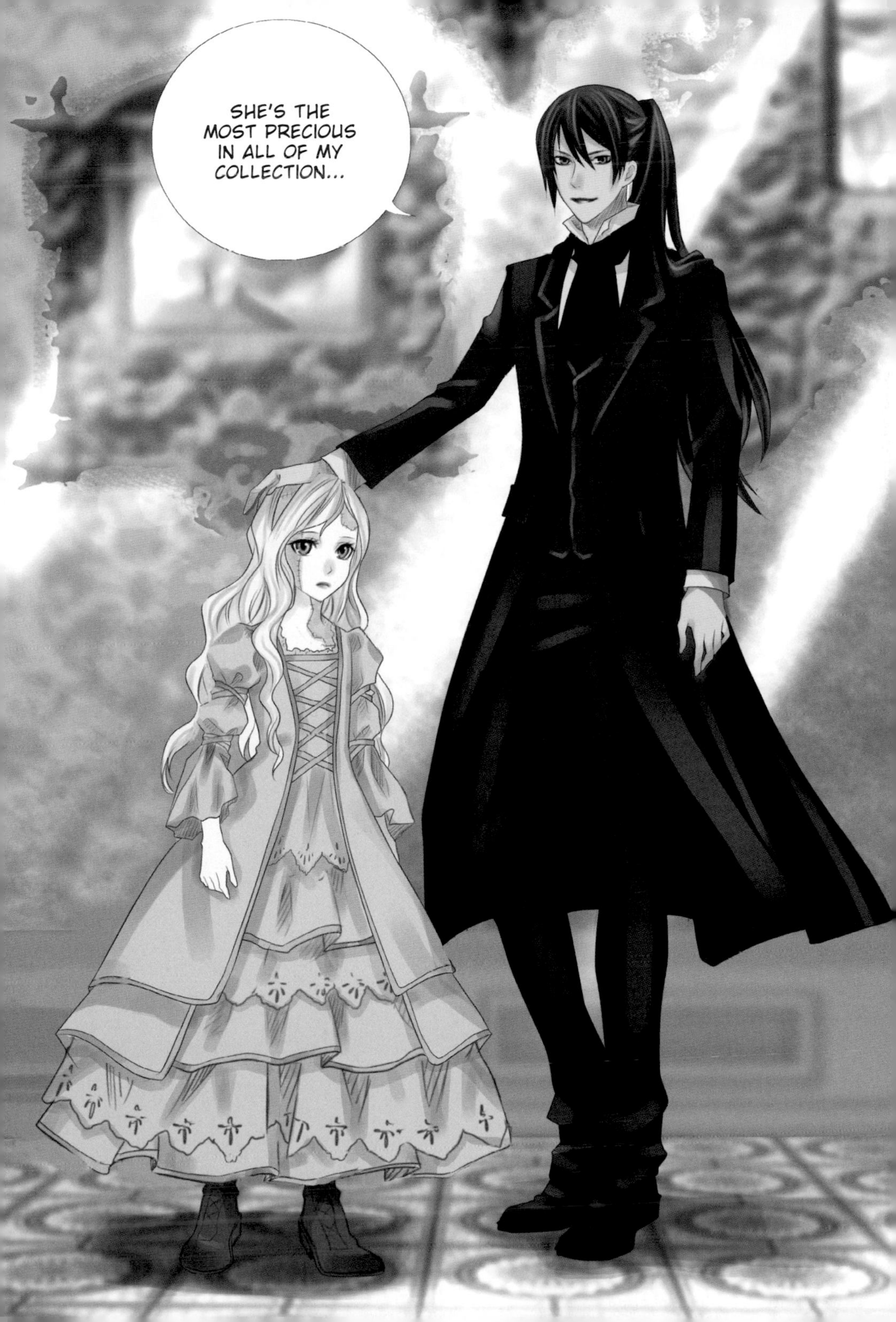
SHE'S THE MOST PRECIOUS IN ALL OF MY COLLECTION...

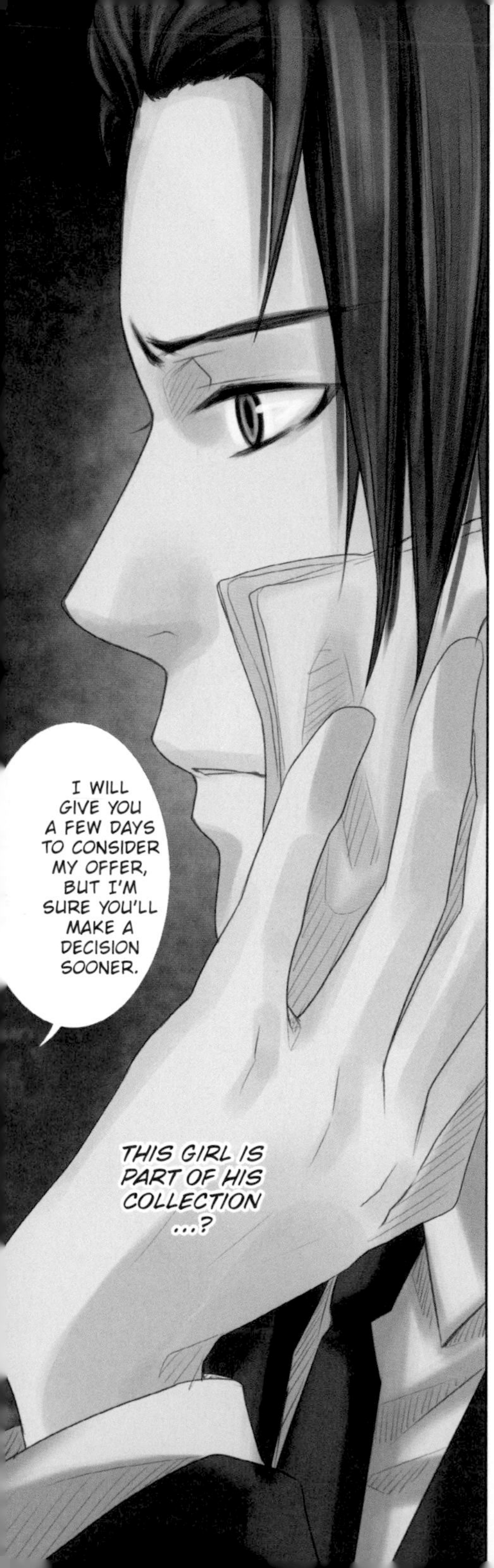
I WILL GIVE YOU A FEW DAYS TO CONSIDER MY OFFER, BUT I'M SURE YOU'LL MAKE A DECISION SOONER.
THIS GIRL IS PART OF HIS COLLECTION ...?
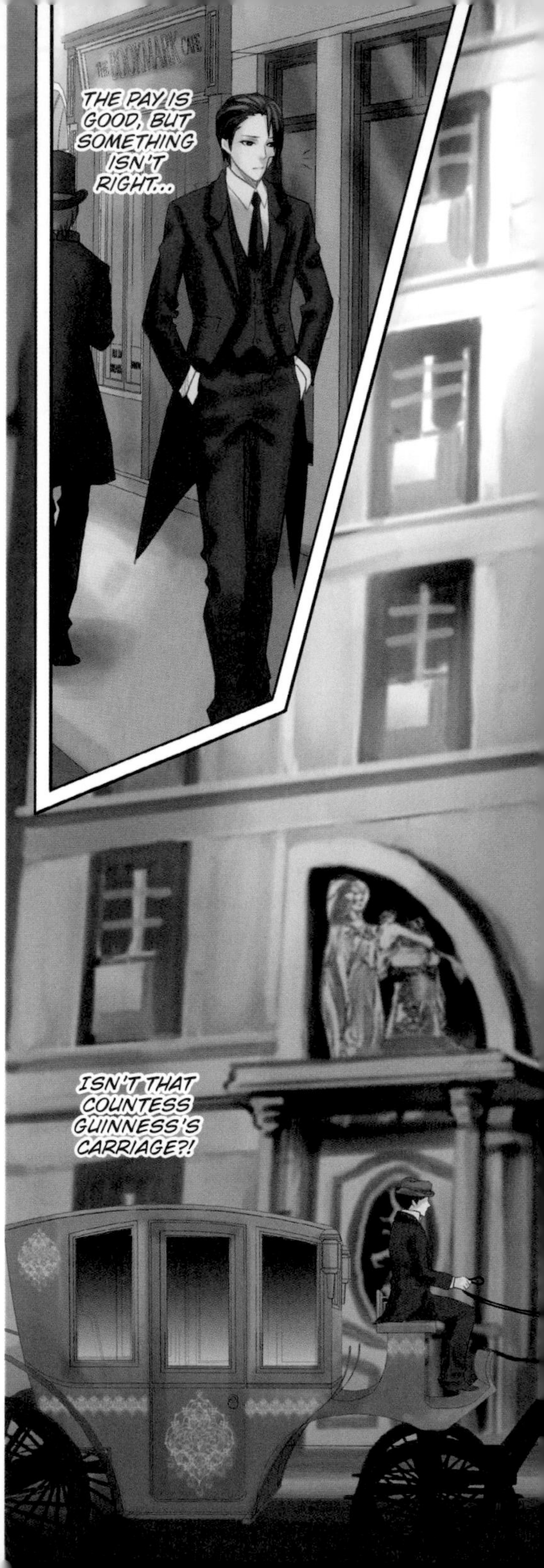
THE PAY IS GOOD, BUT SOMETHING ISN'T RIGHT...
ISN'T THAT COUNTESS GUINNESS'S CARRIAGE?!

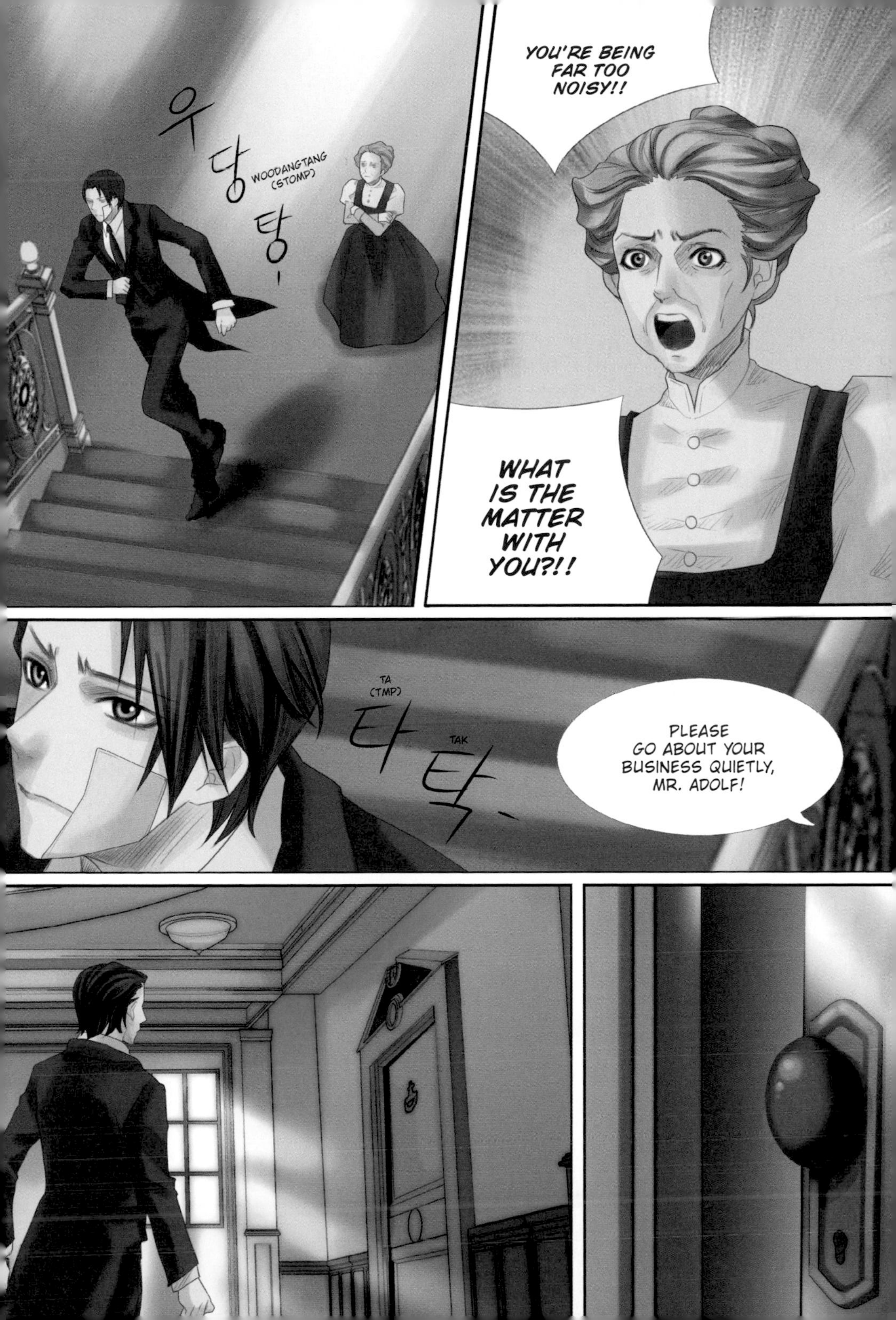

우당탕
WOODANGTANG (STOMP)
YOU'RE BEING FAR TOO NOISY!!
WHAT IS THE MATTER WITH YOU?!!
TA (TMP)
타
TAK
탁
PLEASE GO ABOUT YOUR BUSINESS QUIETLY, MR. ADOLF!

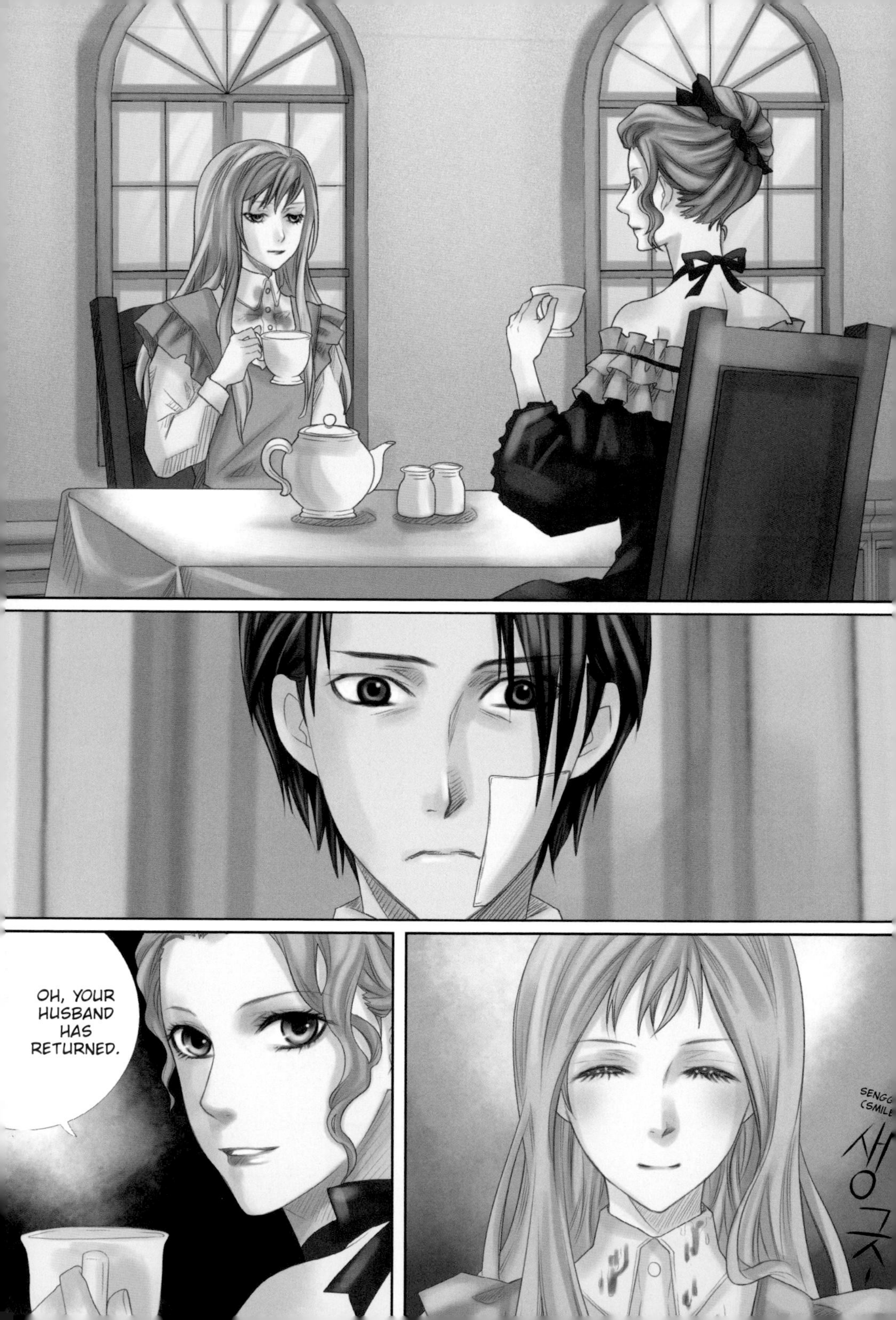
OH, YOUR HUSBAND HAS RETURNED.
SENGG
(SMILE

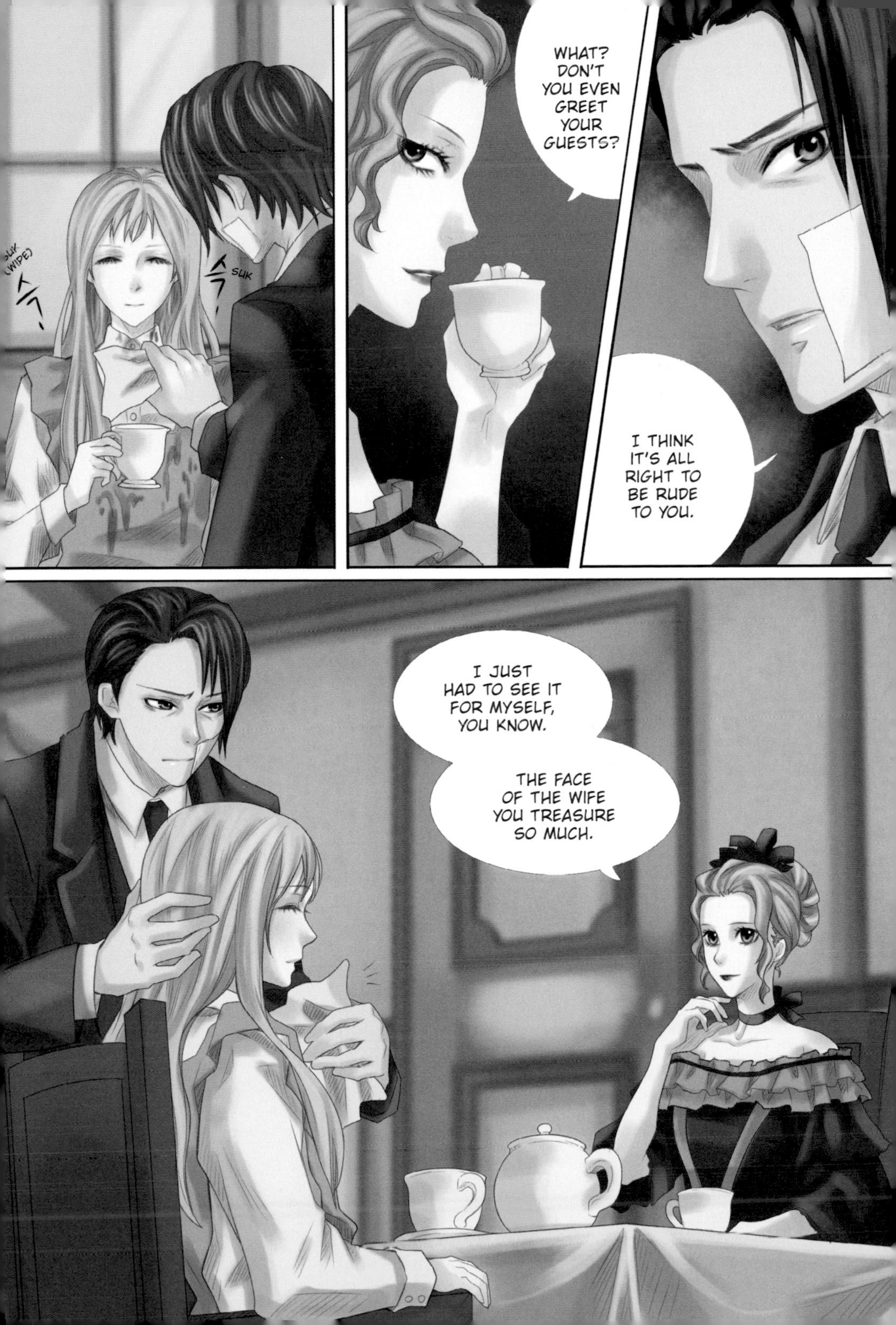
(WIPE)
SUK
WHAT? DON'T YOU EVEN GREET YOUR GUESTS?
I THINK IT'S ALL RIGHT TO BE RUDE TO YOU.
I JUST HAD TO SEE IT FOR MYSELF, YOU KNOW.
THE FACE OF THE WIFE YOU TREASURE SO MUCH.

THOUGH SHE'S NOT THE BEAUTY SHE ONCE WAS, SHE'S STILL LOVELY.
MARI DE ROBERTI, THE ONLY DAUGHTER OF MARQUIS DE ROBERTI. SHE DISAPPEARED THREE YEARS AGO UNDER THE PREMISE OF TRAVELING IN THE COUNTRY FOR HER HEALTH, BUT SHE WAS NEVER SEEN AGAIN.
ABOUT A YEAR AGO, I WAS INVITED TO MARQUIS DE ROBERTI'S MANOR AND GLIMPSED HER PORTRAIT. I REMEMBERED HER BECAUSE SHE WAS SO BEAUTIFUL.
MUMCHIT (PAUSE)
멈칫

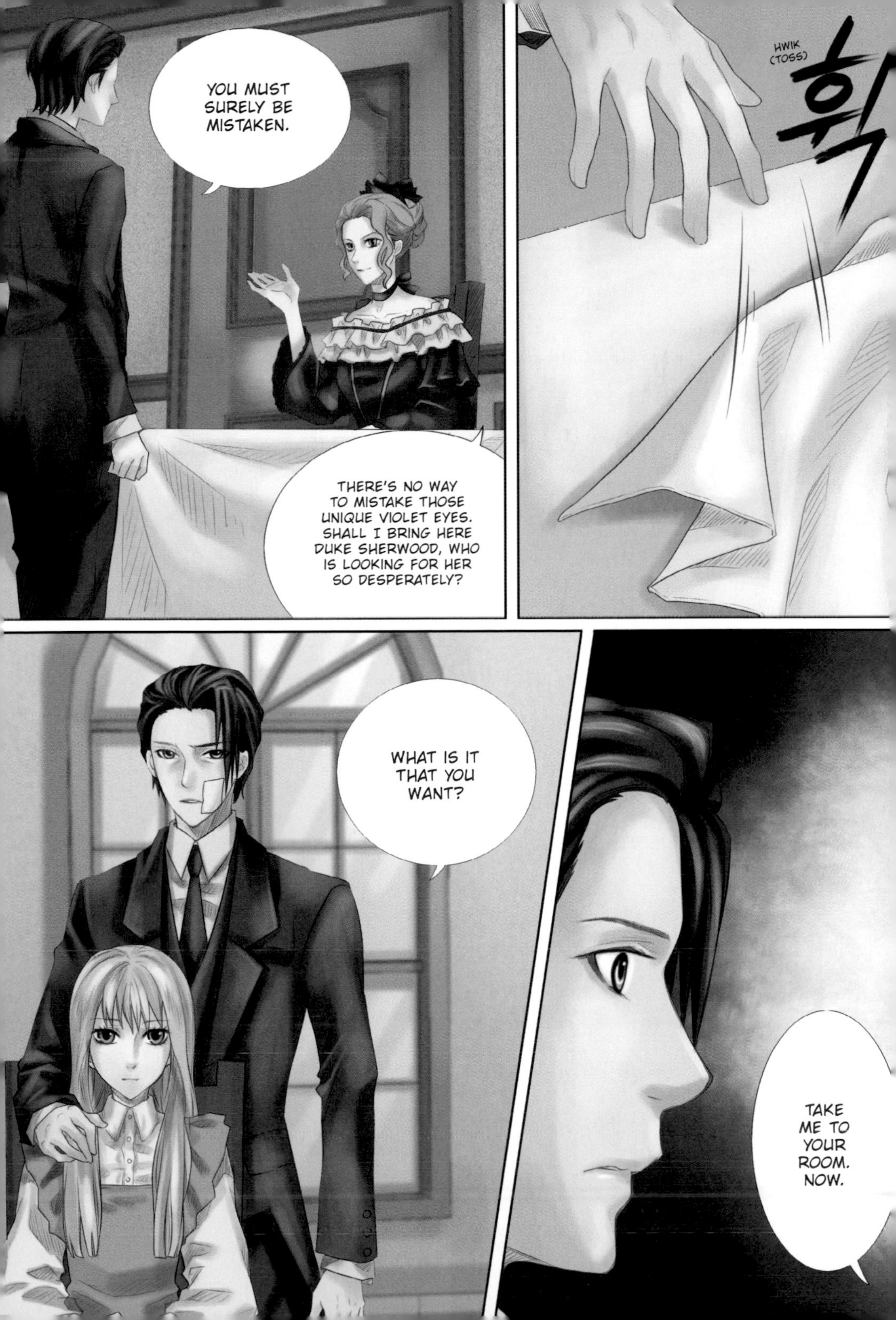
YOU MUST SURELY BE MISTAKEN.
THERE'S NO WAY TO MISTAKE THOSE UNIQUE VIOLET EYES. SHALL I BRING HERE DUKE SHERWOOD, WHO IS LOOKING FOR HER SO DESPERATELY?
HWIK (TOSS)
휙
WHAT IS IT THAT YOU WANT?
TAKE ME TO YOUR ROOM. NOW.

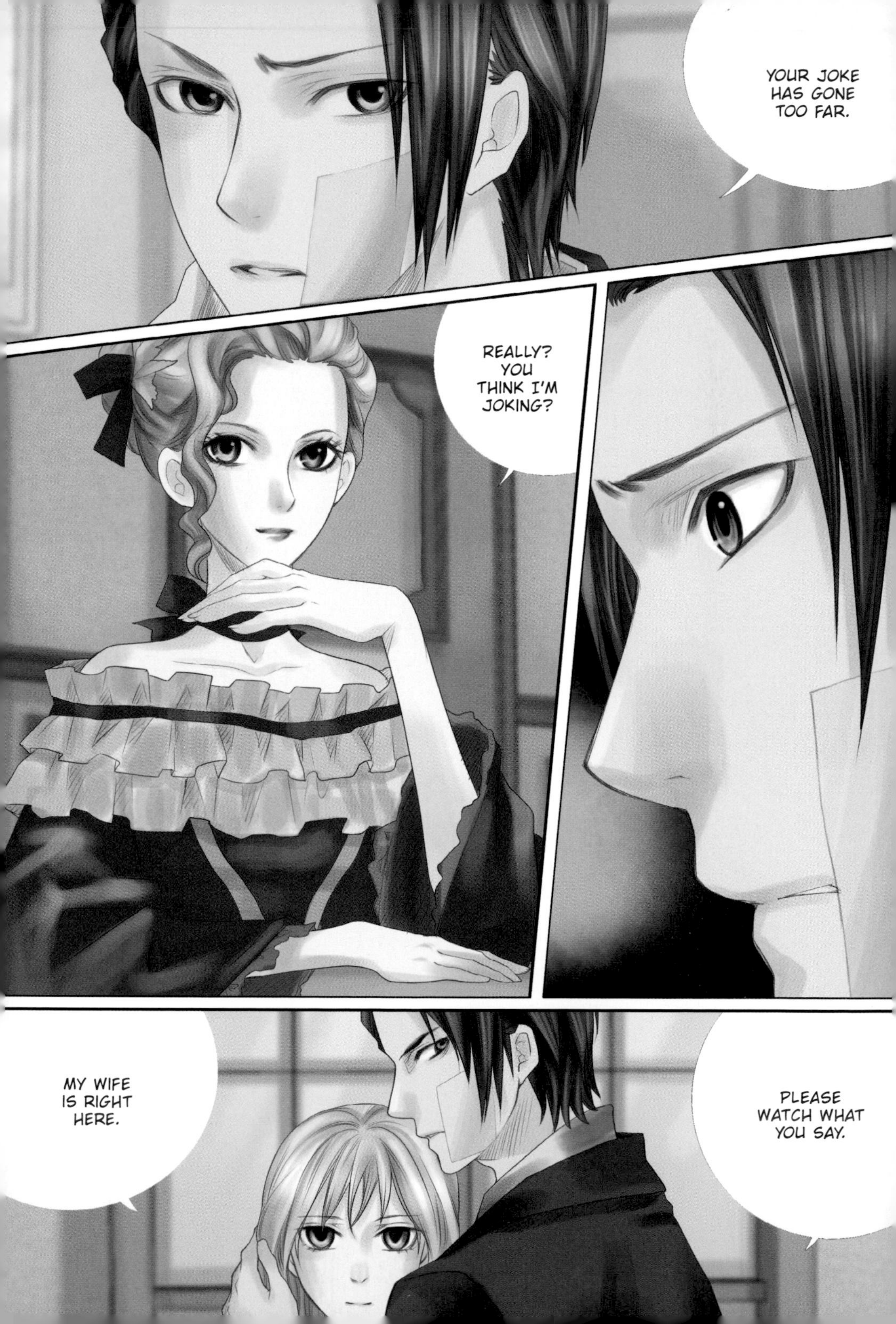
YOUR JOKE HAS GONE TOO FAR.
REALLY? YOU THINK I'M JOKING?
MY WIFE IS RIGHT HERE.
PLEASE WATCH WHAT YOU SAY.

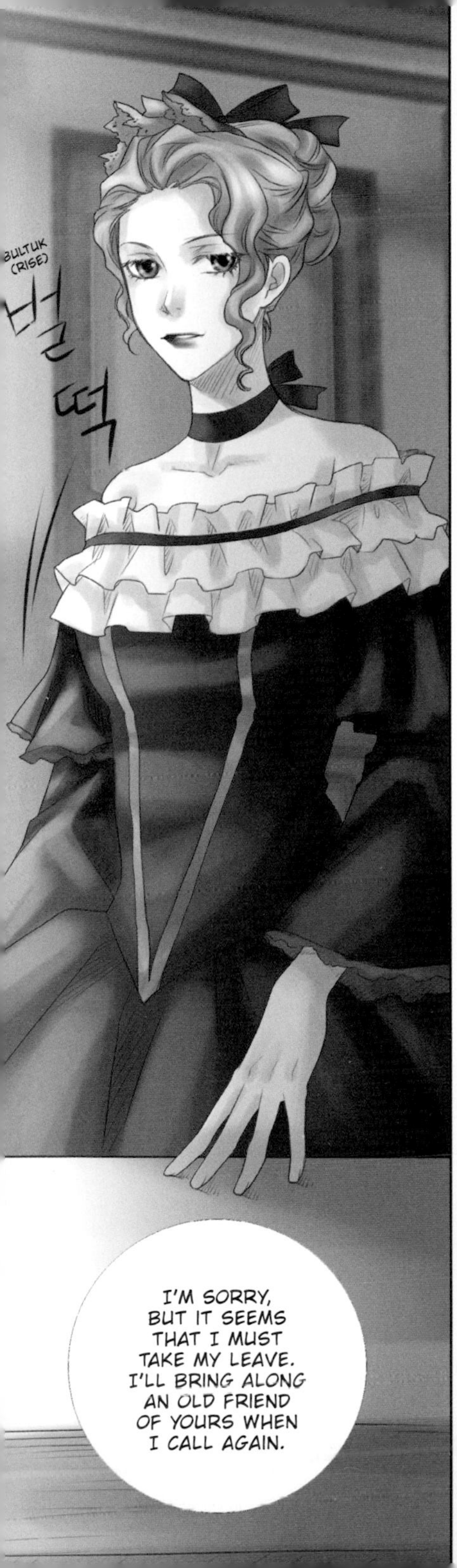
BULTUK (RISE)
벌떡
I'M SORRY, BUT IT SEEMS THAT I MUST TAKE MY LEAVE. I'LL BRING ALONG AN OLD FRIEND OF YOURS WHEN I CALL AGAIN.
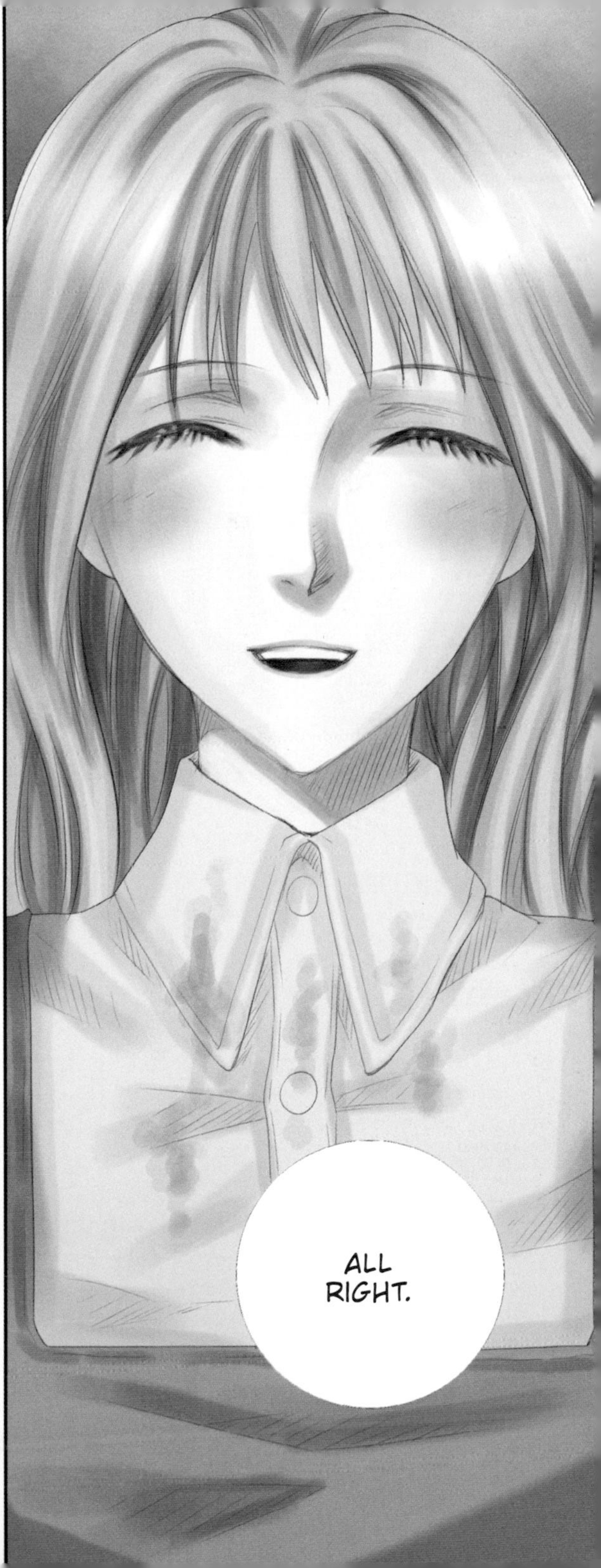
ALL RIGHT.

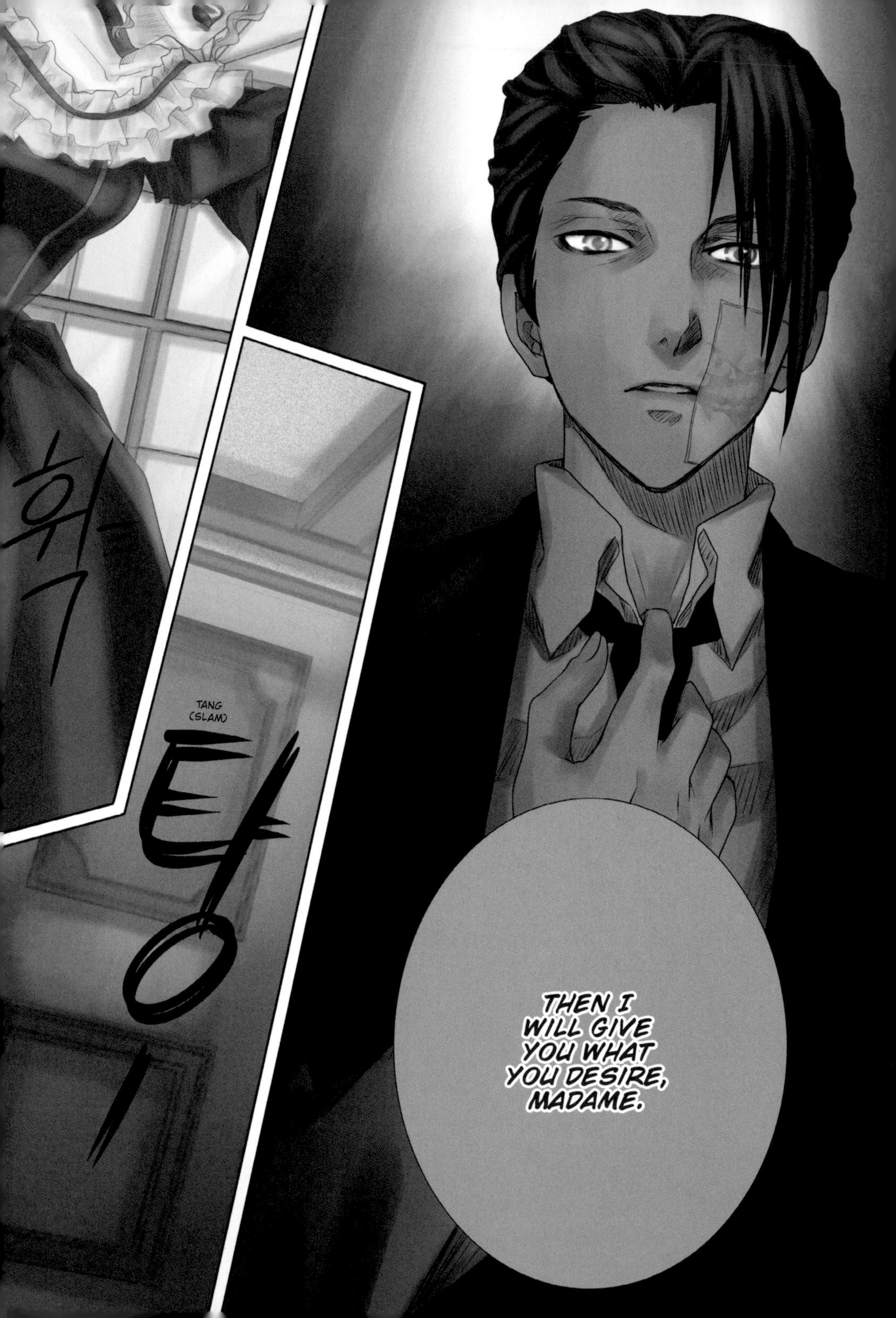
휙—
TANG (SLAM)
탕—
THEN I WILL GIVE YOU WHAT YOU DESIRE, MADAME.

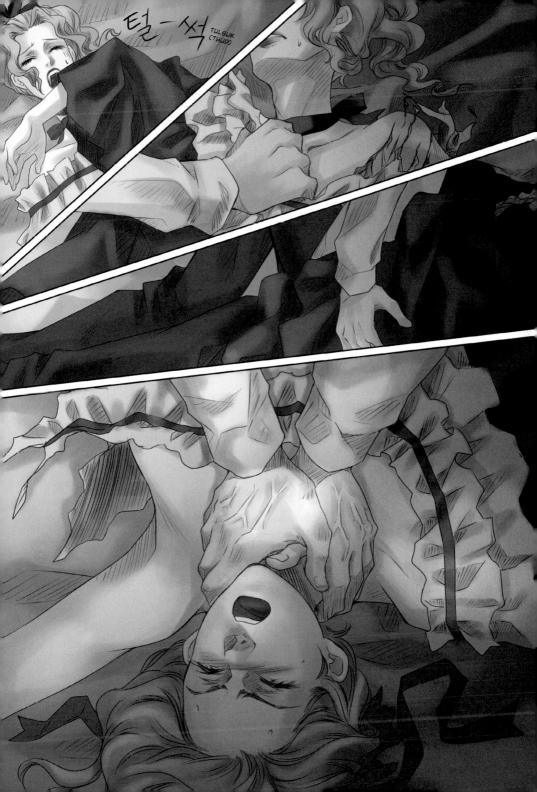

툴—썩
TULGUK
(THUD)

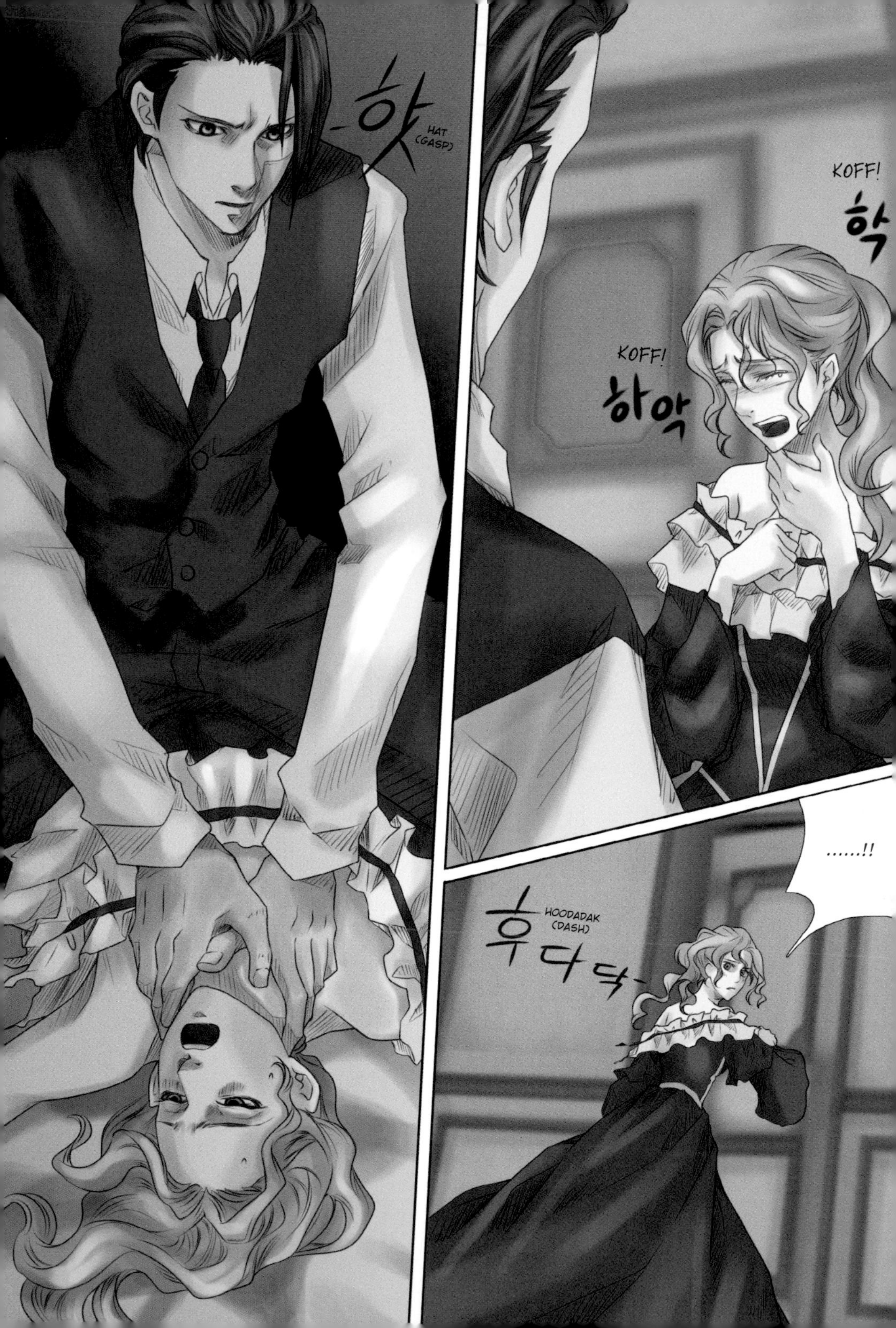

핫
HAT (GASP)
KOFF!
학
KOFF!
하악
후다닥
HOODADAK (DASH)
......!!

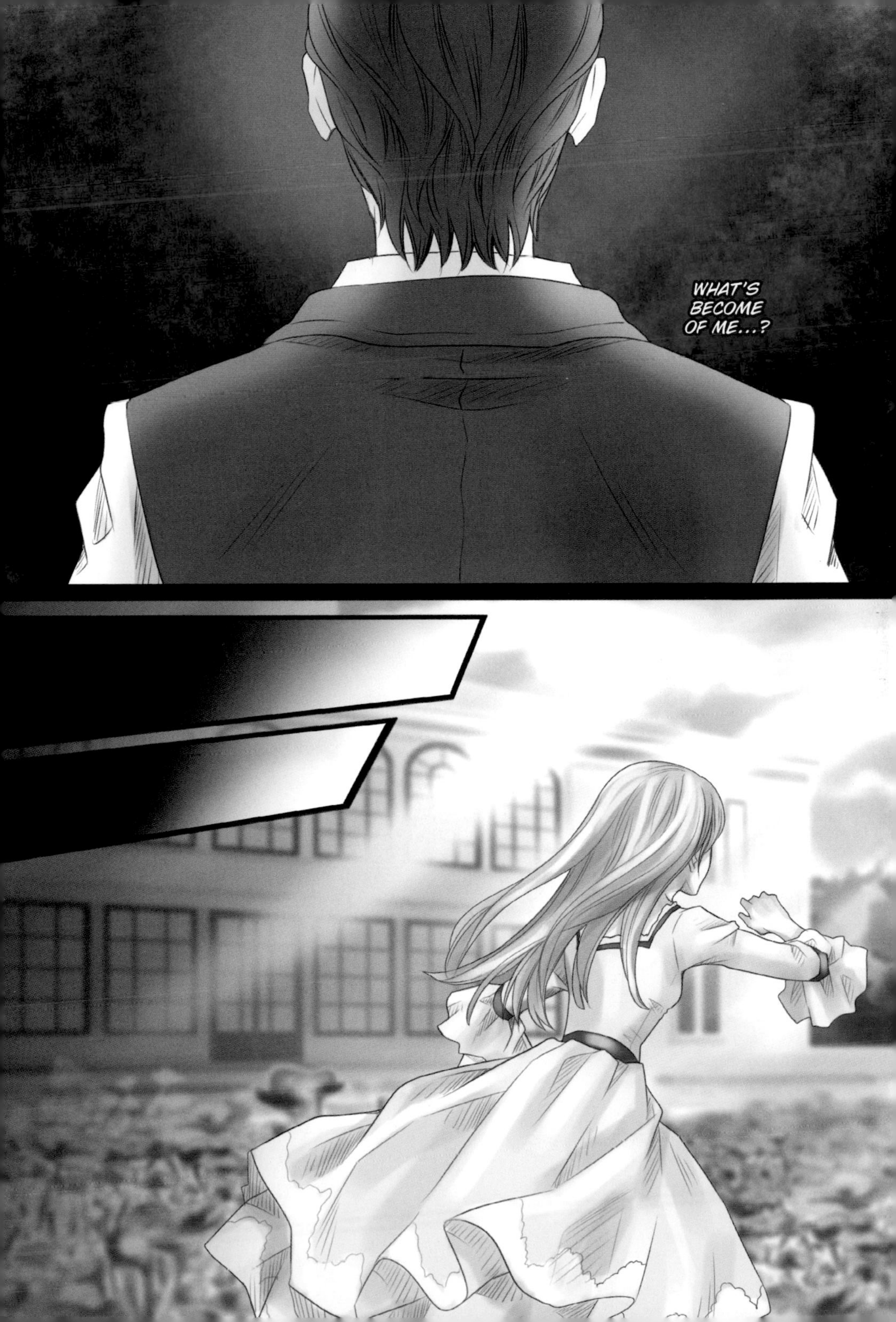
WHAT'S BECOME OF ME...?

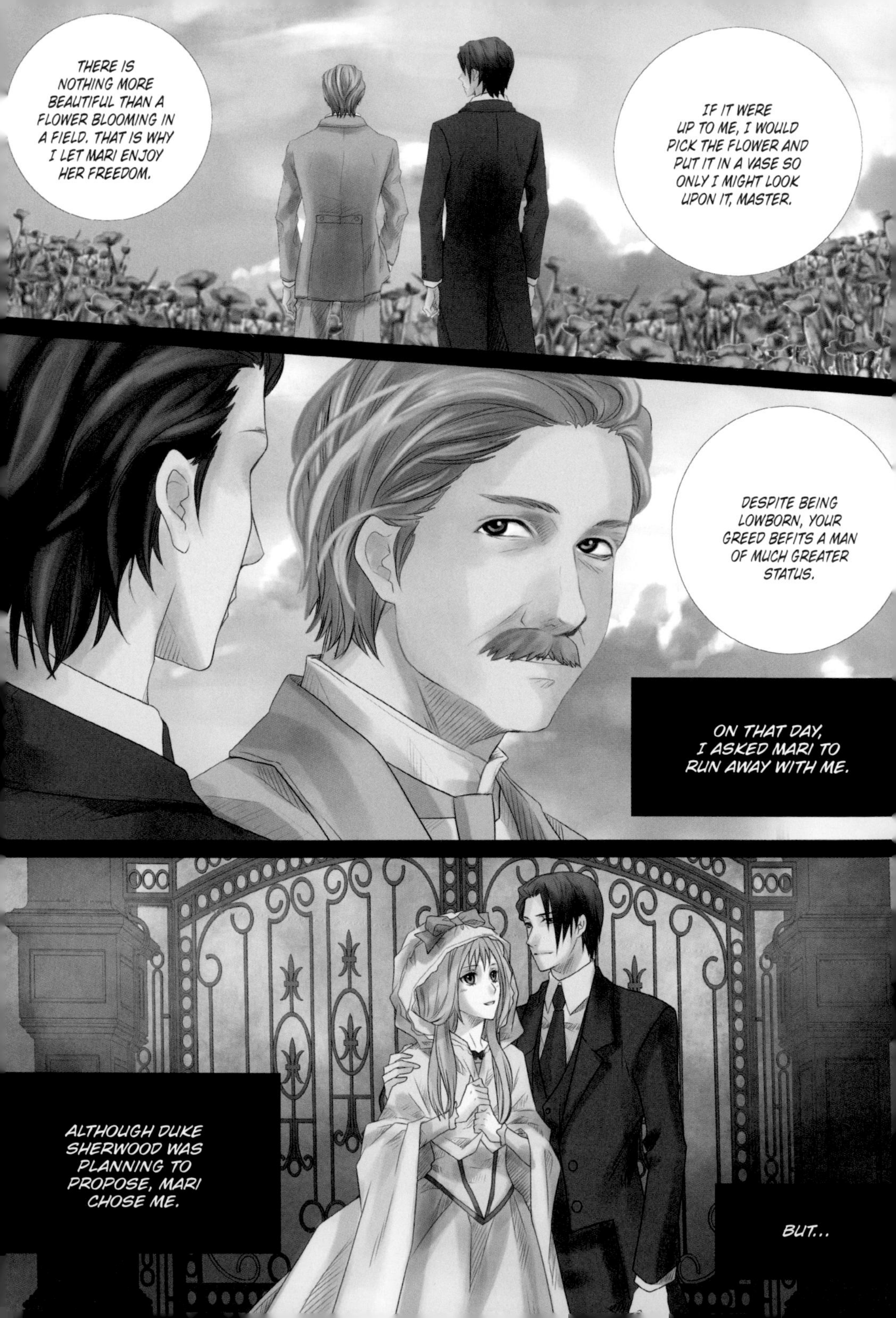
THERE IS NOTHING MORE BEAUTIFUL THAN A FLOWER BLOOMING IN A FIELD. THAT IS WHY I LET MARI ENJOY HER FREEDOM.
IF IT WERE UP TO ME, I WOULD PICK THE FLOWER AND PUT IT IN A VASE SO ONLY I MIGHT LOOK UPON IT, MASTER.
DESPITE BEING LOWBORN, YOUR GREED BEFITS A MAN OF MUCH GREATER STATUS.
ON THAT DAY, I ASKED MARI TO RUN AWAY WITH ME.
ALTHOUGH DUKE SHERWOOD WAS PLANNING TO PROPOSE, MARI CHOSE ME.
BUT...

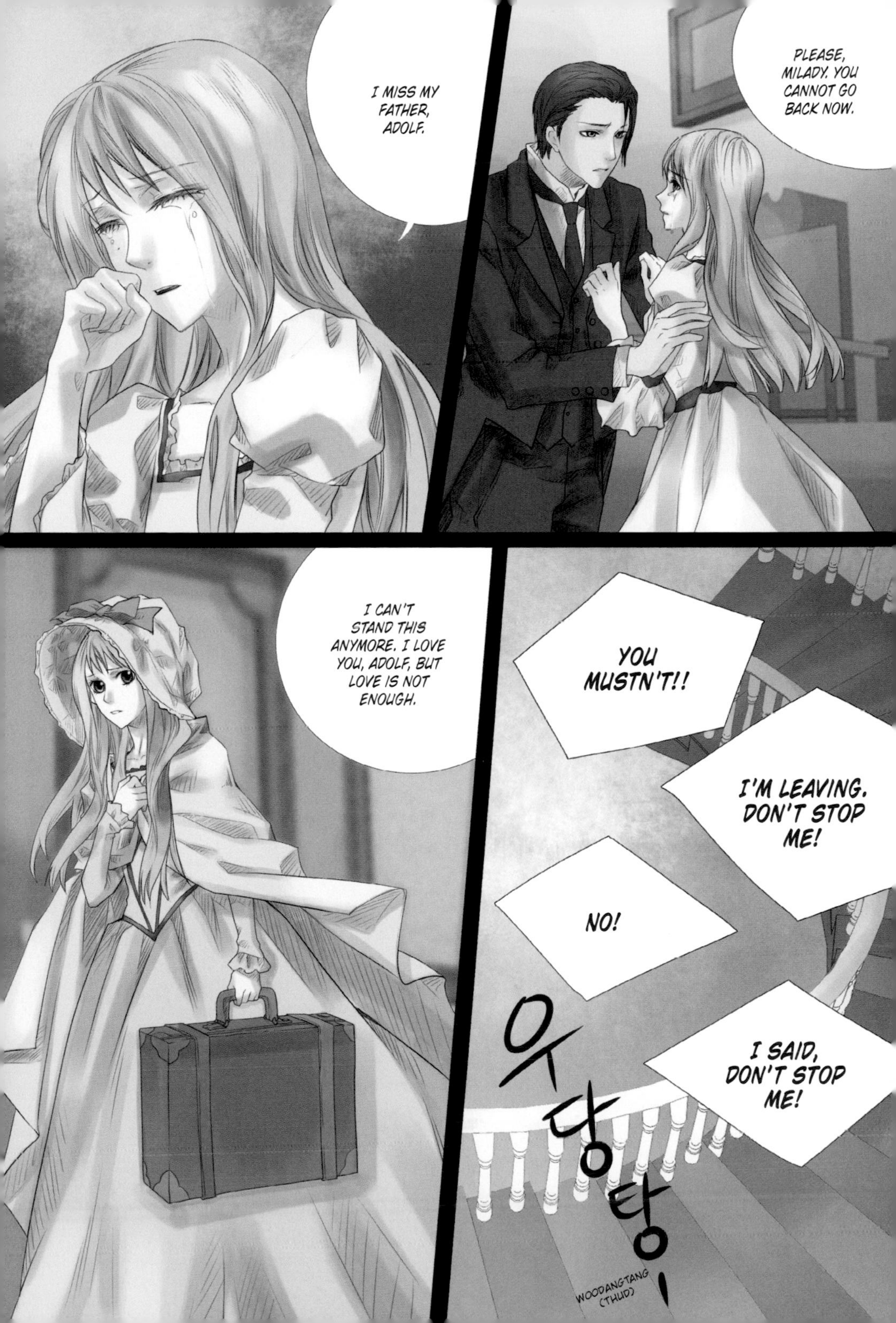
I MISS MY FATHER, ADOLF.
PLEASE, MILADY. YOU CANNOT GO BACK NOW.
I CAN'T STAND THIS ANYMORE. I LOVE YOU, ADOLF, BUT LOVE IS NOT ENOUGH.
YOU MUSTN'T!!
I'M LEAVING. DON'T STOP ME!
NO!
I SAID, DON'T STOP ME!
우당탕
WOODANGTANG (THUD)

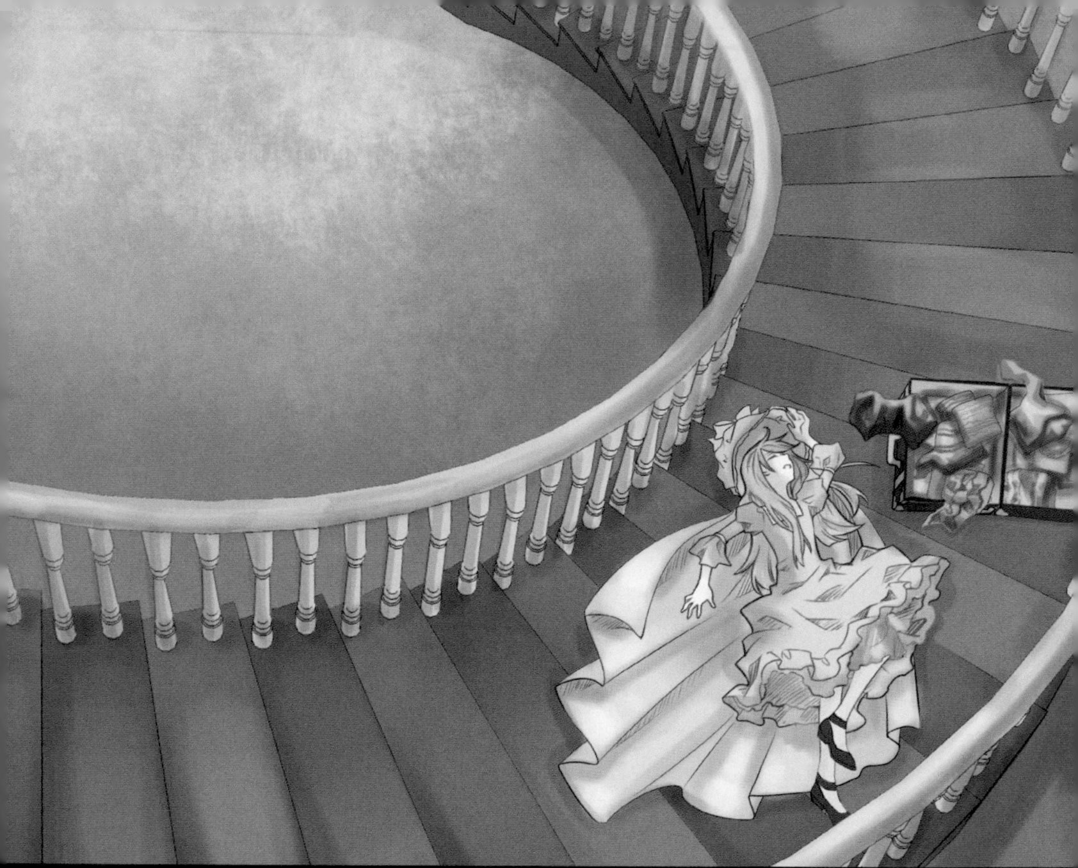
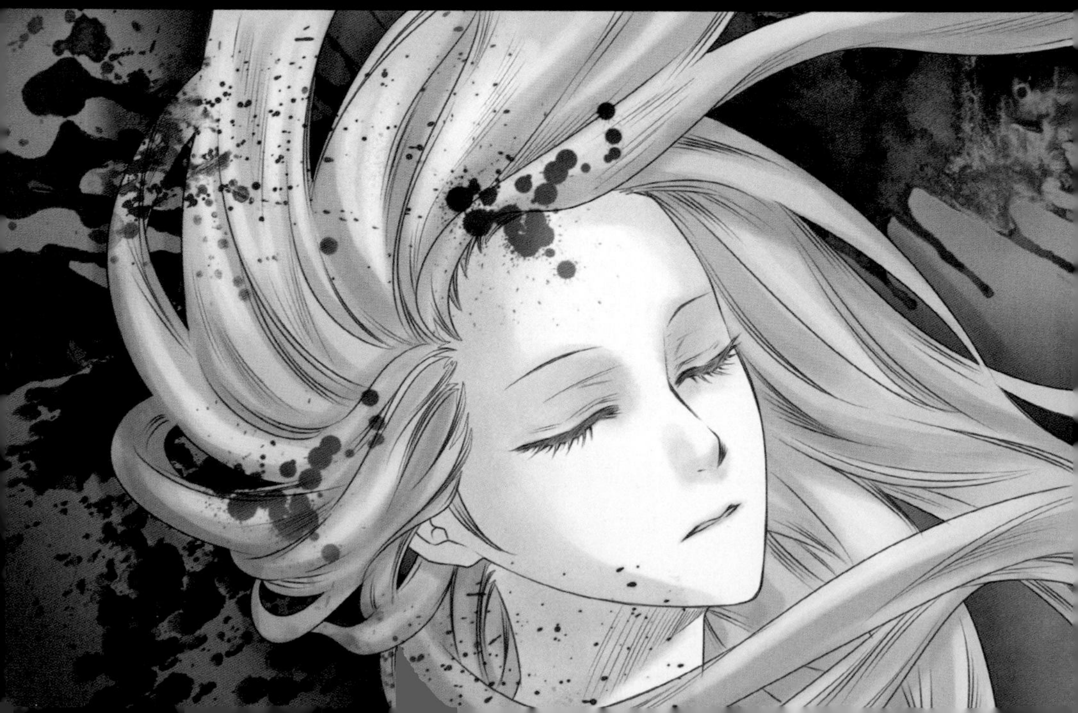

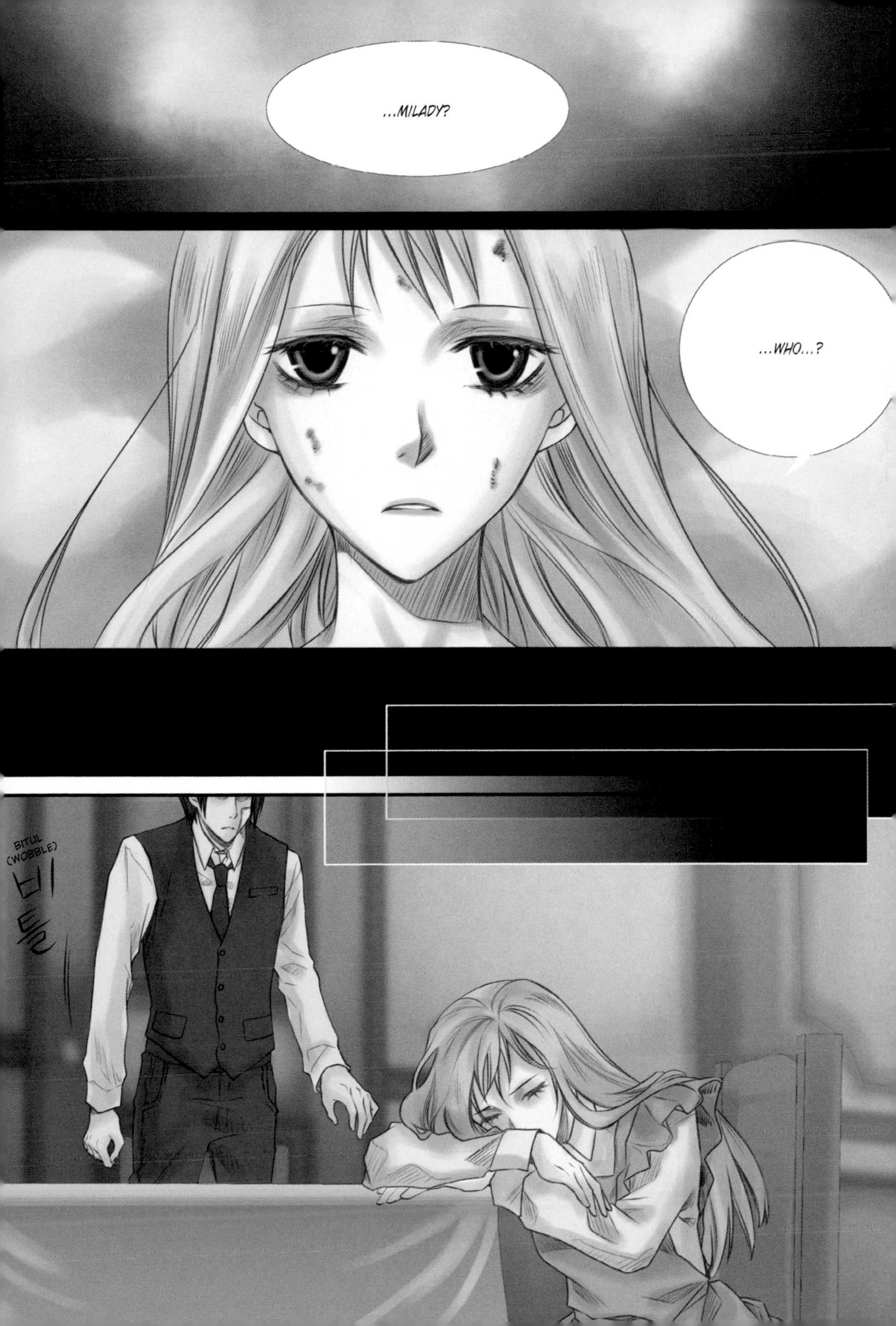
...MILADY?
...WHO...?
BITUL (WOBBLE)
비틀

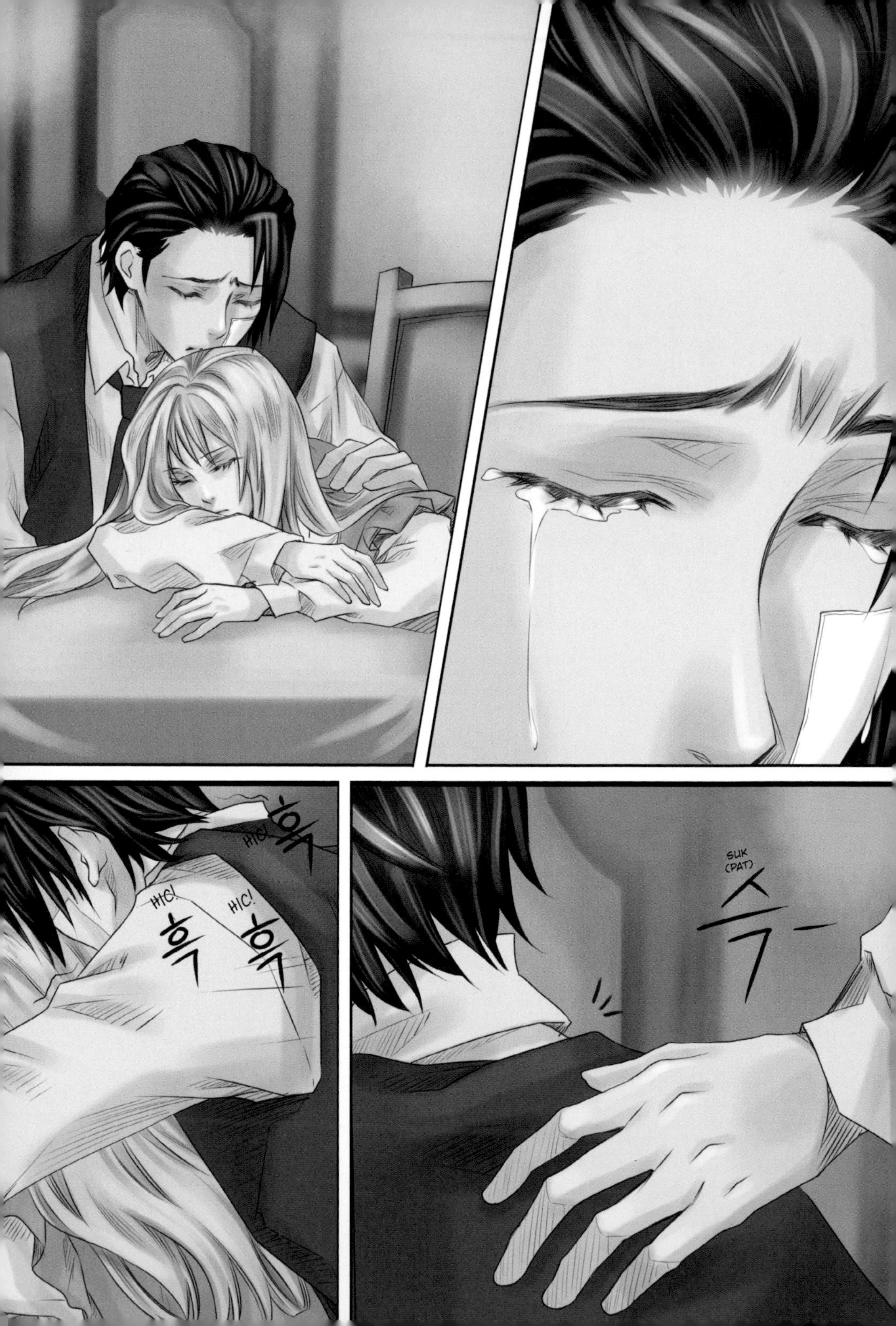
HIC!
흑
HIC!
흑
HIC!
흑
SUK (PAT)
슥

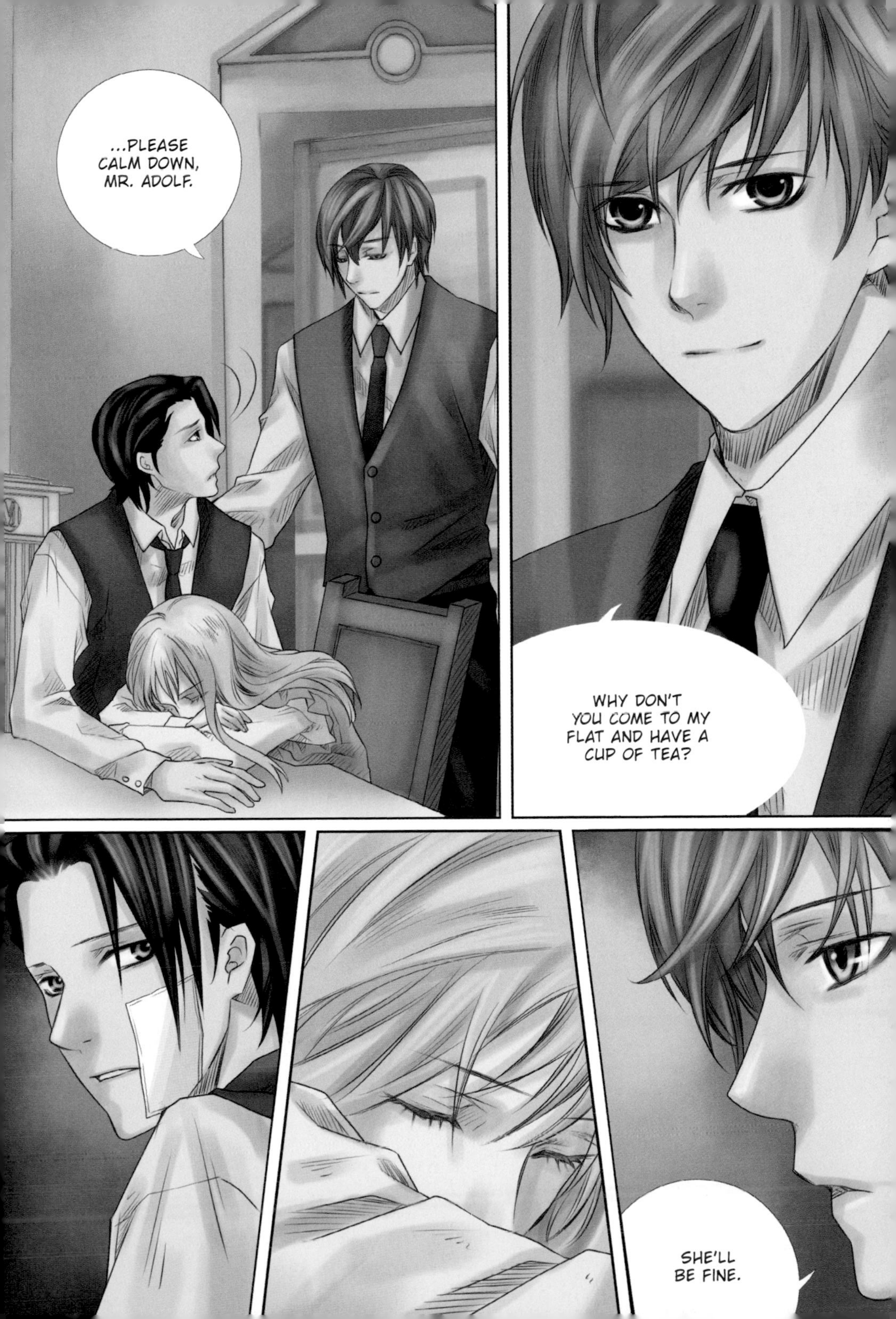
...PLEASE CALM DOWN, MR. ADOLF.
WHY DON'T YOU COME TO MY FLAT AND HAVE A CUP OF TEA?
SHE'LL BE FINE.

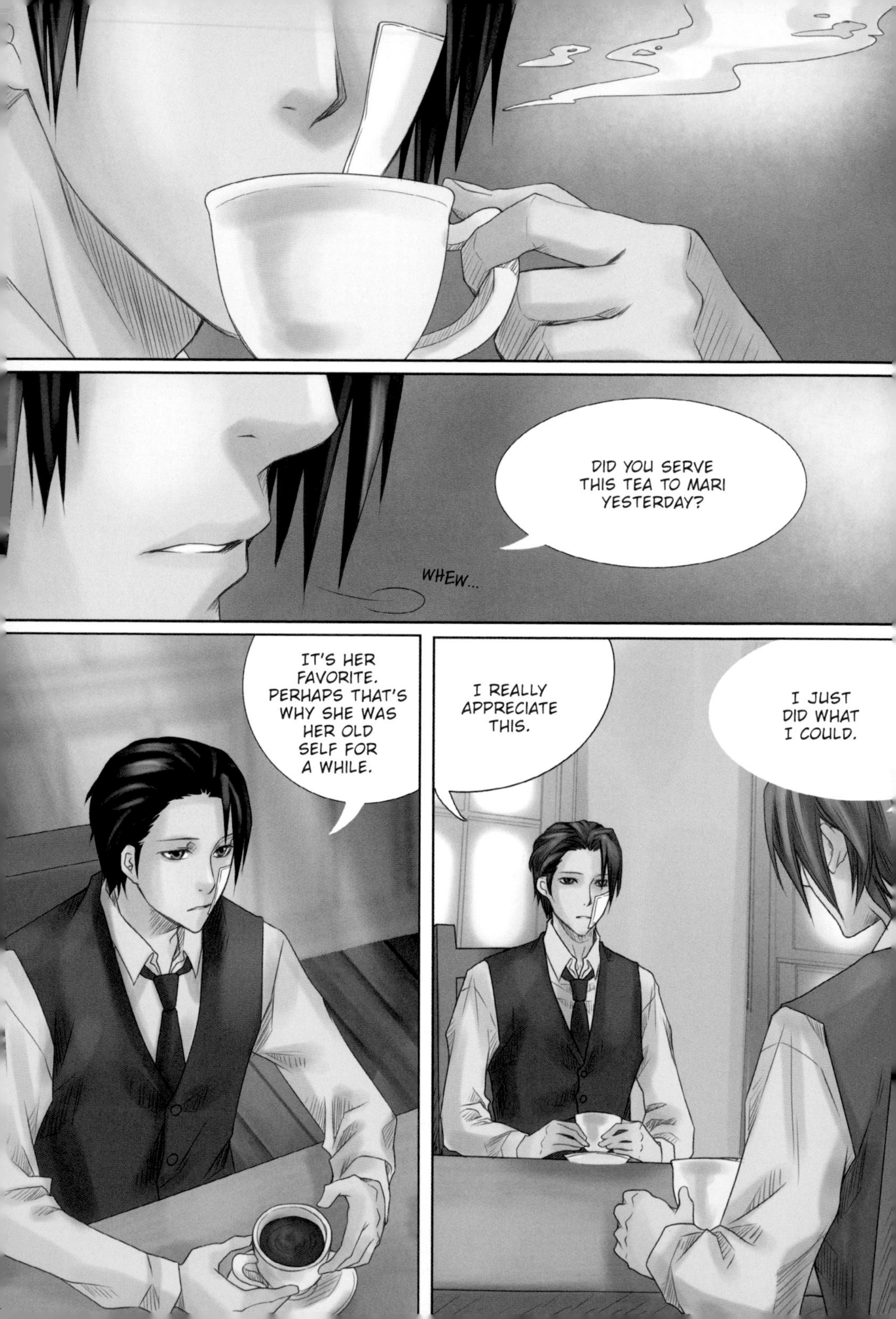
DID YOU SERVE THIS TEA TO MARI YESTERDAY?
WHEW...
IT'S HER FAVORITE. PERHAPS THAT'S WHY SHE WAS HER OLD SELF FOR A WHILE.
I REALLY APPRECIATE THIS.
I JUST DID WHAT I COULD.

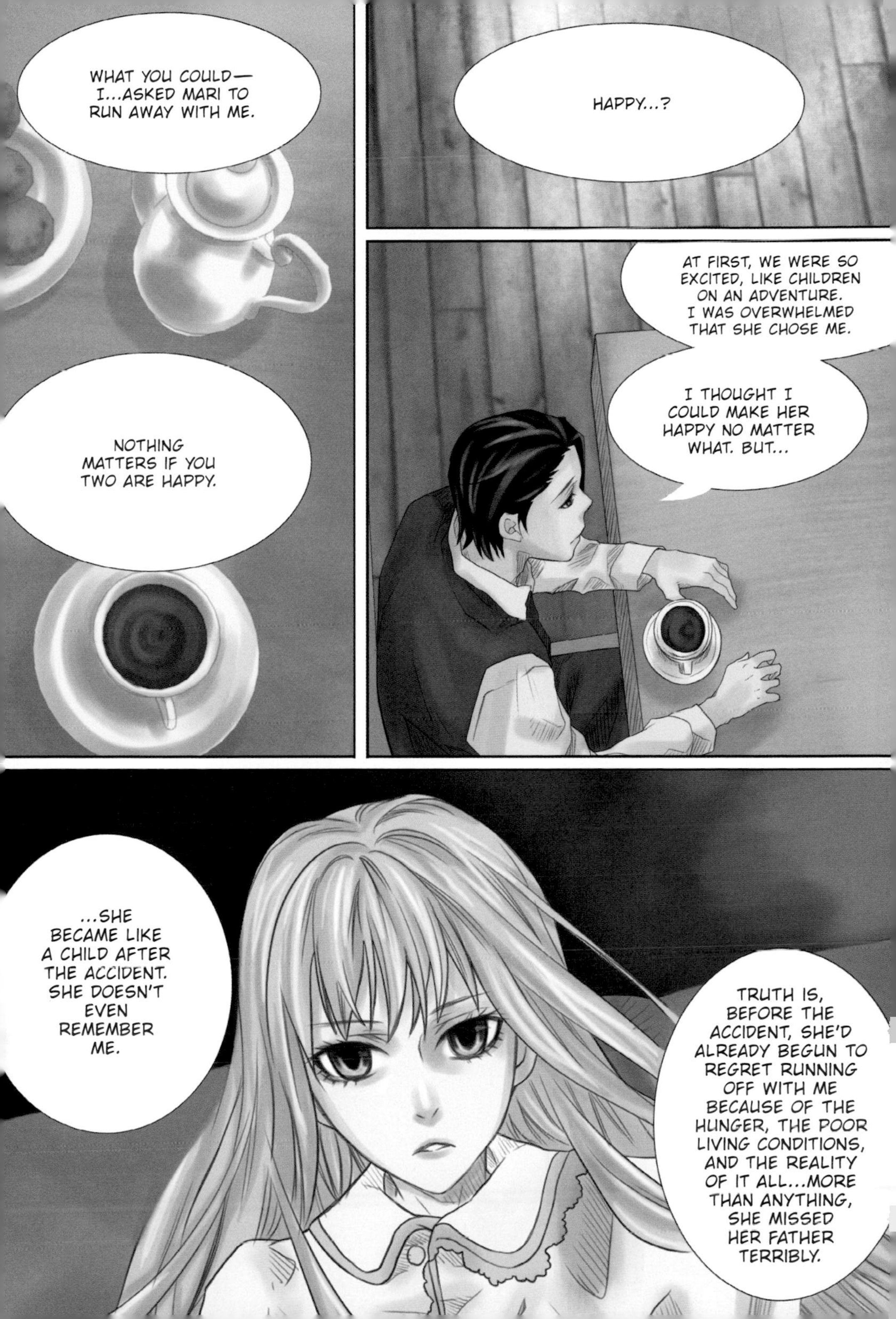
WHAT YOU COULD— I...ASKED MARI TO RUN AWAY WITH ME.
NOTHING MATTERS IF YOU TWO ARE HAPPY.
HAPPY...?
AT FIRST, WE WERE SO EXCITED, LIKE CHILDREN ON AN ADVENTURE. I WAS OVERWHELMED THAT SHE CHOSE ME.
I THOUGHT I COULD MAKE HER HAPPY NO MATTER WHAT. BUT...
...SHE BECAME LIKE A CHILD AFTER THE ACCIDENT. SHE DOESN'T EVEN REMEMBER ME.
TRUTH IS, BEFORE THE ACCIDENT, SHE'D ALREADY BEGUN TO REGRET RUNNING OFF WITH ME BECAUSE OF THE HUNGER, THE POOR LIVING CONDITIONS, AND THE REALITY OF IT ALL...MORE THAN ANYTHING, SHE MISSED HER FATHER TERRIBLY.

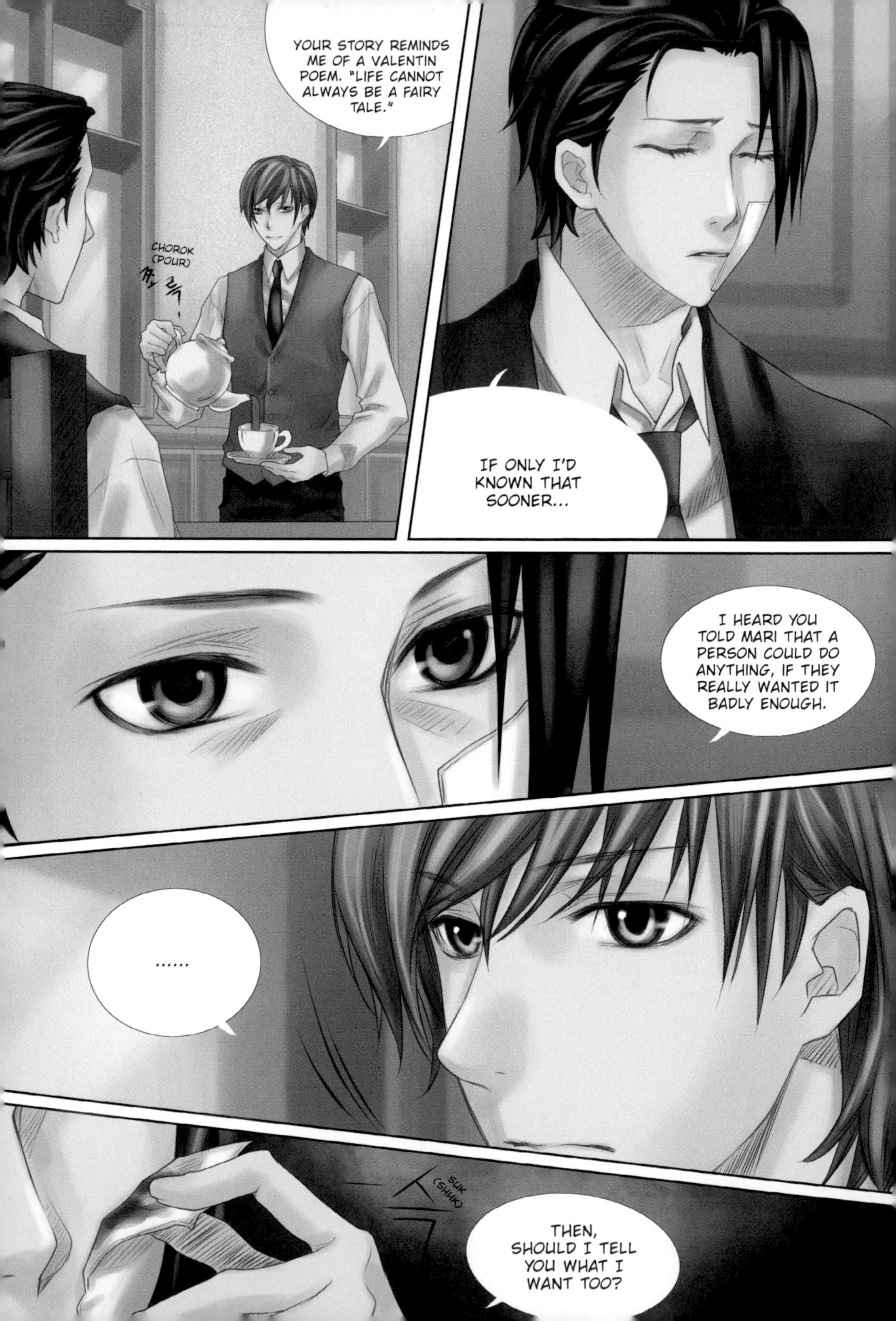
YOUR STORY REMINDS ME OF A VALENTIN POEM. "LIFE CANNOT ALWAYS BE A FAIRY TALE."
CHOROK (POUR)
IF ONLY I'D KNOWN THAT SOONER...
I HEARD YOU TOLD MARI THAT A PERSON COULD DO ANYTHING, IF THEY REALLY WANTED IT BADLY ENOUGH.
......
SUK (SHHK)
THEN, SHOULD I TELL YOU WHAT I WANT TOO?

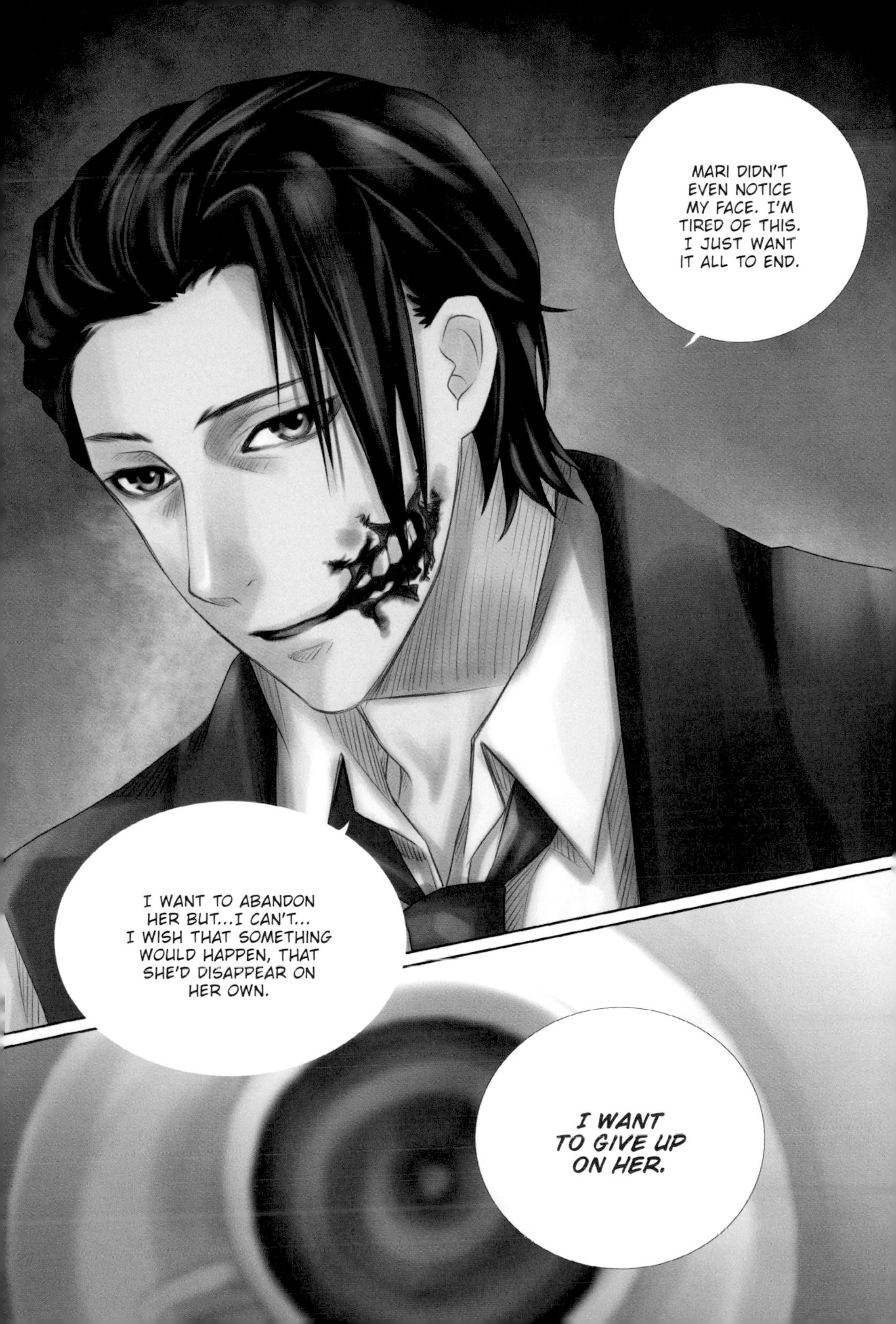
MARI DIDN'T EVEN NOTICE MY FACE. I'M TIRED OF THIS. I JUST WANT IT ALL TO END.
I WANT TO ABANDON HER BUT...I CAN'T... I WISH THAT SOMETHING WOULD HAPPEN, THAT SHE'D DISAPPEAR ON HER OWN.
I WANT TO GIVE UP ON HER.

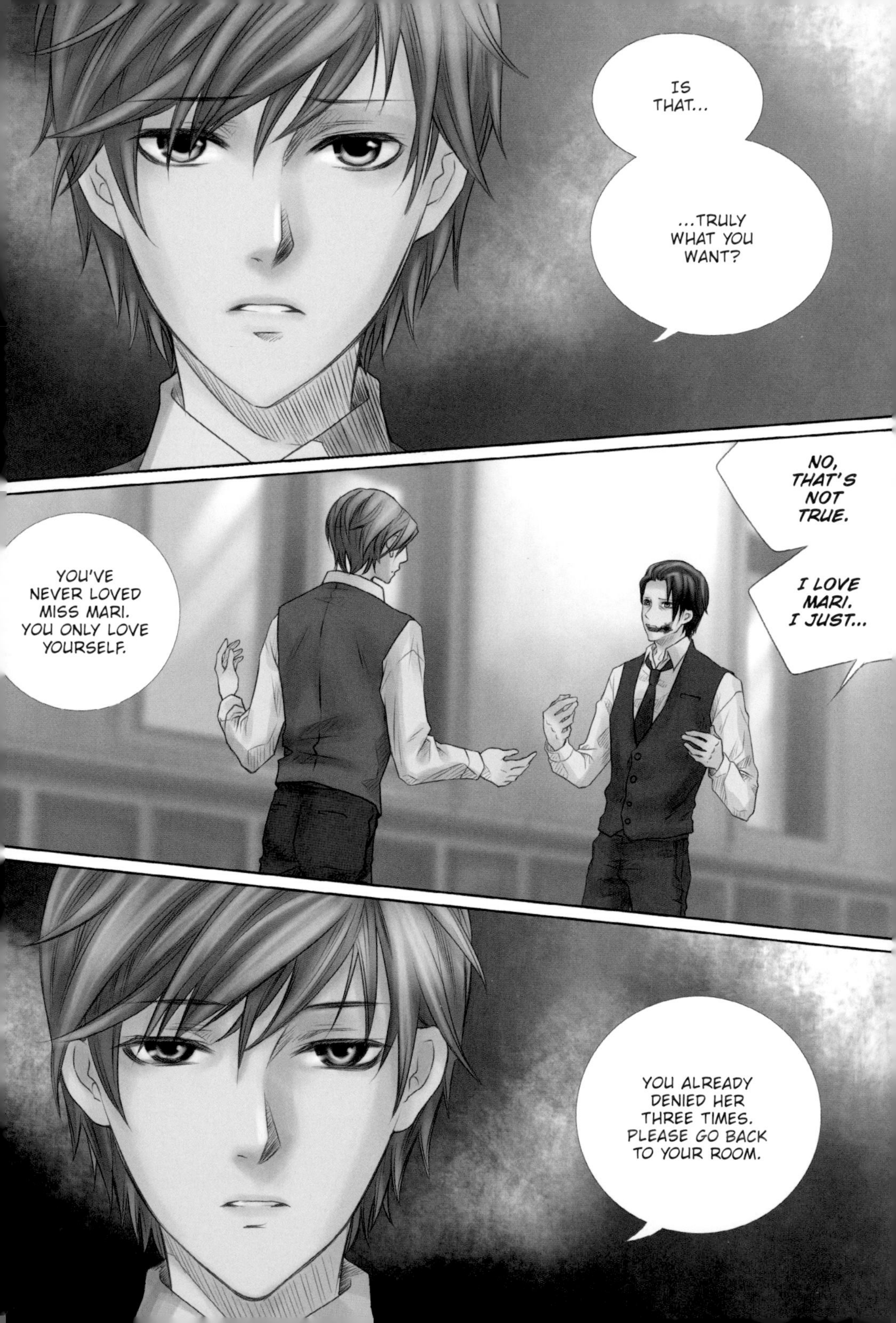
IS THAT...
...TRULY WHAT YOU WANT?
YOU'VE NEVER LOVED MISS MARI. YOU ONLY LOVE YOURSELF.
NO, THAT'S NOT TRUE.
I LOVE MARI. I JUST...
YOU ALREADY DENIED HER THREE TIMES. PLEASE GO BACK TO YOUR ROOM.

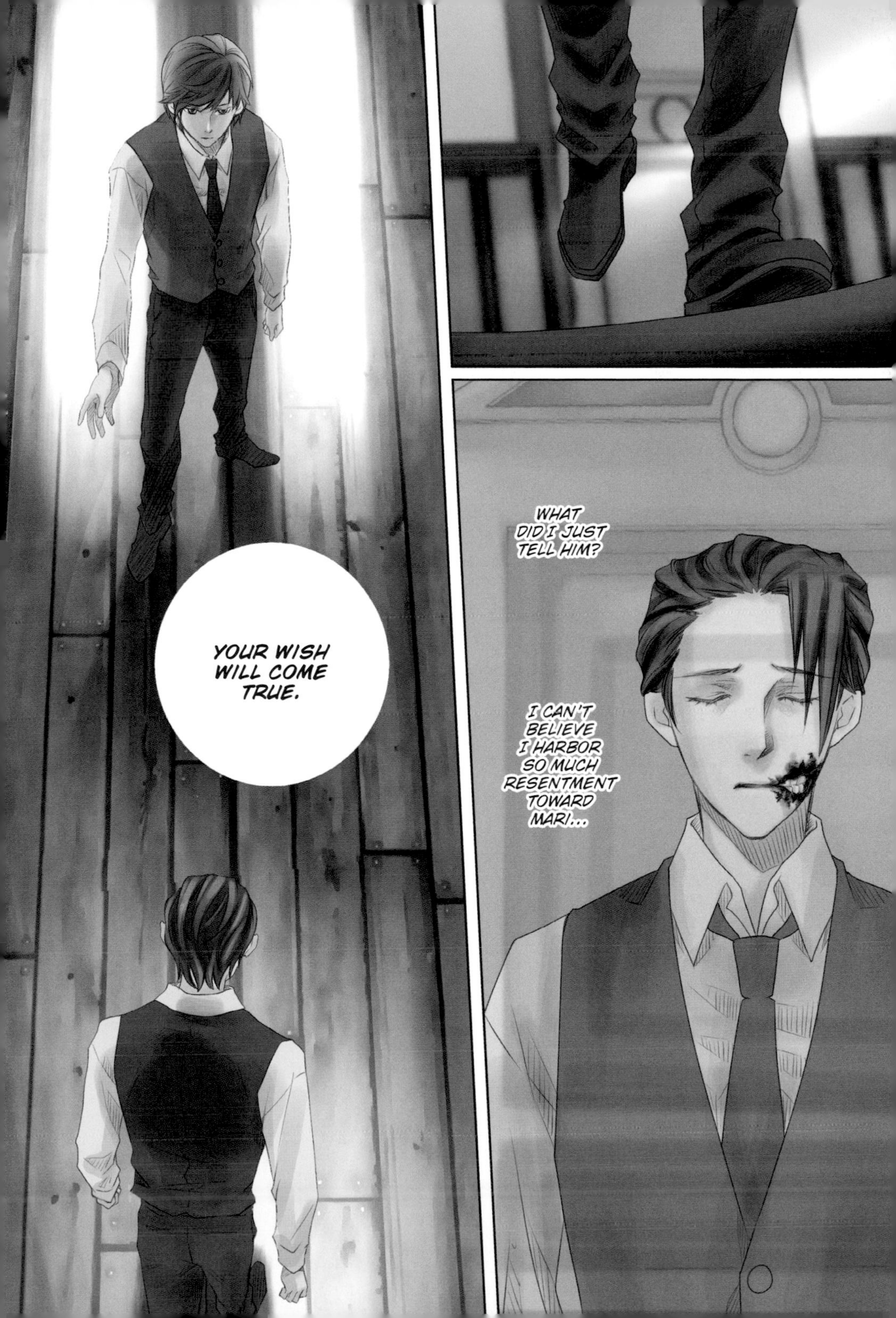
YOUR WISH WILL COME TRUE.
WHAT DID I JUST TELL HIM?
I CAN'T BELIEVE I HARBOR SO MUCH RESENTMENT TOWARD MARI...

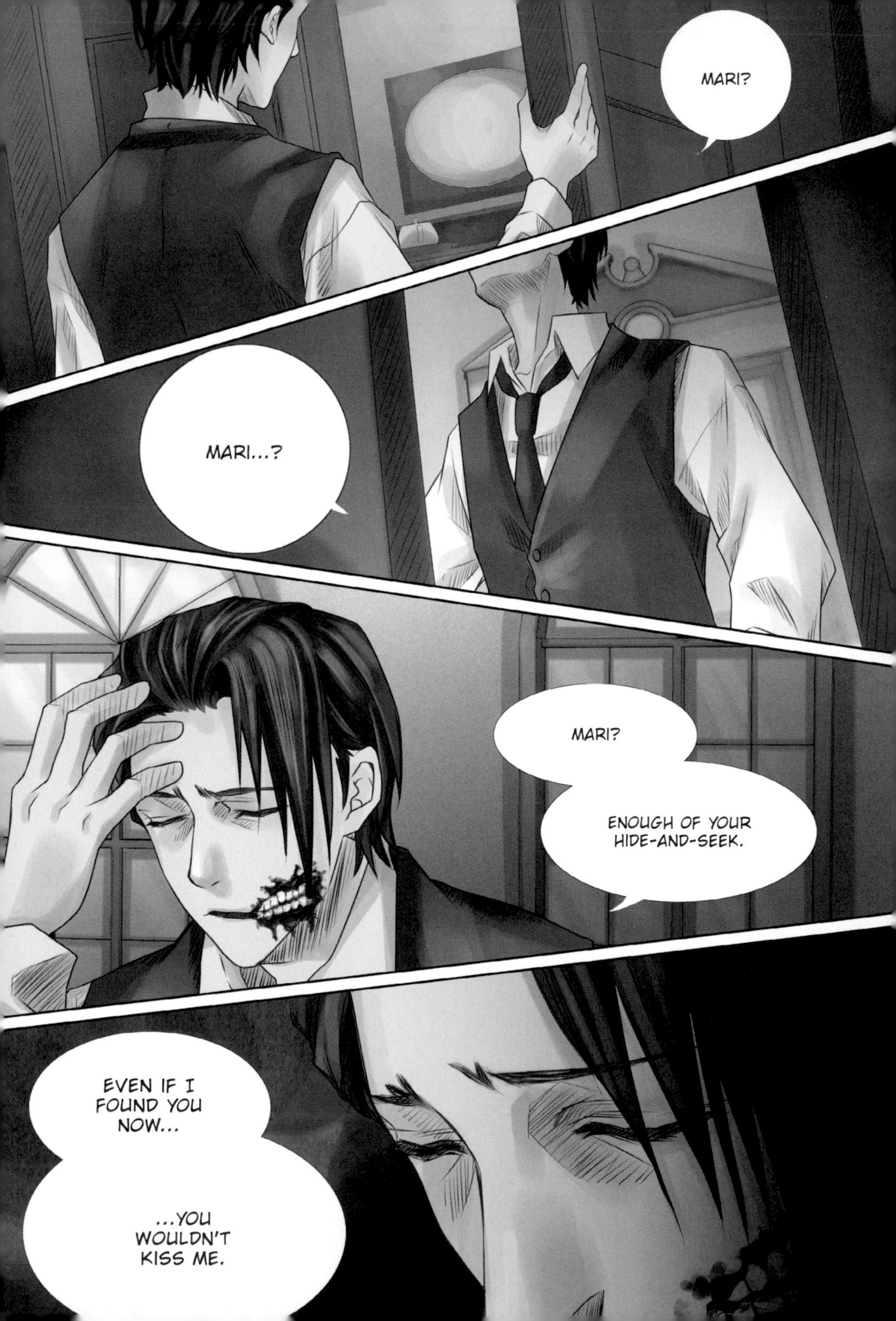
MARI?
MARI...?
MARI?
ENOUGH OF YOUR HIDE-AND-SEEK.
EVEN IF I FOUND YOU NOW...
...YOU WOULDN'T KISS ME.

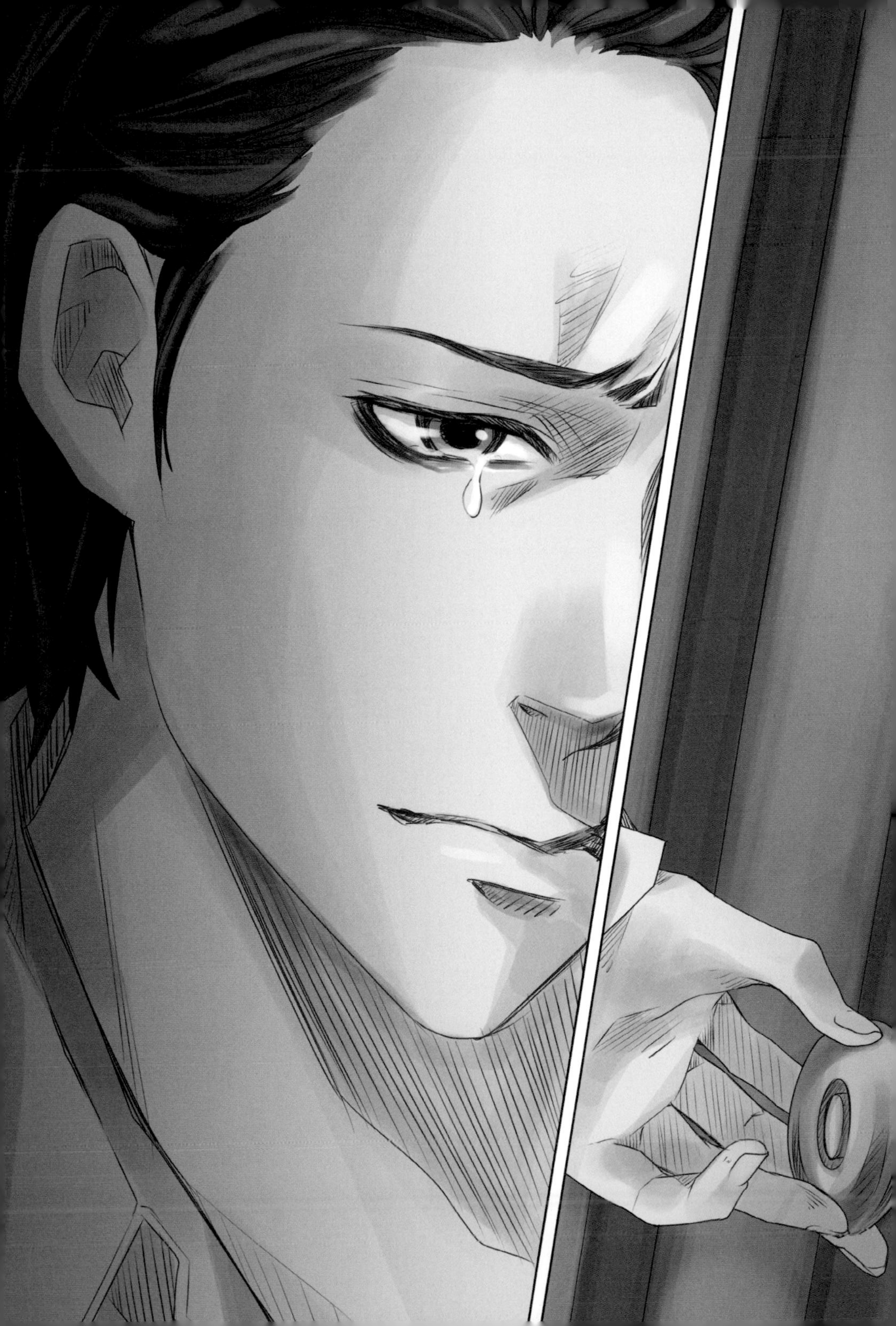

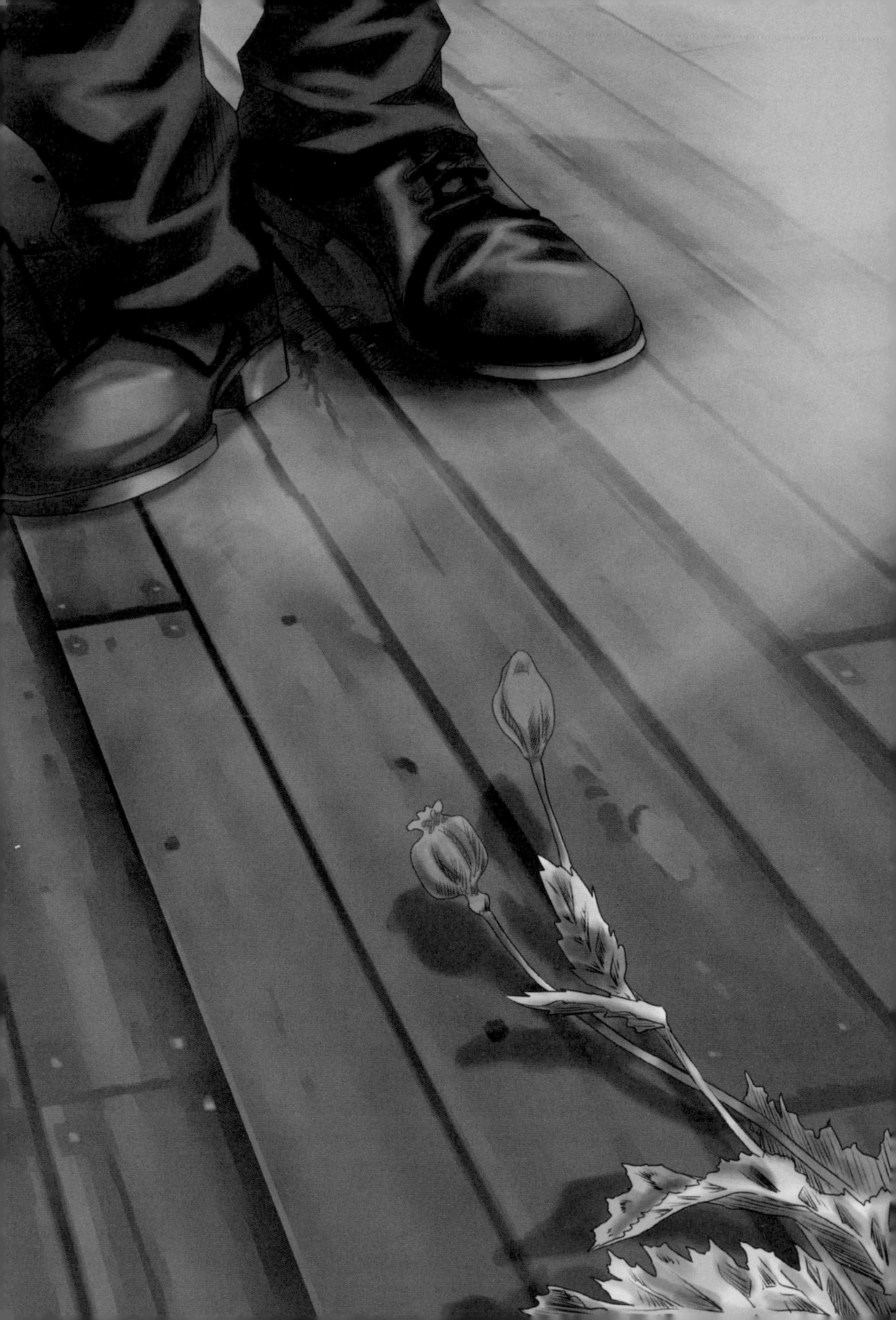

Void's Enigmatic Mansion

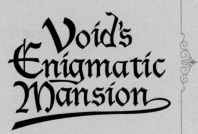

To be continued in Volume 3...

Void's Enigmatic Mansion

Visit artist HeeEun Kim's blog at http://blog.naver.com/kimnoran!

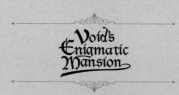

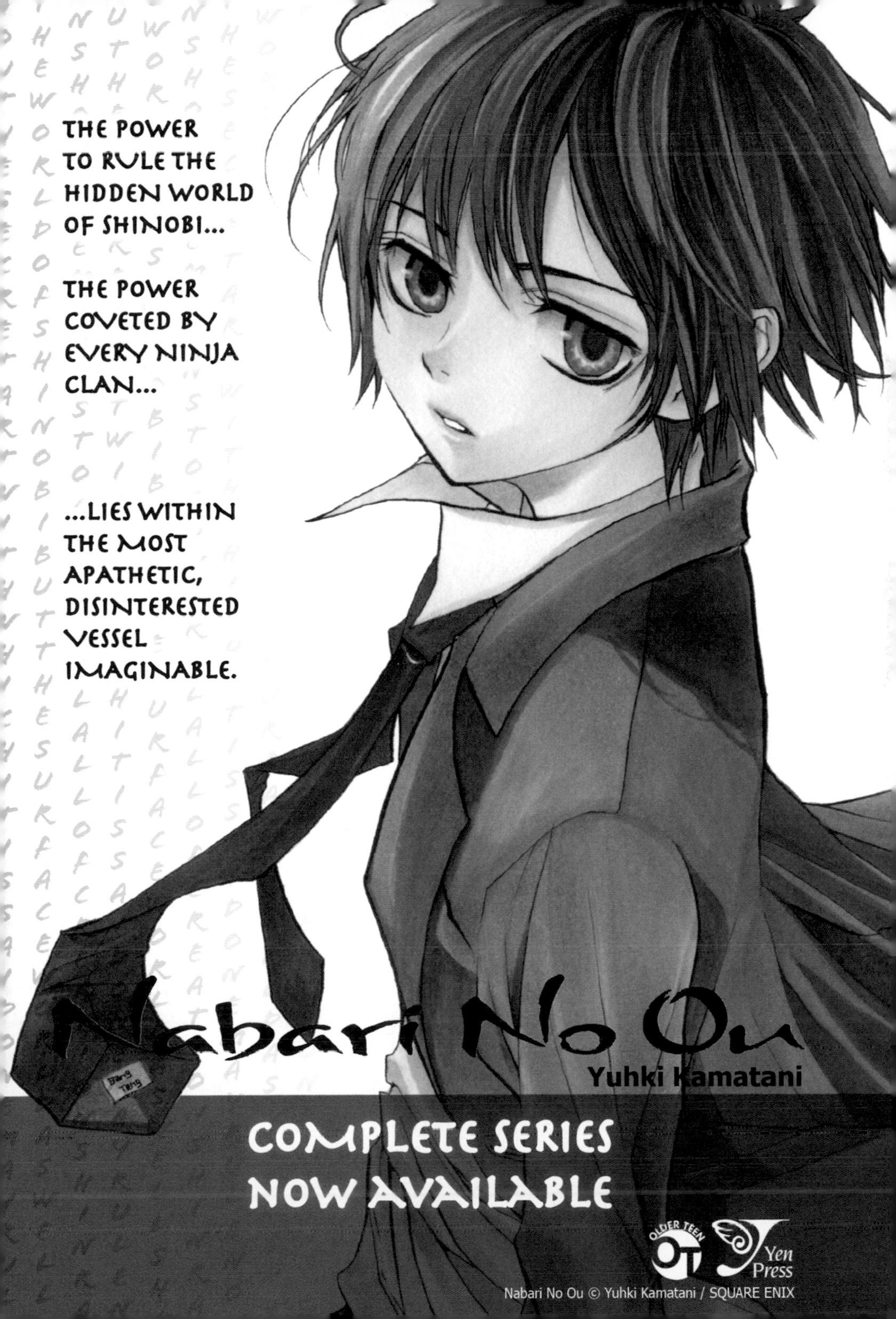
THE POWER TO RULE THE HIDDEN WORLD OF SHINOBI...
THE POWER COVETED BY EVERY NINJA CLAN...
...LIES WITHIN THE MOST APATHETIC, DISINTERESTED VESSEL IMAGINABLE.
Nabari No Ou
Yuhki Kamatani
COMPLETE SERIES NOW AVAILABLE
OLDER TEEN OT
Yen Press
Nabari No Ou © Yuhki Kamatani / SQUARE ENIX

To become the ultimate weapon, one boy must eat the souls of 99 humans...

...and one witch.

Maka is a scythe meister, working to perfect her demon scythe until it is good enough to become Death's Weapon—the weapon used by Shinigami-sama, the spirit of Death himself. And if that isn't strange enough, her scythe also has the power to change form—into a human-looking boy!

Yen
Press

Yen Press is an imprint of
Hachette Book Group

www.yenpress.com

COMPLETE SERIES IN STORES NOW!

WELCOME TO IKEBUKURO, WHERE TOKYO'S WILDEST CHARACTERS GATHER!!

AS THEIR PATHS CROSS, THIS ECCENTRIC CAST WEAVES A TWISTED, CRACKED LOVE STORY...

AVAILABLE NOW!!

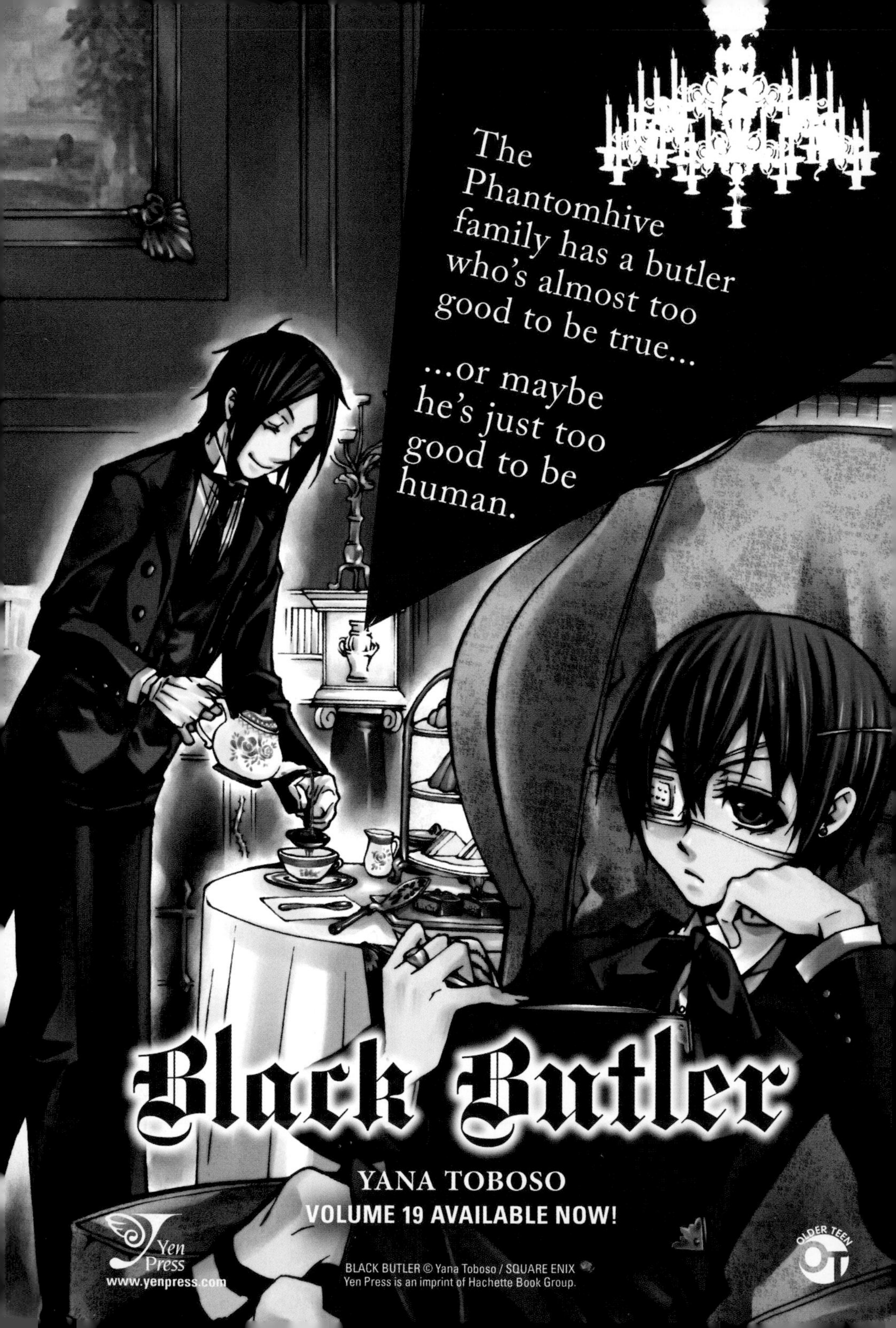
The Phantomhive family has a butler who's almost too good to be true...
...or maybe he's just too good to be human.
Black Butler
YANA TOBOSO
VOLUME 19 AVAILABLE NOW!
Yen Press
www.yenpress.com
BLACK BUTLER © Yana Toboso / SQUARE ENIX
Yen Press is an imprint of Hachette Book Group.
OLDER TEEN
OT

VOID'S ENIGMATIC MANSION 2

HeeEun Kim
JiEun Ha

Translation: HyeYoung Im
English Adaptation: J. Torres
Lettering: Stephanie Lee

VOID'S ENIGMATIC MANSION, Vol. 2
©2014 HeeEun Kim
©2014 JiEun Ha
Supported by KOMACON
All rights reserved.
First published in Korea in 2014 by Haksan Publishing Co., Ltd.

English translation rights in U.S.A., Canada, UK and Republic of Ireland arranged with Haksan Publishing Co., Ltd.
English translation © 2014 by Hachette Book Group, Inc.

Yen Press
Hachette Book Group
1290 Avenue of the Americas
New York, NY 10104

www.HachetteBookGroup.com
www.YenPress.com

Yen Press is an imprint of Hachette Book Group, Inc. The Yen Press name and logo are trademarks of Hachette Book Group, Inc.

The publisher is not responsible for websites (or their content) that are not owned by the publisher.

First Yen Press Edition: June 2015

ISBN: 978-0-316-34218-6

10 9 8 7 6 5 4 3 2 1

WOR

Printed in the
United States of America